BRITISH WILD FLOWERS

VOLUME ONE

BRITISH WILD FLOWERS

VOLUME ONE

by

John Hutchinson

DAVID & CHARLES : NEWTON ABBOT

ISBN 0 7153 5552 X

First published by Penguin Books Limited 1945
First hardback edition, revised 1972
David & Charles (Publishers) Ltd

Reproduced and printed in Great Britain by
Redwood Press Limited   Trowbridge & London

CONTENTS

*The Sequence of Families, Key to Families,
Glossary of Botanical Terms, and Indexes
will be found in both volumes.*

INTRODUCTION

These two volumes comprise the author's three Pelican Books, COMMON WILD FLOWERS, MORE COMMON WILD FLOWERS, and UNCOMMON WILD FLOWERS, first published in 1945, 1948, and 1950 respectively. To these have been added about two hundred new drawings and descriptions of more uncommon wild flowers, making a total of 809.

Instead of further reprints under these titles, it has been considered preferable to rearrange the whole in systematic order in two volumes, thus bringing all members of each family together, irrespective of whether they are common or uncommon.

It is not intended to compete with more general *Floras*, but rather to serve as an introduction to them and to other more popularly written books which have appeared since the second world war, some of them listed on p. xiv.

To save space, instead of keys to genera, a *key to families* is provided, and this should render it easy for the beginner to determine most of the plants which he may meet with around his home or during his rural rides or rambles in any part of the British Isles.

The sequence of families follows that of the author's BRITISH FLOWERING PLANTS published in 1948. In that book he arranged the families in an ascending series, beginning with those that seem to exhibit the most primitive features, such as the Buttercup family (*Ranunculaceae*), and the Rose family (*Rosaceae*), and ending with the more highly evolved such as the Deadnettle family (*Labiatae*) amongst the Dicotyledons, and with the Sedges (*Cyperaceae*) and the Grasses (*Gramineae*) in the Monocotyledons. Grasses, however, are not included, as they were thoroughly dealt with in a companion volume entitled GRASSES by C. E. Hubbard, published in September 1954 (Pelican Book A295).

The three books as originally published were written expressly for a variety of people – both young and old – who have little or no knowledge of botany, but who might want to learn the names and a little about the wild flowers of the countryside. Some, perhaps the great majority, will be content to match the wild flowers they find with the drawings. But others may see more than the pretty posy and look a little further into the structure of the flowers. This, in itself, is an interesting and fascinating study

vii

which will soon bring its own reward in a more extended know-ledge of plants and perhaps lead on to the consultation of the several excellent *Floras*, a selection of which is given on page xiv.

With this object in view, therefore, particular attention has been paid to the illustration of dissections of important parts of the flowers, fruits, and seeds, such as may be seen by the use of a sharp penknife or old razor-blade and a watchmaker's eye-glass or a hand-lens. These usually show the more important characters of the *genus* and *family*. Perspective has sometimes been sacrificed in order to display clearly the shapes of leaves and other features which are of primary importance for recognizing the *species*.

In order to use the key it will be necessary to dissect or study a sectional drawing of a simple type of flower, and for this purpose none is better or more easily obtainable than that of a common buttercup as shown in the illustration below.

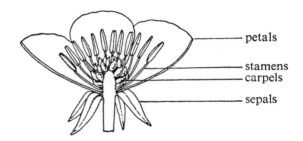

The five outermost green parts are the *sepals* (collectively called the *calyx*), the five yellow organs are, as everyone knows, the *petals* (forming the *corolla*), in this case with a nectary at the base of each; next in succession are the numerous *stamens*, consisting of a filament (stalk) and *anther* (pollen carrier), and finally a num-ber of small green parts in the middle and arranged in a spiral, the *carpels*. These carpels in the buttercup are free from one another, but in most other flowers they are few and joined together to form a single *ovary*. It may be useful to know, but not essential, that the stamens are the *male* element of the flower and collec-tively form the *androecium*, whilst the carpels with their potential seeds, the *ovules*, represent the *female* part and are known as the *gynaecium*.

Having carried out this operation or observation, it should not be too difficult, especially after a little practice, to make use of the simple type of key beginning on page xvii and 'run down' the majority of British wild flowers. Having followed the key to the place indicated by the characters of the leaves, flowers, fruits etc., the observer should be able to check the accuracy of his work by comparing the figures representing the family indicated. If these do not show the plant in hand, it may be either that it is not illustrated in the book, or that some mistake has been made in the use of the key.

HOW TO USE THE KEY

To put the beginner into the way of using the key to families, the Buttercup may be taken as an example. As it is a herb with net-veined leaves, it is obviously a DICOTYLEDON. The DICOTYLEDONS in the key are subdivided into three artificial groups, (1) *petals present*, free; (2) *petals present, united*; and (3) *petals absent*.

The Buttercup clearly belongs to group 1, to which we should turn on p. xvii. As the carpels are free from each other, it belongs to the line numbered 1, and not to 1a, in which the carpels are united into a single ovary. Then it will be observed that there are no stipules appended to the leaf-stalks, so that it falls under 2a. As the carpels are not as described in no. 5a, it belongs to no. 5, and is a herb, no. 6, with numerous carpels, which combination of characters determine it to belong to the family *Ranunculaceae*. A number of species of this family are illustrated in figures 214–241, and they should be examined in order to identify the genus and species.

After a little practice in naming a number of plants, the observer will probably soon begin to recognize related plants or families of flowering plants. In the case of the Rose family, for example, called *Rosaceae*, after the genus *Rosa*, it will be noticed (figures 4–43) that the female part of the flower is usually described as being composed of *free carpels*, which when ripe contain the seeds. The fact that the carpels are free from one another, associated with other features, is therefore one, but only one of the spotting characters by which many of the Rose family may be recognized.

One of the least difficult families to recognize is the Daisy family, *Compositae* (figures 507–600). The apparent single flower is in reality an aggregation of flowers into a head (capitulum). And with a few exceptions it will be found that most plants with a similar head of flowers belong to the Daisy family, and one can soon recognize this group, especially if it be observed that the anthers are joined together around the style.

Some flowers are very small and have no petals. They are often crowded together into a *catkin* (as in the Oak and Birch), which,

ix

like the head of the *Compositae*, is a particular kind of *inflorescence*. Most people are familiar with at least one kind of inflorescence, a *spike*, which suggests at once a stiff dense collection of flowers as found in many orchids.

The notes accompanying the drawings are confined to a short, general, and simple description, combining the more important *family*, *generic*, and *specific* characters. Varieties and forms, which occur in some species, are not usually mentioned. If sufficiently interesting, a few facts are given relating to the biology of the flower, particularly regarding *pollination*, which is of special importance to the bee keeper, the fruit-grower, and the seedsman. In this country Charles Darwin was the foremost investigator in this subject, and there is still a good deal to be learned.

In addition, where space permits, a few notes are added on the uses to which some of our wild plants are put, including those known to be poisonous. Their local use as remedies has now almost completely died out, since there is a chemist's shop in nearly every village. During the second world war, however, when Britain was more or less cut off from overseas supplies, interest in them was revived. The common foxglove, the henbane, the belladonna, and the autumn-crocus played their part. Even the despised nettle provided a useful fibre and was also used for the extraction of chlorophyll, whilst the rose hip, rich in vitamin C, helped greatly as an antiscorbutic in the absence of oranges. National Rose Hip Syrup became a standard rationed commodity and five hundred tons of rose-hips collected from hedgerows during the year 1943 produced two and a half million bottles of syrup, which were considered to be equivalent in Vitamin C content to twenty-five million oranges. Other wild plants of less importance in the war effort were broom-tops, burdock-leaves and roots, coltsfoot leaves, comfrey roots and leaves, dandelion roots, elder flowers and fruits, hawthorn berries, lime-tree flowers, raspberry leaves, valerian root, and wormwood, all being the source of a wide variety of medicines.

The arrangement of the families represented by the plants illustrated follows the author's own system of classification, which aims at a sequence of increasing specialization. The interrelationships of the principal families are shown in the diagram opposite. First come the conifers, of which we have only three native species. These are considered to be more primitive than the remainder of the flowering plants. Then all those plants are grouped together which usually have *net-veined* leaves and *two seed-leaves* (*Dicotyledons*), and the remainder, with *parallel-veined* leaves and only *one seed-leaf* (*Monocotyledons*), come last.

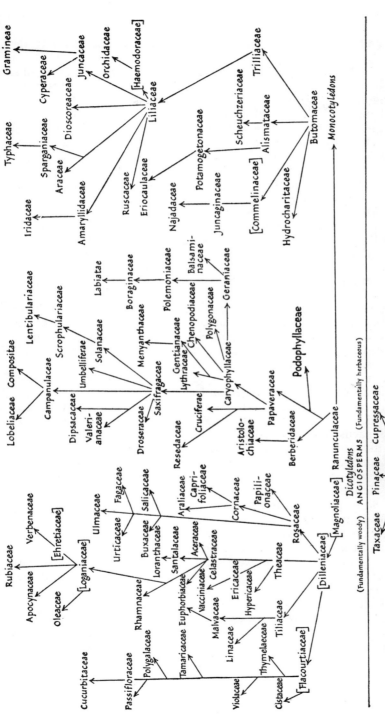

The latter include the lily and orchid families, and end with the sedges and grasses.

The *Dicotyledons* are further arranged into two main groups. First come the trees and shrubs and some herbs related to them (figures 4–213), and secondly the fundamentally herbaceous plants and a few slightly woody plants related to them (figures 214–709). *Monocotyledons* are shown from figures 710 to 809.

The reader with some knowledge of botanical classification may recognize that the families which exhibit the more primitive floral characters are placed first, and the most advanced come last in each of these groups, the sedges and grasses being regarded as being very advanced and greatly reduced in their floral structure.

The Latin names of the plants are in accordance with the International Rules of Botanical Nomenclature, so far as ascertained. A departure from common practice has been made, however, in the case of some of the names of the species. These have all been printed with a small initial letter, as is usual in zoology. Botanists generally spell certain specific names with a capital letter, especially those derived from an old genus name, and those named after persons. Thus *Sorbus Aucuparia* L., the Rowan tree, is usually so printed because *Aucuparia* is an old genus name. The 'L', after the Latin name indicates that Linnaeus, the famous Swedish botanist, often spoken of as the 'father of modern botany', was responsible for giving the name to the tree. The majority of the species of our commoner British plants were named by Linnaeus, as most of them are also found in Sweden. In a few cases the 'L.' is included in brackets after the Latin name, and the name, or abbreviated name, of another botanist follows it. This indicates that though Linnaeus first described the species, the latter is now placed under a different genus name. An example is the Stork's Bill, *Erodium cicutarium* (L.) L'Hérit. Linnaeus described it as *Geranium cicutarium*, and it was later transferred by the French botanist L'Héritier to *Erodium*.

Some groups of plants, such as the many kinds of Brambles, Roses, and Hawkweeds, though including some that are very common, are mostly difficult to distinguish except by intensive study, and have therefore been omitted.

The author, as acknowledged in the introduction to COMMON WILD FLOWERS, is greatly indebted to Sir Edward J. Salisbury, C.B.E., F.R.S., Director of the Royal Botanic Gardens, Kew, at whose suggestion the first book was prepared.

The drawings, with the exception of four kindly drawn by Olive Tait, are the author's own work and have been made at intervals during the last ten years, mainly from living specimens.

Finally the author thanks the publishers, their staff, and the printers for their unfailing courtesy and consideration. His has been the most congenial of tasks, for with his wife and members of his family and many botanical friends, he has explored remote and lovely districts of this much-beloved Britain which, for the botanist, at any rate, is still a land of hope and glory and a precious stone set in the silver sea. Wild flowers are a priceless heritage and should be picked only in moderation, especially those that are less common, and the rare ones not at all, so that they may be left to reproduce their kind and give enjoyment to others.

BOOKS RECOMMENDED FOR
FURTHER STUDY

The system of classification, according to which the plants illustrated in these books are arranged, is different from that to be found in any other botanical works except the present author's *British Flowering Plants* (see below), which deals with their evolution and classification. He recommends it especially to the notice of students who wish to use the general *Floras* enumerated below.

1. Hooker, *Student's Flora of the British Islands* * (Macmillan, 1937).
2. Bentham and Hooker, *Handbook of the British Flora* (L. Reeve and Co., Ashford, Kent).
3. Fitch and Smith, *Illustrations* to Bentham and Hooker's *Handbook of the British Flora*, ed. 7 (L. Reeve and Co., 1924).
4. Butcher and Strudwick, *Further Illustrations of British Plants* (L. Reeve and Co., 1946).
5. Skene, *The Biology of Flowering Plants* (Sidgwick and Jackson, Ltd., London, 1932).
6. Fritsch and Salisbury, *Plant Form and Function* (G. Bell and Sons, Ltd., London, 1943).
7. Hutchinson, *British Flowering Plants* (Evolution and Classification of Families and Genera) (P. R. Gawthorn, Ltd., 55 Russell Square, London, W.C.1, 1948).
8. Summerhayes, *Wild Orchids of Britain* (Collins, 1951).
9. Clapham, Tutin, and Warburg, *Flora of the British Isles* (Cambridge Univ. Press, 1952).
10. C. E. Hubbard, *Grasses* (Pelican A295, 1954).

The most comprehensive work on flower pollination is Knuth, *Handbook of Flower Pollination*, English translation by Ainsworth Davis (Clarendon Press, Oxford, 1908).

*Third edition of 1884, reprinted in 1937.

SEQUENCE OF FAMILIES IN THE
TWO VOLUMES

(The numbers in brackets refer to the illustrations)

VOLUME I

KEY TO THE FAMILIES DESCRIBED AND ILLUSTRATED IN THE TWO VOLUMES

(The numbers in brackets refer to the illustrations)

Part 1. Ovules (potential seeds) not enclosed in an ovary; to this group belong only the three native Conifers, i.e. the Yew, Pine and Juniper . . . . **Gymnosperms** (1–3)

Part 2. Ovules (potential seeds) enclosed in an ovary which later develops into a fruit and contains the seed or seeds; all other native British flowering plants, except the three in part 1 above, belong here . . . . **Angiosperms** (4–409)

*

The families belonging to Part 2 (**Angiosperms**) are further sub-divided into two groups called DICOTYLEDONS and MONOCOTYLE-DONS, determined as follows:

Leaves usually with a net-like venation (such as that of a Birch or Oak leaf, a Buttercup, a Lime tree etc.; seedling with 2 seed-leaves; bundles in the stem arranged in a ring or rings (as seen in a cross-section of a Birch- or Oak-stem); sepals and petals usually 5 or 4 each . DICOTYLEDONS (4–709)

Leaves usually with nerves running parallel to the midrib (as in Grasses, Sedges, Lilies, etc.), often narrow with parallel margins; seedling with only 1 seed-leaf; bundles in the stem not in rings, but scattered; sepals and petals usually 6 or 3, or completely reduced
MONOCOTYLEDONS (710–809) (for key see p. xxix)

*

The DICOTYLEDONS are divided into three groups as follows:

Petals present, free from each other . . . GROUP 1
Petals present, more or less united into a tube GROUP 2
Petals absent . . . . GROUP 3

GROUP 1

(PETALS PRESENT, FREE FROM EACH OTHER, RARELY MUCH REDUCED)

1 Carpels free from each other, sometimes crowded in or on a swollen receptacle (floral axis), more than 1; styles free from each other (to p. xviii):

2 Leaves with stipules, these sometimes joined to the leaf-stalks; trees, shrubs or herbs:

  3 Carpels more than 2, or if few, then fruits with numerous hooks on the outside; leaves simple or more often pinnate, trifoliolate or 5-foliolate; calyx often with an epicalyx
Rosaceae (4–43)

  3a Carpels 2, often partially united below; herbs:

    4 Leaves pinnate . . . . . . **Rosaceae** (4–43)

    4a Leaves not pinnate . . . . **Saxifragaceae** (425–437)

2a Leaves without stipules; mostly herbs:

  5 Carpels not immersed in or enclosed by the floral axis:

    6 Herbs:

      7 Carpels usually numerous, or if few the petals often modified into tubes or spurs and the leaves much divided . . . . . **Ranunculaceae** ((223–241)

      7a Carpels few; petals never modified; leaves fleshy, undivided . . . . . **Crassulaceae** (421–424)

      7b Carpels 5; leaves twice divided **Paeoniaceae** (214)

7c Carpels several; leaves much divided **Helleboraceae** (215–222) and **Podphyllaceae** (244)

    8 Flowers large and showy, solitary; aquatic plants
Nymphaeaceae (242, 243)

    8a Flowers very small in dense spike-like panicles
Rosaceae (4–43)

1a Carpels more or less united into a single ovary, or carpel 1 (as in the Pea family):

  9 Ovary not united to the sepals or calyx-tube (i.e. ovary completely superior or nearly so) (to p. xxii):

    10 Perfect stamens the same number as the petals and opposite to them:

      11 Sepals 3 or more:

        12 Anther opening by valves (flaps); style 1; petals with 2 large nectaries within the base; shrubs or herbs with prickly margined leaves or leaflets . . . . **Berberidaceae** (244–246)

        12a Anthers opening by a slit lengthwise;

          13 Sea-side herbs with pale blue flowers and basal rosette of leaves
Plumbaginaceae (379, 380)

          13a Inland shrubs or small trees, sometimes with thorny branches: flowers greenish
Rhamnaceae (195, 196)

      11a Sepals 2; petals widely notched at the apex
Portulacaceae (353, 354)

10a Perfect stamens as many as the petals and alternate with them, or more numerous or rarely fewer than the petals:

14 Flowers divisable into equal halves in more than one direction (i.e. flowers actinomorphic or regular) (to p. xxi):

15 Filaments of the stamens more or less united into several separate bundles; leaves opposite, often gland-dotted
Hypericaceae (183–189)

15a Filaments of the stamens united into a single central tube around the ovary and styles; leaves often clothed with star-shaped hairs . . . . . **Malvaceae (146–150)**

15b Filaments free or slightly united only at the base:

16 Stamens 6, four longer and two shorter (tetradynamous); sepals 4, petals 4, often clawed; ovary of 2 united carpels often divided by a thin false septum (Wallflower family)
Cruciferae (259–314)

16a Stamens and other floral parts not combined as above, if stamens 6 then more or less equal in length:

17 Leaves opposite or whorled (never all radical, i.e. direct from the root or base of the stem) (to p. xx):

18 Stamens numerous (more than 10); shrublets clothed with star-shaped (stellate) hairs; petals soon falling off . . . . **Cistaceae (128, 129)**

18a Stamens not more than double the number of the petals:

19 Trees with flowers in pendulous racemes or cymes; leaves lobed; fruits with 2 widely spreading winged lobes . . . . **Aceraceae (198, 199)**

19a Trees with very small flowers in broad flat corymbs; leaves pinnate . . . **Caprifoliaceae (97–102)**

19b Woody shrubs or shrublets; fruits not winged as described above:

20 Ovules attached to the walls of the 1-locular ovary; fruit a capsule opening by valves; shrublet with small whorled or opposite leaves **Frankeniaceae (140)**

20a Ovules attached to the central axis of the several-locular ovary:

21 Fruit a small black berry; shrublets with small heath-like leaves . . . . . . **Empetraceae (191)**

21a Fruit a capsule, 4-lobed, red to pink; seeds with a yellow aril . . . . . **Celastraceae (192)**

19c Herbs:

22 Ovary half-inferior (i.e. partly united to the calyx-tube; leaves deeply divided; flowers in a cluster on a common peduncle . . **Adoxaceae (438)**

22a Ovary completely superior (i.e. placed above the insertion of the sepals):
23 Ovary incompletely or not at all divided into loculi, with free-central or basal placentas
Caryophyllaceae (317–352)
23a Ovary completely divided into separate loculi:
24 Leaves with very conspicuous stipules, mostly with stalks of unequal length in each pair; sepals and petals 5 each
Geraniaceae (641–654)
24a Leaves without or with very minute stipules:
25 Stamens united into a short tube . **Linaceae** (151, 153)
25a Stamens not united:
26 Sepals and petals 3–4 each . . . **Elatinaceae** (316)
26a Sepals and petals more than 4 each:
27 Ovules several in each ovary . **Lythraceae** (409, 410)
27a Ovule 1 in each ovary. . **Illecebraceae** (399–402)
17a Leaves alternate or all radical (i.e. from the root or near the base of the stem):
28 Trees or shrubs with broadish elliptic rounded or cordate leaves:
29 Flowers with a large elongated bract partly attached to the peduncle (Lime tree family)
Tiliaceae (144,145)
29a Flowers without such a bract, arranged in slender racemes or on spiny branches or in clusters from scaly buds (Rose family) . **Rosaceae** (4–43)
29b Flowers without a bract as described above, arranged in umbels; climber with aerial roots and evergreen leaves . . . . **Araliaceae** (103)
28a Shrubs or shrublets with woody branches and very small leaves:
30 Tall sea-side shrubs with slender whip-like branches, minute leaves and slender racemes of pink flowers; fruit a capsule, the seeds crowned by a tuft of hairs . . . . **Tamaricaceae** (141)
30a Dwarf shrublet with small narrow leaves with rolled back margins; fruit a berry
Empetraceae (191)
28b Herbs, sometimes aquatic:
31 Stamens numerous, more than 10:
32 Stamens inserted below the ovary (hypogynous):
33 Sepals and petals 5 each
Ranunculaceae (223–241)
33a Sepals 2; petals 4 **Papaveraceae** (249–256)

32a Stamens inserted around the ovary (perigynous):

  34 Terrestrial plants; petals 5   .   .   .   **Rosaceae (4–43)**

  34a Aquatic plants, floating leaves and large yellow or white flowers; petals more than 5

                    Nymphaeaceae (242, 243)

31a Stamens 10 or fewer:

  35 Leaves small and scale-like, yellowish; flowers pale yellow, a saprophyte on the roots of certain trees

                    Monotropaceae (181)

  35a Leaves not like scales, more or less green; not saprophytic:

    36 Anthers opening by a round terminal pore; leaves rounded, long-stalked; flowers in terminal racemes

                    Pyrolaceae (178–180)

    36a Anthers opening by slits lengthwise:

      37 Leaves with stipules:

        38 Leaves trifoliaolate   .   .   .   **Oxalidaceae (655)**

        38a Leaves not trifoliolate:

          39 Ovary 5-locular; leaves more or less lobed or toothed   .   .   .   . **Geraniaceae (641–654)**

          39a Ovary 1-locular; leaves very small and entire

                    Illecebraceae (399–402)

      37a Leaves without stipules:

        40 Flowers with branched glandular staminodes alternating with the stamens

                  Saxifragaceae (425–437)

        40a Flowers without staminodes:

          41 Leaves densely sticky-glandular more or less all over or on the margin

                  Droseraceae (439–441)

          41a Leaves not glandular as described above:

          42 Leaves deeply divided

                  Ranunculaceae (223–241)

          42a Leaves not divided:

          43 Seed solitary in the fruit

                  Illecebraceae (399–402)

          43a Seeds several in the fruit   **Linaceae (151–153)**

14a Flowers divisable into 2 equal halves only in vertical direction (flowers zygomorphic or irregular):

  44 Ovary composed of 1 carpel with 1 style:

    45 Petals not spurred, but often clawed; leaves mostly pinnate or trifoliolate; stamens united into a sheath often with one free from the rest (Pea family)

                  Papilionaceae (44–93)

45a Petals with a spur at the base; stamens free
$\qquad$ **Ranunculaceae** (223–241)
44a Ovary composed of more than 1 united carpels with more than 1 style or stigmas:
46 Ovary 1–2-locular with the ovules inserted on the walls or at the apex of the loculi:
47 Stamens free from each other:
48 Anther-connective produced beyond the loculi; leaves stipulate . . . . . . **Violaceae** (132–139)
48a Anther-connective not produced; leaves not stipulate
$\qquad$ **Resedaceae** (315)
47a Stamens connate into two bundles:
49 Ovules on the walls of the ovary
$\qquad$ **Fumariaceae** (257, 258)
49a Ovules at the apex of the ovary **Polygalaceae** (142)
46a Ovary 5-locular, with the ovules arranged on the central axis; one sepal spurred and petaloid
$\qquad$ **Balsaminaceae** (656–658)
9a Ovary more or less united to the calyx-tube (ovary from $\frac{1}{2}$ inferior to wholly inferior):
50 Leaves alternate or rarely clustered:
51 Flowers in umbels, usually very small (as in the Hemlock) or rarely in a dense head-like cluster (Seaholly); leaves often very much divided:
52 Herbs with more or less hollow ribbed stems, flowering in spring and summer
$\qquad$ **Umbelliferae** (442–485)
52a Climber with aerial roots, flowering and fruiting in autumn; leaves evergreen (Ivy)
$\qquad$ **Araliaceae** (103)
51a Flowers neither in umbels nor in head-like clusters, sometimes in corymbs:
53 Stamens numerous; trees, shrubs or herbs; leaves usually with prominent stipules, entire, pinnate or toothed . . . . . **Rosaceae** (4–43)
53a Stamens 10 or fewer:
54 Ovary 1-locular with numerous ovules on 2 parietal placentas; shrubs, branches armed with 3-forked spines . **Grossulariaceae** (94)
54a Ovary 2-locular; dwarf herbs with small white or pink flowers . **Saxifragaceae** (425–437)
54b Ovary 4-locular; herbs with pink, white or rarely large yellow flowers
$\qquad$ **Onagraceae** (411–418)

50a Leaves opposite or whorled:
  55 Parasitic shrublet with minute flowers and round white
        berries (Mistletoe) . . . . .   **Loranthaceae (193)**
  55a Low cushion-like herbs with bluish-purple solitary flowers
                                        Saxifragaceae (425–437)
  55b Shrubs or herbs not forming cushions:
    56 Flowers in heads surrounded by a whorl of white bracts, or
          in terminal cymes without bracts . **Cornaceae (95, 96)**
    56a Flowers not in heads or cymes:
      57 Herbs with toothed leaves; style simple or divided only at
            the top . . . . **Onagraceae (411–418)**
      57a Aquatic herbs with very minute flowers; styles or stigmas
            separate . . . . .   **Halorrhagaceae (419, 420)**

GROUP 2
(PETALS UNITED)

1 Ovary not united to the sepals or calyx-tube (i.e. ovary
    superior) (to p. xxv):
  2 Stamens the same number as the corolla-lobes and opposite to
      them; herbs often with a basal rosette of leaves;
    3 Sepals or calyx-lobes 5 . . .   **Primulaceae (464–378)**
    3a Sepals 2 . . . .   **Portulacaceae (353, 354)**
  2a Stamens, if the same number as the corolla-lobes, then not
      opposite to them, sometimes more or few than the lobes:
    4 Stamens not inserted on the corolla-tube; anthers mostly
        opening by a terminal pore, rarely by slits lengthwise:
      5 Leaves mostly radical, long-stalked and orbicular or
          spoon-shaped . . . . . . **Pyrolaceae (78–80)**
      5a Leaves not all radical, at most shortly stalked, often very
          small with rolled back margins, alternate or whorled or
          opposite . . . .   **Ericaceae (164–174)**
    4a Stamens inserted more or less on the corolla-tube; anthers
        usually opening by a slit lengthwise:
      6 Stamens twice as many as the corolla-lobes; leaves orbi-
          cular, peltate . . . . .   **Crassulaceae (421–424)**
      6a Stamens as many as or fewer than the corolla-lobes:
        7 Stamens as many as the corolla-lobes (to p. xxiv):
          8 Leaves pinnate; shrub or small tree
                                        Caprifoliaceae (97–102)
          8a Leaves pinnate; small herb, not aquatic
                                        Polemoniaceae (659)
          8b Leaves trifoliolate or orbicular; aquatic plants
                                        Menyanthaceae (362, 363)

8c Leaves simple or toothed:
 9 Leaves opposite:
  10 Ovary deeply divided vertically with the style inserted be-
      tween the lobes; herbs . . . . **Labiatae** (678–709)
  10a Ovary not divided as above; style terminal on the ovary:
   11 Herbs with leafy stems and sometimes also basal rosettes
       or leaves; flowers mostly blue **Gentianaceae** (355–361)
   11a Shrublet with decumbent or prostrate, wiry, leafy stems
        and solitary blue flowers . . . **Apocynaceae** (202)
 9a Leaves alternate, or all radical or crowded into rosettes:
  12 Ovary deeply lobed vertically into 4 parts, especially
      in fruit; style inserted between the lobes (gynobasic);
      plants often covered with rough bulbous-based hairs
                                Boraginaceae (660–677)
  12a Ovary and style not as above:
   13 Tree with evergreen prickly leaves, small white flowers
       and clusters of bright red berries
                                Aquifoliaceae (190)
   13a Herbs or climbers or small cushion-like plants:
    14 Ovary with not more than 2 ovules; twining or creep-
        ing plants with lovely broadly tubular flowers
                                Convolvulaceae (608–610)
    14a Ovary with more than 2 ovules in each loculus:
     15 Woody cushion plantlet found only in the Scottish
         mountains, with dense rosettes of small leaves and
         single stalked white flowers **Diapensiaceae** (182)
     15a Habit not as above:
      16 Corolla dry and scarious; herbs with radical leaves
          and flowers mostly in dense spikes
                                Plantaginaceae (381–384)
      16a Corolla not dry and scarious:
       17 Corolla-lobes contorted; leaves pinnate
                                Polemoniaceae (659)
       17a Corolla-lobes imbricate or plicate; two very
           closely-related families
            Solanaceae (601–607) and **Scrophulariaceae** (611–636)
7a Stamens fewer than the corolla-lobes:
 18 Trees with pinnate opposite leaves: stamens 2; fruit
     winged (Ash tree) or a berry (Privet)
                                Oleaceae (200, 201)
 18a Herbs:
  19 Flowers actinomorphic (regular); ovary 1-locular with
      free placentation; sepals 2
                                Portulacaceae (353, 354)

19a Flowers more or less zygomorphic (irregular):
20 Ovary 1-locular with a free basal placenta; aquatic or bog
    plants, the latter with a rosette of broadish leaves
                            Lentibulariaceae (639, 640)
20a Ovary usually with more than 1 loculus and with axile
     placentas:
21 Ovules numerous in each loculus or ovary:
22 Ovules attached to the central axis of the 2-locular ovary;
     corolla sometimes spurred at the base; stamens 4 or 2
                        Scrophulariaceae (611–636)
22a Ovules attached to the walls of the ovary; stamens 4 in
     two pairs, anthers connivent **Orobanchaceae** (637, 638)
21a Ovule 1 in each loculus; corolla mostly very distinctly 2-
     lipped:
23 Ovary not lobed, with a terminal style
                           Verbenaceae (213)
23a Ovary deeply and vertically lobed with the style in-
     serted between . . . . . **Labiatae** (678–709)
1a Ovary more or less united to the sepals or calyx-tube (i.e.
  ovary inferior):
24 Flowers in heads surrounded by an involucre of bracts
    (as in the Daisy, Dandelion, etc.):
25 Anthers united into a tube around the style; calyx of
     the small individual flowers representd by a pappus
     of bristles or bristle-like hairs, these rarely absent
                         Compositae (507–600)
25a Anthers not united as above; calyx not as above
                        Dipsacaceae (490–493)
24a Flowers not in heads as described above but some-
    times in a dense cluster:
26 Leaves alternate or all radical:
27 Anthers opening by pores at the top of the loculi
                        Vacciniaceae (175–177)
27a Anthers opening by slits lengthwise:
28 Corolla not spurred at the base:
29 Corolla actinomorphic (regular):
30 Climber with tendrils; leaves 5–7-lobed;
     flowers unisexual, yellowish-green
                        Cucurbitaceae (143)
30a Erect or decumbent herbs; flowers bisexual
                      Campanulaceae (479–504)
29a Corolla zygomorphic (irregular); stamens united
     into a column around the style
                      Lobeliaceae (505, 506)

28a Corolla spurred at the base . **Valerianaceae 486–489)**
26a Leaves opposite or whorled:
  31 Leaves stipulate or in whorls (the stipules the same or almost the same as the leaves) . **Rubiaceae (203–212)**
  31a Leaves not whorled, simple or compound; no stipules:
    32 Ovary 1-locular with 1 pendulous ovule
        Valerianaceae (486–489)
    32a Ovary more than 1-locular:
      33 Very small herb with deeply divided leaves and a terminal cluster of small greenish flowers
        Adoxaceae (438)
      33a Shrubs scramblers or climbers
        Caprifoliaceae (97–102)

GROUP 3

(PETALS ABSENT, SOMETIMES THE CALYX PETALOID)

1 Flowers (at least the males) in catkins, very small:
  2 Ovary superior (i.e. not united to the sepals):
    3 Branches and leaves covered by silvery scales; sea-side shrub or small tree . . . . . . **Elaeagnaceae (197)**
    3a Branches and leaves not covered by silvery scales; willows, birches, oaks, nettles etc.:
      4 Ovules attached to the wall of the ovary; trees, shrubs or subherbaceous; willows and poplars
        Salicaceae (105–115)
      4a Ovules attached to the top or bottom of the ovary:
        5 Leaves alternate:
          6 Leaves stipulate; trees:
            7 Ovary superior . . . . . **Betulaceae (117, 118)**
            7a Ovary inferior . . . . . **Fagaceae (121, 122)**
          6a Leaves not stipulate; shrublets with glandular leaves
            Myricaceae (116)
        5a Leaves opposite; herbs with stinging hairs
          Urticaceae (124–126)
  2a Ovary inferior (i.e. united with the sepals or calyx-tube):
      8 Male flowers with a calyx; involucre not leafy and not jagged . . . . **Fagaceae (121, 122)**
      8a Male flowers without a calyx; fruits partially enclosed in a leafy jagged persistent involucre
        Corylaceae (119–120)
1a Flowers not in true catkins, but sometimes in clusters or heads or in slender spikes:

9 Ovary wholly superior (i.e. not united with the sepals or calyx-tube) (to p. xxviii):
10 Flowers enclosed in an involucre (called a cyathium), (see figs. 156–163), with large glands on the margin; stems often exuding milk-like sap when cut or bruised
Euphorbiaceae (154–163)
10a Flowers not arranged as above, but the females sometimes in a dense bracteate head:
11 Leaves opposite or verticillate, never all radical:
12 Leaves with stipules:
13 Ovary with free central placentation (i.e. crowded on the central axis without dividing walls)
Caryophyllaceae (317–352)
13a Ovary with axile, basal or apical placentation:
14 Flowers bisexual, very small   Illecebraceae (399–402)
14a Flowers unisexual:
15 Twiners with 3–5-lobed toothed leaves; female flowers with large bracts . . . . Cannabinaceae (127)
15a Erect herbs with stinging hairs; ovary with 1 ovule
Urticaceae (124–126)
15b Erect herbs but no stinging hairs; ovary with more than 1 ovule . . . Euphorbiaceae (154–163)
12a Leaves without stipules:
16 Shrubs or trees with hard wood:
17 Leaves undivided . . . . . Buxaceae (104)
17a Leaves pinnate . . . . . . Oleaceae (201)
16a Herbs or soft-wooded climbers:
18 Climber with free carpels with long hairy tails in fruit leaves compound
Ranunculaceae (223–241)
18a Erect herbs:
19 Flowers bisexual:
20 Ovules numerous:
21 Placenta free basal   . Primulaceae (364–378)
21a Placenta free central
Caryophyllaceae (317–352)
20a Ovule 1, pendulous from a basal placenta
Illecebraceae (399–402)
19a Flowers unisexual . Chenopodiaceae (399–402)
11a Leaves alternate or all radical:
22 Leaves stipulate:
23 Ovary 2- or more-locular, composed of united carpels:
24 Fruits not winged   Euphorbiaceae (154–163)
24a Fruits winged . . . . . . Ulmaceae (123)

23a Ovary 1-locular or carpels free:
    25 Stipules forming a sheath around the stem or attached to the leaf-stalk:
      26 Leaves entire . . . . . **Polygonaceae (385–398)**
      26a Leaves digitately lobed, trifolioate or simply pinnate
        Rosaceae (4–43)
    26b Leaves twice pinnate:
    26c Ovules several . . . . . **Helleboraceae (215–222)**
    26d Ovule 1 . . . . . . **Ranunculaceae (223–241)**
    25a Stipules neither sheathing nor attached to the petiole:
      27 Flowers without staminodes
        Chenopodiaceae (403–408)
      27a Flowers with staminodes between the fertile stamens
        Illecebraceae (399–402)
22a Leaves without stipules:
    28 Stamens connate; leaves kidney-shaped
      Aristolochiaceae (247–248)
    28a Stamens free from each other:
      29 Woody plants but sometimes shrublets:
        30 Leaves covered with silvery scales; sea-side shrub or small tree . . . . . **Elaeagnaceae (197)**
        30a Leaves not covered by silvery scales, sometimes glandular:
        31 Leaves gland-dotted, odorous when bruised
          Myricaceae (116)
        31a Leaves not gland-dotted:
        32 Stamens perigynous; flowers bisexual, mostly sweet-scented; calyx green or coloured, tubular
          Thymelaeaceae (130, 131)
        32a Stamens hypogynous; leaves very small and heath-like; dwarf shrublets with small crowded leaves and small inconspicuous flowers . . . . . **Empetraceae (191)**
    29a Herbs:
      33 Ovary of several separate free carpels
        Ranunculaceae (214–241)
      33a Ovary of 1 carpel or united carpels
        Chenopodiaceae (403–408)
9a Ovary inferior (more or less united with the calyx):
    34 Woody plants:
      35 Leaves covered with silvery scales; sea-side shrub or small tree **Elaeagnaceae (197)**
      35a Leaves not covered with silvery scales:

36 Plants parasitic on trees; branches brittle (Mistletoe)
$\qquad$ **Loranthaceae (193)**
34a Herbs:
  37 Leaves trifoliolate; carpels free or nearly so with separate
    styles . . . . **Rosaceae (4–43)**
  37a Leaves not trifoliolate:
    38 Leaves alternate:
      39 Leaves kidney-shaped or cordate; calyx coloured; 3-
      lobed or 2-lipped and tubular spoon-shaped
$\qquad$ **Aristolochiaceae (247, 248)**
      39a Leaves lanceolate; calyx green   **Urticaceae (124–126)**
    38a Leaves opposite:
      40 Ovules attached to the walls of the ovary; leaves
      rounded; small herbs in wet places
$\qquad$ **Saxifragaceae (425–437)**
      40a Ovules not attached to the walls of the ovary:
        41 Aquatic or semiaquatic plants:
          42 Leaves in whorls . . . **Halorrhagaceae (419, 420)**
          42a Leaves opposite . . . . **Onagraceae (411–418)**
        41a Not aquatics, leaves narrow . . **Santalaceae (194)**

MONOCOTYLEDONS

1 Ovary superior, i.e. not united to either the calyx or corolla
  (perianth) (to p. xxxi):
 2 Carpels free from each other or only one carpel with 1 stigma;
  mostly aquatic or semi-aquatic plants:
  3 Flowers bracteate:
    4 Flowers in simple umbels; carpels 6; ovules spread all over
    the inside of the carpels . . . . **Butomaceae (710)**
    4a Flowers in panicles or compound umbels; ovules not
    spread over the inner surface of the carpels:
      5 Carpels 6 or more; leaves not ligulate
$\qquad$ **Alismataceae (714–717)**
      5a Carpels 4–3; leaves ligulate . . **Scheuchzeriaceae (718)**
  3a Flowers without bracts:
    6 Terrestrial or marsh herbs with linear radical leaves and
    leafless flowering stems bearing a slender raceme or
    spike of greenish flowers . . **Juncaginaceae (719)**
    6a Fresh-water aquatics with floating leaves; flowers
    bisexual; stamens 4 . . **Potamogetonaceae (720)**
 2a Carpels more or less completely united with usually more
  than 1 stigma;

7 Perianth present:
8 Perianth of 2 separate and usually dissimilar whorls (calyx and corolla):
9 Flowers not in heads surrounded by bracts:
10 Low shrublet with leaf-like cladoiform branchlets; stamens united into a tube; flowers mostly unisexual
Ruscaceae (740)
10a Herb with a whorl of usually 4 obovate leaves sub-tending a single conspicuous flower; stamens free; anther-connective produced beyond the loculi
Trilliaceae (722)
10b Herb with a loose terminal raceme of small flowers
Scheuchzeriaceae (718)
9a Flowers in a head surrounded by bracts; leaves linear in a radical cluster . . . . . **Eriocaulaceae (721)**
8a Perianth of 1 whorl, each part more or less similar, mostly conspicuous and petaloid:
11 Flowers in an umbel or single but subtended by a spathaceous bract or bracts; rootstock a bulb
Amaryllidaceae (745–750)
11a Flowers not arranged as above:
12 Flowers in globose clusters, unisexual, the upper clusters male, the lower female
Sparganiaceae (744)
12a Flowers arranged on a spadix (dense spike), sub-tended by a large spathe, sometimes this narrow and leaf-like . . . . . . **Araceae (742, 743)**
12b Flowers not as above:
13 Branchlets modified and looking like leaves bearing the flowers on their surface; stamens united into a tube; flowers mostly unisexual
Ruscaceae (740)
13a Branchlets not modified as above; flowers bisexual:
14 Leaves in a whorl of 4, 5 or 6 subtending a single flower . . . . **Trilliaceae (722)**
14a Leaves not as above:
15 Flowers without bracts; ovary or 6–3 carpels
Juncaginaceae (719)
15a Flowers with bracts; ovary of 3 or 2 carpels:
16 Perianth petaloid . . . **Liliaceae (723–739)**
16a Perianth glume-like; plants grass-like
Juncaceae (779–784)
7a Perianth absent or represented by hypogynous scales or setae; flowers very small, arranged in spikelets in the axils

of scaly bracts . . . . . . **Cyperaceae (785–809)**
1a Ovary inferior, i.e. united to the calyx or corolla (perianth):
17 Perianth composed of a distinct separate calyx and corolla:
18 Stamens 3 or more; flowers actinomorphic (regular):
19 Aquatics; ovules on the walls of the ovary or on intrusive placentas . . . **Hydrocharitaceae (711–713)**
19a Terrestrial plants; ovules on the inner angles of the
loculi . . . . **Iridaceae (751–754)**
18a Stamens 2 or 1; ovary or pedicel or both often spirally
twisted; flowers zygomorphic (irregular)
Orchidaceae (755–778)
17a Perianth-segments more or less alike and often petaloid,
mostly 6, free or united at the base into a single tube,
in orchids the third petal often often much modified
into a lip:
20 Flowers more or less actinomorphic (regular), if less so
then stamens 3 or more:
21 Ovules spread all over the walls of the ovary; aquatic
plants . . . . . **Hydrocharitaceae (711–713)**
21a Ovules on the placentas in the inner angle of the
loculi:
22 Stamens 6:
23 Inflorescence scapose, umbellate, subtended by an
involucre of one or more spathaceous bracts,
sometimes reduced to one flower; not climbing
Amaryllidaceae (745–750)
23a Inflorescence raceomose, axillary; climbers; flowers unisexual . . . . **Dioscoreaceae (741)**
22a Stamens 3; herbs, not climbing; flowers bisexual,
showy . . . . . . **Iridaceae (751–754)**
20a Flowers very zygomorphic (irregular), the third petal
often very different and modified into a lip; stamens
2 or 1; ovary and often the pedicel spirally twisted
Orchidaceae (755–778)

GLOSSARY OF BOTANICAL TERMS

Achene: a small, dry seed-like fruit.

acuminate: gradually pointed.

adnate: attached the whole length to another structure.

alternate: not opposite to something else.

annual: lasting only one year or season.

anther: portion of stamen bearing the pollen.

apiculate: with a little point.

aquatic: living in water.

aril: outgrowth from seed-stalk (common in *Euphorbia* family).

astringent: contracting or binding.

axil: the angle between leaf and branch or stem.

axillary: in the axil.

berry: succulent fruit with seeds immersed in the pulp.

biennial: lasting two years.

bisexual: having two sexes (i.e. stamens and pistil in the same flower).

bract: modified leaf at base of flower-stalk, or leaves around a flower-head.

bracteole: small bract on the flower-stalk.

bullate: blistered or puckered.

calcareous: chalky or limy.

calyx: outermost, usually green, floral envelope.

capitate: arranged in a head, or head-like.

capsule: dry fruit which opens.

carpel: one or more divisions of ovary or fruit.

caruncle: wart or protuberance near stalk of seed.

catkin: slender, often pendulous spike of flowers.

compound: formed of many similar parts.

concave: scooped out.

connate: united similar parts.

connective: portion of filament connecting lobes of the anther.

convex: humped.

cordate: heart-shaped.

corolla: collective name for the petals.

corymb: more or less flat-topped collection of flowers.

crenate: with blunt, curved teeth.

crenulate: diminutive of crenate.

cross-pollination: transference of pollen from one flower to stigmas of another.

cyme: an inflorescence repeatedly divided with the oldest flower in the middle of each fork.

cystoliths: mineral markings in the leaves as found in the Nettle family.

deciduous: falling off.

decumbent: lying on the ground.

decurrent: running down.

dentate: toothed.

dioecious: male and female flowers on different plants.

disk: a fleshy portion of floral axis, often secreting nectar.

disk-flower: flowers in the middle of a flower head with rays.

drupe: stone fruit such as a plum.

elliptic: shaped like an ellipse.

endosperm: reserve food material in a seed.

entire: not divided or toothed.

B (I)

epicalyx: collection of bracteoles like an extra calyx.

falcate: sickle-shaped.
female: the fruiting part of the flower (ovary or carpels).
filament: stalk of stamen.
fruit: the fertilized and mature ovary or carpel.

glabrous: not hairy.
glaucous: with a whitish-blue lustre like the 'bloom' of a grape.
globose: round like a globe.

hastate: like an arrow, but with the barbs turned outwards.

imbricate: overlapping, with one part wholly outside.
inferior: below.
inflexed: turned inwards.
inflorescence: collection of flowers on the shoot.
introrse: facing inwards.
involucre: a ring of bracts surrounding one or more flowers.
irregular: applied to a flower (like that of a pea) which cannot be divided into equal halves in more than one direction.

lanceolate: lance-shaped.
leaflet: unit of a compound leaf.
lenticels: corky spots on bark.
lobulate: divided into small lobes.
locular: divided into chambers.
loculus: a chamber or cavity of an ovary, fruit, or anther.
longitudinal: lengthwise.

male: a plant or flower which bears stamens.

monoecious: male and female flowers on the same plant.
mucronate: bearing a little tip.

nectary: organ in which nectar is secreted.
node: point of insertion of a leaf or leaves.
nutlet: little nut.

oblanceolate: reverse of lanceolate.
obovate: reverse of ovate.
opposite: inserted at same level, as leaves on a shoot.
orbicular: circular.
ovary: the female part of the flower, represented by the carpels.
ovate: egg shaped.
ovoid: ovate in outline.
ovule: the organ which after fertilization develops into a seed.

panicle: a branched raceme.
papillous: clothed with short, knob-like hairs.
pappus: modified calyx of the *Compositae.*
pectinate: divided like a comb.
pedicel: the ultimate flower-stalk.
peduncle: common stalk of several flowers.
peltate: attached in the middle (like the stalk of a mushroom).
pendulous: hanging down.
perennial: lasting more than two years.
perianth: the collective outer covering of the flower.
persistent: not falling off.
petal: the usually coloured inner part of the floral leaves.
petiolate: stalked leaves.
petiole: leaf-stalk.

pinnate: divided like a feather.

placenta: the part of the ovary or carpel which bears the ovules.

plumose: feather-like.

pollen: the fertilizing, dust-like powder in the anthers.

procumbent: lying down.

pubescent: hairy.

pustulate: covered with little warts.

raceme: unbranched inflorescence with individual flowers stalked.

radical: from the root.

ray-flower: marginal flower of the *Compositae.*

receptacle: floral axis.

reflexed: bent back.

regular: symmetrical.

reticulate: like a net.

rootstock: underground stem.

scabrid: rough.

segment: division of an organ.

self-pollination: pollen from the same flower.

serrate: with saw-like teeth.

serrulate: diminutive of serrate.

sessile: without a stalk.

spadix: spike with a fleshy axis (as in *Arum*).

spathe: envelope around the spadix.

spike: stiff unbranched inflorescence with the flowers not stalked.

stamen: the male organ of the flower.

stigma: tip of the style.

stipule: appendage at base of leaf of leaf-stalk.

stolon: basal branch which roots.

style: narrow portion of pistil between ovary and stigma.

superior: placed above.

tendril: thread-like production.

terminal: at the top or end.

ternate; in threes.

tomentose: densely covered with short hairs.

truncate: cut off abruptly.

tuber: fleshy underground part of the stem.

tuberculate: with small outgrowths like warts.

umbel: inflorescence branched like the ribs of an umbrella.

unisexual: of one sex.

valve: portion into which a fruit or other organ separates or opens.

villous: with long shaggy hairs.

viscid: sticky.

vitta: oil tubes of fruits of *Umbelliferae.*

whorl: arranged in a circle around an axis.

YEW

Taxus baccata L. (A, male shoot, $\times\frac{2}{5}$ B, shoot with 'fruit', $\times\frac{2}{5}$)

Small tree often used as a garden hedge and in topiary work; 'flowers' very inconspicuous, the males (A1, $\times 1\frac{1}{4}$) on one tree, the females (C, $\times 2$) on another (dioecious); the pollen from the male is blown by the wind to the female, the latter consisting of an exposed ovule on a short shoot of its own and surrounded by small overlapping scales (C, $\times 2$); unlike other conifers, Yew trees have no cones, and so there is no real fruit; but the seed (D, E, $\times 1\frac{1}{4}$) is surrounded by a red sweet fleshy cup-like structure (aril) which is a great attraction to birds, who pass the seed without injury, for

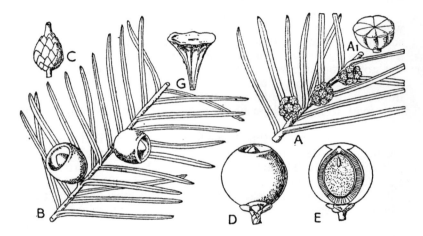

the seed itself is very poisonous; it is thus distributed away from the parent tree (G, ripe male scale, $\times 2\frac{1}{2}$) (family *Taxaceae*).

The Yew is very widely spread in most parts of Europe, from Britain and Scandinavia to western Russia, and from Algeria to as far east as Burma and even the Philippines. The further south it occurs, the higher it ascends the mountains, for example up to 5400 ft. in the Pyrenees.

One can nearly always find a Yew in a country churchyard. It was of value in olden times for making bows. In this country it is best seen as a wild tree in the chalk downs of southern England. Yews live to a great age, up to about 3000 years, the highest recorded being about 30 ft., with a trunk 12 ft. in diameter. The wood throws out a great heat when burned.

Pinus sylvestris L. ($\times \frac{2}{5}$)

Branches of two kinds, long and short shoots, the former growing on without interruption each year, the latter bearing the pair of needle-like leaves which arise in the midst of small scales; after persisting for three or four years these leaf-bearing short shoots fall off, and are really deciduous (term for leaves falling off), though the tree is of course always green (evergreen); the male or staminate 'cones' are crowded towards the top of the shoot (A), and about the end of May when the branches are disturbed by the wind clouds of pollen are dispersed; the pollen-grains are provided with two air-filled bladders, which makes them very buoyant; they are thus transported to the more familiar female cones (B, C) which bear the ovules and eventually the seeds (E, $\times 2$); when these are mature one may hear in a pine-wood on a warm summer day little explosions at intervals, indicating the release of a small winged seed from the cone, formerly more or less erect, but now drooping, which facilitates the escape of the seed; this falls with a rotatory movement which carries it well away from the shade of the parent tree, where it stands a better chance of germination (D, scale bearing the two inverted ovules, $\times 4$) (family *Pinaceae*).

Most people know a Pine tree when they see one, and the drawing may help them to distinguish the native from the numerous cultivated kinds. Those familiar with Scotland and parts of the Lake District in Cumberland, and, nearer London, Bagshot Heath, will realize how much the scenery owes to this most beautiful tree. Though young specimens are of rather formal pyramidal growth, older examples spread out their tops like a Cedar of Lebanon, and rarely clash with other types of vegetation. Usually the Pine is associated with Heather, Ling, and Bracken.

Scots Pine is greatly valued for its timber and as firewood. Like all Conifers, it is a 'softwood', as compared with Oak, a 'hardwood'. One can travel far abroad and still meet with the tree, sometimes in most diverse climates, even as far as eastern Siberia, where the temperature in winter falls to $-40°$ F., and in southern Spain, with a summer temperature up to $95°$ F. There are several varieties, some of which, however, are not at all constant and are dependent on soil conditions. For example, Pines which have been small and stunted assume the ordinary tall form when the condition of the soil is changed by draining.

D

A

B

C

E

J.H.

39

JUNIPER
Juniperus communis L.

Evergreen shrub, much branched, with very sharp prickly short narrow evergreen leaves, these in whorls of 3 and glaucous above;

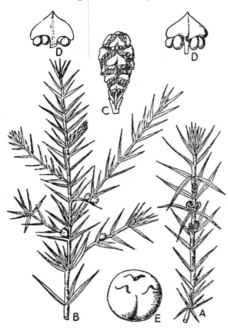

male and female cones usually on different plants (dioecious), axillary, very small, the male (C, ×2) consisting of several broad shortly pointed scales D, ×3) each with about 4 anther-loculi attached to the lower margin, the female with a few empty scales at the base and 3 fleshy ones above which unite to form the depressed globose cone ('fruit') (E, ×1½) which is dark purple-blue and about ⅓ in. in diam.; seeds hard; very widely distributed in North Temperate regions from the Mediterranean to the Arctic and across Asia into North America; (A, male shoot, ×⅖; B, female shoot, ×⅖); usually grows on open downs and hillsides and is locally common; a second species is *J. sibirica* Burgsd. (*J. nana* Willd.), very dwarf and in these islands found only in Scotland and the western half of Eire.

Oil of Juniper is obtained from the dried ripe female cones ('fruits'), and is colourless or pale greenish-yellow, with a characteristic odour and a burning somewhat bitter taste. It is used medicinally, and the berries are also employed for flavouring gin (family *Cupressaceae*).

The Juniper 'berry' is not a real berry in the botanical sense, such as a Cherry or Blackberry, but consists of naked seeds united together into a berry-like structure. It is not therefore a real fruit, for a fruit is derived from closed carpels or carpels united into an ovary, in which the seeds are enclosed.

Laurocerasus officinalis Roemer ($\times \frac{2}{3}$)

Bush or small tree, much branched; leaves evergreen, shining, green, alternate, oblong-elliptic, shortly pointed, averaging about 6 in. long and 2 in. broad, leathery, denticulate, often with 2 conspicuous glandular pits (A, $\times \frac{2}{3}$) towards the entire base on the lower surface; lateral nerves 9–10 pairs, looped; stalk $\frac{1}{2}$–$\frac{3}{4}$ in. long; stipules soon falling off and leaving a scar; flowers strongly scented, arranged in axillary semi-pendulous racemes, the stalks spreading at a right angle; calyx (B, $\times 5$) pinkish-brown outside, orange-yellow inside; lobes greenish-white, inflexed, woolly-hairy inside; petals (C, $\times 4$) white, obovate, $\frac{1}{5}$ in. long; stamens (D, $\times 4$) 20, in two whorls, the inner slightly shorter; filaments white;

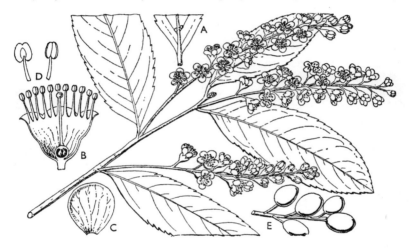

anthers pale yellow; ovary green, 2-ovuled; stigma disk-like; fruit (E, $\times \frac{2}{3}$) a black berry about $\frac{3}{4}$ in. long, with a hard stone (synonym *Prunus laurocerasus* L.) (family *Rosaceae*).

The Cherry Laurel is one of our commonest garden shrubs, and is frequently planted as a hedge; it grows well in shade, stands a lot of cutting about, and is readily propagated by cuttings and layers. There are several cultivated varieties. As a wild plant it is found in the Balkans, Asia Minor, the Caucasus, and northern Persia.

The fresh leaves are sometimes used for flavouring sweetmeats, custards, creams, etc., but should be employed with great caution, as they have poisonous qualities (prussic acid). (See also notes under Bird Cherry (fig. 5).)

5   BIRD CHERRY, HECKBERRY
Padus racemosa Schneider ($\times \frac{2}{3}$)

A shrub or small, much-branched tree with dark-coloured bark; mature leaves obovate-elliptic, pointed, rounded at the base, 2–3 in. long and up to 2 in. wide, the several pairs of lateral nerves with a tuft of hairs in their axils (B, ×2); serrate with pointed teeth; stalks sometimes bearing large glands, but these mostly paired near the leaf-base (A, ×1⅓); stipules soon falling off, toothed; flowers appearing with the young leaves, arranged in slender more or less pendulous racemes at the end of the young shoots from the previous season's growth; calyx widely bell-shaped, 5-lobed, lobes rounded, with a gland between the base of each (C, ×2); petals (D, ×2) white, shortly clawed, rounded and with jagged edges; stamens (E, ×4) numerous; ovary (F, ×4) superior, of one carpel with 2 pendulous ovules; fruit (G, ×1) small, globose, black, and shining, with a hard stone in the middle (synonym *Prunus padus* L.) (family *Rosaceae*).

Grows in woods and hedges, mostly in the northern parts of Britain, flowering in May; fruit extremely bitter, when eaten causing the tongue to become nearly black and dried up; flowers strongly perfumed; the stigmas are receptive before the anthers are ripe; but if insect visits fail automatic self-pollination takes place.

The Bird Cherry is a very widely distributed tree, occurring over most of Europe eastwards as far as Manchuria and Japan, south to Persia and the Himalayas; the wood is hard and yellowish, but not put to much use.

I recognize the genus **Padus** as distinct from the true Cherries (*Prunus*) because, as in the case of *Pyrus* (*Sorbus*, *Malus*, etc.), *Prunus* is divisible into more than one genus. In **Padus** the racemes of flowers are always borne at the ends of the young shoots, in **Laurocerasus** (see fig. 1) the racemes are axillary, whilst in **Prunus** proper the flowers are clustered and not arranged in racemes, or only rarely and very shortly so.

Formerly the Bird Cherry was much sought after in France by cabinet-makers and turners for the attractively grained wood, the beauty of which was increased by sawing the trunk diagonally instead of parallel with its length.

Although the fruits are so sour to human beings, birds eat them readily, hence the origin of the common name, whilst caterpillars devour the leaves of this tree more than any others of the family.

SLOE
Prunus spinosa L. (×$\frac{2}{5}$)

Flowers appearing before the leaves on short lateral spine-tipped branchlets; calyx (A, ×1) with 5 lanceolate lobes, lined inside with a 10-lobed disk; petals (B, ×$2\frac{1}{4}$) white; stamens about 12–15, the yellow anthers attached at the back above the base (C, ×6); carpel (D, ×2) 1, free within the calyx-tube, gradually narrowed into a rather long slender style tipped with a head-like (capitate) stigma; largest leaves (E, ×$\frac{2}{5}$) on the longer shoots, which bear neither flowers nor fruit, more or less elliptic and rather shortly toothed; fruit (F, ×$\frac{2}{5}$) blue-black and globular or broadly elliptic (family *Rosaceae*).

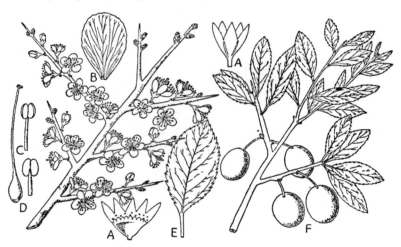

The fruit of the Sloe, like that of the cherry (fig. 5), is known as a drupe or stone fruit, in which the outer part is fleshy, and the inner part is hard and stony and contains a single seed; it is very astringent, but makes a fairly good jam; formerly used in making British 'Port Wine', and the juice for marking-ink; wood tough and used as teeth for rakes. The spine-tipped branchlets protect the young foliage from browsing animals and the plant is useful for hedges. Damsons and the various kinds of Plums of our gardens are derived from forms of the Sloe. It is not likely to be confused with other wild species of the genus, *Prunus avium* L. (see fig. 8), and *P. padus* L., the Bird Cherry, or Heckberry, as it is often called in the north; the latter has rather long racemes of small white flowers and black very bitter shining fruits.

Cotoneaster integerrimus Medik ($\times\frac{1}{2}$)

A dwarf deep-rooted shrub with long and short shoots, the older branches with a dark purplish-red glabrous bark; young branchlets covered with short cottony hairs; leaves broadly ovate-elliptic to nearly rounded, entire, 1–2 in. long and nearly as much broad, glabrous or nearly so above, densely and softly woolly below, with rather obscure looped lateral nerves; stipules conspicuous, acute, brownish; flowers (C, $\times2\frac{1}{2}$) pink, few at the ends of the short shoots; bracts linear, hairy on the margin; calyx 5-lobed, lobes erect, hairy on the margin; petals (B, $\times4$) 5, erect, obovate, pink, finely veiny; stamens (A, $\times4$) numerous in a ring at the base

of the calyx-lobes; ovary inferior, composed of usually 3 carpels, each with a lateral style about as long; fruits (D, $\times\frac{3}{4}$) pendulous, covered with a fine 'bloom', red, globose, about $\frac{1}{4}$ in. diam.; pyrenes (E, $\times3$) 3-sided, rounded on the back, very hard (family *Rosaceae*). – Synonym *Cotoneaster vulgaris* Lindl.

Found in Britain in only one locality in north Wales, but otherwise widely distributed as far east as Siberia and south to Spain and Persia. Nectar is secreted by the fleshy inner wall of the receptacle, and wasps are the principal visitors.

Numerous species of this genus are cultivated, mainly for their ornamental berries; a favourite is *C. microphyllus* Wall., which makes a pretty covering for rocky slopes.

8

WILD CHERRY or GEAN
Prunus avium L. ($\times\frac{1}{2}$)

In woods and hedges, and generally distributed; common in beech woods; sometimes nearly 100 ft. high, with a girth up to 12 ft.; trunk often unbranched to a considerable height, and covered with a thin smooth greyish bark which peels off in transverse strips; branches long and spreading, of two kinds, long shoots (A, $\times\frac{1}{2}$), and very short shoots (B, $\times\frac{1}{2}$), the long shoots continuing to elongate, the short shoots bearing an annual crop of flowers and, or, leaves; long shoots smooth between the short shoots, and tinged with purple; short shoots scarred by the stalks of the leaves of previous years; current season's leaves produced from within a cluster of leaf-scales (C, $\times\frac{1}{2}$) of various shapes; inner scales very hairy inside; leaf-stalks bear a pair of glands (extra-floral nectaries) near the top or almost on the base of the leaf-margin (D, $\times 1$); flowers appear at the same time as the leaves which attain their full size when the fruit is ripe; young leaves often with gland-tipped teeth; mature leaves elliptic or obovate, pointed, rather coarsely but bluntly toothed; hairs confined to the axils of the nerves (E, $\times 2\frac{1}{2}$) and to the nerves; stipules narrow, margined by glands; flowers 2–6 in a cluster, with stalks up to $1\frac{1}{2}$ in. long; calyx-lobes reflexed; petals white, finely veined; stamens (F, $\times 2$) about 25, with long slender filaments and small rounded anthers attached in the middle; style 1, slender, as long as the stamens; fruit (G, $\times\frac{3}{4}$) globose, reddish, 1-seeded, seed furrowed along one edge (family *Rosaceae*).

Prunus avium is a very widely distributed tree, found in nearly the whole of Europe, as far north as Bergen in Norway, and south to Asia Minor and the Caucasus; being very ornamental in flower, it has been much planted, especially in parts of Germany, where it is grown alongside the highways. It is considered to be a native of the southern counties of England. In Scotland it is usually called Gean. The wood is scarce, but is one of the best native timbers for inside work, possessing a fine even grain and taking a good surface and polish. It is likely to be confused with only one other native species, *P. cerasus* L., which, however, never becomes a tree, but remains a bushy shrub with much-branched stems, and from the roots are produced numerous suckers.

A characteristic feature of *Prunus avium* is the presence of curious glands on the leaf-stalk, just below the leaf-blade, and shown clearly in fig. D. Each bunch of leaves is produced from a cluster of bud-scales varying in shape (fig. C).

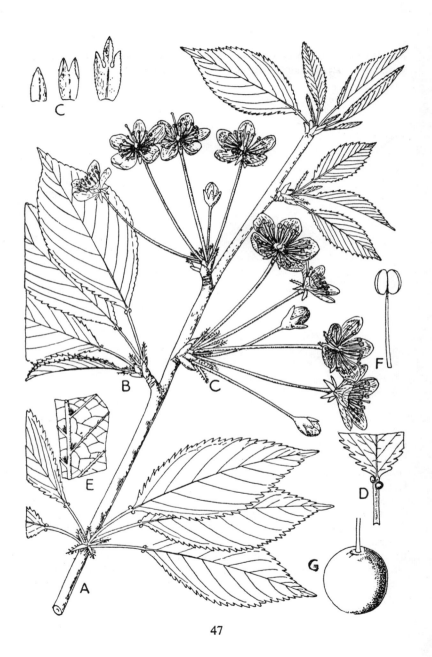

47

9

MEDLAR
Mespilus germanica L. ($\times \frac{1}{3}$)

Small tree with axillary spines; young shoots more or less villous with soft whitish hairs; stipules oblanceolate, small and leafy, with

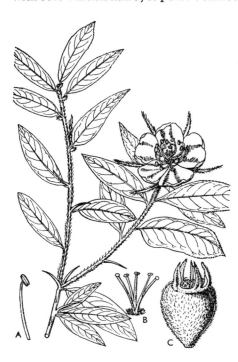

glandular teeth; leaves deciduous, alternate, oblong-obovate to lanceolate, rounded at the base, triangular at the apex, $2\frac{1}{2}$–4 in. long, 1–$1\frac{1}{2}$ in. broad, entire or finely toothed in the upper half, very softly pubescent on both surfaces especially when young; flowers terminal on the young lateral branchlets; pedicel and calyx densely villous; calyx widely turbinate, deeply 5-lobed, lobes spreading between the petals, linear-lanceolate, about $\frac{3}{4}$ in. long; petals 5, white, broadly obovate; stamens (A, $\times 1\frac{1}{2}$) numerous; anthers attached in the middle; ovary inferior, very hairy on top; styles (B, $1\frac{1}{2}$) usually 5, sometimes 2 or more partly united; fruit (C, $\times \frac{2}{3}$) rounded-ovoid, obtusely angular, hairy, crowned by the persistent incurved calyx-lobes and remains of stamens and styles (family *Rosaceae*).

In hedges and woods in various parts of England, usually as an escape from cultivation; the fruit is not palatable until it has become soft and pulpy, and it should be left on the tree as long as possible – to about the end of October; it should then be stored until fit to eat. The white conspicuous flowers are produced in May and June. They are bisexual and the half-concealed nectar is secreted by a yellow fleshy ring in the receptacle within the stamens. The species is a native of Europe and Asia Minor.

HAWTHORN 10
Crataegus monogyna Jacq. ($\times\frac{3}{5}$)

A shrub or small tree, the branchlets often ending in stiff sharp thorns; leaves born on very short annual shoots, stalked, with a pair of lanceolate acute leafy stipules at the base of the stalk (A, $\times 1\frac{1}{4}$); blade obovate-wedge-shaped in outline, 3-lobed, lobes ascending coarsely 2–3-toothed, bright green and glabrous or slightly hairy below in the axils of the main nerves; flowers (B, $\times 2\frac{1}{2}$) fragrant, arranged in short broad corymbs at the ends of the short leafy shoots; bracts very small and soon falling off; stalks hairy

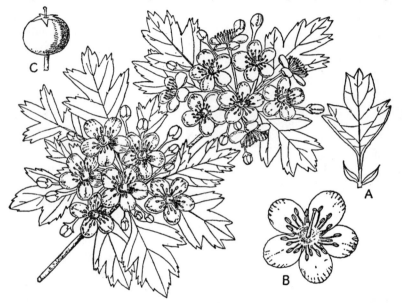

towards the top and on the calyx-tube; calyx-lobes 5, widely separated, oblong-lanceolate, not hairy; petals 5, white or tinged with pink, much overlapping in bud (imbricate), free from one another, rounded-obovate; stamens about 25; anthers pink; ovary inferior, with 1 rather thick style woolly at the base and a head-like stigma; fruit (C, $\times 1\frac{3}{4}$) a red 'berry', more or less globose, crowned by the short calyx-lobes, with a mealy exterior and containing a hard nut (drupe) containing a single seed (family *Rosaceae*).

There are two species in Britain, that described above and *Crataegus oxyacanthoides* Thuill, with less cut leaves.

Malus sylvestris Mill. (syn. Pyrus malus L. ($\times \frac{2}{5}$)

One of our most beautiful small native trees, especially when in flower or fruit; bark scaly and fissured; leaves scattered on the long shoots, clustered on the short shoots, narrowly obovate, sharply serrate; flowers A, $\times \frac{4}{5}$, petals removed) 5–6 in a cluster (umbel) and appearing with the leaves at the top of a short shoot; calyx-lobes pointed, woolly inside; petals (B, $\times \frac{4}{5}$) 5, pink outside, white inside; stamens (C, $\times 2$) about 20; anthers ovate, tipped by a gland; ovary inferior; styles 5, united in the lower part (D, $\times 1\frac{1}{4}$; E, $\times 3\frac{1}{4}$); fruit (F, $\times \frac{2}{5}$) almost globular, about 1 in. diam., green flushed with red, very acid (family *Rosaceae*).

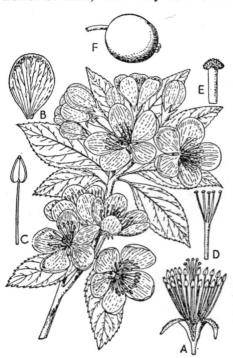

During the day the flowers of the Crab Apple give off only a very slight odour of honey, but at night they possess an agreeable fragrance which attracts numerous night-flying insects. When the flower opens the erect stamens are crowded together in the middle, and their close, yellow anthers are usually well below the level of the five already mature stigmas. The latter are thus almost certain to receive pollen from other flowers carried by insects searching for the nectar, which is secreted inside the calyx-tube (receptacle). Cross-pollination, as in our garden apples, is necessary for a good crop of crab apples. The tree grows apparently wild from about the Forth and Clyde areas southwards, and in many parts of Eire. Some trees have been reported up to 45 ft. high.
Synonym *Malus pumila* Mill.

Sorbus aria (L.) Crantz ($\times \frac{1}{2}$)

A shrub or moderate-sized tree up to about 40 ft. high, easily recognized by the snow-white under-surface of the leaves; branchlets brownish-crimson, marked with very small rounded pore-like
lenticels; leaves simple, ovate to slightly obovate, shortly wedge-
shaped at the base, rounded or slightly pointed at the apex, averaging about 3 in. long and 2 in. broad, woolly-hairy on both surfaces when young, but the hairs only persisting below, rather
coarsely and doubly crenate-dentate, with 6–9 pairs of nearly

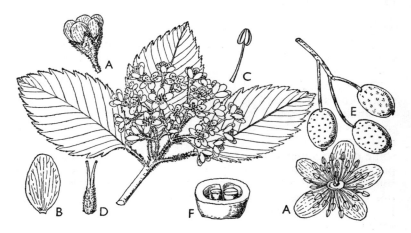

straight prominent nerves; flowers (A, $\times 1\frac{1}{4}$) arranged in a terminal corymb (see figure) at the end of the new shoots, covered
all over with cottony white hairs; petals (B, $\times 2$) white; stamens
(C, $\times 2$) about 25, in two rows; styles (D, $\times 2\frac{1}{2}$) 2, hairy at the
base; fruits (E, $\times \frac{1}{2}$) ellipsoid, red, $\frac{1}{2}$–$\frac{3}{4}$ in. long (F, $\times 1\frac{1}{4}$ section
of fruit) (synonym *Pyrus aria* (L.) Ehrh.) (family *Rosaceae*).

The White Beam is a tree in woods, on good soil reaching 40–50
ft. or sometimes a little higher. In rocky mountainous situations,
however, it is usually shrubby. It is easily recognized by the
snowy-white under-surface of the leaves, but outside Britain it
exhibits a great variety of forms in a wild state, ranging as it does
over a wide area throughout Europe, Algeria, Asia Minor, and as
far east as Siberia and central China.

Sorbus aucuparia L. ($\times\frac{1}{2}$)

An elegant tree up to about 30 ft. high with numerous spreading branches; bark brownish-grey, smooth, branchlets reddish-brown; winter-buds ovoid, hairy; leaves alternate, pinnate, with with about 6–8 pairs of leaflets and an end one, and a slightly winged common stalk; leaflets oblong, toothed (dentate), smooth or more or less hairly below; stipules very small and soon falling off and leaving a slight scar; flowers (B, $\times4$) small, rather densely arranged in a more or less flat cluster (corymb), scented; calyx (A, $\times4$) adnate to the lower part of the carpels, with 5 short tri-angular teeth; petals creamy-white, rounded; stamens (C, $\times3$) 20–25; anthers (D, $\times5$) brownish-yellow; styles (E, $\times4$) usually 3, hairy at the base; fruit more or less globular, fleshy, about $\frac{1}{3}$ in. diam., scarlet or rarely orange, soon eaten by birds (F, flower bud, $\times4$) (family *Rosaceae*).

This beautiful tree will scarcely be confused with any other native kinds because of its distinctive characters. It is a favourite for small gardens, and is often planted as a street tree, where it provides food for birds in the autumn. It is more common in the northern parts of Britain, and in the past was put to many uses, some due to superstition. For instance, it was supposed to be a protection against witchcraft, a twig being carried about the person for this purpose. The wood is hard with a fine grain, but the tree should not be confused with the true Ash, *Fraxinus excelsior* L., described under fig. 201 and which has opposite leaves and dry winged fruits.

There are several exotic species of *Sorbus* related to the Rowan which are becoming increasingly popular, not only because of their elegant form and foliage, but because of the beauty of their autumn colours and their ornamental fruits. One of the most in-teresting species is the south European *Sorbus domestica* L., a single tree of which grew in the middle of the Wyre forest in Worcestershire, where it was probably introduced in Roman times. It was regarded as an old tree in 1678, and lasted until 1862, when it was maliciously burnt down. It is pleasant to recall that descendants of this tree, which was known to everyone and vener-ated in the neighbourhood, are still growing in the forest. The fruits are interesting, being of two shapes, on one tree being shaped like a pear, and on another like an apple.

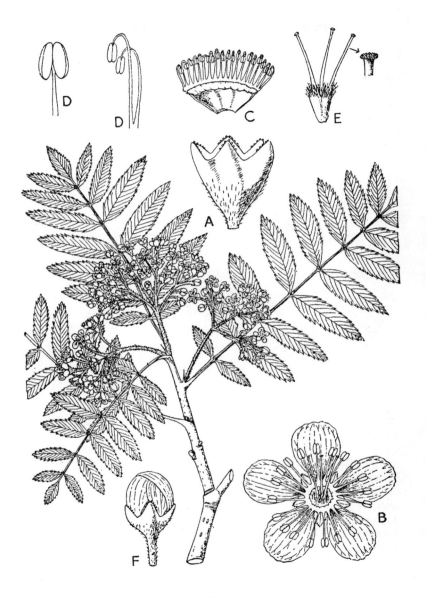

Sorbus torminalis (L.) Crantz ($\times\frac{1}{3}$)

A large shrub or medium-sized tree with purplish-brown branch-lets; leaves borne on short lateral barren shoots and also on the young flowering terminal shoots, deciduous, ovate-elliptic in out-line, rounded or slightly cordate at the base, pinnately divided into about 7–8 lobes, these sharply pointed and serrulate, the main lateral nerves as many as the lobes and very slightly hairy in their axils below, the remainder of the hairs below soon falling off; stipules not evident; flowers (B, ×1) in terminal corymbs, their branches more or less woolly-hairy; upper part of calyx-tube (A, ×1) less hairy than the lower, lobes triangular, glandular on the

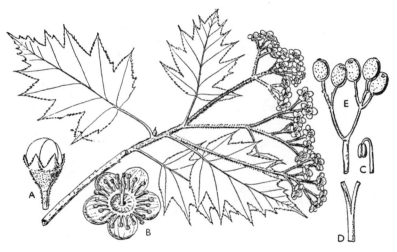

margin; petals white, larger than in the Rowan (Mountain Ash) (fig. 13); stamens (C, ×2) about 25, inflexed in bud; styles (D, ×2) usually 2, united below; ovary inferior; berries (E, × $\frac{1}{3}$) ellip-soid, brownish, with warty lenticels, about $\frac{1}{2}$ in. long (synonym *Pyrus torminalis* (L.) Ehrhart) (family *Rosaceae*).

Not wild in Britain, but planted in the southern half of Eng-land; it prefers a soil rich in humus; known as the 'Service' or 'Griping' tree, and in Kent and Sussex the fruits are called 'Chequers'. They ripen late in October, are eaten by birds, and have a wine-like flavour when over-ripe; leaves reddish-yellow in autumn.

Amelanchier arborea Fernald ($\times\frac{1}{3}$)

A shrub or small tree with slender often arched stems; branches somewhat crimson and with a glaucous 'bloom' like that on a bunch of grapes; leaves and flowers appearing together; stipules (A, $\times\frac{2}{3}$) thread-like, softly hairy, $\frac{1}{3}$ in. long; leaves (B, $\times\frac{2}{3}$) oblong-elliptic, rounded at the base, sharply and rather suddenly pointed, at flowering time about $1\frac{1}{2}$ in. long and $\frac{3}{4}$ in. broad, softly hairy on both surfaces but the hairs soon falling off, closely toothed with sharp incurved teeth on the margin; stalk about $\frac{1}{3}$ as long as the blade, softly hairy; flowers (C, $\times\frac{1}{2}$) several in a terminal raceme; bracts and bracteoles linear, reddish, hairy; calyx with 5 spreading triangular awl-shaped lobes woolly-hairy above; petals (D, $\times 1\frac{1}{3}$) 5, spreading to a diameter of about $1\frac{1}{2}$ in., white, oblanceolate; stamens about 15, incurved in bud, opening in turn from the outside; ovary somewhat below the calyx with a smooth cushion-like top from the middle of which arises the shortly 5-lobed style with fringed stigmas; fruit campanulate, reddish purple, about $\frac{1}{3}$ in. diam., topped by the persistent sepals, filaments and style (family *Rosaceae*). – Synonym *Amelanchier canadensis* of many authors, not of Medic; also *A. laevis* var. *villosa*.

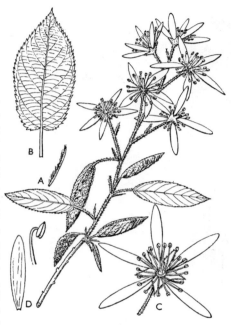

Naturalized on the Bagshot Heath, Hurtwood Common, Surrey, etc.; native of the eastern United States of America as far north as Quebec.

Filipendula vulgaris Moench (× ½)

Perennial with the roots swollen here and there into oblong tubers (A, ×½) (hence the common name Dropwort); stems erect, up

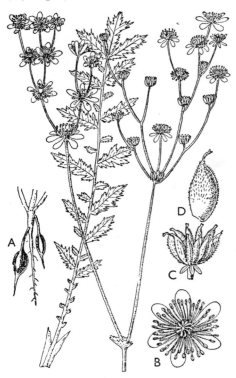

to about 2 ft. high, but usually about 1 ft.; leaves mostly crowded at the base of the stem, pinnately divided into several separate often alternately longer and shorter segments, which increase in length upwards and are coarsely toothed, glabrous or nearly so; stipules broad and adnate to the leaf-stalk nearly their full length; flowers (B, ×1½) in a terminal cyme with raceme-like branches, and the flowers on one side, the lateral ones very shortly stalked; calyx 5-lobed, lobes oblong, rounded at the apex, glabrous; petals 6–5, rounded-obovate, shortly clawed, pure white or sometimes tinged with red; stamens numerous; carpels (C, ×3) free, 6–12, not twisted in fruit (D, ×4) shortly hairy (synonym *Spiraea filipendula* L.) (family *Rosaceae*).

This plant bears various names in different *Floras*, such as *Spiraea filipendula* L., *Ulmaria filipendula* Hill, and *Filipendula hexapetala* Gilib. The companion species in the British flora, the Meadow-Sweet, is shown in fig. 17, and it is there explained why a separate generic name is necessary for them. *F. hexapetala*, so named from having usually six petals, ranges right across Europe and Asiatic Russia, and flowers in summer. It is found mainly in dry chalky and limestone pastures. The flowers have a faint scent, but secrete no nectar.

Filipendula ulmaria (L.) Maxim. ($\times \frac{2}{5}$)

Rootstock short and creeping; stem purplish, up to 4 ft. high; basal leaves (A, $\times \frac{2}{5}$) large, pinnate; terminal leaflets deeply 3–4-lobed; lateral leaflets more or less elliptic, doubly and finely toothed (serrulate); between the larger leaflets are pairs of small leaflets; all with a dense felt of white hairs or sometimes almost without hairs below; stipules leafy, ear-shaped; upper stem-leaves smaller and usually only 3-lobed; flowers (B, $\times 2$) arranged in a cyme with the lateral branches longer than those in the middle, $\frac{1}{4}$-in. diam.; calyx-lobes ovate, reflexed; petals (C, $\times 3$)

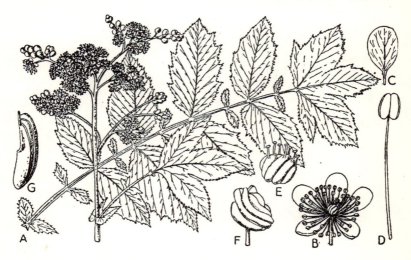

creamy-white, clawed; stamens (D, $\times 12$) numerous; carpels (E, $\times 4$) free, and with short subterminal styles and head-like (capitate) stigmas, becoming more twisted and falcate in fruit (F, $\times 1\frac{1}{2}$; G, $\times 2\frac{1}{2}$) (family *Rosaceae*).

This is one of our most attractive wild plants, generally distributed in wet meadows and near water; it will not always be found in botanical books under the genus name *Filipendula*, but often as *Spiraea*. The genus *Astilbe* (family *Saxifragaceae*), a common greenhouse pot plant, is often called by gardeners *Spiraea*. True Spiraeas, however, are woody, and our plant is sufficiently distinct to bear a different generic name. Botanists do not always agree about points such as these, though there is not much difference of opinion regarding the genera of our common plants.

RASPBERRY
Rubus idaeus L. ($\times\frac{1}{3}$)

Stems biennial, flowering and fruiting the second season, woody, to about 5 ft. high, prickly (A, $\times1$); rootstock short; leaves pin-

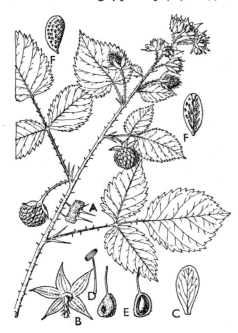

nate, the lower often with two pairs, the upper with one pair of leaflets and an end leaf-let; leaf-stalk some-times with a few short prickles; leaflets broad-ly ovate, doubly cut in-to sharp-pointed teeth, end leaflet broader and larger, with a soft felt of white hairs below; sti-pules paired above the base of the leaf-stalk, thread-like; flowers few together at the top of the stem, with single or paired flowers in the upper axils, these ma-turing first and ripen-ing their fruits; flower-stalks (pedicels) slen-der, with soft short hairs and small prickles; sepals 5, with a long point from a triangular base, softly hairy (B, $\times1$); petals 5, white (C, $\times1\frac{1}{3}$); stamens (D, $\times3$) numerous; carpels (E, $\times3$) numerous on a conical receptacle, free and woolly when young, becoming red or yellow and juicy in fruit; style slender (F, seed $\times5$) (family *Rosaceae*).

The Raspberry is easy to recognize among the many British species, forms, and hybrids of the genus *Rubus*. It grows in par-tially open spots in woods and is often common on the sides of railway embankments and cuttings. It flowers from June on-wards, and soon produces a crop of the juicy red berries so much sought after by country people. Nectar is secreted in a fleshy ring on the margin of the flower-axis (receptacle) within the stamens. The styles form a convenient landing-place for insects, which effect cross-pollination, but self-pollination may also take place.

Rubus chamaemorus L. (×⅔)

Dwarf perennial herb of the moors and mountains; lower part of the stem with a few large sheathing brown persistent stipules; leaves 1–3 on each plant, long-stalked, rounded-kidney-shaped in outline, deeply palmately 5-lobed and 5-nerved, cordate at the base, about 1½–2 in. broad, slightly hairy on the nerves below; flowers unisexual, dioecious, solitary, terminal, long-stalked, stalks shortly hairy and with some gland-tipped hairs; sepals 5, broadly elliptic, pointed, glandular-pubescent petals white, rounded-obovate, ¾ in. long; stamens numerous; ripe carpels orange-yellow, ellipsoid, reticulate, ⅕ in. long, surrounded by the persistent calyx (family *Rosaceae*).

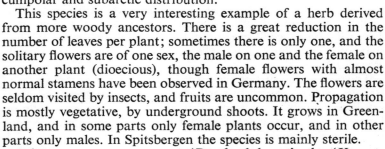

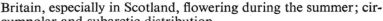

Grows in turfy bogs on the mountains in northern Britain, especially in Scotland, flowering during the summer; circumpolar and subarctic distribution.

This species is a very interesting example of a herb derived from more woody ancestors. There is a great reduction in the number of leaves per plant; sometimes there is only one, and the solitary flowers are of one sex, the male on one and the female on another plant (dioecious), though female flowers with almost normal stamens have been observed in Germany. The flowers are seldom visited by insects, and fruits are uncommon. Propagation is mostly vegetative, by underground shoots. It grows in Greenland, and in some parts only female plants occur, and in other parts only males. In Spitsbergen the species is mainly sterile.

Other common names are 'Roe-buck-berry', the 'Knowtberry' of the Scotch, and 'Knotberry' in old English. In Germany it has several names, 'Moltebeere', 'Multbeere', 'Schellbeere', 'Kranichbeere', and 'Torfbeere'.

MOUNTAIN AVENS
Dryas octopetala L. ($\times \frac{1}{2}$)

Woody perennial with short much-branched prostrate or creeping stems and forming dense tufts; leaves (A, $\times 1\frac{1}{4}$) alternate, on fairly long hairy stalks, oblong or ovate-oblong in outline but deeply toothed on the margin and rounded-cordate at the base, glabrous and green above with impressed nerves and veins, snow-white below with woolly hairs, $\frac{1}{2}$–$\frac{3}{4}$ in. long; stipules thin, united to the leaf-stalks, but with free linear tops; flowers on long slender hairy stalks terminating the short leafy shoots; sepals (B, $\times 1\frac{1}{4}$) about 8, narrow, nervose on the inside, woolly hairy outside; petals (C, $\times 1$) white, about 8 to 10 or rarely fewer, narrowly obo-

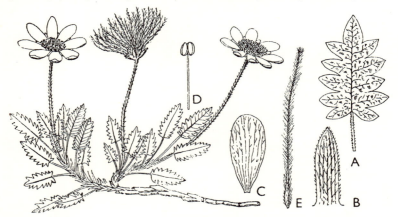

vate, veiny; stamens (D, $\times 6$) very numerous, with slender filaments, and rounded anther-loculi; achenes (E, $\times 2$) numerous, free, silky hairy, each in fruit ending in a long plumose tail like that of 'Traveller's Joy', *Clematis vitalba* (fig. 241) (family *Rosaceae*).

This lovely and distinctive plant is not found over the whole of Britain, but is frequent in northern England, northern and western Eire, and the mountains of northern Scotland, especially on limestone soil. It is widely distributed in arctic and alpine regions of the northern hemisphere.

The flowers are *protogynous*, i.e. the stigmas are receptive before the anthers release their pollen. Failing insect visitors to effect cross-pollination, automatic self-pollination may take place owing to the higher position of the anthers. Nectar is secreted by a ring below the filaments.

Perennial herb growing in hedgebanks and on the borders of woods, and generally distributed, but rarer in the north of Scotland; the basal leaves (A, $\times \frac{2}{5}$) have longish stalks with a large end-lobe which is either shortly 3-lobed or divided to the base' into 3 separate leaflets; stem-leaves variably lobed from above the middle to nearly the base; stipules (B, $\times \frac{2}{5}$) large and leafy; flowers terminal and solitary; sepals 5, united in the lower part, with a small bracteole between each; petals (C, $\times 2\frac{1}{2}$) bright yellow; stamens (D, $\times 8$) numerous; carpels numerous, free, in fruit (E, $\times \frac{4}{5}$), produced into a hooked prickle (F, $\times 2\frac{1}{2}$) (family *Rosaceae*).

This plant flowers from late spring til autumn, and the fruits are readily distributed by means of the hooked prickles, which catch on to the clothing of passers-by and the coats and fur of animals. Nectar is secreted by a green fleshy ring within the stamens. Cross-pollination is effected by insect visitors, and self-pollination is also possible. The plant was formerly used in medicine and the roots to impart a clove-like flavour to ale.

A second species of the genus is also found in Britain, the Water Avens, *Geum rivale* L., (fig. 22) which grows in marshy places and ditches, and is common in northern England, Scotland, and Eire. In this the petals are orange streaked with red, and where the two species grow together hybrids between them are often found.

WATER AVENS
Geum rivale L. ($\times \frac{1}{2}$)

Perennial herb with a rather slender rhizome covered with persistent leaf-sheaths fringed with hairs; roots sometimes hairy; basal
leaves (A, $\times \frac{1}{2}$) on long hairy stalks, irregularly pinnate, the leaflets increasing in size upwards, the end one the largest, and widely
cordate to wedge-shaped (cuneate) at the base, the lower becoming very small, all coarsely toothed or lobed, finely but thinly hairy
on both surfaces; stipules leafy, entire or lobed, clothed with long
slender hairs; stem-leaves becoming much smaller and with very
short stalks; flowers (B, $\times \frac{1}{2}$) few (2–3) at the top of the stems,

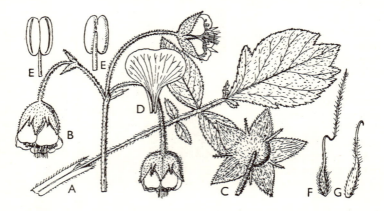

with leafy bracts; sometimes some flowers are unisexual, the males
having only rudiments of carpels; stalks very softly hairy; calyx
(C, $\times 1$) reddish-brown, with 5 ovate-triangular pointed lobes and
very narrow lobes (bracteoles) between them; petals (D, $\times 1\frac{1}{2}$) 5,
yellow, streaked with red, obovate, narrowed into a claw, strongly
nerved; stamens (E, $\times 4$) numerous; carpels arranged in a stalked
bunch, densely covered with long soft hairs, with a long slender
style which in fruit (F, G, $\times 2$) becomes bent like a hook in the
upper part and clothed with long spreading hairs (family *Rosaceae*).

Grows in marshy places and ditches, and widely distributed in
the temperate regions all around the northern hemisphere; common in northern Britain and in Eire. Nectar is stored in numerous
drops in the receptacle. Either cross- or self-pollination is possible,
some humble-bees stealing nectar by inserting their proboscis between the calyx and petals.

Potentilla fruticosa L. (×½)

A more or less erect much-branched shrub up to 2½ ft. high but sometimes dwarfer; bark on older branches split longitudinally; annual shoots and leaves covered with long silvery silky hairs; stipules about ½ in. long, oblong-lanceolate, acutely acuminate, longitudinally nerved, with membranous margins; leaves pin-

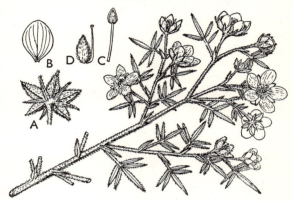

nately 5-foliolate (rarely 7-foliolate), leaflets oblong-lanceolate, entire, acute, about ¾ in. long; flowers about 1–1¼ in. diam., numerous and dotted all over the plant, with silky stalks about as long as the leaves; calyx (A, ×1½) double, i.e. composed of an epicalyx of 5 lanceolate bracteoles as long as the 5 ovate-acuminate calyx-lobes, both sets silky hairy; petals (B, ×1) 5, yellow, spreading, veiny; stamens (C, ×1½) numerous; carpels (D, ×1½) numerous, with a basal style, silky hairy (family *Rosaceae*).

Confined to hilly limestone districts in northern England and along the western edge of the central plain of Eire, flowering in summer; widely distributed around the north temperate zone as far south as the Himalayas. Nectar is secreted by the receptacle. The chances of cross- and self-pollination are about equal in this species, for insects on alighting may touch either the stigmas first or the anthers which open at the sides.

Owing to its very wide range this species varies very much and there are several varieties in cultivation which are described in Bean's *Trees and Shrubs Hardy in the British Isles*; one of these, var. *grandiflora* Willd., has leaves and flowers much larger than the type form, the flowers averaging as much as 1¼ in. in diam.; var. *leucantha* Spath has white flowers, as also var. *veitchii*, a fine form from Hupeh originally described by Wilson as *P. veitchii*.

24   SILVERY-LEAVED CINQUEFOIL
Potentilla argentea L. ($\times \frac{1}{2}$)

Low perennial with slender brown rootstock; leaves (F, ×1) green and very minutely hairy above, white below with short woolly hairs; blade divided to the base into 5 parts, each part (F1, ×2) narrowly wedge-shaped to the base, deeply lobed, the lateral nerves impressed above, prominent below; stipules paired at the base of the stalk and joined to it for a short distance; flowers (A, ×1, petals removed) in short leafy cymes, the bracts leaf-like and sessile; flowers in the forks maturing first and on a slender stalk; calyx 'double' (B, ×1), made up of 5 leafy bracteoles and 5 ovate lobes, hairy outside; petals (C, ×2) 5, bright yellow, rounded;

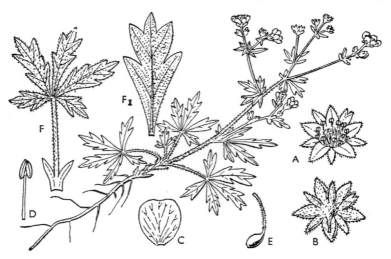

stamens (D, ×4) several, with short yellow anthers and brownish connective; carpels (E, ×3) numerous, surrounded by shaggy white hairs (family *Rosaceae*).

This very distinctive species is locally distributed in England and south-eastern Scotland, but does not occur in Eire. It grows in dry, sunny pastures, heaths, and by roadsides, flowering in summer. It is common in Norway, and is found through central Europe and across Asia. Bees and flies effect pollination.

In Britain there are about fifteen species of *Potentilla* (see also notes under *P. fruticosa*, fig. 23), and for their identification a modern *Flora* such as recommended on p. xiv should be used.

Potentilla anglica Laichard (× ½)

Perennial with short thick rootstock, bearing a cluster of radical leaves and slender trailing stems rooting at the nodes; basal leaves on slender stalks and divided into 3–5 wedge-shaped coarsely toothed leaflets about ¾ in. long and ⅔ in. broad, thinly hairy on both surfaces, especially on the nerves below; stem-leaves shortly stalked, with leaflets similar to the basal ones but smaller; stipules large and resembling lower leaflets; flowers solitary in the upper leaf-axils, on very slender stalks about 1½ in. long; calyx (A, ×2½) double, of 4–5 narrow bracteoles and 4–5 ovate hairy sepals; petals (B, ×4) 4 or 5, yellow, obovate and broadly notched;

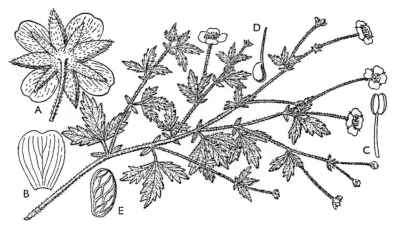

stamens (C, ×5) several; carpels (D, ×6) several inserted on a densely setose-hairy axis, in fruit (E, ×6) ellipsoid and coarsely reticulate (family *Rosaceae*). Synonym *Potentilla procumbens* Sibth.

A locally common species in woodlands, hedgebanks, and amongst bushes on commons, but widely distributed in Europe.

Potentilla is a very large genus of more than three hundred species, most of them herbs, but a few shrubby. It is a good example to demonstrate how some herbs have been derived from woody ancestors. Several of these herbaceous species, besides being reduced to herbs, show a corresponding reduction in the number of carpels and stamens, an example being *P. sibbaldii* Hall. f. (fig. 31).

Potentilla erecta (L.) Rausch ($\times\frac{1}{3}$)

Perennial herb with numerous slender erect pubescent stems from a thick many-headed rootstock; leaves nearly sessile, divided to the base into 3 narrowly wedge-shaped segments, with a pair of leafy lobulate stipules at the base, the segments coarsely and sharply toothed; pedicels axillary and terminal, often collected into a loose leafy cyme, very slender; sepels (A, ×2) 4, narrowly triangular-lanceolate, acute, with a narrow bracteole between each; petals (B, ×1¾) 4 or rarely 5, yellow, broadly obovate, veiny; stamens (C, ×3) 15–20; carpels (D, ×4) few, obliquely obovoid, hairy around the base, with a slender lateral style, glabrous; fruits (E, ×3) ovoid, reticulate (F, fruits, ×1) (family *Rosaceae*).

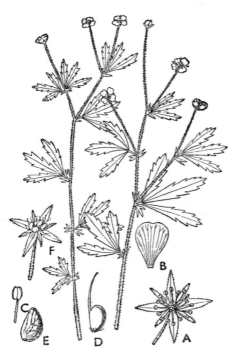

On heaths and dry pastures, widely distributed; flowering in summer. In most British *Floras* this is usually included in the aggregate species, *P. tormentilla*. Nectar is secreted on the inner side of the calyx-tube (receptacle), and the anthers are only covered with pollen on their narrow outer edges. Cross-pollination is effected by insects, but during dull weather the flowers are half shut, when self-pollination may take place.

Although most of the British species of *Potentilla* are herbs, many of the exotic species are shrubs. The herbaceous species, therefore, are probably the most highly evolved, for their shrubby ancestry is indicated by the possession of a woody underground rootstock, a device which ensures their preservation in winter and during excessive droughts.

Potentilla sterilis (L.) Garcke ($\times \frac{1}{3}$)

Perennial with the habit of the Wild Strawberry, covered with long silky hairs; leaves on long stalks, divided into 3 leaflets, these broadly obovate, nearly sessile, wedge-shaped at the base, very coarsely toothed, silky hairy on both surfaces; stipules large and thin, joined to the leaf-stalks, persisting on the older part of the stem; flowers (B, $\times 1$) solitary, on long slender stalks, nearly $\frac{1}{2}$ in. diam.; calyx (A, $\times 1$) of 5 narrowly triangular lobes with a narrow bracteole between each almost as long; petals (C, $\times 1\frac{1}{2}$) white, broadly obovate; stamens (D, $\times 3$) about 20; anthers elliptic; carpels (E, $\times 4$) rounded, glabrous, with a long slender style attached at the side; in fruit (F, $\times 5$) obovoid and reticulate; receptacle not enlarging as in the Strawberry (synonym *Potentilla fragariastrum* Ehrh.) (family *Rosaceae*).

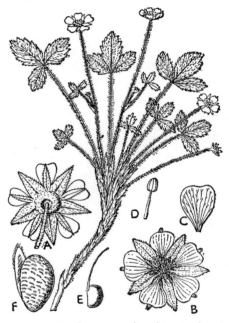

This species flowers in early spring, and grows on banks, dry pastures, and in open woods in Europe, extending eastwards as far as the Caucasus; it is rare in northern districts of Britain. It greatly resembles the wild Strawberry (fig. 32), having very similar white flowers but borne singly, and with quite different fruits. Between the stamens and the carpels is a pentagonal hairy coloured nectar-ring. After a time the stamens bend inwards and touch the stigmas, when self-pollination results. The hairs on the upper surface of the leaves have a bulbous swelling at the base.

CREEPING CINQUEFOIL
Potentilla reptans L. ($\times\frac{1}{2}$)

Perennial herb with a slender rootstock and slender creeping stems which root at the nodes and form new plants; leaves on long slender stalks, divided fan-wise into 5 separate leaflets, the latter oblanceolate and rather coarsely toothed; stipules ovate, large, not divided; flowers $\frac{3}{4}$–1 in. across, on slender stalks (pedicels) usually longer than the leaves; calyx with 5 ovate-triangular lobes and narrower lobes (bractlets) between (A, $\times\frac{3}{5}$); petals (B, $\times 1\frac{1}{2}$) bright yellow, widely notched at the top; stamens about 20; anthers (C, $\times 5$) egg-shaped (ovoid), opening at the sides; achenes

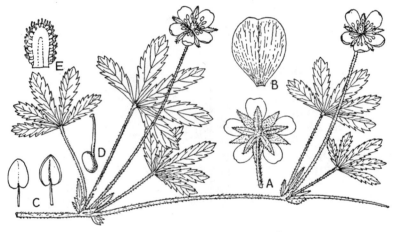

(D, $\times 8$) numerous, inserted on a hairy conical axis (E, $\times 2$), with the slender style inserted on one side and crowned by a small head-like (capitate) stigma (family *Rosaceae*).

This is a very common species in meadows and by roadsides mixed with other 'herbage', and it flowers during summer and autumn. It becomes rather scarce north of the Forth and Clyde. One other is common and liable to be mistaken for *P. reptans*. This is *P. tormentilla* Sibth., which has only 4 petals in all or nearly all the flowers, and the upper leaves are not stalked.

As in other species of the genus, the nectar is secreted in the form of a shining layer on the inner wall of the calyx-tube or receptacle around the base of the stamens. Cross-pollination is usually effected by insect visitors, but automatic self-pollination also takes place owing to the closing of the flowers in dull weather and during the night.

Argentina anserina (Linn.) Rydb. ($\frac{2}{5}$)

Perennial with slender rootstock, giving off procumbent runners; leaves all radical, more or less horizontally spreading, silky and silvery-white on both sides; leaflets up to about 15 pairs, sessile, oblanceolate, sharply toothed, with smaller pairs of leaflets between; flowers about 1 in. diam., solitary on slender stalks from the rootstock or in the leaf-axils on the runners; sepals and bracts of the epicalyx together 10, almost equal, but in two distinct whorls, hairy (see fig. A, flower from below, $\times \frac{3}{4}$); petals (B, $\times 1$) yellow, finely veined, almost orbicular; stamens about 20; anthers

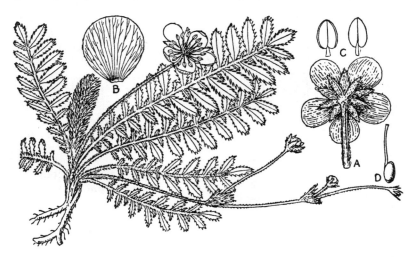

(C, $\times 3$) ovate, opening at the side; carpels (D, $\times 2$) numerous, elliptic, with the slender style inserted towards the top (family *Rosaceae*).

If South Africa has its Silver tree, we have a similarly coloured weed, for it is silky and silvery-white all over; it grows in damp meadows and banks of ditches as well as damp places on roadsides. In this species the nectar is secreted as a thin shining film on the inner wall of the calyx-tube around the base of the stamens, and is of a dark or reddish-yellow colour. If insect visitors alight in the middle of the flower they effect cross-pollination, but if this does not occur automatic self-pollination takes place on account of the flowers closing up completely at night or in dull weather.

Potentilla palustris (L.) Scop. ($\times \frac{2}{5}$)

In marshy places and spongy peat-bogs, especially in hilly districts; whole plant strongly astringent; rootstock blackish, creeping in the mud; lower leaves stalked, with a terminal and 2–3 pairs of lateral leaflets; stalk hairy, with the large stipule joined to it for some distance from its base; leaflets elliptic, very coarsely toothed (serrate); upper leaves (A, $\times\frac{1}{3}$) much smaller and very shortly stalked with only 3 leaflets, and with a pair of large ear-like stipules at the base; flowers (B, $\times\frac{1}{2}$) dark-purple, up to $1\frac{1}{2}$ in. diam., very few in a terminal leafy cluster, stalked; calyx-lobes 5, broad and sharply pointed, alternating with much smaller bractlets (*epicalyx*), opposite which are the quite small petals (C,

$\times 2\frac{1}{2}$); stamens 20–25, inserted on a broad flat hairy disk; anthers (D, $\times 5$) purple, opening at the side; carpels (E, $\times 3$) numerous, with the slender style arising from near the base; roots formerly used in tanning; they yield a yellowish dye (family *Rosaceae*).

In this flower the duty of attracting insects has been largely assumed by the calyx, which is dark purple in the lower part, the petals being quite small and not at all conspicuous. The stamens are in two whorls and at first erect over the stigmas. But the latter are not mature and receptive until after the anthers have opened and shed their pollen. Afterwards the filaments bend outwards, leaving the space they occupied in the middle of the flower free for the styles to receive pollen carried from another flower by insects collecting the nectar secreted in the large disk.

Perennial with creeping or decumbent rootstock, forming dense spreading tufts, the short stems densely covered by the persistent leaf-bases; leaves long-petiolate, with a large adnate stipule at the base, 3-foliolate, leaflets obovate-wedge-shaped, truncate and deeply 3-toothed at the apex (A, ×1), about ½–¾ in. long, with long bristle-like hairs on both surfaces; flowers (B, ×1¼) in shortly pedunculate corymb-like cymes with large leafy bracts; calyx (C, ×3) 'double', i.e. with an epicalyx of 5 subulate bracts between the sepals, the latter ovate-triangular, strongly nerved; petals 5 or sometimes absent, small, narrow, and inconspicuous, pale greenish yellow; stamens usually 5–7; achenes (D, ×5)

mostly 5, in fruit ovoid, pale yellow-brown, shining; style lateral (family *Rosaceae*). – Synonym *Sibbaldia procumbens* L.

Found only in the hills and mountains of northern England and in Scotland, where it is more common; circumpolar in distribution and at greater elevations in the mountains of western and central Europe and in Asia; sometimes regarded as a separate genus from *Potentilla*, but hardly distinguishable from it by any definite characters.

The flowers of this species are greenish-yellow and not at all conspicuous. The nectar is exposed and secreted by the broad fleshy disk which surrounds the carpels and is eagerly sought for by short-tongued insects which effect cross- and self-pollination.

WILD STRAWBERRY
Fragaria vesca L. ($\times\frac{1}{2}$)

In appearance this is just a garden strawberry in miniature, and sometimes as tasteful; in woods and shady hedgebanks, often plentiful; perennial herb with runners (A), softly hairy all over; leaves long-stalked, divided to the base into three leaflets, the latter obovate, wedge-shaped at the base, coarsely toothed (serrate), the teeth curved upwards; stipules dry and thin; flowers few on a long common stalk (peduncle) up to about a foot long; bracts leafy; calyx (B, $\times 1\frac{1}{4}$) of 5 broadly lanceolate lobes and with narrow bracteoles between nearly as long, pubescent; petals (C, $\times 3$)

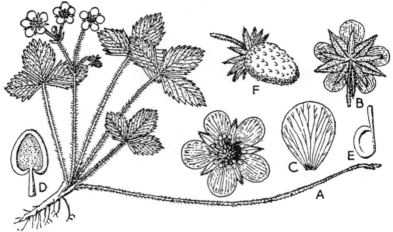

pure white, broadly obovate-rounded; stamens 15–20; anthers (D, $\times 10$) horse-shoe shaped, heart-shaped at the base, opening at the sides; carpels (E, $\times 10$) free, crowded in the middle of the flower and inserted on a conical axis, quite smooth (glabrous), with the short style inserted on one side; the fruit (F, $\times 1\frac{1}{4}$) axis enlarges, juicy and sweet and bears the small ripe fruitlets (achenes) on the outside (family *Rosaceae*).

This wild plant is the parent of all our cultivated varieties of Alpine strawberries, and propagates itself by means of runners on which buds arise at the nodes as well as at the tip. These develop into new plants after the connecting portions have died away. Suppose a strawberry plant sends out three runners during a season, each takes root at five nodes, and from every node a new plant develops, so that the following year the mother plant is surrounded by fifteen offspring!

Shrublet usually not much more than 1 ft. high, much branched, the branches densely covered with unequal-sized prickles mixed with shorter gland-tipped hairs; leaves with 3–5 pairs of leaflets and an odd stalked leaflet at the end; leaflets sessile, almost orbicular, about $\frac{1}{2}$ in. long, rather sharply toothed, not hairy; stipules green, joined (adnate) to the stalk, about $\frac{1}{2}$ in. long, finely glandular-toothed; flowers mostly solitary at the end of short shoots, stalked, about $1\frac{1}{2}$ in. diam.; calyx-lobes narrow, $\frac{1}{2}$ in. long, margins at most finely toothed but not lobed as in some other roses;

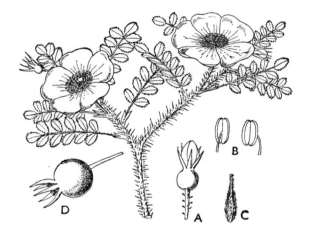

petals pink or white, spreading widely; stamens numerous, the stalks very short; carpels numerous, enclosed by the enlarged floral receptacle which really forms a false fruit around the little fruitlets (achenes) lining the inside; false fruit globose, purplish-black, crowned by the persistent calyx-lobes (family *Rosaceae*).

This pretty little rose grows on sandy heaths, especially near the sea, and is to be found on some of the commons around London. In its widest (i.e. aggregate) sense it is distributed in the cooler parts of Europe, northern Asia, and south to the Himalayas. There are several varieties, and it hybridizes freely with other species; **var. pimpinellifolia** has smooth flower-stalks, though intermediate states are found.* Rose flowers have no nectar, but are sweetly scented, and attract insects by their abundant pollen.

* See A. H. Wolley-Dod, *Journal of Botany*, 1930, *Supplement*, p. 10.

Rosa canina L. ($\times \frac{1}{2}$)

The plant illustrated is the common form of one of our most beautiful hedgerow plants, but those who use this book will probably not be at first much concerned with the many other species and varieties which are to be found; * a shrub; branchlets prickly; leaves with usually 2 pairs of leaflets and a terminal one, with a large 2-lobed stipule joined to the stalk; stipule and stalk lined with a few shortly stalked glands; leaflets narrowly elliptic, doubly and rather sharply toothed (crenate), the teeth tipped with a small gland (A, $\times 2$); flowers sweet-scented, $1\frac{1}{2}$–2 in. in diam., usually only one open at a time in each cluster of 3; sepals (B, $\times 1$) broadly lanceolate, narrowed into a slightly broader top, the outer ones with a variable number of side-lobes margined with stalked glands, the innermost without side-lobes and shortly hairy more or less all over the outside; petals white or pink; stamens (C, $\times 3$) numerous, the anthers rather deeply lobed at each end; styles (D, $\times 5$) about 25, hairy, with an oblique concave stigma; fruits (E, $\times \frac{3}{4}$) red, usually 3 together, the middle one larger and more pear-shaped than the side ones, from all of which the sepals fall off; in vigorous shoots the prickles are larger, as shown in the drawing (F, $\times \frac{3}{4}$) (family *Rosaceae*).

There is no nectar in the flowers of many wild roses, but they produce abundant pollen, which is collected by insects, and either cross- or self-pollination occurs. The fruits of many are rich in vitamin C, and a large quantity were gathered during the war and made into syrup for the benefit of children as an anti-scorbutic in place of oranges.

As already stated on p. x, in the year 1943 over five hundred tons of rose-hips were collected from the hedgerows and woods of Britain, and from these no fewer than two and a half million bottles of National Rose Hip Syrup were prepared, equivalent in Vitamin C content to twenty-five million oranges. In general the roses in northern districts were richer than those further south.

     * See " A Revision of the British Roses," by A. H. Wolley-Dod in *Journal of Botany*, 1930–31, *Supplement*.

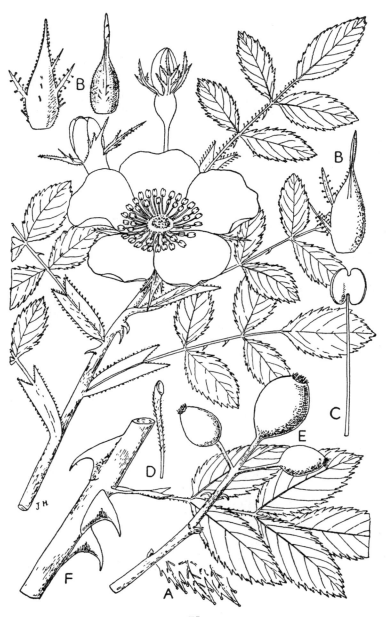

SWEET BRIAR
Rosa rubiginosa L. (×⅓)

Shrub with woody rootstock; young stems (A, ×⅓) succulent and very prickly, with downwardly curved prickles mixed with slender straight prickles here and there; leafy branchlets also armed with slender straight prickles; stipules (B, ×1) large, adnate to the leaf-stalk and densely margined with glands; leaf-stalk glandular and prickly; leaflets 3 pairs and a terminal leaflet (C, ×⅔), rounded, sharply and doubly serrate, rather densely glandular below and aromatic when rubbed; flowers pink, solitary or in threes, about 1½ in. diam.; usually 3 calyx-lobes pinnately lobed, 2 entire, some

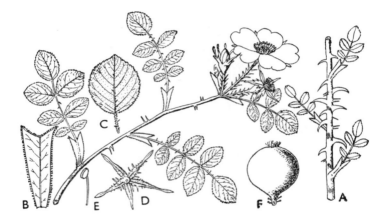

glandular, others softly tomentose outside (D, ×⅓); petals rather deeply notched; stamens (E, ×2) numerous; carpels numerous in-side the receptacle; fruit (F, ×⅔) rounded, smooth or occasionally with very few slender prickles, the stalk armed with stiff gland-tipped prickles, sepals at length falling off (family *Rosaceae*).

This differs from the Dog Rose (fig. 34) by the densely glandular leaflets, which are sweet scented when rubbed, and, like the fragrant flowers, help to attract insects.

In most roses nectar is not secreted in the flowers, insects visiting them for their pollen, but the Sweet Briar is an exception. On the broad fleshy margin of the receptacle or calyx-tube there is a thin layer of nectar. The flowers appear in early summer and are open from very early morning until about 9 p.m., the stigmas being receptive before the stamens release their pollen.

Perennial herb found in dry thickets, hedgebanks, and sides of fields, and in waste places, where it grows more luxuriantly up to 3 ft. high. No basal leaves, but only stem leaves, pinnate with coarsely-toothed leaflets (A, $\times \frac{2}{5}$), with numerous smaller leaflets between, and large leafy stipules (B, $\times \frac{2}{5}$) at the base; whole plant covered with soft hairs; flowers (C, $\times \frac{1}{2}$) in a stiff terminal spike, with a 3-lobed bract (D, $\times \frac{2}{5}$) below each; calyx-tube top-shaped, with a ring of hooked bristles at the top, becoming furrowed and hard in fruit (E, $\times 1\frac{1}{4}$), lobes 5, without intermediate bracts; petals (F, $\times 1\frac{1}{5}$) yellow; stamens 15–20, or fewer; carpels usually 2, in fruit enclosed by the hardened calyx (family *Rosaceae*).

This species was formerly a favourite remedy for liver complaints and a multitude of other diseases, and the whole plant yields a yellow dye. It flowers in summer and autumn, and the individual flowers remain open for three days. The flowers are adapted to both cross- and self-pollination. When they first open, the anthers are well away from the stigma, leaving ample room for an insect visitor to dust pollen on it from another flower or plant. Later they bend towards the stigma, rendering possible self-pollination, and finally the anthers drop off.

The floral axis (receptacle) is dry and woody and furnished with numerous stiff hooked bristles and acts as a fruit, the one or two real fruits (achenes) being enclosed by it. This false fruit readily attaches itself to clothing and to animals, by means of which it is widely distributed. Synonym *Agrimonia eupatoria* L.

Perennial herb, stems erect, up to 3 ft. high; odour resinous on account of numerous glands on the lower surface of the leaves (A, $\times 3$);

stems zigzag, clothed with long slender hairs; leaves alternate, pinnately divided into 4–5 pairs of coarsely toothed sessile leaflets with several small but very unequal-sized leaflets between them, hairy on nerves and margin; stipules large and leaflike, deeply cut into acute lobes; racemes spike-like, nearly 2 ft. long, soon developing fruit in the lower part; bracts 3-lobed, narrow; calyx-tube bell-shaped, with several rings of hooked bristles; lobes 5; petals (B, $\times 2$) 5, yellow; stamens numerous; carpels (C, $\times 2$) usually 2, in fruit enclosed by the hardened bristly, not furrowed, calyx (D, $\times 3$) (family *Rosaceae*).

Very similar to the Common Agrimony (fig. 36), but differs on account of the resinous odour, due to the numerous glands on the lower surface of the leaves, and the smooth (not furrowed) fruiting calyx-tube. The biological notes given for the Common Agrimony apply equally to this species. Both kinds flower from June onwards.

A nearly related genus is *Aremonia* Neck., *A. agrimonioides* (L.) Neck., which is introduced from south Europe and naturalized in woods in Scotland. The yellow flowers are arranged in cymes and there are no hooked bristles on the outside of the receptacle as in *Agrimonia*.

Perennial herb with a woody rootstock and annual stems up to about 2 ft. high; leaves mostly basal and from the lower part of the stem, pinate with opposite stalked broadly oblong coarsely toothed (dentate) glabrous leaflets; stipules of the basal leaves thin, adnate to the petiole, of the stem-leaves leaf-like and dentate; upper part of stem branched into rather long peduncles each bearing an oblong-cylindric head of dark crimson or purple bisexual flowers (A, $\times4$); calyx-tube enclosed in 2–4 bracts, 4-ribbed, the 4 lobes coloured like petals; no petals; stamens (B, $\times4$) 4, opposite the lobes; globular disk around the style at the base of

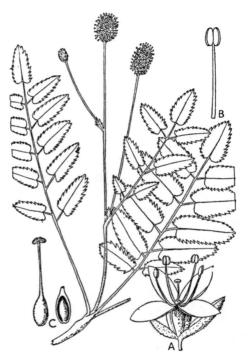

the calyx-lobes; ovary (C, $\times5$) embraced by the calyx-tube but quite free from it, 1-locular, with 1 ovule; style slender, with a very large disk-like papillous stigma; fruit dry, enclosed by the persistent ribbed calyx-tube; grows in moist meadows, mainly in northern Britain (family *Rosaceae*).

Surrounding the base of the style is a nectar-secreting ring, and the four calyx-lobes act as nectar receptacles. A striking feature of the flower-head is that the flowers open in succession from below upwards, so that only a zone one flower deep is in bloom at the same time. Insect visitors effect cross-pollination, though self-pollination may also take place automatically.

Poterium sanguisorba L. ($\times\frac{1}{2}$)

Perennial herb about a foot high, glabrous or sprinkled with long, many-celled hairs (A, $\times 10$); leaves mostly towards the base of the

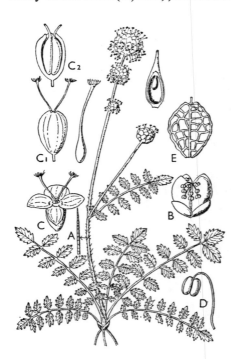

stem, pinnate with an odd terminal leaflet; leaflets opposite or nearly so, rounded to elliptic, coarsely toothed; stem or branches ending in a rounded head of flowers sometimes with one or two smaller heads below, each head bearing three types of flowers, the lower male (B, $\times 3$), the middle bisexual, and the upper female (C, $\times 3$), all light green or rarely purplish; calyx of the male 4-lobed; no petals; stamens (D, $\times 3$) numerous; calyx of female (C1, C2, $\times 3$) ellipsoid, tubular, contracted into four small teeth between which are the one or two styles with brush-like stigmas; fruit (E, $\times 3$) composed of the quadrangular, coarsely-reticulate persistent calyx-tube enclosing one or two seeds (family *Rosaceae*).

This pretty plant may be confused with the Greater Salad Burnet (fig. 38), but it has very different greenish unisexual and bisexual flowers, and numerous stamens. The yellow anthers of the male flowers hang down limply on long, thin white filaments. In some plants, however, the filaments are red and the anthers yellowish-red or red. The style and stigma are red to yellow or white. There are no nectaries in the flowers, and the pollen is borne by the wind.

It was at one time largely used as a salad plant, and was a common ingredient in 'cool tankards'. The leaves when bruised taste and smell like cucumber and are said to be refreshing.

Perennial herb; roostock thick; basal leaves on long stalks, kidney-shaped in outline, heart-shaped at the base, shortly and broadly 5–7-lobed, margin sharply toothed; main nerves as many as lobes, radiating fan-wise from the top of the stalk; not hairy below; upper stem-leaves alternate, becoming much smaller and less stalked, with a pair of coarsely toothed stipules like small leaves; flowers A, ×4) greenish-yellow arranged in small irregular clusters on slender stalks, with leafy bracts; sepals 4, with alternate smaller ones (bracts), green, 3-nerved; petals none; stamens (B, ×8) 4, alternating with the larger sepals and opposite the small sepals

(really small bracteoles forming an *epicalyx*); ovary (C, ×6) composed of one 1-locular carpel in the middle of a large fleshy disk, with the slender style arising from the base, and with a head-like stigma (family *Rosaceae*).

The roots taste like parsnip and are much sought after by pigs. It flowers from spring to autumn, in pastures and by streams. The popular name refers to the shape of leaves resembling a lady's mantle of olden times. If the young leaves be examined in bud it will be found that they are plaited and folded like a fan (D, $\times \frac{2}{5}$) and the green parts between the main radiating nerves are deeply folded and closely packed. The flowers vary a good deal in their structure and tend to become unisexual; in some the stamens are developed and the style is very short, or the stamens are vestigial or partly so and the style is well developed.

41   PARSLEY PIERT
Alchemilla arvensis (L.) Scop. ($\times\frac{1}{3}$)

Low-growing annual forming a flat carpet, with numerous branches radiating from the root; stems softly hairy with very delicate hairs; leaves (A, $\times2\frac{1}{2}$) fan-shaped, stalked, divided into 3 main parts, each part deeply lobed, thinly hairy; stipules (B, $\times2$) encircling the stem and adnate to the leaf-stalk, with a bunch (fascicle) of unisexual flowers in the axil and opposite to the leaf (leaf-opposed); pedicels short; calyx-lobes (C, $\times5$) 4, ovate, ciliate; no petals; fertile stamens 1 or 2, the others much reduced; anthers with 2 separate loculi (D, $\times8$); no ovary in the male; in the female a similar calyx and with 1–3 free carpels (E, $\times3$) which

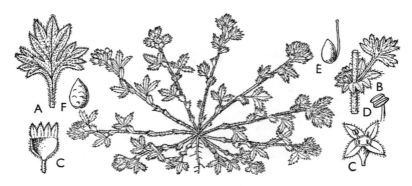

form the tiny fruits (F, $\times4$) (synynonym *Aphanes arvensis* L.) (family *Rosaceae*).

In fields and waste places, and often on lawns; widely distributed over the world by cultivation. The tiny flowers are hidden by the large leafy stipules, in the axil of which they are bunched together, and on the side of the stem opposite to the leaf. The small greenish semi-unisexual flowers have no petals, and the nectar is secreted by a fleshy ring on the inner wall of the floral axis (receptacle).

In many families, and even in some genera, one or more species often show considerable reduction in their flowers, especially by dispensing with their petals; or the flowers have become unisexual. Both these conditions are found in this interesting little species, an additional advanced character being its annual habit, most of the other species being perennials.

82

Spiraea salicifolia L. ($\times \frac{2}{5}$)

Erect shrub with greenish straw-coloured stems and branches; axillary buds with hairy tips; leaves alternate, broadly lanceolate, narrowed at each end, about 2–3 in. long and usually about 1 in. broad, thin, sharply toothed, usually glabrous, with a prominent midrib below and several forked lateral nerves; no stipules; petioles set in a pocket-like callus at the base; flowers (A, ×3) in dense spike-like panicles, each branch of the panicle with a small leaf-like bract at the base; calyx 5-lobed, lobes triangular, becoming reflexed; petals 5, obovate, pink, veiny; stamens (B, ×5) about 30, filaments spreading, thread-like; anthers small and rounded; carpels 5, free at the base of the calyx-tube; styles 5, free, stigma rounded; fruit (C, ×2) composed of 5 ovoid free beaked achenes (family *Rosaceae*).

Found in a wild state on wet river banks and bushy places across the north temperate zone, but in Britain an escape from gardens and naturalized in hedges and on river banks.

Nectar is secreted in abundance by an annular orange yellow thickening on the inner wall of the receptacle and within the stamens; these elongate and curve in such a way that the pollen can reach the stigmas of neighbouring flowers. In the related genus *Ulmaria* there is no nectar.

ACAENA
Acaena anserinifolia (Forst.) Druce ($\times\frac{1}{3}$)

Shrublet often forming a dense mass with numerous decumbent herbaceous branches and densely leafy; stems and branches softly pilose; leaves alternate, pinnate with an odd terminal leaflet; leaflets few pairs, crenate-serrate, softly pilose; stipules sheathing and adnate to the petiole, with leaflet-like lobes; flowers numerous in dense globose heads, on slender terminal peduncles; calyx (A, ×4) turbinate, 4-lobed, with harpoon-like processes (epicalyx) between the lobes which elongate and persist in fruit (E, ×$\frac{2}{3}$);

petals absent; stamen 1, anther didymous; carpel (D, ×4) 1, enclosed by the calyx-tube; style 1, with a large fimbriate stigma; fruit (B, ×1$\frac{1}{4}$) a 1-seeded achene enclosed by the hardened calyx which bears the persistent harpoon-like processes (C, ×3) (Synonym *Acaena sanguisorbae* Vahl.) (family *Rosaceae*).

An alien, native of Australia, Tasmania, and New Zealand, introduced with wool; in gravelly places and on sand-dunes; well established in a few localities, particularly in Holy Island, Northumberland.

Genista anglica L. ($\times\frac{1}{2}$)

A tiny shrub up to about a foot high; roots long and creeping; stems woody, branched from the base, branches armed with long slightly curved sharp spines, these being the hardened leafless branchlets of the previous season; young leafy shoots produced below the spines, some barren, some bearing flowers; leaves small, simple, obovate, acute; no stipules; flowers yellow, about $\frac{1}{2}$ in. long; calyx (A, $\times 2\frac{1}{2}$) bell-shaped, shortly 5-toothed; standard-petal (B, $\times 2$) ovate; wing-petals (C, $\times 2\frac{1}{2}$) obliquely oblong, shortly clawed; keel-petals (D, $\times 2\frac{1}{2}$) very similar but with a lobule

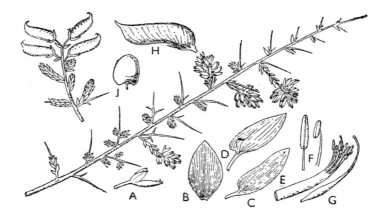

towards the base; stamens (E, $\times 2\frac{1}{2}$) 10, united into a single tube; anthers (F, $\times 6$) alternately short and attached in the middle (versatile) and long and attached at the base; ovary (G, $\times 2\frac{1}{2}$) glabrous; style longer than the stamen, glabrous; fruits (H, $\times 1\frac{1}{2}$) inflated like short broad pea-pods and tipped by the curled style, obliquely nerved; seeds (J, $\times 5$) rounded, dark brown, and shining (family *Papilionaceae*).

This small shrublet grows on heaths and moors, flowering in spring and early summer and sometimes again in the autumn. It is confined to western Europe, extending eastward only to Denmark and north-west Germany. It is absent from Eire. As in other species of the genus, there is no nectar secreted in the flowers, which discharge their pollen by an explosive mechanism on to the ventral surface of visiting bees, which collect the pollen in their pollen-baskets.

Genista tinctoria L. ($\times\frac{1}{2}$)

Shrublet with stems up to $1\frac{1}{2}$ ft. long; stems ribbed, slightly hairy to glabrous; leaves alternate, sessile, oblong-lanceolate to nearly ovate, at most about 1 in. long, entire, more or less hairy on the margin; flowers in a leafy or bracteate raceme, each with a pair of small bracteoles at the base of the calyx; calyx (A, $\times1\frac{1}{2}$) 2-lipped, the upper lip 2-lobed, the lower 3-lobed, lobes equal in length; petals yellow, the standard (B, $\times1\frac{1}{2}$), wings (C, $\times2$) and keels (D, $\times2$) as shown in the drawing; stamens (E, $\times2$) 10, united into one sheath, the anthers alternately long and basifixed, and short and medifixed; style (F, $\times2$) longer than the ovary; fruit (G, $\times1$) 1 in. long, with 7–9 dark-coloured seeds (family *Papilionaceae*).

Found over the greater part of England, but in Scotland in the south only; extends to eastern Asia, and introduced into North America. The flowers do not secrete nectar, but possess an explosive mechanism, the stamens and pistil coming into contact with pollen-collecting bees, which effect cross-pollination. Explosion has not been observed to occur naturally.

Cytisus scoparius (L.) Link ($\times \frac{2}{5}$)

Shrub up to 5 ft. high; branches numerous, long, straight, and whip-like, angular; leaves (A, $\times 1\frac{1}{4}$) divided into 3 small leaflets; flowers forming leafy racemes, bright yellow; calyx gaping and 2-lipped, lips minutely-toothed; standard petal (B, $\times 1\frac{1}{4}$) broad and rounded, notched at the apex; wing-petals (C, $\times 1\frac{1}{2}$) oblong, with a rounded lobe; keel-petals (D, $\times 1\frac{1}{4}$) bent like a golf-club; stamens (E, $\times 2$) all united into a tube, 5 long and 5 shorter; ovary hairy on the margins; style rounded-curved in the open flower; stigma terminal; pods (F, $\times 1$) compressed, about $1\frac{3}{4}$ in. long, margins covered with long slender hairs; seeds (G, $\times 3$) several, broadly oblong,

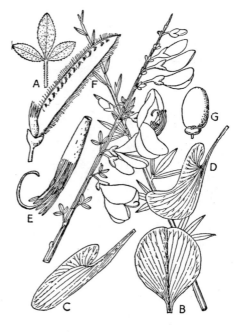

with a large fleshy aril at the base (family *Papilionaceae*).

Though there is no nectar, humble- and honey-bees visit the flowers and set in motion a very interesting explosive mechanism which releases the stamens and style from within the petals. The anthers are concealed within the boat-shaped keel-petals, and discharge their pollen very early, and it collects in the front part of the keel. When the insect alights on the keel and wings, the weight of its body presses them down and the pollen is discharged on to its undersurface, whence it is carried away and deposited on the stigma of another flower.

Broom tops, both fresh and dried, are used in medicine as a slight stimulant for the kidneys. The green angular switch-like branches are quite flexible and are useful for basket-work. When peeled they have the appearance of cane.

Ulex europaeus L. ($\times \frac{2}{5}$)

Shrub, or rarely a tree up to 20 ft. high; flowers golden-yellow, slightly scented, in spring and early summer, and again in autumn; each branchlet and leaf ends in a sharp spine; calyx with blackish hairs outside, divided into two large lobes (A, $\times 1$); standard petal bilobed at the apex (B, $\times 1\frac{1}{2}$); wing-petals hairy on the lower side (C, $\times 1\frac{1}{4}$); keel-petals also hairy (D, $\times 1\frac{1}{2}$); stamens 10, all united into a sheath (E, $\times 2$), the anthers alternately large and small, the large attached at the base, the small in the middle (F, $\times 4$); ovary (G, $\times 1\frac{1}{2}$) densely hairy; stigma terminal; pod $\frac{3}{4}$ in. long, densely hairy. On a warm day the pods burst with a little

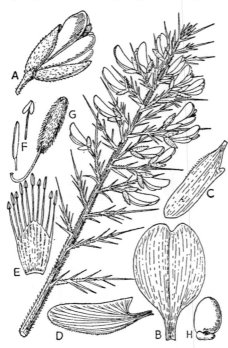

crack and fling out the seeds; these are brown and shining and have at the base a large fleshy aril (H, $\times 3$) (family *Papilionaceae*).

Some consider the spiny character of the gorse to be the result of its environment, as it grows most frequently in exposed dry places in shallow and often stony soil. They point out that many plants which grow in deserts are also spiny. Others say that the spines have been developed to protect them from browsing animals. It seems probable that a combination of the two reasons supplies the answer; that spines in gorse and other plants are a direct outcome of environment (exposure, drought, and soil), and, once formed, have been retained because of the protection they afford. The flowers have no nectar, but bees alight on the wings and release the pollen with an explosive action which dusts their bodies below.

DWARF GORSE 48
Ulex minor Roth ($\times\frac{1}{2}$)

Dwarf more or less prostrate shrublet with densely pilose-pubescent ribbed branches; leaves (H, $\times 2\frac{1}{2}$) awl-shaped, spine-tipped, up to about $\frac{1}{2}$ in. long, more or less hairy, bearing in their axils short branchlets clothed with similar but shorter leaves; flowers (A, $\times 2$) axillary and crowded towards the ends of the shoots and forming a short head or elongated 'tail'; stalks hairy; calyx 2-lipped, $\frac{1}{3}$ in. long, upper lip cleft at the apex, lower boat-shaped, shortly hairy; corolla yellow, the standard (B, $\times 1\frac{3}{4}$), wings (C, $\times 2$), and keel (D, $\times 2$) as shown in the drawing; stamens (E, $\times 3$) 10, united into a single sheath; filaments free in the upper

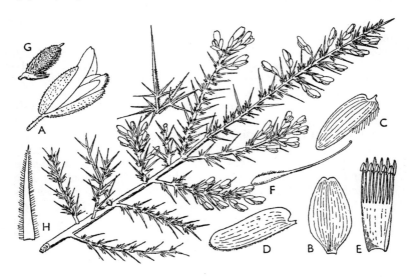

part and bearing alternately oblong and sagittate anthers of un-equal length; ovary (F, $\times 3$) hairy on the upper side, style glabrous; fruit (G, $\times 2\frac{1}{2}$) $\frac{1}{3}$ in. long, hairy (synonym *Ulex nanus* Forst.) (family *Papilionaceae*).

Very closely related to the common Gorse, of which it has been considered to be a small variety; besides its dwarf habit, most of its other features are on a much smaller scale than those of the commoner kind. Bees visiting the flowers set in motion the explosive mechanism, which, though in this case feeble, completely discharges the pollen on to the ventral surface of the insect, and after its visit scarcely a vestige of pollen is left behind.

Anthyllis vulneraria L. ($\times\frac{3}{5}$)

Perennial herb covered with very short appressed hairs; root-stock woody, branched; stems annual, spreading or ascending, up to about 1½ ft. long, each terminating in 1 or more often 2 de-pressed-globose clusters of flowers, girt by leafy bracts (see note below); basal leaves (A, $\times\frac{3}{5}$) with broader leaflets than the stem-leaves, the terminal leaflet much larger than the others and oblong-lanceolate, entire; stem-leaves subsessile, pinnate, leaflets linear to linear-lanceolate, the lowermost pair resembling stipules; flower-heads (see note below) up to 1½ in. diam. girt by narrow leafy bracts (B, ×1) shorter than the flowers; calyx (C, ×2) tubu-lar and inflated, somewhat 2-lipped, the back lip unequally 4-toothed, the front lip entire or slightly toothed, covered with long hairs outside; petals usually yellow, but varying to deep red; for standard, see fig. D, ×2½, wing, fig. E, ×2½, and keel-petals, fig. F, ×2½; stamens (G, ×1½) 10, their stalks united into 1 sheath; anthers equal, short; ovary (H, ×4) long-stalked, oblong, gla-brous, 2-ovuled (J, ×6); style slender, bent in the upper part, glabrous; fruits enclosed in the calyx, with 1 or 2 seeds (family *Papilionaceae*).

In this plant the beginning of the formation of a head of flowers surrounded by an involucre of bracts (capitulum) may be clearly traced. The head of flowers is really composed of a number of smaller clusters, each of which is subtended by a much-reduced modified leaf divided nearly to the base into several narrow leaflets (B, ×1); the lowest pair of leaflets often look very like stipules, but the absence of real stipules may be checked by examining the basal leaves, in which there is no trace of them; a striking feature of the floral structure is the stalked (stipitate) ovary (H, ×4).

The pollen is collected into threads and is discharged from the flowers by a pumping arrangement, the ends of the filaments of the stamens being thickened and club-like. The pollen is stored up in the tip of the keel-petals before the flower opens, and is re-leased by insect visitors. Not until the pollen is carried away does the stigma of the same flower become receptive, and this is caused by insects rubbing against it. The species is found chiefly in hilly districts throughout Europe and western Asia. It flowers in early summer, and grows in dry places on shallow soils, being most abundant on chalky soils. *Anthyllis* consists of about twenty species distributed in Europe and north Africa to western Asia.

NOOTKA LUPIN
Lupinus nootkatensis Donn. ($\times\frac{1}{3}$)

Perennial herb $1\frac{1}{2}$–2 ft. high; stems villous, with long slender hairs; leaves alternate, divided, like those of the Horse-Chestnut, into 6–

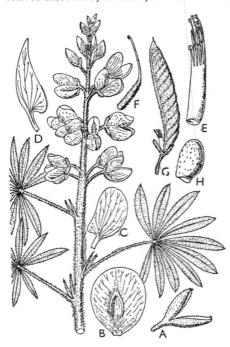

10 separate leaflets on a common stalk, the leaflets oblanceolate, 1–2 in. long, short and softly hairy on both surfaces; stipules paired at the base of the stalk, linear, about $\frac{1}{2}$ in. long, hairy; flowers in a terminal raceme up to 8 in. long; calyx (A, $\times1\frac{1}{2}$) 2-lipped, upper lip bifid, lower trifid, hairy; petals pale blue and pink, the spotted standard (B, $\times1$), wings (C, $\times1\frac{1}{2}$), and keel (D, $\times2$) as shown in the drawing; stamens (E, $\times3$) 10, all united into a sheath, 4 of the lower anthers elongated, the remainder very short and rounded; ovary (F, $\times1$) hairy, style with a swollen tip; fruit (G, $\times1$) $1\frac{1}{2}$ in. long, obliquely grooved between the seeds, hairy; seeds (H, $\times3\frac{1}{2}$) slightly mottled (family *Papilionaceae*).

A native of north-west America, from Vancouver Island, north-west to Alaska; thoroughly naturalized in great abundance by rivers, especially in Scotland (banks of the Dee and Tay), and on bare hillsides in the Orkney Islands.

The flowers are visited mainly by bees, which set in motion a pumping arrangement by which strings of pollen are released. *Lupinus* is a genus of about 200 species, abundant in the western mountains of North America, some being highly ornamental and now available through hybridization in a great range of colours. Easily grown from seed, they have become popular in British gardens. Another introduced species is *L. arboreus* Sims, a shrub with yellow flowers rarely tinged with blue.

Lotus corniculatus L. ($\times \frac{1}{2}$)

Perennial herb with long taproot; stems decumbent or ascending up to 1 ft.; leaves divided into 3 separate leaflets with a pair of large leaflet-like stipules at the base; leaflets obovate to ovate, slightly hairy; flowers about $\frac{1}{2}$ in. long, in a cluster on a long common stalk, with 3 leaflets close under, bright yellow, the upper (standard) petal usually red on the outside; calyx (A, $\times 2\frac{1}{2}$) with 5 sharply pointed equal-sized lobes, thinly hairy; standard (B, $\times 2$) petal erect or recurved in the upper half, narrowed to the base with incurved margins; wing-petals (C, $\times 2$) blunt; keel-petals

(D, $\times 2$) beaked; one of the 10 stamens (E, $\times 2\frac{1}{2}$) free from the others; pods (F, $\times 1$) linear, $\frac{3}{4}$–1 in. long, spirally twisted after opening; seeds (G, $\times 5$) broadly ellipsoid, grey, mottled with dark brown (family *Papilionaceae*).

The back petal (standard or vexillum) is erect and often marked with red streaks which serve as nectar guides to bees, which effect cross-pollination. There is not space here to describe fully the wonderful floral mechanism of the pumping arrangement as it is called, by which the pollen, previously discharged into the tip of the keel-petals and held there by the elongated club-shaped stalks of the five outer stamens, is released. This is brought about by the weight of the insect pressing on the wing- and keel-petals. Self-pollination is ineffective because the stigmatic portion of the style must be rubbed before it becomes receptive to the pollen.

Lotus uliginosus Schkuhr. ($\times \frac{2}{5}$)

Perennial; stems erect or ascending, up to about 2 ft. long, rather zigzag, glabrous or thinly pilose; leaves petiolate, trifoliolate,

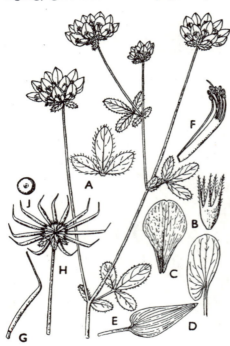

leaflets very shortly stalked, obovate to oblanceolate, glabrous to thinly pilose; stipules large and leafy, elliptic to obovate, looking like a pair of basal leaflets; flowers orange-yellow, several in a head on a long slender peduncle, the head about 1 in. diam. and with a trifoliolate leafy bract (A, $\times 1\frac{3}{5}$) at the base; calyx (B, $\times 1\frac{3}{5}$) bell-shaped, equally 5-lobed, lobes narrow, ciliate; standard petal (vexillum) (C, $\times 1\frac{3}{5}$) obovate, gradually narrowed into the rather broad claw, notched at the apex; wing-petals (D, $\times 1\frac{3}{5}$) oblong-elliptic, produced on one side at the base, with a slender claw; keel-petals (E, $\times 1\frac{4}{5}$) ovate-acuminate; stamens (F, $\times 1\frac{4}{5}$) in 2 bundles, 1 stamen free, the other 9 united in a sheath open along the top; filaments alternately longer and shorter, but anthers equal; ovary (G, $\times 1\frac{4}{5}$) long and narrow, glabrous, with a longish smooth style bent at an angle; ovules numerous; fruits (H, $\times \frac{3}{5}$) spreading in star fashion, about 1 in. long, almost rounded, slightly keeled, slightly reticulate, at length splitting with the halves slightly curled; seeds (J, $\times 3$) very small, globose, greenish, with a very small circular scar (family *Papilionaceae*).

The pollen mechanism is similar to that described in the Bird's-Foot Trefoil in fig. 51; as in that species the stalks of the stamens are club-shaped at the top.

Lotus tenuis Wald. & Kit. ($\times\frac{1}{3}$)

Perennial herb with long woody taproot; stems very slender, numerous, glabrous; leaves divided into 3 separate leaflets with a pair of large leaflet-like stipules at the base; leaflets very narrowly oblanceolate, glabrous or slightly hairy; flowers (A, $\times 1\frac{1}{2}$) $\frac{1}{2}$ in. long, few in a cluster on a common stalk, with 3 smaller leaflets close under, bright yellow; calyx equally 5-lobed, lobes subulate, slightly hairy; standard (B, $\times 1\frac{1}{2}$), wings (C, $\times 1\frac{1}{2}$) and keel (D, $\times 1\frac{1}{2}$) petals as shown in the drawing, the keel sharply pointed; stamens (E, $\times 2$) united in a sheath except the upper which is free, 5 of the stamens below the other 5; ovary (F, $\times 2$) curved, glabrous, style as long and slender; pod (G, $\times \frac{3}{4}$) 1 in. long, glabrous, twisting slightly after opening;

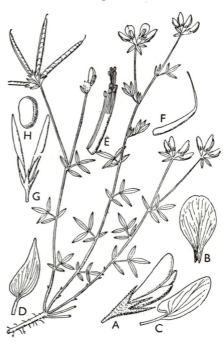

seed (H, $\times 3$) dark brown, smooth (family *Papilionaceae*).

This species is very closely related to the Bird's-foot Trefoil, *Lotus corniculatus* L., shown in fig. 51. The stems of *L. tenuis* are more slender and the leaflets and stipules narrower than in that species.

There are five species in Britain, the one shown above and *L. corniculatus* L. (see fig. 51), besides three others, *L. uliginosus* Schkuhr (fig. 52), a perennial, with the calyx-teeth spreading in bud, the upper two with an acute sinus, *L. angustissimus* L., the calyx-teeth with an obtuse sinus and peduncles very short, and long pods, and *L. hispidus* Desf., also with an obtuse calyx-sinus but with long peduncles.

Tetragonolobus maritimus (L.) Roth ($\times\frac{1}{3}$)

Perennial herb; stems decumbent in the lower part, thinly pilose; leaves trifoliolate, with a pair of large ovate leafy stipules at the base; leaflets sessile, oblanceolate, about $\frac{3}{4}$ in. long, thinly pilose and often closely mottled with fine purple lines; stipules shortly adnate to the petiole; flowers solitary, terminal, on long stalks with a 3-leaved bract at the apex; calyx (A, $\times 1$) tubular, 5-lobed, lobes long-pilose; petals orange-yellow, the standard (vexillum) as in fig. B, $\times\frac{2}{3}$, the wings (fig. C, $\times 1$) and the keel (fig. D, $\times 1$); stamens (E, $\times 1$) 10, in two bundles, the upper stamen free, remainder united in a sheath open down the upper side; anthers equal; ovary (F, $\times 1$) linear, quadrangular; style winged on one

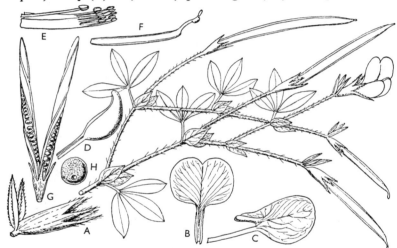

side below the stigma; fruit (G, $\times\frac{2}{3}$) 2–2$\frac{1}{2}$ in. long, opening by 2 spirally curved valves, each of the olive-green globose seeds (H, $\times 2$) enclosed in a thin partition (family *Papilionaceae*). – Synonyms *Lotus siliquosus* L., *Tetragonolobus siliquosus* Roth.

An introduced plant in the southern counties of England, often in waste ground but sometimes in hilly pastures; there is no general English name but it is known locally in Gloucestershire as 'Wild Tom Thumbs'.

The flowers secrete nectar, which is concealed so deeply that it can be reached only by long-tongued kinds of humble-bee; shorter-tongued species steal the nectar by perforating the flowers at the base of the petals.

Perennial with zigzag spreading stems, usually not hairy; leaves pinnate, with about 7 pairs of opposite leaflets and an odd terminal leaflet, more or less elliptic, entire; stipules large, free, about ¾ in. long, sharply eared at the base on one side; flowers several in axillary long-stalked racemes; bracts slender and thread-like; calyx (A, ×1½) cup-shaped, with 5 equal narrow lobes; petals greenish yellow; standard (B, ×1½), wings (C, ×1½), and keel (D, ×1½) petals as shown in the drawings; stamens (E, ×1½) 10, one free, the others united in a sheath open on the upper side; anthers short, equalsized; ovary (F, ×1½) shortly stalked; style with a head-like stigma; fruits (G, ×¾) crowded, slightly bladdery, 1–1¼ in. long, divided lengthwise by a partition; seeds (H, ×2) kidney-shaped, smooth, light yellowish green (family *Papilionaceae*).

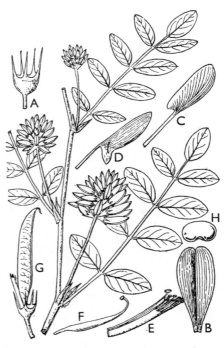

Recognized by the spreading habit, large stipules, very narrow, thread-like bracts, greenish-yellow flowers, and the pods divided by a partition arising from the keel-margin. The flowers secrete nectar, and honey-bees steal it from the side between the claws of the wing- and keel-petals. Humble-bees and other long-tongued bees suck it legitimately.

Two other species of this genus are found in Britain, *A. danicus* Retz., fig. 56, with stipules connate at the base, and *A. alpinus* L., in Scotland, with stipules free to the base.

A. glycyphyllos is called Milk Vetch because of the sweetness of its roots and leaves, at first pleasant to taste, but which leave a bitter and disagreeable flavour on the tongue. On this account cattle leave the plant untouched when it occurs in pastures.

PURPLE MILK VETCH
Astragalus danicus Retz. ($\times \frac{1}{2}$)

Slender prostrate perennial herb; stems glabrous to slightly hairy; leaves pinnate with an odd terminal leaflet (imparipinnate) and up

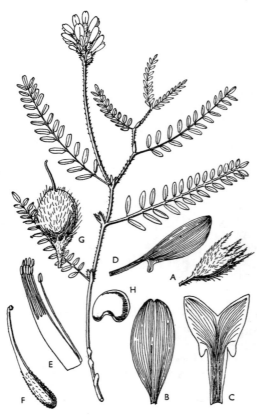

to 15 pairs of narrowly oblong-lanceolate obtuse lateral leaflets, these with long slender hairs on the upper surface and margin; stipules rather large and conspicuous, united half way up opposite the leaf-stalk; peduncles 2–3 or solitary on each shoot, longer than the leaves, thinly covered with short blackish hairs; bracts ovate, hairy; flowers bluish purple; calyx (A, $\times 1\frac{1}{4}$) 5-toothed, covered with blackish hairs, teeth subulate; standard (B, $\times 1\frac{1}{2}$), wings (C, $\times 1\frac{1}{2}$), and keel petals (D, $\times 1\frac{1}{2}$); stamens (E, $\times 2$) 10, one free, the others united in a split sheath; ovary and style as shown in the figure (F, $\times 2$); fruit (G, $\times 1\frac{1}{2}$) broadly ellipsoid, densely covered with long soft white hairs, imperfectly 2-locular by the inflexed margins of the lower suture; seeds (H, $\times 3$) several, kidney-shaped, smooth (family *Papilionaceae*). Flowers from early summer on chalky soils or sand-dunes chiefly on the eastern side of Britain, also in Eire; extends eastwards to Siberia and south to Italy.

Perennial almost stemless herb; lower part covered with the persistent withered remains of stipules and leaf-stalks; leaves pinnate with an odd terminal leaflet (imparipinnate); leaflets opposite, about 8–12 pairs, narrowly oblong-lanceolate, entire, thinly covered with long silky hairs; stipules large, persistent, very acuminate, pilose with long hairs; flowers pale yellow tinged with purple, crowded at the top of axillary peduncles covered with fine hairs; bracts large, lanceolate, about as long as the calyx; calyx (A, $\times\frac{5}{6}$) campanulate, with 5 narrow equal teeth, hairy outside; standard (B, $\times 1$), wings (C, $\times 1$), and keel (D, $\times 1$) petals as shown in the drawing, the keel with a sharp point at the apex; stamens (E, $\times 2$) 10, one free, the others connate into a sheath split along the upper side;

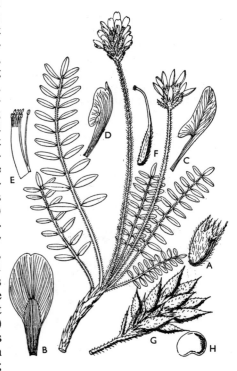

anthers small and uniform; ovary (F, $\times 2$) hairy, with about 12 ovules; style curved, with a terminal stigma; fruit (G, $\times\frac{1}{3}$) membranous, about 1 in. long, style persistent; seeds (H, $\times 2$) kidney-shaped, smooth (family *Papilionaceae*). (Synonym *Astragalus campestris*).

In rocky places only in Scotland, but otherwise almost circumboreal distribution. The flowers secrete nectar and are pollinated by bees.

A second species, *O. halleri* Bunge, the Purple Oxytropis, is also found only in Scotland; this has pale purple flowers and the peduncles exceed the leaves at flowering time, in June and July.

BIRD'S-FOOT
Ornithopus perpusillus L. ($\times \frac{1}{3}$)

Much-branched prostrate annual with slender leafy stems; leaves alternate, pinnate, with about 6–8 pairs of almost stalkless elliptic leaflets and an odd terminal leaflet, all slightly hairy; flowers in a cluster at the end of axillary branchlets and subtended by a small pinnate leaf (A, $\times$2); calyx (B, $\times$4) tubular, with 5 equal lobes, pubescent; petals yellowish white or tinged with pink; standard petal (C, $\times$3) spoon-shaped with a long claw and streaked with purple; wing-petal (D, $\times$3) very similar but a little broader; keel-petals (E, $\times$3) also similar but with a rounded auricle (ear) on one side at the base; stamens (F, $\times$3) 10, 1 free, the others united in a

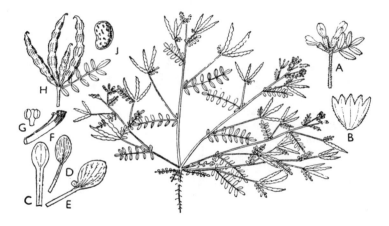

sheath; anthers with separate loculi (G, $\times$10); ovary with several seeds, hairy; style incurved; fruits (H, $\times$1) curved, about $\frac{3}{4}$ in. long, breaking up into about 5–7 1-seeded joints, thinly hairy, terminated by the hook-like stigma; seeds (J, $\times$3) ellipsoid, brown and mottled (family *Papilionaceae*).

This is called Bird's-Foot because the fruits with their hooked tips resemble a bird's claws. The plant belongs to the interesting tribe *Hedysareae*, mostly found in the tropics, and distinguished at once in the family by the jointed pods, which split up into 1-seeded units.

It grows in dry pastures, and flowers in spring and summer. The stamens and stigma are mature at the same time, and automatic self-pollination is quite effective. As there is no nectar secreted in the flowers, insect visitors are very few.

Weak branched herb with long internodes; stems ribbed, glabrous; leaves pinnate, with about 6–8 pairs of leaflets and an odd terminal leaflet (imparipinnate), the lowermost pair at the very base of the common stalk; stipules very small and narrow; leaflets oblong, entire, apiculate, glabrous; flowers clustered at the ends of long axillary peduncles; bracts very small and linear; stalks about $\frac{1}{3}$ in. long; calyx (A, $\times1\frac{1}{3}$) short, 5-toothed; petals yellow, the keel purple-crimson at the top; standard (B, $\times1$), wings (C, $\times1$), and keel (D, $\times1$) petals as shown in the drawing; stamens (E, $\times2$) 10, one free the others connate into a sheath

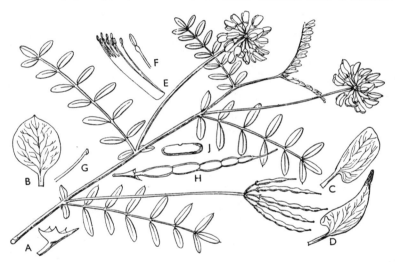

split along the upper side; filaments (F, $\times6$) swollen at the top; anthers equal; ovary with few ovules and a slender style with lateral papillous stigma (G, $\times3$); fruits (H, $\times\frac{2}{3}$) up to about 10 in a bunch, about 8-seeded, breaking up into as many joints, these 1-seeded; seeds (J, $\times2$) narrowly oblong, attached in the middle, dark brown, smooth (family *Papilionaceae*).

Distributed in south and central Europe from Spain to the Balkans and to north Persia and Syria; naturalized in North America, where it is known as 'Axseed' or 'Axwort'.

There is no nectar in the usual place inside the flowers, but on the outside of the short fleshy calyx, where it is sought out by bees.

HORSE-SHOE VETCH
Hippocrepis comosa L. ($\times\frac{1}{2}$)

Perennial herb with a woody rootstock; branches ascending or spreading on the ground, up to 1 ft. long, glabrous; leaves alternate, pinnate; leaflets 4–5 pairs, opposite, with an odd terminal leaflet, oblong-elliptic, at most about $\frac{1}{4}$ in. long, very slightly hairy; stipules paired, ovate; flowers umbellate on a common long axillary stalk, up to about 10 together and with very short individual slightly hairy stalks but no leaflet below; calyx (A, $\times2\frac{1}{2}$) equally 5-lobed, lobes triangular-subulate, glabrous; petals yellow, the standard (B, $\times3$), wings (C, $\times3$), and keel (D, $\times3$) as shown in the drawing; stamens (E, $\times4$) in 2 bundles, the upper filament

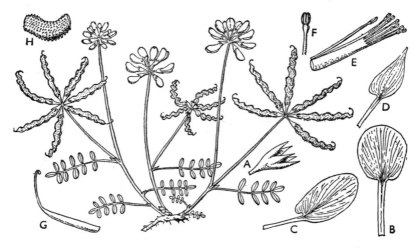

free from the others, all dilated at the apex; anthers (F, $\times6$) equal-sized; style (G, $\times2\frac{1}{2}$) with an incurved tip; fruit spreading starwise, strongly undulate, loosely covered with sessile glands (H, $\times1$) (family *Papilionaceae*).

In pastures and on banksides, mostly in limestone districts, but rare in Scotland, flowering in spring and summer.

The flowers secrete nectar and have a pumping arrangement by which threads of pollen are ejected. The nectar is cunningly concealed, the claw of the standard bearing a projecting triangular plate on the underside at the base by which the two nectar-passages are completely closed.

SAINFOIN

61

Onobrychis viciifolia, Scop. ($\times\frac{1}{3}$)

Perennial; stems up to 2 ft. high, laxly branched, distinctly ribbed; leaves alternate, pinnate, with 6–10 pairs of either alternate or opposite leaflets (H, $\times\frac{3}{4}$), these lanceolate, not toothed, slightly hairy below, especially on the midrib; stipules free from the stalk, triangular, very acute, about $\frac{1}{3}$ in. long, soon becoming brown; flowers in very long-stalked racemes in the axils of the upper leaves, the lower flowers soon developing into fruit; bracts small, awl-shaped; calyx (A, $\times1\frac{1}{4}$) slightly unequally 5-lobed, lobes very narrow (subulate), fringed with white hairs; corolla tinged with pink or mauve, especially the standard (B, $\times1\frac{1}{4}$) lined with crimson; wings (C, $\times1\frac{1}{4}$) very small, keel (D, $\times1\frac{1}{4}$) nearly as long as the standard; upper stamen free, the other 9 (E, $\times1\frac{1}{4}$)

connate into a sheath; anthers equal, versatile; ovary with 1 ovule; style (F, $\times2$) slender, smooth; fruit (G, $\times1$) strongly reticulate and dentate on the margin (family *Papilionaceae*) (synonym *Onobrychis sativa* Lam).

Probably native in southern and eastern England, elsewhere mostly following cultivation; widely distributed in central and southern Europe and temperate Asia. The early summer flowers secrete nectar, and cross-pollination is brought about by a simple valvular mechanism. The wing-petals are very small, and cover only the claws of the keel-petals, serving as nectar-covers by which access at the side is prevented or rendered difficult. The stigma projects beyond the anthers.

WOOD VETCH
Vicia sylvatica L. ($\times \frac{2}{5}$)

Climber over bushes up to 8 ft. high; stems and leaves glabrous; leaves pinnate with about 6 pairs of opposite or subopposite ellip-

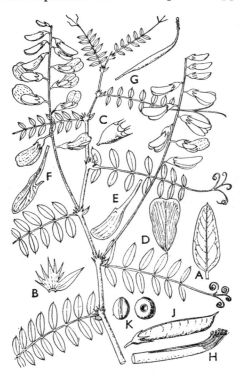

tic leaflets (A, $\times \frac{4}{5}$) rounded to a short point at the apex, the main stalk ending in a branched tendril; stipules (B, $\times 1\frac{1}{2}$) leafy, rounded and deeply cut into sharp lobes; flowers white with blue veins, arranged in axillary one-sided racemes; peduncle as long or longer than the leaves; stalks shorter than the calyx, slightly hairy; calyx (C, $\times 1\frac{1}{2}$) oblique, with short narrow teeth; standard petal (D, $\times \frac{4}{5}$) narrowly obovate; wing-petals (E, $\times 1$) half spoonshaped; keel-petals (F, $\times 1$) narrower, with a reflexed lobe on one side near the middle; stamens (H, $\times 3$) in 2 bundles, the upper one free except in the lower part; ovary (G, $\times 1\frac{1}{2}$) glabrous; style with a brush of hairs all around below the stigma; fruits (J, $\times \frac{4}{5}$) about 1 in. long, with several seeds (K, $\times 1\frac{1}{4}$), these rounded and with a circular depression on one side (family *Papilionaceae*).

Mostly in woods in hilly districts, flowering in summer; widely distributed into Asiatic Russia and central Asia.

All species of this genus are nectar-yielding bee-flowers, with a brush of hairs on the style. In addition there are often extrafloral nectaries, sometimes indicated by deeply coloured spots on the under-side of the stipules. These secrete nectar in sunny weather. This nectar is eagerly sought for by ants, which in turn serve to protect the plant from caterpillars and such-like.

COMMON VETCH 63
Vicia sativa L. ($\times \frac{2}{5}$)

Long cultivated as a fodder plant and widely distributed in temperate regions; annual or biennial herb, with weak ribbed ascending stems; leaflets 4–7 pairs, obcordate to narrowly linear (the narrow-leaved form is regarded as the wild or ancestral form of *V. sativa* and is usually distinguished as *V. angustifolia* Roth), with a longish point in the middle of the usually V-shaped apex; common stalk ending in a single or branched tendril; stipules (A, $\times 1\frac{1}{4}$) leafy, much lobed, and with a dark spot in the middle; flowers reddish-purple, axillary, solitary, or in pairs, on very

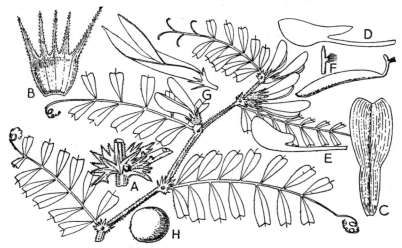

short stalks; calyx (B, $\times 1\frac{1}{4}$) 5-lobed to the middle; standard (C, $\times 1\frac{1}{2}$) contracted below the middle, V-shaped at the top; wing-petals (D, $\times 2$) with a long backwards-directed lobe; keel-petals (E, $\times 1\frac{1}{2}$) with a shorter lobe; ovary hairy; style bent; stigma terminal, with a beard-like tuft of hairs (F, $\times 3$); pod (G, $\times \frac{1}{2}$) about 2 in. long, smooth, twisted after opening; seeds (H, $\times 1\frac{1}{2}$) several, rounded, dark brown, velvety, with a short narrow scar.

Other British kinds of Vetch have very shortly stalked flowers; these are *V. lutea* L., with solitary yellow flowers and hairy pod; *V. sepium* L., with 2–4 reddish-purple flowers on a short common stalk and smooth pods; *V. lathyroides* L., with much smaller flowers, small stipules, and granular seeds. The Bithynian Vetch, *V. bithynica* L., has longer flower-stalks and usually only 2 pairs of leaflets (family *Papilionaceae*).

TUFTED VETCH
Vicia cracca L. ($\times \frac{1}{2}$)

This is the most easily recognized species because of the numerous bluish-purple flowers borne on one side of the flattened axis of the raceme; a perennial with slender annual stems up to 4 or 5 ft. high or even more, the whole plant hairy to nearly glabrous; leaves with numerous leaflets and the common stalk (rhachis) ending in a branched tendril; leaflets alternate to subopposite, linear to oblong, rounded at the apex and markedly pointed (mucronate); stipules divided into 2 lobes, but not conspicuous; flowers (see above) arranged in a dense raceme and more or less reflexed, about $\frac{1}{2}$ in. long (A, $\times 2\frac{1}{2}$); calyx short, the upper lobe broadest; standard (B, $\times 2\frac{1}{2}$) contracted above the middle; wing- and keel-petals with long slender claws, and tightly clasped together by the unilateral lobes of the former (C, $\times 3$); stamens connate into a sheath split at the top with one free stalk (D, $\times 3$); anthers short and broad (E, $\times 10$); style shortly hairy all around and with a dense tuft of longer hairs below the terminal stigma (F, $\times 4$); pods (G, $\times \frac{3}{4}$) flat, about $1\frac{1}{2}$ in. long, with several dark velvety-brown seeds (H, $\times 2\frac{1}{2}$) $\frac{1}{8}$ in. diam., marked nearly their full length by a scar (family *Papilionaceae*).

When a bee visits the flower it settles on the wing-petals, and these, being firmly held by the keel-petals, act like a lever and are depressed by the weight of the insect, which deposits pollen from another flower. They close up again as soon as the latter flies away. In several other species of this genus there are extra-floral nectaries, which show as more deeply coloured spots on the outside (lower) of the stipules (see *Vicia sativa*, fig. 63).

This ornamental species is not likely to be confused with any others, except perhaps *Vicia orobus* DC. and *Vicia sylvatica* L., both of which have the flowers on a longish common stalk (peduncle) but have much fewer and paler flowers and broader leaflets; the leaf-stalk of *V. orobus* ends in a single point and not a branched tendril, and the stipules of *V. sylvatica* are much more toothed than in *V. cracca*.

Anne Pratt, who published several volumes of wild flowers in colour, remarks that during the months of July and August, the handsome crowded spikes of the Tufted Vetch climb to the topmost boughs of the hedges or droop down in luxuriance among the branches of the wood, and that the farmer welcomes it there too, knowing that it affords a large amount of fodder for animals grazing in the fields.

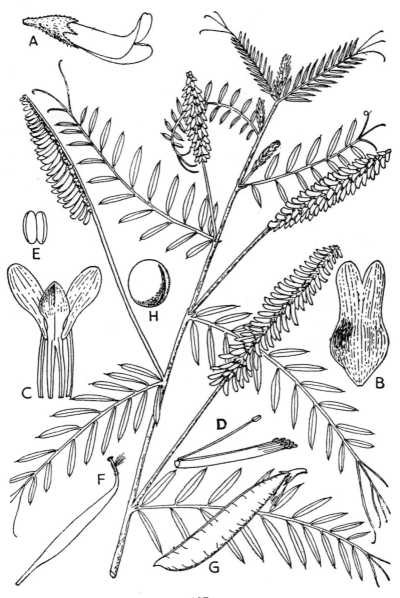

HAIRY VETCH
Vicia hirsuta (L.) S. F. Gray ($\times \frac{2}{5}$)

Slender annual with weak stems rambling among grasses and other herbs; stems ribbed, hairy to nearly glabrous; stipules (B, $\times 1\frac{3}{5}$) deeply divided into very narrow parts; leaves pinnate, nearly sessile, the common stalk ending in a branched tendril; leaflets (A, $\times 1$) 6–10 pairs, narrow, scooped out at the apex and with a sharp point; flowers very small, few on axillary peduncles shorter than the leaevs, pale blue; calyx (C, $\times 3$) deeply and equally 5-lobed, hairy outside; petals about a third longer than the calyx (for shapes see figures) standard (D), wings (E) and keel (F) $\times 2$; stamens (G, $\times 8$) 10, the upper partly free,

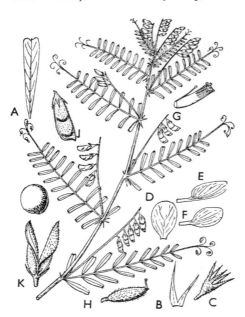

the other united; ovary (H, $\times 3$) pubescent; style glabrous, very short; fruit (J, $\times \frac{4}{5}$) a small pod, at length twisted (K, $\times 1\frac{1}{5}$), reticulate and hairy all over, with 2 rounded slightly flattened seeds (L, $\times 2\frac{1}{2}$) mottled with dark purple (family *Papilionaceae*).

A widely distributed species, and recognized by its small 2-seeded fruits; the style is very short and not hairy below the tip, as in several other species of the genus.

The small bluish flowers secrete abundant nectar, which collects in the form of a large drop and emerges on each side of the base of the free filament. Insect visitors are numerous, and they effect cross- and self-pollination with equal facility.

This species flowers in July and August and is often to be found in cultivated fields in the southern counties. It grows in a similar habitat in many parts of the world.

Perennial with creeping rootstock; stems slightly zigzag, glabrous except towards the top; leaves rather distant, spreading or recurved, pinnate, branched at the end into slender threads (tendrils); leaflets nearly opposite, ovate to ovate-lanceolate, rounded at the base, rounded and mucronate at the apex, glabrous or thinly pubescent; stipules divided into 2 lobes, more or less dentate, green but small; flowers dull lilac to pale purple, yellowish at the base, few in very short subsessile racemes in the upper axils; stalks and calyx pubescent; calyx (A, ×1) with 5 almost equal sharp teeth; standard (B, ×1) obovate, contracted in the middle; wing-petals (C, ×1) obliquely obovate, with a reflexed lobe; keel-petals (D, ×0) golf-club-shaped; stamens (E, ×2) 10, all but one united in a sheath; ovary (F, ×3) stalked, glabrous; style with 2 brushes of hairs below the stigma, the inner of shorter hairs (G, ×5); fruits (H, ×$\frac{3}{5}$) 1–1½ in. long, like small pea-pods, sharply pointed, glabrous, the valves curling after opening; seeds (J, ×2½) purple-black, with a broad hilum reaching more than half the way around (family *Papilionaceae*).

In this species the style is provided with 2 brushes just below the stigma; that on the inside of the bend is shorter than that on the outer side, as shown in fig. G, ×5; the latter encloses a plate-like depression; access to the nectar is much the same as described for the Tufted Vetch (fig. 64).

BITTER VETCH
Vicia orobus DC. ($\times\frac{1}{3}$)

Perennial with a short creeping rootstock; stems erect, not climbing, becoming almost woody, angular, thinly hairy; leaves alternate, pinnate with about 8–10 pairs of opposite or alternate leaflets, the latter oblong-lanceolate, rounded to a sharp tip, $\frac{1}{2}$–$\frac{3}{4}$ in. long, with several distinct lateral nerves, the tip of the common stalk sometimes ending in a hook-like point (tendril) or the upper leaves with a terminal leaflet; stipules large, with sharp pointed basal lobes; flowers in axillary stalked racemes except in the upper leaves, purplish white; calyx (A, $\times 1$) obliquely 5-lobed, the lowermost lobe longest and very narrow; standard (B, $\times 1\frac{1}{4}$), wings (C, $\times 1\frac{1}{4}$) and keel (D, $\times 1\frac{1}{4}$) petals as shown in the drawing; stamens (E, $\times 2$) in 2 bundles, 1 free; anthers ovoid, equal; ovary (F, $\times 2$) stalked, style hairy all around below the tip; pods (G, $\times\frac{1}{2}$) flattened, about 1 in. long, the valves at length twisting spirally; seeds (H, $\times 1\frac{1}{2}$) few, rounded, velvety-purple-black, with a long hilum (family *Papilionaceae*).

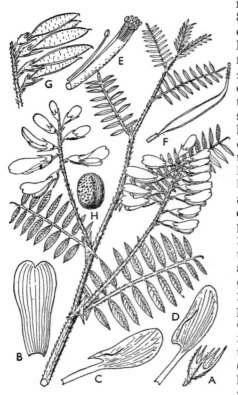

Very local, mostly in western and northern Britain; rare in Eire; flowers in early summer in western Europe.

A most interesting species because of the erect habit and the imperfect evolution of tendrils; perhaps a primitive type of vetch.

SPRING VETCH 68
Vicia lathyroides L. ($\times\frac{1}{2}$)

A low-spreading much-branched annual or biennial, sometimes forming quite a carpet, very slightly hairy more or less all over; leaflets (A, $\times 2\frac{1}{2}$) 2–3 pairs, sessile, oblanceolate, rounded at the top with a sunken apex, about $\frac{1}{3}$ in. long, slightly hairy on the nerves below; common leaf-stalk ending in an unbranched tendril; stipules small and awl-shaped; flowers (B, $\times 4$) solitary in the leaf-axils, nearly sessile; calyx equally 5-lobed, lobes very narrow, hairy; petals purple, the standard (C, $\times 2\frac{1}{2}$), wings (D, $\times 4$) and keel (E, $\times 4$) as shown in the drawing; stamens 10, united in a

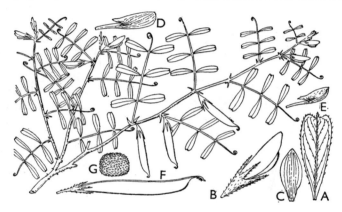

split sheath, the upper free; ovary glabrous, style short, with a line of hairs below the apex; fruit (F, $\times 1\frac{1}{2}$) $\frac{3}{4}$ in. long, flattened, smooth, about 6-seeded; seeds (G, $\times 3$) rounded-quandrangular, closely warted (family *Papilionaceae*).

A dainty little plant with several distinctive features, especially the awl-shaped stipules and closely warted seeds, which easily distinguish it from *V. sativa* (fig. 63); to be looked for in dry pastures and open woods and on banksides; Europe to the Caucasus and in north Africa.

The genus *Vicia* is well represented in Britain there being as many as twelve species recognized in the latest *Flora* (see p. xiv), which provides a key for their determination. Important characters are the presence or absence of tendrils, the colour of the flowers, and the number of seeds in the pods.

111

Annual with slender much-branched stems and often climbing amongst low bushes and on banksides, not hairy; leaves pinnate,

with usually about 5 to 10 very narrow leaflets and ending in a simple or branched tendril; stipules narrowly lanceolate and sharply pointed; flowers (A, $\times 1\frac{1}{2}$) few (often only 2) on very slender axillary stalks; calyx equally 5-lobed, slightly hairy; petals pale blue; the standard (B, $\times 2$), wings (C, $\times 2$) and keel (D, $\times 2$) as shown in the drawing; fruit (E, $\times 1$) usually 4-seeded, but sometimes 5 or 6, about $\frac{1}{2}$ in. long, the valves twisting after opening; seeds (F, $\times 2$) rounded, smooth (family *Papilionaceae*).

Distributed in Europe, western Asia, and north Africa, introduced into many other parts of the world.

This species has very small flowers, and, in spite of the specific name, the number of seeds varies from 4 to 6, though there are generally only 4. The difference between the genera *Vicia* and *Lathyrus* is very slight. In *Vicia* the style is hairy all around the tip or on the lower side, and in *Lathyrus* it is hairy only on the upper side.

Vicia tetrasperma is a very slender annual, its small pale purple flowers appearing in June and July; it is often to be found in corn-fields and by hedges but becomes rarer in Scotland. There is a variety, var. *tenuissima* Druce, with much narrower leaflets.

A weak annual branching from the base, branches 1–2 ft. long; stem angular, glabrous or very slightly hairy; leaves with 2 pairs of narrow leaflets and a branched tendril, slightly hairy below; stipules leafy and conspicuous, 3-nerved, coarsely toothed, the basal tooth pointing downwards; flowers (A, $\times 2$) axillary and solitary, the stalk often nearly as long as the leaf and jointed near the top, the upper portion, especially, hairy; calyx nearly equally 5-lobed, lobes with weak spreading hairs; standard petal (B, $\times 1\frac{1}{2}$) mauve-purple, faintly darker veined, deeply notched at the top;

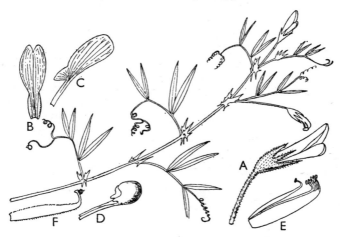

wings (C, $\times 1\frac{1}{2}$) much paler (nearly white), rounded at the top; keel-petals (D, $\times 1\frac{1}{2}$) also pale but with a purple blotch at the top; stamens (E, $\times 4$) in 2 bundles, the free stamen with a very broad filament; ovary (F, $\times 3$) hairy along the margins; style curved, with a brush of hairs on the outside below the stigma; fruit 1–1$\frac{1}{2}$ in. long, slightly hairy (family *Papilionaceae*).

Often to be found on sea-cliffs, but distributed inland as a cornfield weed; extends eastward to the Caucasus.

This is by some botanists treated as a separate species, *V. angustifolia* (L.) Reichard, but it is very variable and there are intermediate forms.

Lathyrus pratensis L. ($\times \frac{2}{5}$)

Perennial herb with creeping rootstock; stems weak, sharply angular; stipules arrow-shaped (sagittate); one pair of lanceolate

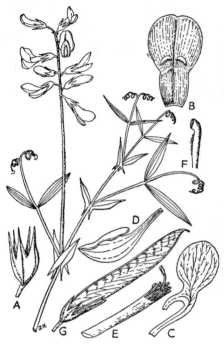

very acute leaflets with 3 parallel nerves, and a terminal simple or branched tendril; flowers bright yellow, about $\frac{3}{4}$ in. long, several on an axillary common stalk (peduncle); calyx (A, $\times 1\frac{1}{4}$), equally 5-lobed; standard (B, $\times 1\frac{1}{2}$) contracted in the middle, oblique appendix on each side; wing-petals (C, $\times 1\frac{3}{5}$) with a recurved hook-like lobe; keel-petals with a folded upper margin (D, $\times 1\frac{3}{5}$); stamens (E, $\times 2$) all united into a sheath; style (F, $\times 6$) with a terminal oblique stigma and a line of hairs on the upper side; pods (G, $\times \frac{4}{5}$) $1\frac{3}{4}$ in. long; seeds globose, dark brown or olive mottled with black, with a scar; widely distributed into Asia (family *Papilionaceae*).

The only other yellow-flowered species in Britain is the much less common *Lathyrus aphaca* L., mainly found as a cornfield weed in the south. It has no real leaflets, but large leafy stipules. The observer may find some difficulty in distinguishing the genus *Lathyrus* from *Vicia*, the Vetches (see figs. 62–70). In *Lathyrus* the stigma is as described above, namely, with a line of hairs on the upper side below the stigma, whilst in *Vicia* there is a bunch of hairs as shown in figure 63, F.

Although the stigma of the flower of this species is surrounded by the pollen of the same flower, automatic self-pollination apparently does not take place, the stigmatic surface needing to be rubbed by visiting bees before it becomes receptive.

Lathyrus montanus (L.) Bernh. ($\frac{1}{3}$)

Perennial herb with creeping rootstock swollen like tubers at some of the nodes (A, ×1); stems erect, usually unbranched, an-gular, glabrous; stipules green, unequally 2-lobed, lobes sharply pointed; leaves few, pinnate, with 2–3 (rarely 4) pairs of opposite oblanceolate leaflets acute at the apex, with 3–5 main parallel nerves; common stalk of leaves ending in a long sharp point; flowers few in terminal and upper axillary racemes; calyx (B, ×1) unequally 5-lobed, upper 2 lobes shorter and ovate; petals bright reddish-purple, fading to brown; stan-dard (C, ×1$\frac{1}{2}$) wings as in fig. D, ×1$\frac{1}{2}$, keel as in fig. E, ×1$\frac{1}{2}$; stamens as in fig. F, ×1$\frac{1}{2}$; ovary (G, ×1$\frac{1}{4}$) pods (H, ×$\frac{1}{2}$) about 2 in. long, with

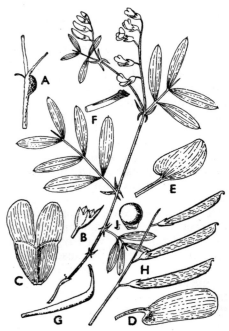

slightly thickened margins, finely reticulate, beak curved; seeds (J, ×1$\frac{1}{2}$) brown, rounded, with a rim-like caruncle at the base (family *Papilionaceae*).

The style is almost vertical and covered on the inner side with short hairs directed obliquely upwards. These sweep out the pol-len from the anthers and deposit it on the ventral surface of bees, who dust it on the stigma of the next flower visited, bringing about cross-pollination. Although the stigma is surrounded by the pol-len of the same flower, it is not receptive until rubbed against by insects.

In woods, thickets and hedgebanks in hilly country; west and north Europe.

Lathyrus nissolia L. ($\times\frac{1}{2}$)

Slender annual up to about 3 ft. high and very grass-like; stems slender, green, ribbed, not hairy; stipules minute, soon falling off; true leaves not present, but represented by the leaf-like stalk, these much like the leaves of a grass, very narrow and tapered to the apex, with 5–7 nerves parallel with the margins; flower-stalks solitary in the axils of the leaves and about equal in length, bearing 1 or 2 flowers; calyx (A, $\times 6$) obliquely bell-shaped, with 5 narrow lobes slightly hairy on the margin, the lowermost lobe a little longer than the others; petals bright red, turning crimson or bluish in the upper parts; standard as in fig. B, $\times 1$; wing-petals as shown in fig. C, $\times 1\frac{1}{2}$; keel-petals fig. D, $\times 1\frac{1}{2}$; stamens (E, $\times 1\frac{1}{2}$) all united into a single closed sheath; anthers rounded, equal; ovary (F, $\times 1\frac{1}{2}$) linear, with several ovules, glabrous; style short, flattened back and front, slightly hairy above; fruits (G, $\times\frac{2}{3}$) like very narrow peas, strongly marked with nerves, about 2 in. long, becoming spirally twisted when old; seeds (H, $\times 3$) slightly 4-sided, dark and minutely roughened (family *Papilionaceae*).

This is a species of more than ordinary interest. Not only does it mimic, but it grows amongst grasses, and is quite difficult to distinguish from them when not in flower or fruit. It can easily be recognized, however, because the base of the leaf is not sheathing and there is no ligule, as in most grasses. There is a parallel example in the South African flora, and one with which botanists in that country are fond of catching out the uninitiated stranger. But the South African plant, *Cliffortia graminea* Linn. f., belongs to the family *Rosaceae*. Secondly, this species exhibits a very high stage in evolution, having completely dispensed with its leaflets and tendrils, and developed the leaf-stalks to function as leaves, whilst the several- or many-flowered raceme characteristic of most other species of this genus is here reduced to 1 or 2 flowers. Indeed, if plants could divulge their pedigree, this would have a very interesting story.

The flowers contain nectar and have a brush of hairs on the style below the stigma to sweep out the pollen. Sometimes, however, the flowers do not open, though they set fertile fruits.

This plant is only locally common in Britain, but ranges into western Asia and north Africa. In Britain it occurs from Cornwall and Kent north to Cheshire and south-east Yorkshire, flowering in June and July. Some of the flowers do not open, though they may produce seeds.

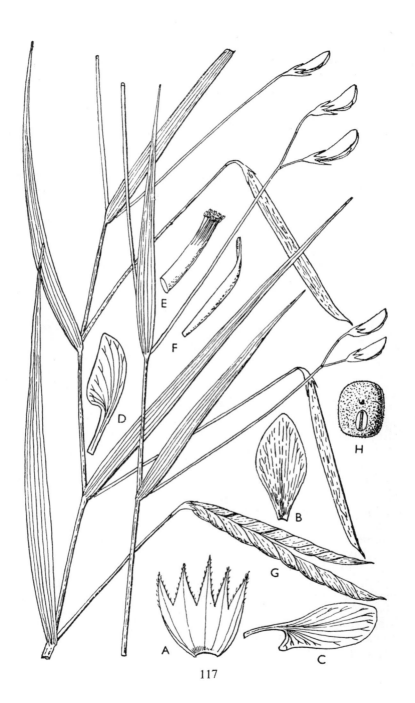

Lathyrus japonicus Willd. ($\times \frac{1}{3}$)

Perennial with a long thick black rootstock (rhizome); stems several, procumbent, usually not hairy, pale glaucous-green, very sharply angled; leaves pale glaucous-green, even paler below, spreading at a right angle, pinnate, ending in a 2- or 3-forked tendril at the top; stipules large and leaf-like but ear-like (auriculate) at the base; leaflets alternate, 5–6 on each side, sometimes somewhat bent back, nearly sessile, elliptic, rounded to an acute tip, with about 4 pairs of oblique nerves; flowers (A, $\times 1$) few in erect

stalked racemes, purple and fading to blue; calyx unequally 5-lobed, 2 upper broadly triangular, the 3 lower narrowly so, acute, and longer; standard (vexillum) (B, $\times 1$) about 1 in. long, rounded, with a short broad claw and with 2 oblique lumps just below the middle, notched at the apex and arched with crimson lines like a butterfly; wing (C, $\times 1$) and keel-petals (D, $\times 1$), smaller and paler blue or violet; stamens (E, $\times 1$) 10, united into a sheath except the upper one; style bent upwards at a right angle, bearded along the inner side; ovary (F, $\times 1$) very finely hairy, containing about 8 ovules; fruit (G, $\times \frac{1}{2}$) compressed, pea-like, nearly 2 in. long, with oblique branched nerves; seeds (H, $\times 1\frac{1}{2}$) nearly black, rounded, with a fairly long scar (hilum), about $\frac{1}{4}$ in. diam. (family *Papilionaceae*).

This is one of the least difficult plants of the family and genus to identify, because it is found only in one kind of habitat, i.e. on shingle beaches in south-eastern England, from Aldeburgh in Suffolk to Dorset; and there is a narrow-leaved form in the Shetlands. The species is found also from Scandinavia to north Germany and Normandy; in some places there is a hairy form. It also grows on the coast of North-west America, around the Great Lakes, and north-east America from southern Greenland southwards to Long Island and in Japan.

In nearly all British books of botany so far published this plant is called *Lathyrus maritimus* – a very appropriate name indeed, but one which should not be used, according to International Rules, which govern the naming of plants. The story of the names of this particular species has been well told by a very discriminating American botanist, the late Dr Fernald,* and it will be sufficient to say here that it was first described by Linnaeus in 1753 as *Pisum maritimum*. It remained so called until the year 1833, when this species name, *maritimum*, was transferred to *Lathyrus* by Fries, and it became *Lathyrus maritimus* (L.) Fries. But between these dates, Bigelow had described in 1824 a supposedly different species as *Lathyrus maritimus*, so that this name already existed and precluded the introduction of Linnaeus' name into *Lathyrus*. And it is in this manner that the names of plants are sometimes changed, usually for very good reasons, There are no half measures; one must follow the International Rules either completely or not at all.

As in some other flowers, the stigmas only become receptive to pollen after being rubbed against by an insect. Pollination is brought about by long-tongued humble-bees seeking the nectar.

It is related that in 1555 the people in the neighbourhood of Aldeburgh and Orford, Suffolk, suffering from famine, supported themselves to a great extent by the seeds of this plant, which grew in great abundance on the sandy hills along the coast. It had not been noticed by the inhabitants before, and its supposed sudden growth was generally regarded by them as a miraculous intervention of Providence, though some attributed it to the wreck on that coast during the previous year of a vessel laden with peas. The seeds, however, are bitter and very unpalatable.

* See *Rhodora* 34 : 177 (1932).

Lathyrus sylvestris L. ($\times \frac{1}{3}$)

Perennial with a creeping rootstock; stems climbing by tendrils, green and broadly winged between the nodes; stipules narrow, acute, with 1 side-lobe at the base; leaves with a single pair of leaflets; the stalk winged, the upper portion ending in a 3-forked tendril; leaflets forming a V, lanceolate, very acute, up to about 4 in. long, with 3 parallel nerves, not hairy, but microscopically dotted; main flower-stalk (peduncle) axillary, usually accompanied by a short branchlet, few-flowered, up to about 6 in. long; flowers (A, $\times \frac{2}{3}$) on rather recurved stalks; calyx (B, $\times 1$) bell-shaped, with 2

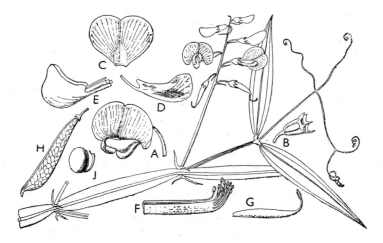

short triangular upper teeth, the lowest tooth about twice as long; petals of rather indeterminate colour, the standard (vexillum) (C, $\times \frac{2}{3}$) broad and more or less flushed with pink, the wings (alae) (D, $\times 1$) purplish in the upper half, the keel-petals (E, $\times 1$) united on the upper side and dull green; stamens (F, $\times 1\frac{1}{2}$) 10, in 2 bundles (diadelphous), the upper one completely free, the others united in a tube open along the top; ovary (G, $\times 1\frac{1}{4}$) not hairy; style up-curved, hairy below the apex; fruit (H, $\times \frac{1}{4}$) flattened, loosely net-veined (reticulate), about $2\frac{1}{2}$ in. long; seeds (J, $\times 1\frac{1}{4}$) $\frac{1}{4}$ in. nearly globular, purple-black, with a broad scar running nearly their whole length (family *Papilionaceae*).

Grows in hedges, woods, and copses, flowering during summer; widely distributed in Europe.

Lathyrus aphaca L. ($\times\frac{1}{2}$)

Annual straggly herb with stems up to 1½ ft. long, glabrous all over; the apparent leaves are really stipules which are opposite on the stem, broadly ovate, broadly arrow-shaped at the base, about 1 in. long and ¾ in. broad, entire and marked with numerous closely parallel nerves; the real leaves are completely reduced to tendrils; flowers single or paired on a common stalk 2–3 times as long as the stipules; bracts minute and soon falling off; calyx sub-equally lobed to below the middle, lobes acute, 3-nerved; petals yellow, the standard (A, $\times 1\frac{1}{4}$), wings (B, $\times 2\frac{1}{2}$) and keel (C, $\times 2\frac{1}{2}$) as shown in the drawing; stamens (D, $\times 3$) 10, one free from the others, which are united in a sheath; anthers uniform; ovary (E,

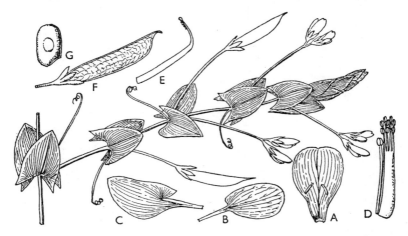

$\times 2$) papillous, with a style at right angles and hairy on the inner side; pod (F, $\times 1$) 1¼ in. long, reticulate; seeds (G, $\times 2\frac{1}{2}$) almost rectangular, often with a large paler areole in the middle (family *Papilionaceae*).

A cornfield weed in the southern counties, flowering in early summer; a very interesting and easily-recognized species because the opposite stipules are large and leaf-like, and the real leaf-blade is reduced to a tendril; distributed into north Africa and as far east as India.

There are ten or more species of *Lathyrus* in Britain, some of them introduced into fields and waste places. A key to all the species is given in the *Flora* recommended on p xiv.

BLACK PEA
Lathyrus niger Bernh. ($\times\frac{1}{3}$)

Perennial which turns black in drying; stems glabrous, angular or ribbed; leaves pinnate, with a barren tip but no tendrils; leaf-

lets 4–5 pairs, opposite or subalternate, oblong-elliptic to broadly lanceolate, with a distinct cuspidate tip, 1–1½ in. long, with several ascending lateral nerves; stipules obliquely lanceolate, acute, produced at the base on one side into a sharp point; flowers in axillary one-sided pedunculate racemes, the peduncles as long as or exceeding the leaves; pedicels shorter than the calyx, slightly pubescent; calyx (A, ×1) widely cup-shaped, shortly dentate but with 2 longer teeth below the petals; petals bluish-purple, the standard (B, ×1¼), wings (C, ×1) and keel (D, ×1) as shown in the drawings; stamens (E, ×1¼) in two bundles, the upper one free, the others connate into a split sheath; anthers uniform; ovary (F, ×1¼) glabrous; style bent, flattened towards the tip and hairy in the upper flat part, with a small terminal stigma; fruit (G, ×½) twisting when ripe, 2 in. long, obliquely nerved; seeds (H, ×2½) rounded-quadrangular, nearly black, with a large hilum nearly all along one side (family *Papilionaceae*).

Only in Scotland and very rare; extends eastward to Caucasus and south to Algeria.

It grows in rocky woods in mountain valleys up to about 1200 ft. The plant is well named *niger* (black) for it turns black when dried and the seeds are also nearly black.

Shrublet to about 2 ft. high, much branched and leafy, with short branchlets ending in a sharp needle-like point; stems crimson, covered with curly and gland-tipped hairs; leaves (A, ×1) alternate, most on the long shoots with 3 leaflets, on the short shoots with 1 leaflet; stipules leafy, joined to the leaf-stalk, rather sharply toothed like the leaflets, these jointed at the base; flowers (B, ×1) axillary on the short spine-tipped branchlets, bright pink; standard and keel streaked with numerous crimson lines; or rarely all pure white; calyx (C, ×1) green, with numerous gland-tipped

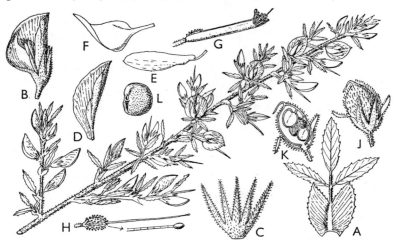

hairs and a few longer hairs, 2-lipped, the upper lip of 4 equal narrow lobes, the lower of 1 slightly longer lobe; standard (vexillum) (D, ×1) recurved in the open flower, slightly glandular outside, pink (or white), $\frac{3}{4}$ in. long; wing-petals (alae) (E, ×2) a little shorter than the sharply beaked keel-petals (F, ×1$\frac{1}{3}$); stamens (G, ×1$\frac{1}{3}$) 10, united into a sheath open along the top; anthers equal; ovary (H, ×1$\frac{1}{3}$) with long gland-tipped several-celled hairs; ovules 6–8; style thread-like, stigma terminal; fruit (J, K, ×1) ellipsoid, densely glandular; seeds (L, ×2) rounded, finely warted (family *Papilionaceae*).

A very pretty plant with a profusion of bright pink, rarely white, pea-like flowers. They are without nectar, but are visited mainly by bees which set in motion the pumping arrangement, when threads of pollen are thrown off.

Ononis repens L. ($\times \frac{2}{5}$)

Diffuse spreading herb; branches densely leafy, covered with long weak whitish several-celled hairs; leaflet (A, $\times 1\frac{1}{2}$) 1, with a large

leafy stipule adnate to the very short stalk, oblong-obovate, rounded at the top and sharply toothed, covered with very short sticky glandular hairs; flowers (B, $\times 1\frac{1}{4}$) axillary, solitary, shortly stalked, pink, the standard streaked a deeper shade; calyx (C, $\times \frac{4}{5}$) equally and rather deeply 5-lobed, lobes lanceolate, with long slender hairs and numerous short gland-tipped hairs; standard (D, $\times 1\frac{1}{5}$) rounded-obovate, with many nerves, slightly apiculate; wing-petals (E, $\times 1\frac{1}{5}$) oblong, blunt, with an acute basal lobe; keel-petals (F, $\times 1\frac{1}{5}$) beaked; stamens (G, $\times 1\frac{3}{5}$) all united into a closed sheath; style slender, with an apical stigma; pod about as long as the calyx, with 2 or 3 seeds (family *Papilionaceae*).

Rest-harrow flowers in summer and autumn and grows in grassy places, dry pastures, and sand-dunes; it is partial to calcareous soil. The flowers have no nectar, but bees visit them to collect the pollen, which is squeezed out of the pollen-chamber formed by the tip of the keel-petals when these are depressed by the weight of the insect.

The genus *Ononis* may be recognized particularly by the stamens, which are all united together into a single sheath (monadelphous), and not in two bundles (diadelphous) as in most other members of the family to which the Broad Bean and Garden Pea belong.

Melilotus altissima Thuill ($\times\frac{1}{2}$)

Annual or biennial herb up to 4 ft. high, sometimes much branched; stems glabrous, ribbed; leaves alternate, divided into 3 separate leaflets, the lateral pair nearly sessile, the end leaflet stalked but jointed near the top; leaflets oblong to narrowly obovate, narrowed to but rounded at the base, shortly dentate, with several straight side nerves; stipules 2 to each leaf, awl-shaped, about $\frac{1}{4}$ in. long; flowers in slender one-sided axillary racemes, reflexed; calyx (A, $\times 4$) with 5 awl-shaped lobes; petals yellow, the standard, wings, and keel equal in length and as shown in figs. B, C, D, $\times 2\frac{1}{2}$; stamens 10, 1 free from the others (E, $\times 2\frac{1}{2}$); ovary (F, $\times 2\frac{1}{2}$) shortly stalked, with a style about as long; fruit (G, $\times 2\frac{1}{2}$) transversely nerved, shortly beaked, 1-seeded; seed (H, $\times 3$) ellipsoid, smooth (synonym *Melilotus officinalis* (Willd.) (family *Papilionaceae*).

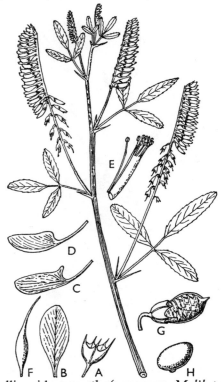

Found mostly in waste places, ranging throughout Europe and Russian Asia. The flowers are produced in summer, secrete nectar, and smell like cumarin (like new-mown hay). Cross-pollination is effected by insects, which dust the stigma projecting beyond the anthers. The wing- and keel-petals are loosely fused together on each side and are depressed by the weight of the insect, when the stamens and pistil are exposed.

The species are very closely related, and there are four represented in Britain, one of them, the White Melilot, having white flowers (see fig. 81).

WHITE MELILOT
Melilotus alba Desr. ($\times\frac{1}{3}$)

Biennial or perennial erect herb up to $2\frac{1}{2}$ ft. high with several erect or ascending branches; stem hollow, ribbed, glabrous; leaves al-

ternate, stalked, pinnately divided into 3 leaflets, these obovate to oblong-oblanceolate, narrowed to the base, the lateral leaflets nearly sessile, the end one stalked, $\frac{1}{2}$–1 in. long, repand-dentate, with as many lateral nerves as teeth into which they are produced; stipules paired, very narrow and awl-shaped; flowers numerous and small ($\frac{1}{4}$ in. long), in slender axillary racemes 3–4 times as long as the leaves, but which become much longer in fruit; calyx (A, $\times 2$) bell-shaped, equally 5-lobed, lobes short and awl-shaped; petals white, falling after fading, the standard (B, $\times 2$), wings (C, $\times 2$) and keel (D, $\times 2$) as shown in the drawing; stamens (E, $\times 3$) in 2 bundles, the upper one free, the remainder united in a sheath open on the upper side; ovary with few ovules; style glabrous; fruits (G, $\times 1$) pendulous, ovoid-elliptic, scarcely $\frac{1}{4}$ in. long, transversely wrinkled, not opening, style persistent (family *Papilionaceae*).

Widely distributed in Europe and Asia, flowering from June to September. This species is considered to be an introduction and is naturalized in fields and on waste ground mainly in the southern half of England and Wales.

Melilotus is one of the least difficult of the genera of *Papilionaceae* to recognize, because of its trifoliolate leaves, elongated raceme of small flowers, and small fruits which do not open like those of most other British members of the family.

Trigonella ornithopodioides (L.) DC. (×½)

A dwarf tufted annual herb with numerous short spreading glabrous branches; leaves 3-foliolate, very clover-like, leaflets obovate-wedge-shaped, truncate at the top, rather sharply toothed;
stipules (J, ×1½) large and partly united to the leaf-stalk, the free
part tapering to a fine point, prominently nerved; flowers (A, ×2)
purplish white, usually in pairs on a short common stalk in the leaf-
axils; calyx equally 5-lobed to the middle, lobes narrow with
subulate points, glabrous; standard (B, ×2), wings (C, ×3) and
keel (D, ×3) petals as shown in the drawing; stamens (E, ×3) 10,
one free, the others united into a split sheath; anthers small and

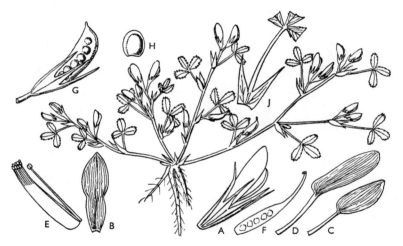

all alike; ovary (F, ×3) with about 5–8 ovules; style curved with a
terminal head-like stigma; fruit (G, ×2) twice as long as the calyx
and well exserted from it, opening along the lower side, smooth,
containing about 5–8 rounded smooth seeds (H, ×4); (synonyms
Trifolium ornithopodioides Sm.; *Trigonella purpurascens* Lam.)
(family *Papilionaceae*).

This rather outstanding species has by some botanists been
transferred to *Trifolium*. I prefer to keep it in *Trigonella*, however,
for it does not seem to be related to any other species of *Trifolium*
but has undoubted affinity with at least two other species of
Trigonella, *T. laciniata* L., and *T. occulta* Del., natives of the Near
East.

TOOTHED MEDICK
Medicago polymorpha L. ($\times \frac{1}{2}$)

A glabrous annual branching from the base; leaves alternate, divided into 3 leaflets on a common stalk, leaflets obovate, wedge-shaped at the base, rounded at the apex, slightly toothed in the upper half, the lateral nerves parallel and running out into the teeth; stipules large and deeply divided into narrow lobes; flowers few together in little heads on a common stalk in the axils of the leaves; bracts small and awl-shaped; individual flower-stalks very short; calyx (A, $\times \frac{1}{2}$) deeply divided into 5 narrow pointed parts; petals yellow, the standard (B, $\times 6$), wings (C, $\times 7$), and keel (D, $\times 7$) as shown in the drawing; stamens (E, $\times 7$) 10, in 2 bundles, one stamen being free; anthers of one size and shape; ovary (F,

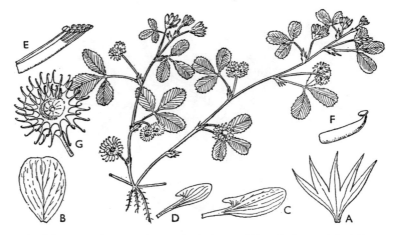

$\times 7$) oblong, style very short; fruit (G, $\times 1\frac{1}{2}$) spirally twisted into a circle like a watch-spring and formed of 2 or 3 loose flat coils armed with hooked bristles (family *Papilionaceae*).

Grows mainly in cultivated and waste ground, flowering in spring and summer; widely distributed in many parts of the world.

The flowers secrete nectar, and visiting insects, on alighting, release the stamens and pistil which spring out of the keel and discharge the pollen on to their bodies.

The fruits of *Medicago* (fig. G) are very characteristic, being spirally coiled up and armed with hooked prickles which are readily distributed by attaching themselves to the fur of animals and to the clothing of human beings. Synonym *Medicago denti-culata* Willd.

Medicago lupulina L. (×½)

Annual, with slender mostly procumbent branches from the base
and up to 2 ft. long; stipules large and toothed; leaflets 3, obovate,
shortly toothed (dentate), apiculate; common stalk short; flowers
(A, ×3) in small rounded heads in the axils of the leaves, heads
on slender stalks (peduncles); calyx (B, ×5) equally 5-lobed to
the middle, lobes lanceolate, hairy on the margins (ciliate); petals
yellow, the standard (C, ×2½) broadly obovate; keel and wings
blunt at the apex, free from the staminal tube; 1 stamen free, the

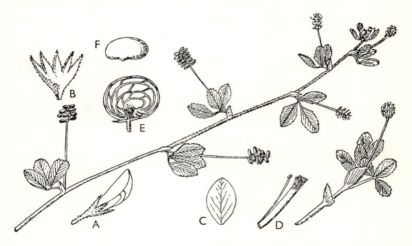

other 9 united in a sheath split along the top (D, ×5); anthers
small and equal; ovary with a glabrous style, stigma terminal;
fruits (E, ×1½) crowded into an oblong cluster, very short, curved,
black when ripe, reticulate, 1-seeded; seed (F, ×3½) kidney-
shaped, straw-coloured, smooth (family *Papilionaceae*).

A weed in waste places and fields, widely distributed in temperate regions and naturalized in many countries.

The chief pollinator of this plant is the honey-bee, which does
not disdain even this flower's tiny store of honey. The whole inflorescence is pulled down by the weight of the insect, which then
sucks the flower's head downwards. It visits a few flowers at a
time, and then flies away to another plant. On alighting the insect
causes the column of reproductive organs (stamens and style) to
spring out of the keel, to which in this case it does not return after
the pressure is removed.

A low much-branched annual; stems ribbed, covered with long soft hairs; leaves with longish stalks and divided into 3 separate obovate leaflets about $\frac{3}{4}$ in. long, these with strong parallel nerves forked towards the finely toothed margin; stipules joined to the leaf-stalk, and ending in a free sharp point, strongly nerved, hairy; flowers in dense axillary and terminal sessile clusters embraced at the base by the broad stipules; calyx (A, $\times4$) equally divided into 5 awl-shaped lobes, hairy and ribbed, persistent and embracing the fruit; vexillum (B, $\times3\frac{1}{2}$) wings (C, $\times3\frac{1}{2}$), and keel (D, $\times3\frac{1}{2}$) petals as shown in the drawing, rose-coloured; stamens (E, $\times3\frac{1}{2}$) united in a sheath with the upper free, filaments slightly dilated at the top;

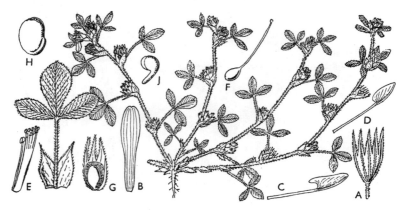

ovary (F, $\times3\frac{1}{2}$) ellipsoid, with a long slender style; fruit (G, $\times3\frac{1}{2}$) enclosed by the persistent calyx, rounded, 1-seeded; seed (H, $\times5$) brown, containing a large green embryo (J, $\times4$) (family *Papilionaceae*).

Flowers in summer and grows in dry fields and waste places; distributed in Europe generally and east as far as the Caucasus.

There are as many as twenty-one species of Clover in Britain, eight of which are shown in these drawings. For the determination of the remainder a comprehensive *Flora* should be consulted (see p. xiv). The genus is recognized by the trifoliolate leaves, flowers in a dense head, some of which are sterile, and by the short pod which rarely exceeds the calyx.

Trifolium striatum occurs throughout Britain, but is sometimes very local; in Eire mostly near the coast.

Strong-growing perennial with ascending glabrous stems up to about 2 ft. long; leaves with 3 leaflets, these very broadly obovate (almost rounded), wedge-shaped at the base, rounded at the apex, averaging about 1 in. long, finely and closely toothed, with numerous parallel nerves, glabrous; stipules large, united for $\frac{1}{3}$ their length to the leaf-stalk, with long sharp points, conspicuously nerved; flowers (A, $\times 2\frac{1}{2}$) pinkish white, in axillary and terminal long-stalked globose heads about 1 in. diam.; flower-stalks about $\frac{1}{6}$ in. long; calyx-lobes 5, awl-shaped, glabrous; standard (B, $\times 4\frac{1}{2}$), wing (C, $\times 4\frac{1}{2}$), and keel petals (D, $\times 4\frac{1}{2}$) as shown in the drawing; stamens (E, $\times 5$) 10, the upper one free, the other 9 united in a sheath split along the top; anthers equal-sized; ovary (F, $\times 6$) with several ovules; style glabrous; fruit with 2–4 seeds (family *Papilionaceae*).

Originally introduced for fodder, and found by roadsides throughout Britain; widely distributed in the northern hemisphere.

The flowers are at first white and erect, afterwards rose-red and curved downwards, the heads then presenting a white centre and a rose-red margin. They are then very conspicuous to insects.

87   ZIGZAG CLOVER, MEADOW CLOVER

Trifolium medium L. ($\times \frac{1}{2}$)

Perennial with more or less zigzag branches thinly clothed with very fine long hairs; leaves rather few and distant, long-stalked,

with three leaflets, these oblong-oblanceolate, rounded to a short tip at the apex, narrowed to the base, 1–1½ in. l o n g, n o t toothed, with numerous lateral nerves whose branches run out to the margin, glabrous or with silky hairs on the lower surface; stipules large and joined for nearly half their length to the leaf stalk, closely nerved and more or less hairy; flowers (A, ×2) in terminal shortly stalked heads 1–1½ in. diam.; calyx tubular, with 5 very narrow hairy lobes, the lobes nearly equal but the bottom one longer; standard (B, ×1½), wing petals (C, ×2), and keel (D, ×2) as shown in the drawing; stamens (E, ×2) 10, the upper one free from the others which are united in a sheath open on the upper side; ovary (F, ×2) rounded, style slender, glabrous; pod rounded, 1-seeded (family *Papilionaceae*).

In open woods, in bushy fields, and on banks and roadsides; widely distributed into eastern Asia, becoming a mountain plant in south Europe. Generally distributed throughout Britain, though often rather local and more common in northern districts.

Recognized by the shape of the leaflets with numerous closely set lateral nerves, very large stipules with subulate tips, and ellipsoid shortly stalked heads of reddish-purple flowers.

Perennial herb with procumbent stems; leaves on long slender stalks, with three leaflets, these obovate or elliptic, closely parallel-nerved to the very finely-toothed margins, averaging about 1 in. long; stipules large and united for about half their length with the leaf-stalk, the free parts narrow and sharply pointed and strongly marked with green nerves; flowers (A, $\times 3\frac{1}{2}$) in very long-stalked more or less globose heads which soon fruit and form a net-like pinkish ball (J, $\times 1$) due to the calyx becoming inflated and strongly reticulate; head subtended by deeply lobed bracts; calyx (in flower) equally 5-lobed, hairy on and just below the

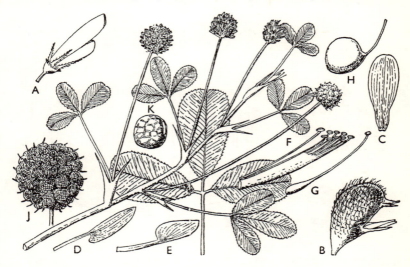

lobes; petals pink, the standard (C, $\times 3\frac{1}{2}$), wings (D, $\times 3\frac{1}{2}$), and keel (E, $\times 3\frac{1}{2}$) petals as shown in the drawing; stamens (F, $\times 5$) 10, one free above, the others united in a sheath; ovary and style (G, $\times 5$) glabrous; fruit (H, $\times 5$) globular, enclosed in the inflated net-like calyx (B, $\times 7$); seed (K, $\times 4$) rounded, slightly mottled (family *Papilionaceae*).

In moist meadows and pastures, flowering in summer and autumn; enjoys a wide distribution from the Atlantic Islands to eastern Asia.

The Latin and popular names refer to the head of fruits around which the calyx becomes inflated and reticulate.

Perennial herb, with numerous spreading stems often rooting at the nodes; stipules inconspicuous, not $\frac{1}{2}$ in. long, with a short sheath and long narrow lobes; leaflets broadly obovate to rounded, sharply toothed, with a lighter band across the middle; leaf-stalks long; flowers (A, $\times 2\frac{1}{2}$) white or tinged with pink, in globose heads on a long (sometimes very long) common axillary stalk; individual flowers on slender stalks; calyx equally 5-lobed, not hairy; standard (B, $\times 2$) petal with a narrow claw with ridged

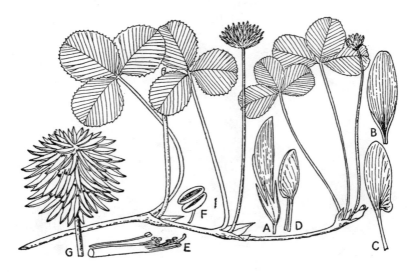

margins, slightly notched at the apex; wing-petals (C, $\times 2$) with an obtuse lateral lobe; keel-petals (D, $\times 2$) slightly joined, with slender claws; upper stamen free, the others united in a sheath split at the top (E, $\times 2\frac{1}{2}$); anthers (F, $\times 15$) very short, attached in the middle; style hairy only at the tip; pod with 2–4 seeds, enclosed in the withered corolla (family *Papilionaceae*).

The notes on pollination given for *T. pratense*, fig. 90, apply equally well to this species, which is also a valuable pasture and bee-plant. The genus *Trifolium* is quite richly represented in this country, there being over twenty native species. Some of these are very rare and of exceptional interest because of their geographical distribution; for example, two or three which are found only in Cornwall and in Spain and Portugal.

Trifolium pratense L. ($\times \frac{1}{2}$)

Perennial herb; stems ascending, up to 2 ft. long, more densely hairy in the upper part; stipules (A, $\times 1\frac{1}{2}$) very conspicuous, about $\frac{3}{4}$ in. long, connate with the leaf-stalk and with sharply pointed lobes, veiny; leaflets obovate, with numerous parallel nerves radiating into the minute teeth; flowers (B, $\times 2$) reddish-purple or rarely white, in dense terminal rounded clusters girt by two sessile leaves at the base; calyx-lobes (C, $\times 1\frac{1}{2}$) very prominent in bud and bristle-like, purple, one slightly longer than the others; standard petal (D, $\times 2$) like a narrow draining spade, long-clawed; wing-petals (E, $\times 2\frac{1}{2}$) oblong, with a very long slender claw; keel-petals (F, $\times 2\frac{1}{2}$) very similar; upper

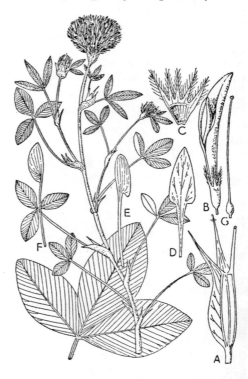

stamen free, the remainder united into a sheath; ovary (G, $\times 2$) ellipsoid, very short, with a long slender style and head-like stigma; an important field crop (family *Papilionaceae*).

Clovers are important bee-flowers, and these insects effect cross-pollination when searching for the abundant nectar. This is brought about through a simple valvular arrangement by which the stamens and pistil are caused to protrude from the keel-petals so long as pressure is exerted by the weight of the insect. When this happens the pollen is dusted on the underside of the bee's head, and is transferred to the stigma of another flower. Nectar is also stolen by other insects which perforate the flowers from the outside and thrust their proboscis through the hole.

Trifolium campestre Schreb. ($\times \frac{1}{2}$)

Annual, on dunes, waste places, and in fields; stems wiry, much branched and procumbent and clothed with very short hairs; leaves (H, $\times 1$) divided into 3 separate leaflets (trifoliolate), the end leaflet with a longer stalk than the others, all obovate and broadly wedge-shaped (cuneate), in the lower half, upper half shortly toothed; nerves numerous and parallel, each ending in a tooth; stipules large and leafy, united for a short distance to the stalk, narrowly ovate, clothed with a few long hairs; flowers (A,

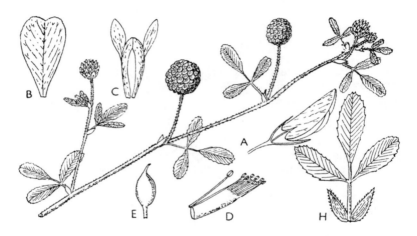

$\times 3$) very small in a congested head-like raceme, greenish-yellow, the standard petal enlarging and becoming membranous over the ripe fruit; calyx with 5 very narrow lobes of unequal length; standard petal (B, $\times 5$) slightly toothed in the upper part; wing- and keel-petals partly united (C, $\times 3$); stamens (D, $\times 3$) 10, 1 free, the others united into a sheath; anthers very small and rounded; ovary (E, $\times 4$) shortly stalked, with 1–2 ovules; fruit ovoid-ellipsoid, 1- or rarely 2-seeded; seed ovoid, yellowish and shining (family *Papilionaceae*).

Widely spread in Europe, Asia, and north Africa, and the Atlantic Islands, and introduced into North America.

Trifolium is the largest genus of *Papilionaceae* represented in the British flora, there being 23 species in the latest list of plants. Included in these are 5 species which are introduced, either as crop plants or weeds of cultivation.

Trifolium arvense L. ($\times \frac{2}{5}$)

Annual herb with erect slender root; stems wiry, slender, much branched, softly pubescent with appressed hairs; leaves (A, $\times 1\frac{1}{2}$) divided into 3 separate leaflets on a very short common stalk, the leaf-lets oblanceolate, entire or slightly toothed near the apex, softly hairy below; stipules joined to the leaf-stalk, about $\frac{1}{3}$ in. long, marked with parallel nerves and sharp-pointed; flowers (B, $\times 3$) very small, white to pale pink, densely crowded into an oblong, cylindric, brush-like stalked spike $\frac{1}{2}-\frac{3}{4}$ in. long; no bracts; calyx (C, $\times 2$) much longer than the petals, 5-lobed to below the middle, lobes linear-awl-shaped, very acute, fringed with long hairs; petals white or pale pink, very small; stan-dard (D, $\times 3$) obovate, with a very broad claw;

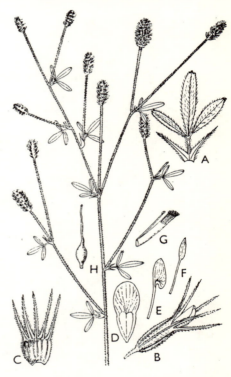

wing- and keel-petals as shown in figs. E, F, ($\times 3$); stamens (G, $\times 4$) 10, the upper one free, the remainder united in a sheath (diadelphous); anthers minute, rounded; ovary (H, $\times 4$) very small, shortly stalked (stipitate), containing 1 ovule; fruit a tiny 1-seeded pod embraced by the calyx (family *Papilionaceae*).

Grows in dry sandy fields, flowering from July to September; widely distributed across the northern hemisphere.

As in most other species of Clover, the flowers secrete nectar. Cross-pollination is effected mainly by bees, though self-pollina-tion also produces fertile seed.

Galega officinalis L. ($\times\frac{1}{3}$)

Perennial herb up to 3 ft. high; stems mostly glabrous; leaves pinnate with 6–7 pairs of opposite lanceolate leaflets and an odd terminal leaflet, leaflets with several fan-like nerves and a sharp tip; stipules large, conspicuous, narrowly triangular, deeply sagittate at the base, strongly nerved; flowers lilac or rarely white, in axillary racemes; bracts long subulate; calyx (A, $\times2$) campanulate with 5 equal subulate teeth; standard (B, $\times1\frac{2}{3}$), wings (C, $\times1\frac{2}{3}$) and keel (D, $\times1\frac{2}{3}$) as shown in the drawing; stamens (E, $\times1\frac{2}{3}$) 10, all united; anthers equal; ovary (F, $\times1\frac{2}{3}$) with about 8

ovules, a curved slender style and minute terminal stigma; fruit (G, $\times\frac{3}{4}$) about 1½ in. long, with parallel nerves converging into the middle of the valves; seeds (H, $\times2$) transversely ellipsoid, smooth (family *Papilionaceae*).

An alien plant on rubbish-heaps, by roadsides and in chalk pits in the south of England; native of southern Europe.

WILD GOOSEBERRY **94**
Ribes uva-crispa L. (× ⅓)

Small shrub with long and short shoots; branches armed with 3-forked spines (A, ×3½) below the short shoots; leaves produced annually and clustered on the short shoots, singly on the long shoots, on long rather slender stalks, orbicular or kidney-shaped in outline, up to about 2 in. broad, 3–5-lobed to about the middle, the lobes coarsely toothed, thin, very slightly hairy; flowers (B, ×1) 1–3 together on the short shoots, shortly stalked, stalks softly hairy; calyx-lobes reflexed, purplish, the tube bearded with hairs; petals (C, ×2) white, erect, wedge-shaped, very small, strongly nerved; stamens (D, ×2) 5, opposite the sepals; anthers attached in the middle at the back; ovary inferior, with a few gland-tipped bristles, 1-locular, with numerous ovules on 2 parietal placentas (E, ×3); fruit (G, ×⅓) an ellipsoid-globose berry, up to 1 in. diam., smooth or bristly-hairy (F, style, ×2) (family *Grossulariaceae*).

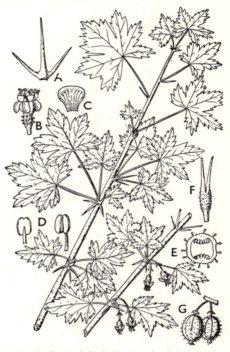

A very widely spread species in open woods and hedges and often more common near villages; extends into western Asia and north Africa.

The flowers are pendulous to horizontal. The anthers shed their pollen as the flowers open, but the styles are not then at full length and the stigmas are not receptive. Nectar is secreted in the base of the bell-shaped floral axis (receptacle), and is protected by stiff hairs projecting vertically from the style. Some bushes bear female flowers, in which the anthers are rudimentary and do not open. Synonym *Ribes grossularia* L.

Swida sanguinea (L.) Opiz ($\frac{2}{5}$)

Shrub up to about 6 ft., leaves opposite, without stipules, ovate, entire, thinly clothed below and on the flower-stalks, ovary and

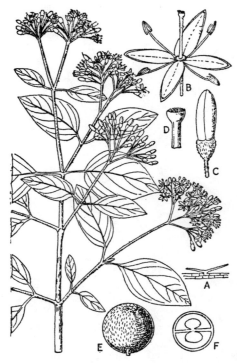

young fruit with white T-shaped hairs (A, ×4); flowers (B, ×1½) numerous, small, collected into terminal lax clusters (cymes) about 2 in. in diam.; no bracts; calyx very minute on top of the ovary; ovary inferior and 2-locular (F, ×4); petals 4, dull white, not overlapping in bud (C, ×1½) (valvate); free from one another; stamens 4, alternate with the petals, and inserted around a ring-like disk which secretes nectar; style undivided, grooved, the disk-like papillous stigma (D, ×3) reaching the same level as the anthers; either self- or cross-pollination; fruit (E, ×1½), globose, fleshy, black, bitter, the hard inner stone (drupe) containing the seed (family *Cornaceae*).

A second native species, the Dwarf Cornel, *Cornus suecica* L., is widely distributed and has a slender creeping rootstock with annual stems only a few inches high. These have opposite ovate leaves, and a little terminal umbel of flowers surrounded by four large white petal-like bracts. The real petals are very minute and a dark purple colour. Certain continental botanists consider it distinct, its name being rather formidable, *Chamaepericlymenum suecicum* (L.) Asch. & Graebn. (see fig. 96).

Dogwood is common on limy soils in the south of England, but rare in the north. The slender annual shoots can be used for basket-making. Synonym *Cornus sanguinea* L.

DWARF CORNEL

96

Chamaepericlymenum suecicum (L.) Aschers & Graebner ($\times \frac{1}{2}$)

A perennial herb with slender creeping rootstock; stems annual, up to 6 in. high, usually unbranched; leaves opposite, sessile, ovate, entire, about 1 in. long and $\frac{3}{4}$ in. broad, with 5–8 nerves lengthwise, glabrous below, but with scattered appressed T-shaped one-celled hairs above (D, ×6); flowers (A, ×5) in a terminal cluster surrounded by 4 large yellowish-white obovate bracts streaked with reddish nerves and resembling petals; flower-stalks and calyx clothed with appressed hairs; calyx bell-shaped, shortly toothed; petals 4, free, very small, dark purple; stamens (B, ×8) 4, alternate with the petals; ovary inferior, 2-locular; style undivided; ovules solitary in each loculus; fruit (C, ×1) a bunch of berry-like red drupes (synonym *Cornus suecica* L.) (family *Cornaceae*).

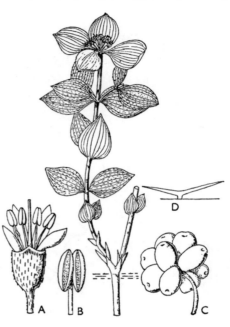

Confined to the hills and mountains of northern England and of Scotland, and with a circumpolar distribution in the northern hemisphere; of exceptional interest, being a highly advanced species of herb clearly descended from woody ancestors. The hairs are 1-celled and T-shaped, and on the leaves they are confined to the upper surface. To compensate for the diminutive size of the flowers, the latter are surrounded by an involucre of large petal-like bracts (modified upper leaves) which resemble petals and serve to attract insects.

In the genus *Cornus* in a restricted sense there are no bracts below the flowers. This I consider to be a very important character. The Dogwood, *Cornus sanguinea* L., is a typical example of *Cornus* proper and an illustration of this will be found at fig. 95.

Sambucus nigra L. ($\times \frac{2}{5}$)

A small spreading tree with rough bark, the stem and branches full of pith; young annual shoots from the main branches soft; leaves deciduous, opposite, pinnate, with an odd terminal leaflet, and 2 or 3 pairs of leaflets; leaflets opposite, shortly stalked, elliptic to obovate, acutely acuminate, rather sharply toothed, glabrous or nearly so; flowers (A, $\times 2$) scented, numerous, arranged in flat terminal corymbs, with about 5 primary branches; no bracts; middle flower at each fork nearly sessile, lateral flowers stalked; sepals 5, very small and green; petals 5, yellowish-white, united at the base into a very short tube and spreading horizontally; stamens 5, alternate with the corolla-lobes, the rather large anthers (B, $\times 3\frac{1}{2}$) facing outwards; ovary (C, $\times 3$) at first nearly quite superior but becoming inferior in fruit; stigmas 3–5, sessile; fruits (D, $\times 1\frac{1}{2}$) purple-black and juicy, densely arranged (family *Caprifoliaceae*).

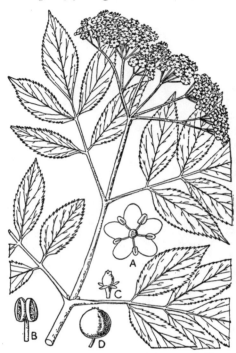

This flowers in early summer and grows in woods and waste places; it is one of our most useful British plants, the fruit making excellent wine and jam or jelly; the flowers are used medicinally; the pith is employed by botanists for embedding specimens for section cutting; the wood is very hard and has been used by mathematical instrument makers and for butchers' skewers, shoemakers' pegs, etc.; leaves, avoided by stock, were formerly used to make an insecticide. Although the flowers of this species are scented, there is no nectary.

Sambucus ebulus L. ($\times\frac{1}{3}$)

Perennial with annual herbaceous stems up to 3 ft. high; rootstock short; leaves opposite, pinnate, leaflets 7–11, lanceolate, serrate, the terminal one the largest, the basal pair much smaller and resembling stipules; flowers (B, ×2) in a terminal corymb with 3 primary branches, pure white or tinged with purple outside, sweet scented, rounded in bud (A, ×2); calyx with 5 small teeth; corolla with a very short tube and 5 spreading lobes; stamens (C, ×2) 5, inserted at the base of the corolla-tube; stigma sessile on the inferior ovary (D, ×4) 3–5-lobed; fruit (E, ×$\frac{1}{2}$) a small black berry (family *Caprifoliaceae*).

Certain species of herbs have clearly descended from ancestors which were woody or at any rate more woody; the Dwarf Elder is a very good example, the more woody relative being the Common Elder, *Sambucus nigra* L., shown in fig. 97. It flowers in summer and somewhat later than the Common Elder, though it is probably not truly native, being found in hedges, on banks and roadsides near villages. It was formerly cultivated for making a dye and is widely distributed from the Atlantic Islands and north Africa through Europe as far east as India.

Though not usually touched by stock, the berries of this plant have been known to cause poisoning in turkeys, the bark, leaves, and berries having decided purgative properties.

The scent of Vanilla is very widely distributed amongst flowering plants, the Dwarf Elder being one of them.

A third species of this genus, *S. racemosa* L., is commonly planted and sometimes naturalized, especially in Scotland. It has red fruits and the flowers are arranged in a more pyramidal panicle.

Viburnum lantana L. ($\times \frac{2}{5}$)

A large shrub or small tree; young shoots and leaves below covered with short star-shaped (stellate) hairs (A, $\times 3$); leaves deciduous, opposite, rounded-ovate, not pointed, rounded or heart-
shaped at the base, rather sharply toothed (dentate), somewhat
wrinkled (rugose) on the upper surface, with very prominent
lateral nerves below; stalks about $\frac{1}{2}$ in. long, with a small ridge between them at the base, but no stipules; flowers odoriferous, small
and white, in dense flat cymes up to 3 in. diameter; calyx-lobes 5,
very small on top of the ovary; corolla with a very short tube and

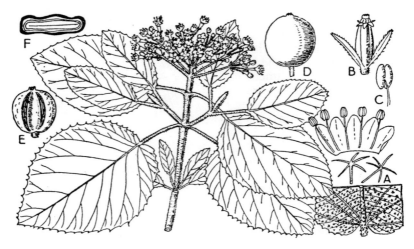

5 spreading rounded lobes; stamens (C, $\times 4$) 5, alternate with the
lobes, and arising from the base of the tube; anthers rounded, facing inwards; ovary (B, $\times 4$) below the calyx (inferior), with a small
disk on top and 2–3 very short stigmas; fruit (D, $\times 1\frac{1}{2}$) a purplish-
black berry with one hard flattened seed (F, $\times 1\frac{1}{2}$). (E, $\times 1\frac{1}{4}$, berry
with flesh removed) (family *Caprifoliaceae*).

A hedgerow plant flowering in early summer, and mainly found
in southern England. It is a widely distributed species, occurring
all over temperate and southern Europe as far as the Caucasus.
The stamens are curved inwards when the flower opens and the
anthers are over the stigmas. Automatic self-pollination is therefore easy. Nectar is secreted in a flat layer on top of the ovary and
immediately below the stigmas. Later the stamens spread towards
the outside of the flower.

A shrub or very small tree with attractive Hydrangea-like flowers arranged in a terminal umbel-like cluster (cyme); the outer flowers (A, $\times 1\frac{1}{4}$) are sterile and white, and serve to attract insects; garden forms often have all the flowers so transformed; the short leafy flowering shoots have brown bud-scales at the base; leaves opposite, rounded in outline but divided nearly to the middle into 3 or rarely 5 coarsely toothed and pointed lobes; principal nerves as many as the lobes and radiating from the base; leaf-stalks with a pair of sessile glands at the top (B, $\times \frac{3}{5}$), and towards the base

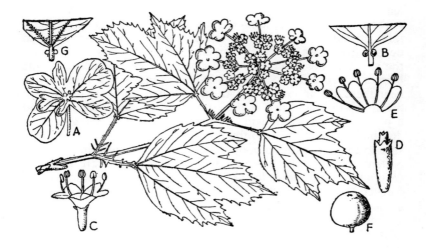

about 2 pairs of very narrow outgrowths, but no stipules; flowers (C, $\times 1\frac{1}{2}$) white, scented like hawthorn; sepals (D, $\times \frac{4}{5}$) 5, very small, above the ovary (ovary inferior); corolla (E, $\times 2$) short and 5-lobed; stamens 5, inserted at the base of the corolla-tube, the anthers facing inwards (introrse); ovary 1-locular and containing 1 ovule; fruit a small 1-seeded berry (F, $\times \frac{4}{5}$) (G, shows lower side of leaf) (family *Caprifoliaceae*).

Viburnum is a large genus and very widely distributed, with numerous species in eastern Asia, especially China, many of which are grown in our gardens. *V. opulus* flowers in early summer and ranges across Europe into Asiatic Russia and into the Arctic regions. Pollination is either by the agency of bees and other insects, or self-pollination may take place.

Lonicera periclymenum L. ($\times \frac{3}{4}$)

Probably our most lovely climbing shrub, with deliciously sweet-scented flowers. These exhibit most interesting features concerned with cross-pollination. The flower-buds (A) are at first vertical, and the anthers open within them between 6 and 7 p.m., the stigma becoming receptive at the same time; but it is placed higher than the anthers, so automatic self-pollination cannot normally take place (B, $\times 1$). The first flowers open about 7 p.m. The lower lip of the corolla separates first and the anthers stick out, the stigma still being held by the hook-like upper lip. The corolla now moves from the vertical to the horizontal and the style is released and curves down as far as the lower lip and well below the anthers (C). At the same time a strong odour is exhaled, which is faint during the day. Hover flies now settle on the anthers and devour the pollen, and they may effect pollination by alighting on the stigma. Hawk-moths then probe for nectar, which is at the base of the corolla-tube. On the following morning if insects have been there, the anthers are destitute of pollen, and have exchanged position with the style (D), the latter being in place between 7 and 8 p.m., when a fresh batch of flowers opens. The stigma now dominates the entrance to the flower and a visiting hawk-moth is sure to touch it with its body, probably already well dusted with pollen from another flower. During the process there is also a very interesting and indeed remarkable change in colour of the corolla. Originally white inside and red outside, it becomes yellow after pollination, and the newly opened flowers present a fresh attraction to hawk-moths, drawn from a distance by the fragrance of the flowers, when near, by the conspicuous collection of them (inflorescence), and when quite close, by the more clearly visible newly opened white flowers. Eventually the successfully fertilized flowers become a dirty orange brown and gradually lose their scent altogether. Humble-bees sometimes visit honeysuckle, but find it difficult to reach the nectar, and they are not supposed to have had any influence in developing the special characters of the flower.

The leaves are opposite and not toothed (entire) and there are no stipules, though there is a connecting line between their bases. The calyx is glandular and on top of the ovary (ovary inferior) (E, $\times 5$), and the corolla is 2-lipped, the upper lip of 4 united lobes, the lower of a single lobe. The red berries are crowded into a cluster (F, $\times 1$) (family *Caprifoliaceae*).

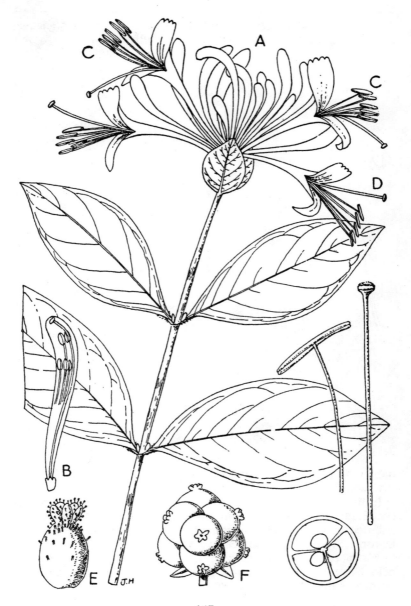

147

TWIN-FLOWER
Linnaea borealis L. (A, ×1)

An evergreen shrublet; branches thinly and softly hairy; leaves opposite, rounded-ovate, with a few teeth and usually a few stiff hairs on the margin, averaging about ½ in. long and broad, ştalks fringed with hairs; flowers drooping, fragrant, in pairs, each flower-stalk with a pair of oblong bracteoles towards the top; calyx (B, D, ×2) of 5 narrow lobes on top of the ovary, thinly hairy; corolla (E, ×3) pale pink or white, about ½ in. long, 5-lobed, lobes ovate-rounded; stamens (F, ×2½) 4, inserted near the base of the corolla-tube, anthers attached in the middle; ovary (C, ×2) inferior, 3-locular (G, ×5),

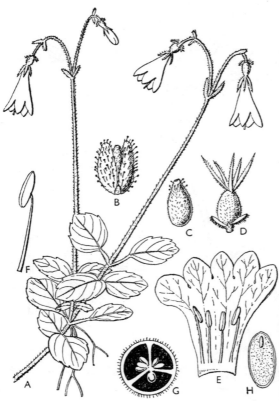

hairy and glandular; fruit like a berry, 1-seeded; seed (H, ×4) with small embryo (family *Caprifoliaceae*).

In Britain found only in pine-woods in the mountains of northern England and central and eastern Scotland, but widely distributed in northern latitudes and in the mountains of southern Europe. Students should remove their hats when they find this lovely plant, for the genus commemorates the name of the most beloved naturalist of all time, that of *Carl Linnaeus*, of Sweden, known as the Father of Modern Botany.

Hedera helix L. ($\times \frac{2}{5}$)

Woody evergreen shrub or creeping on the ground or climbing up trees or walls to a considerable height by means of sucker-like out-growths; leaves alternate, thick, evergreen and shining, those lobed prominently nerved, those of the flowering shoots less lobed and ovate elliptic to obovate and sometimes broadly notched; petioles very variable in length; flowering branches short, from the main climbing stem, ending in an umbel of yellowish green flowers (A, $\times \frac{2}{5}$; B, $\times 1\frac{1}{4}$); calyx short, saucer-like, toothed; petals (C, $\times 1\frac{1}{4}$) 4, free, not overlapping in bud; stamens 4, alternate with petals; ovary half-below the calyx, 3-locular; berry (D, $\times 1\frac{1}{2}$) depressed-globose; seeds

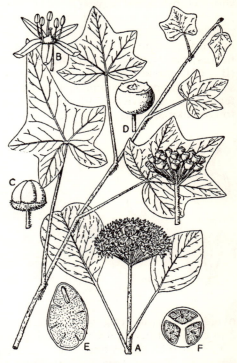

2–5, with very small embryo and the seed-coat intruding into the abundant endosperm; flowers in late autumn, fruits lasting until spring and eaten by pigeons (E, vertical section of seed, $\times 1\frac{3}{4}$; F, cross-section of fruit, $\times 1\frac{1}{2}$) (family *Araliaceae*).

In this country the ivy is one of the latest plants to flower. Insects effect cross-pollination by crawling about amongst the flowers conveniently arranged in umbels, an abundance of nectar being secreted in a yellowish green disk. After the anthers have released their pollen they quickly drop off, and the stigma becomes receptive to pollen from other younger flowers, the disk secreting nectar more actively. If self-pollination takes place it is said to be ineffective, for in Sweden it failed to set seed when grown in a greenhouse, probably owing to the absence of insects.

Buxus sempervirens L. ($\times\frac{1}{2}$)

Evergreen shrub or small tree up to 30 ft. high with very hard wood; stem up to 3 ft. diam.; young branchlets pubescent with short whitish hairs; leaves (A, ×1) opposite, obovate to oblanceo-late or elliptic, narrowed to the shortly stalked base, more or less notched at the apex, $\frac{3}{4}$–$1\frac{1}{2}$ in. long (usually about 1 in.) entire, leathery, shining above, with numerous but rather obscure lateral nerves; no stipules; flowers white, unisexual, axillary, the males (B, ×2) and females (C, ×2) clustered in the same leaf-axils; sepals 4; no petals; stamens 4 in the male flowers; styles 3 in the female flowers; ovary 3-locular (D, E, ×2), with 3 divergent tongue-like stigmas; fruit (F, ×$1\frac{1}{2}$) a 3-locular capsule, sessile,

ovoid, about $\frac{1}{2}$ in. long, with 3 divergent beaks; seeds (G, H, ×4) 2 in each loculus, black and shining (family *Buxaceae*).

Confined to chalky and limestone Downs in southern England, flowering in spring; much planted and naturalized in other places, often used as an edging to garden paths; distributed in western Europe and the Mediterranean region, as far east as the Caucasus and northern Persia.

The wood is very hard with a very fine grain, and has been compared with ivory. It is unrivalled for wood engraving, turnery, and for making drawing instruments; all parts of the plant are bitter, and have caused poisoning in pigs and horses.

The genus *Buxus* has been classified in various families, usually as a member of the *Euphorbia* family, *Euphorbiaceae*, but it is now generally regarded as distinct and placed near to the Witch Hazel family, *Hamamelidaceae*.

Populus tremula L. ($\times\frac{1}{3}$)

An erect tree up to 80 ft. high, the leaves of which are rarely still, shaking or 'trembling' in the slightest disturbance of air, due to the very slender compressed leaf-stalks and wide almost orbicular blade; older branchlets rough with the knobs of the old leaf-scars, with shining bark; leaves 2–3 in. wide, prominently 3-nerved from the base, finely reticulate; flowers unisexual, the males and females on separate trees (dioecious); male catkins (A, $\times\frac{1}{3}$) enclosed in bud by shining sticky scales, about 3 in. long; bracts (B, $\times1\frac{1}{3}$) deeply incised and fringed with long hairs;

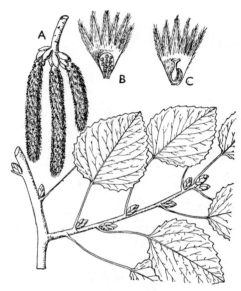

stamens about 8–10, inserted on an obovate flat scale; female catkins and bracts (C, $\times1\frac{1}{3}$) very similar to the male; ovary inserted on a fleshy obovoid 'disk'; style short, 2-lobed (family *Salicaceae*).

This fine tree is widely distributed through Europe, northern Africa, Asia Minor, the Caucasus, and into Siberia. It covers extensive tracts in Scandinavia, Russia, and Siberia. In Britain it is most abundant in the Highlands of Scotland, where it ascends to the limit of tree-growth. The tree is short-lived, however, and is one of the most beautiful in northern latitudes on account of the splendid red and yellow tints assumed by the leaves in the autumn, though such colours are rarely seen in this country. The wood is soft, and is largely used in Sweden for making matches and for wood-pulp in the manufacture of paper.

Populus canescens Smith ($\times\frac{1}{3}$)

Tree up to 100 ft. or more, trunk to 15 ft. in circumference; bark thin, grey, breaking into small roughened dark-coloured cavities, making it deeply furrowed; young branchlets covered with dense whitish hairs; buds ovoid, shortly tomentose; leaves on the long shoots covered below with a thick greyish felt of hairs, on the short shoots glabrous or with traces of hairs; all more or less ovate or suborbicular, 2–$2\frac{1}{2}$ in. diam., coarsely and bluntly toothed but teeth few; stalks nearly as long as the blade, compressed laterally; flowers unisexual, dioecious (male (A, $\times\frac{1}{3}$) and female on different trees), in pendulous stalked catkins up to 4 in. long; stamens (B, $\times2$) 8–15; scales (C, $\times1\frac{1}{2}$) obovate; female catkins much shorter, but elongating in fruit to 4 in. long; ovary (D, $\times2$) glabrous, with spreading shortly divided stigmas; capsule 2-valved (family *Salicaceae*).

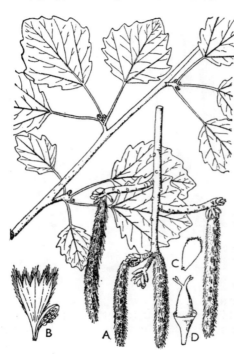

Considered to be a native species in the south-eastern counties and planted elsewhere; male trees much more common than the female; also found wild in France, Belgium, and Holland; wood light and very strong. By old authors this tree is referred to as the White Poplar, *Populus alba* L., a native of south Europe and the Mediterranean region east to the Himalayas and Tibet; *P. alba* is much less common in Britain than *P. canescens*.

The genus *Populus* is closely related to the Willow genus *Salix*. In *Populus*, however, the flowers are wind-pollinated (anemophilous), whilst in *Salix* they are insect-pollinated (entomophilous); in consequence hybrids are more numerous in *Salix*.

Salix pentandra L. (×⅓)

A tree up to 40 ft., but usually a large shrub; branchlets dark brown, shining; winter-buds sharply keeled, shining; leaves fragrant when bruised, ellip-
tic, sharply pointed (acuminate), about 4 in. long
and 1½ in. broad, not
hairy (glabrous), closely
and bluntly toothed, with
about 10 pairs of lateral
nerves much branched to-
wards the margin; stalks
short, clothed with a few
large glands; stipules represented by one or two
large glands; catkins ap-
pearing with or just after
the leaves, terminating
short leafy shoots; males
(A, ×⅓) about 1½ in. long;
scales (B, ×3) conspicu-
ous, pubescent in the
lower half; stamens (C,
×4) usually about 5, with
hairy filaments; glandular
scale large and fleshy; female (D, ×⅓) catkins nar-
rower than the male, the

scales (E, ×2) covered with long silky hairs; ovary stalked (stipitate), glabrous, the style shortly divided into two arms; gland
rounded and fleshy; capsules stalked, glabrous (family *Salicaceae*).

This is a handsome tree, and the fragrant flowers have an odour
similar to that of the Bay Laurel (*Laurus nobilis*). The leaves exhale the same scent when bruised. On river-banks and in marshy
places, ranging east as far as Kamchatka.

About 20 species of *Salix* are found wild in Britain and they
hybridize very readily which sometimes makes their exact determination difficult. In the latest *Flora* (see p. xiv) three keys are
provided, one based on male plants, one on female plants, and
the third on plants with mature leaves. Even with the use of these
a specialist may have to be applied to for a more critical determination.

108   ALMOND-LEAVED WILLOW

Salix triandra L. ($\times\frac{1}{3}$)

Tree 20–30 ft. high; branchlets purplish or purplish brown, slightly hairy when young; stipules (A, ×1) large and leaf-like, obliquely rounded-ovate, slightly cordate at the base, about $\frac{1}{3}$ in. wide; leaves produced just after the flowers, when mature green and shining above, paler or glaucous below, oblong-lanceolate, acute at the apex, about $2\frac{1}{2}$ in. long and $\frac{3}{4}$ in. broad, closely serrulate, glabrous, with numerous lateral nerves; leaf-stalks $\frac{1}{4}$ in. long; male catkins (B, ×$\frac{1}{3}$) $1\frac{1}{4}$ in. long, produced on numerous very short lateral shoots and forming a long narrow oblong 'spray', each catkin with 2 or 3 very young leaves at the base; stamens (C, ×2) 3, with a rounded club-shaped gland at the base; female catkins terminating short leafy branchlets, about $1\frac{1}{4}$ in.

long, with conspicuous narrow bracts rounded at the tip; gland wedge-shaped; ovary (E, ×2) stalked, with 2 spreading stigmas; fruiting catkins (D, ×$\frac{1}{3}$) about 2 in. long (family *Salicaceae*).

Grows by the sides of streams and in wet woods and osier grounds, common and generally distributed in England and Eire; rarer in Scotland.

The stipules in this species are quite a prominent feature, being especially conspicuous on the non-flowering shoots.

It has a wide range in distribution, extending as far east as Japan, south to Persia and into Algeria in north Africa.

Salix caprea L. ($\times \frac{2}{5}$)

Tall shrub or bushy tree; winter buds (A, $\times \frac{2}{5}$) ovoid, with brown leathery smooth scales; leaves (B, $\times \frac{2}{5}$) broadly elliptic or obovate-elliptic, shortly pointed at the apex, base rounded to acute, rather wrinkled and irregularly crenate on the margin, cottony-hairy below; stipules leafy, usually soon falling; catkins very silky, the males (C, $\times \frac{2}{5}$) a little longer and thicker than the females (D, $\times \frac{2}{5}$), about 1 in. long; basal bracts densely silky; male floral bracts (E, $\times 1\frac{3}{4}$) with a fringe of long hairs at the top; stamens 2; anthers long-exserted from the bracts; female catkins about 2 in. long in fruit; bracts much narrower than in the male, with a small scale between the ovary stalk and the axis; ovary and style

hairy (F, $\times 2$); fruits (G, $\times 2\frac{1}{2}$) about 1 in. long, silky, stalked; seeds (H, $\times 3$) narrow, with a fringe of long hairs from the base (family *Salicaceae*).

This Willow is rather variable and widely distributed, and there are several named varieties. It is common in all parts of our country, growing in woods and copses and in waste places. It is the only willow which commonly grows from seed, and in some places is almost a forest weed. It makes good fences, and sheep-hurdles made of it are said to last longer than those made of hazel. As it is so readily propagated by cuttings, it is useful for planting to hold the soil on river banks.

A shrub or small tree up to 30 ft., with long slender branches minutely hairy; leaves produced after flowering, linear to very nar-

rowly linear
lanceolate, nar-
row at the base,
very acutely
a c u m i n a t e,
glabrous above,
softly silvery
silky below,
with very short
hairs, with nu-
merous arched
lateral nerves;
stipules linear,
sub-persistent;
winter catkin-
buds (A, $\times 1$)
ovoid, $\frac{1}{2}$ in.
long, covered
with a rather
thin shining
scale; male
catkins (B, $\times\frac{1}{2}$)
sessile, with or
without a few
very young
leaves at the
base, and with
scattered short
shoots here and
there between
them, about 1
in. long; bracts (C, $\times 3$) narrowly ovate, long-ciliate; scale rod-
like; stamens 2; anthers on long filaments; female catkins (D,
$\times\frac{1}{2}$) sessile, with no leaves developed at flowering time, about 1 in.
long; bracts densely silky with long hairs; female flowers (E, $\times 3$)
stalked within the bract (family *Salicaceae*).

This is the true Osier extensively cultivated for its long pliant
shoots, which are longer than those of any other native species
and are the best for basket-making.

WHITE WILLOW
Salix alba L. ($\times \frac{1}{3}$)

A fairly large tree, silvery in colour because of the dense silky hairs on the lower surface of the leaves; young twigs green, purplish or bright yellow; flowers developed with the leaves on short leafy softly hairy shoots; axillary buds of the mature leafy shoots narrow and silky hairy; matures leaves (A, $\times \frac{1}{3}$) shortly stalked, narrowly lanceolate, acute at both ends and tapered to a slender point at the apex, usually about 4 in. long and at most 1 in. broad, finely toothed on the margin, soon becoming glabrous or nearly so above, closely silky hairy below and nearly white; male catkins (B, $\times \frac{1}{8}$) stalked, about $1\frac{1}{2}$ in. long; floral bracts (C, $\times 2$) elliptic, fringed with hairs; stamens 2, with a pair of glands at

the base; female catkins (D, $\times \frac{1}{3}$) very slender and loosely flowered; ovary (E, $\times 2$) glabrous, with a very short bifid style, and a fleshy gland at the base; capsule glabrous (family *Salicaceae*).

This Willow is widely spread through central and southern Europe, south to Algeria and Morocco, and eastwards to western and northern Asia. In Britain it is supposed to be native from Sutherland southwards, and it is found in Eire.

It is a tree up to 90 ft. high and with a stem as much as 20 ft. in circumference. The wood is tough and valuable, but the best cricket-bats are made from that of *S. caerulea*, formerly considered to be a variety of *S. alba*.

The bark is deeply fissured, greyish, and does not peel off so readily as that of many other willows.

Salix fragilis L. ($\times \frac{1}{2}$)

A bushy tree differing in aspect from *S. alba* (fig. 111) in its green and glabrous (not white and hairy) leaves; young twigs brown

or purplish, slightly hairy towards the tips; flowers developed with the leaves on short leafy shoots; axillary buds (A, $\times 1$) of the mature leafy shoots narrowly ovoid, keeled, hairy at the tip; mature leaves on fairly long stalks, broadly oblong, taper-pointed, rather coarsely toothed on the margins, glabrous on both surfaces, very finely reticulate below, with numerous lateral nerves; male catkins (B) stalked, slender, about 2 in. long; male flowers (C, $\times 3$) with oblong-elliptic silky-hairy bracts; stamens 2, with 2 unequal-sized glands (D, $\times 6$) at the base; female catkins (E, $\times \frac{1}{2}$) $2\frac{1}{2}$–3 in. long, very slender and loosely flowered; bracts narrow, pubescent; ovary (F, $\times 3$) stalked, very slender, and with a slender style, glabrous; capsules stalked, tapered to the apex (G, gland of female) (family *Salicaceae*).

This is a tree up to 70 ft. high, with the bark rough, strongly ridged and divided into broad deep fissures.

Salix aurita L. ($\times\frac{1}{2}$)

A bushy shrub, with short twiggy branchlets knotted with the prominent leaf-scars of previous seasons; leaves developed after the flowers, elliptic, more or less rounded at each end, wrinkled (bullate) above, shortly toothed, densely covered below with soft short hairs; stipules large and leafy; catkins flowering before the leaves, sessile on the shoots and with a few densely silky-hairy bracts at the base, $\frac{3}{4}$–1 in. long; floral bracts very silky hairy (C, ×4), each enclosing a stalked bottle-shaped gland (D, ×7) and a pair of stamens; female flowers (E, ×2$\frac{1}{2}$) stalked; ovary shortly hairy, ending in a short 2-lobed style; the two halves of the capsule (F, ×3) diverging and recurving, releasing the tiny seeds (G, ×5) bearing a basal tuft of long fine silky hairs (A, male, B, female catkins) (family *Salicaceae*).

In moist woods and bushy places on damp heaths, flowering in early spring; widely distributed into Asiatic Russia, from the Mediterranean to the Arctic.

GREY WILLOW
Salix atrocinerea Brot. ($\times\frac{1}{2}$)

A much branched shrub or small tree; leaves developed after the catkins, oblanceolate to obovate, triangular at the base and apex, covered on both surfaces with very short soft hairs, not toothed or very minutely so; stipules kidney-shaped, soon falling off; male catkins (A, $\times\frac{1}{2}$) on short stalks with a few small partially developed leaves at the base, the males about $1-1\frac{1}{4}$ in., the females (B, $\times\frac{1}{2}$) about the same length when in flower but elongating to 2 in. long in fruit (C, $\times\frac{1}{2}$), with small silky leaves towards the base; male flowers (D, $\times2\frac{1}{2}$) with a narrowly elliptic bract, 2 stamens, and a thick fleshy bottle-shaped gland (E, $\times10$); female flowers (F, $\times2\frac{1}{2}$) stalked within the bract, with a very small gland at the base (G, $\times5$); ovary shortly hairy; fruits (H, $\times2$) with recurved halves, silky-pubescent; seeds with a coma of pure white hairs (J, $\times4$) (family *Salicaceae*).

Like many other species of willow, this grows where there is plenty of moisture in the soil. The wood was formerly used for

Salix repens L. ($\times\frac{1}{2}$)

A low straggling shrublet with decumbent branches, these rooting at the lower nodes, minutely hairy in the upper parts; winter-buds covered with smooth leathery scales; mature leaves (A, $\times\frac{1}{2}$) elliptic, about 1 in. long, becoming glabrous above, remaining grey-silky below with appressed hairs; male catkins (B, $\times\frac{1}{2}$) about $\frac{1}{2}$ in. long, at flowering time with a few partially developed silky leaves at the base (sub-precocious); male flowers with a flask-shaped

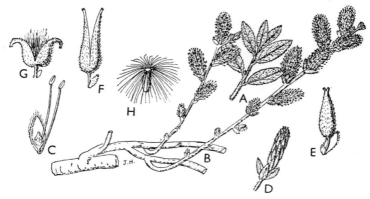

scale at the base (C, $\times 5$); bract elliptic, fringed with long hairs; stamens 2; anthers on long slender filaments; female catkins (D, $\times\frac{1}{2}$) also sub-precocious (see above), shorter when in young flower than the male, about 1 in. long in fruit; ovaries (E, $\times 2\frac{1}{2}$) pubescent; fruits (F, $\times 3$, G, $\times 1\frac{1}{2}$) splitting into 2 recurved halves; seeds (H, $\times 6$) with a fringe of long delicate hairs (family *Salicaceae*).

This is the smallest and dwarfest British species of willow and grows on heaths, moors, and in sandy places, flowering in spring; widely distributed in the Arctic regions of the Old World, extending into Asiatic Russia.

Salix atrocinerea (*contd.*) :—

charcoal in the manufacture of gunpowder.

For a long time this species was known as *Salix cinerea*. Then it was shown that the British shrub was different from the Grey Sallow that is widely distributed on the continent of Europe, from France and Germany eastwards. Our shrub is the same as that which grows in western France, Portugal, and Spain.

116 BOG-MYRTLE

Myrica gale L. (flowering and leafy shoots ×⅓)

Small shrub up to 3 ft. in boggy acid soils; stems purplish; leaves produced after flowering, oblanceolate, toothed (serrate), gland-dotted below (A, ×¾) and aromatic when bruised; male and female flowers on separate plants (dioecious) produced before the leaves in early spring; male spikes (B, ×⅓) catkin-like but stiff, up to 1½ in. long; bracts broad, acuminate, below the stamens (C, ×4) (no sepals and petals); filaments very short; anthers 2-locular; female spikes (D, ×⅓) short and ellipsoid, each flower (E, ×4) with an ovate bract, two scale-like sepals, and a sessile

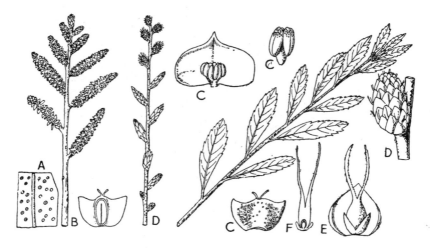

ovary with two styles and one erect ovule; fruit (G, ×3) small, winged (F, vertical section of female flower; ×2½) (family *Myricaceae*).

The pollen is discharged from the anthers and falls on the scales of the spike and is blown away in clouds by the wind. A remarkable feature about the Bog-Myrtle is that plants which bear flowers of one sex during one season may change to the other sex the next year.

It is only locally a common plant, and is found in lowland peat bogs and on wet peaty slopes in various parts of the country. Near London it is very abundant on Bagshot Heath.

Betula pendula Roth. (A, leafy fruiting shoot, ×⅖)

A graceful tree with silvery-white papery bark; smaller branches pendulous; young branchlets glabrous except for scattered minute glands; leaves broadly triangular in outline, broadly wedge-shaped at the base, acutely acuminate at the apex, distinctly lobulate and the lobules toothed, with scattered glands on the upper surface when young; male catkins up to about 2 in. long, pendulous; female catkins about 1½ in. long and ⅓ in. thick, very shortly and sparingly pubescent; scales (B, ×3) 3-lobed, the lateral lobes longer than broad and larger than the middle one, glabrous except

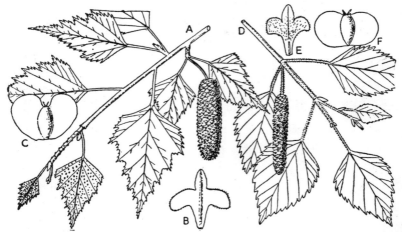

for short hairs on the margins; fruits ('seeds') (C, ×3) with broad ascending membranous wings.

Red Birch, *Betula pubescens* Ehrh. (D, ×⅖); similar to the above but young and two-year-old shoots densely covered with short soft hairs, more ovate and not lobulate leaves more or less simply toothed and more or less hairy below, especially in the axils of the nerves; rather narrower female catkins, the scales (E, ×3) more equally 3-lobed with the lateral lobes about as long as broad, and the fruit (F, ×3) with more horizontally spreading wings with a tuft of hairs at the top of the fruit-body.

These two Birches were formerly regarded as one rather variable species and called *Betula alba* Linn. Hybrids between them are common. Birches provide valuable timber and birch brooms; wood used principally for furniture, utensils, clogs, etc. (family *Betulaceae*).

118   ALDER

Alnus glutinosa Gaertn. ($\times \frac{2}{5}$)

Moderate-sized tree with dark foliage, flowering in early spring before the leaves, the catkins formed in the previous autumn;

leaves obovate, rounded to wedge-shaped at the base, rounded or widely notched at the top and irregularly toothed in the upper part; lateral nerves straight, prominent, with tufts of hairs in their axils; stipules large, soon falling off; flowers unisexual (monoecious); male catkins (A, $\times \frac{2}{5}$) few in a cluster and pendulous in flower, with broad nearly sessile scales, each male with 12 stamens; female catkins (B, $\times \frac{2}{5}$) separate from the male, very short and ellipsoid, with the styles protruding; old fruiting catkins (C, $\times \frac{2}{5}$) with loose open scales like a small fir cone; nuts small and seed-like, not winged; the pollen is carried by the wind (family *Betulaceae*).

The timber of the Alder is used for making artificial limbs, brush-backs, general turnery, toys, etc. The tree is very widely spread through nearly all Europe, Siberia, western Asia, and in Algeria and Morocco. It grows in wet woods, borders of streams and low-lying wet fields. The behaviour of the seeds is interesting. These are shaken out of the 'cones' by the wind during autumn and winter, and their shells have air-tight cavities which enable them to float in water, and they secrete an oil which protects them from wet. If they fall in water, they float undamaged during winter, germinating in spring, the young seedlings at length drifting to the banks where they establish themselves.

Corylus avellana L.

Shrub or small much-branched tree; young shoots (A, $\times\frac{1}{2}$) clothed with gland-tipped hairs; leaves more or less orbicular, widely cordate, shortly acuminate, coarsely and doubly toothed with several prominent lateral nerves; stipules lanceolate; flowers unisexual (monoecious), males very numerous in pendulous catkins (B, $\times\frac{1}{2}$), females (D, $\times\frac{1}{2}$) in a sessile scaly cluster, and with

protruding red stigmas; scales of male catkins (C, $\times 3\frac{1}{2}$) each with two adherent scales within bearing the stamens (about 8); female flowers (E, $\times 3\frac{1}{2}$) 2 within each scale; ovary small with two long styles; fruits (F, $\times\frac{2}{5}$) solitary or clustered on a stalk, each hard nut partly enclosed by a leafy jagged involucre; the edible portion is the embryo, which enlarges to fill the nut when ripe; flowers in early spring before the leaves (family *Corylaceae*).

The shoots of the hazel are used for making walking-sticks, hurdles, crates, etc., and living specimens are bent or partially cut and interlaced for fencing. The slender one-year-old shoots that spring up from the roots are quite useful for basket-making.

Carpinus betulus L. ($\times \frac{1}{2}$)

A tree up to 90 ft. high, with a maximum girth of 12 ft.; bark smooth, thin, grey; leaves deciduous, elliptic, rounded at the base, pointed at the top, about 3 in. long and $1\frac{1}{2}$ in. broad, doubly serrate on the margin, upper surface dark green, glabrous or nearly so, pale green below with appressed hairs on the nerves and with tufts of hairs in the axils of the 10–15 pairs of parallel lateral nerves (A, $\times 1$); stalk $\frac{1}{4}$–$\frac{1}{2}$ in. long; stipules (C, $\times 2$) lanceolate, $\frac{1}{2}$ in. long, falling off very early; flowers appearing with the young leaves, unisexual, the males in pendulous catkins (B, $\times \frac{3}{4}$) about $1\frac{1}{4}$ in. long arising from buds produced near the ends of the lateral branches of the previous year; scales (D, $\times 2\frac{1}{2}$) rounded-ovate, acute; no petals; stamens 12–20, each of the separated yellow anther-loculi tipped with a cluster of long hairs (E, $\times 4$); female flowers (F, $\times 4$) in loose catkins at the top of the young branchlets, about 1 in. long, with ovate ciliate scales; each flower subtended by a small bract and 2 minute bracteoles; ovary 2-locular, rimmed by a minute calyx and with 2 elongated styles; loculi with 1 ovule; fruits (G, $\times 1$) in pendulous 'cones' up to 3 in. made up of overlapping leafy enlarged bracts and bracteoles each with a nutlet (fruit) at the base; nutlet ovoid, $\frac{1}{3}$ in. long, ribbed, glabrous, topped by the 6-lobed calyx with the style in the middle; seed filling the cavity, without endosperm (family *Corylaceae*).

The Hornbeam is probably native in the south of England, and is common especially in Essex and Kent, providing good autumn colour; formerly it was the chief tree in the ancient forests which existed to the north and east of London. It is widely distributed in Europe and extends east to the Caucasus and Persia.

The wood is the hardest, heaviest, and toughest of our native trees, though little used in Britain except for fuel. It burns slowly with a bright flame and gives out a good heat. As it decays quickly when exposed to moisture, it is unsuitable for outside work, and it will not take creosote.

Under cultivation the Hornbeam has developed varieties; in var. *incisa* the leaves have larger sharply serrated teeth; in var. *quercifolia* the leaves are smaller and irregularly and deeply cut or lobed.

Very large trees are found in Britain, some with a girth of stem of as much as 12 ft.

BEECH
Fagus sylvatica L. ($\times \frac{2}{5}$)

Large tree with thick smooth trunk and large dense crown; winter buds (A, $\times \frac{2}{5}$) with numerous brown scales; leaves deciduous, appearing with the flowers early in May, ovate-elliptic, acute at the apex, with several straight lateral nerves and slightly toothed, soft and silky when young, glabrous or nearly so when older; lateral nerves with tufts of hairs in their axils; stalk short; flowers unisexual (monoecious), the males (B, $\times \frac{2}{5}$) in globular pendulous stalked clusters appearing with the young leaves; female clusters on a short erect stalk; bud-scales falling off early; calyx of the

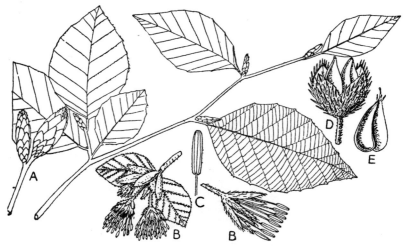

male deeply 4–6-lobed, covered with long silky hairs; no petals; stamens (C, $\times 2$) about 8, on rather long slender filaments; anthers oblong, rather large; ovary of the female flower 3-locular, with 2 pendulous ovules in each division; styles 3; fruits enclosed in a hard bristly involucre (D, $\times \frac{2}{5}$) splitting low down into 4 divisions and containing 2–3 sharply 3-angular nuts (E, $\times \frac{1}{2}$) crowned by the small narrow sepals and style (family *Fagaceae*).

This is one of the largest and most important of our native trees. It occurs as far east as the Caucasus and north to southern Scandinavia. In Britain it is common in chalky districts such as the North and South Downs and the Chilterns, where there are local industries using the valuable timber for chair-manufacture, tool handles, etc., and it provides excellent firewood. The nuts are a favourite food for pigs.

There are two native species of oak in Britain, and they are so similar to each other that they were formerly often regarded as

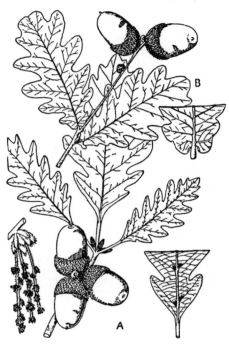

varieties or forms of one species; there are rather good differences, however, the pedunculate oak, *Quercus robur* L. (synonym *Quercus pedunculata* Ehrhart), having very shortly stalked leaves which are ear-shaped (auriculate) at the base, and are quite glabrous beneath, whilst the acorns are borne on a slender common stalk (peduncle); in the sessile oak, *Quercus petraea* (Matt.) Liebl. (synonym *Quercus sessiliflora* Salisb.), the leaves have fairly long stalks, are wedge-shaped at the base, hairy beneath (especially between midrib and nerves), and the acorns are sessile on the branch or borne on a very short stalk (family *Fagaceae*).

Most people can recognize an oak tree, and the above description is probably sufficient. The pedunculate oak is more naturally adapted to a wettish soil, and is essentially a tree of the plains and low hills in northern latitudes, and is found wild in the greater part of Europe, Asia Minor, and the Caucasus; the sessile oak is not found in the plains, favours less wet places, and ascends quite high up the mountains – for example, up to 5,300 ft. altitude in the Pyrenees.

The flowers are unisexual and produced in spring as the leaves unfold. The uses to which these fine trees can be put are legion, and they have played an important part in the history of our race, for shipbuilding and constructional work of all kinds, besides being good firewood.

WYCH ELM

Ulmus glabra Huds.

A tree; mature leafy branchlets (A, ×⅓) with purplish bark and marked with a few small brown lenticels, slightly hairy; mature leaves all with a small nearly glabrous bud in their axils, very unequal-sided at the base, elliptic or slightly obovate-elliptic, rather long-pointed (acuminate) at the apex, averaging about 5½ × 2½ in., rather densely hairy in the axils of the main nerves below and in the fork towards the margin, otherwise very thinly hairy; lateral nerves about 15 pairs, most of them forked and forming a prominent Y ⅔ towards the margin; margin doubly and

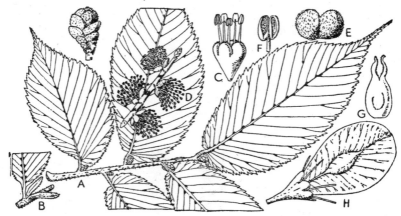

rather coarsely toothed (serrate); leaf-stalk short and pubescent; stipules (B, ×⅓) oblong-spathulate, about ½ in. long, soon falling off; flowers (C, ×1½) bisexual, appearing in early spring, arranged in clusters (D, ×⅓) and at first enclosed by broad usually deeply notched brown hairy bracts (E, ×⅔); calyx (C) top-shaped, 5-lobed to about the middle, pale and thin, the lobes obovate and flushed with crimson and fringed with short brown hairs on the margin; stamens 5; anthers (F, ×4) large, at first bright crimson, becoming purple after opening and releasing the minute white pollen; ovary (G, ×1⅓) sessile, 2-locular, bright green, compressed, with pink stigmas; fruit (H, ×1¼) thin and compressed, about ¾ in. long; pollination by the wind, or failing that automatic self-pollination; all the flowers of one cluster not open at the same time; the filaments grow out rapidly from the bud before they shed their pollen, which only escapes in dry weather (family *Ulmaceae*).

Parietaria judaica L. (× ½) 124

Perennial herb with long pubescent stems, often erect the first year and afterwards spreading or procumbent, usually on old walls, and in waste, stony places, flowering the whole summer; leaves alternate, entire, oblanceolate to elliptic, with slender stalks, apex rather bluntly acuminate, usually with only 2 pairs of lateral nerves, closely dotted on both sides with small cystoliths (A, ×1½); no stipules; flowers in small dense sessile axillary clusters surrounded by a small involucre of a few bracts, bisexual (male and female) or unisexual (one sex); male and bisexual flowers (B, ×4) with a short 4-lobed calyx and 4 stamens opposite the lobes; female (C, ×4) flowers with a tubular shortly 4-lobed

calyx, which adheres to the seed-like or nut-like fruit (D, ×3); seed (E, ×3) solitary with a long embryo (family *Urticaceae*).

A peculiarity of this plant is that some stigmas are red and others white. They protrude from the bud of the bisexual flowers whilst the calyx is still shut up, and are shrivelled up before this opens and the anthers release their pollen. This is brought about by an explosive mechanism similar to that of the nettles. Their stalks are incurved in bud, and when this opens they expand and spring out, scattering their pollen in a small cloud. Gardeners are familiar with a related plant, the so-called Artillery plant (*Pilea muscosa* Lindl.), the flowers of which burst open with little explosions when syringed. Synonym *Parietaria ramiflora* Moench

Urtica urens L. ($\times \frac{2}{3}$)

Erect annual covered with stiff stinging hairs (A, $\times 15$); leaves opposite, ovate or elliptic, coarsely toothed, 3-nerved from the

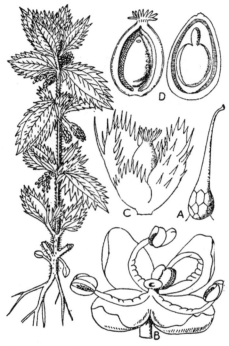

base; flowers without petals, unisexual (monoecious), the males and females intermixed and arranged in loose axillary stalked or almost sessile clusters; male flowers (B, $\times 15$) with 4 obovate sepals and opposite each a stamen which is incurved in bud and springs outwards and scatters the pollen when the flower opens; ovary rudimentary in the male flowers; female flowers (C, $\times 15$) with 4 unequal-sized sepals, some with bristly hairs on the back; ovary ovoid, with a sessile papillous stigma; fruit (D, $\times 12$) a small nutlet containing a single erect seed; grows mostly in waste and cultivated places, often as a garden weed, but more easily destroyed than the common stinging nettle (*Urtica dioica* L.), which is a perennial with flowers in branched spikes, and broader ovate stalked leaves (family *Urticaceae*).

The smaller stinging nettle has been described and figured here because everyone knows the ordinary kind. Some, however, who have not the necessary botanical knowledge, mistake the two Dead Nettles for the common nettle because of the similarity in their leaves. One of these Dead Nettles, *Lamium purpureum*, is shown in Vol. 2, fig. 688, and the flowers are very different from those of the stinging nettle. *Lamium album* L. has larger, white flowers (Vol. 2, fig. 687).

A strong-growing perennial with creeping rootstock; stems erect, 2–3 ft. or more in rich soil or shade, covered all over with stinging bristly hairs (A, ×3), 4-angled; leaves opposite, stalked, the lower widely ovate and cordate at the base, pointed and coarsely toothed, the upper leaves gradually narrower and becoming lanceolate and less cordate; stipules narrow, about $\frac{1}{4}$ in. long; flowers unisexual, usually on separate plants (dioecious), clustered in axillary panicles up to as long as but usually much shorter than the leaves, sepals of the male flower (B, ×3) 4, green, very small; stamens 4; ovary (C, ×3) with a single tufted stigma; fruit (D, ×2½; E, section, ×5) a flattened

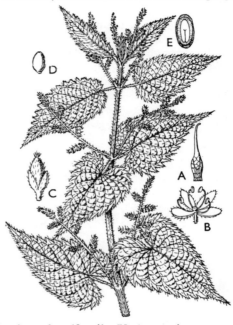

seed-like nutlet enclosed in the calyx (family *Urticaceae*).

The common stinging nettle will be known to everyone, and it need only be touched by the hand to distinguish it from the somewhat similar leaves of the White Dead Nettle shown in Vol. 2, fig. 687, when the difference will be at once apparent, for the latter does not sting.

The leaves of the larger stinging nettle are valuable as a source of chlorophyll, used in medicine, etc., and the stems yield a very tough fibre.

HOP
Humulus lupulus L. ($\times\frac{1}{3}$)

Perennial herb with a thick branched rootstock; stems annual, twining to a considerable height over other plants and in hedges, very tough and rough; leaves opposite, stalked, deeply and broadly heart-shaped at the base, the larger ones deeply 3–5-lobed and sharply toothed (serrate), the floral leaves less divided or only toothed, rough to the touch (scabrid); stipules in pairs; flowers unisexual, dioecious, the males (A, $\times\frac{1}{3}$) in loose panicles with small bracts, small and yellowish-green; sepals (B, $\times 3$) 5; petals none; stamens (C, $\times 3$) 5, the large anthers on very short filaments

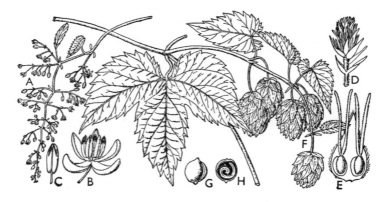

and opening by terminal pore-like slits; female flowers in shortly stalked axillary ovoid heads covered with green overlapping bracts (D, $\times 3$), each bract with 2 sessile female flowers (E, $\times 8$) in its axil; calyx much reduced and scale-like; ovary crowned by a pair of long styles free from the base; fruiting cone (F, $\times\frac{1}{3}$) covered with broad green or yellow bracts hiding the fruits, the scales covered with resinous glands at the base, as also the fruits (G, H) (family *Cannabinaceae*).

The Hop plant is well known for its use in brewing, being widely cultivated in certain counties, such as Kent and Worcestershire; it is considered to be native from Yorkshire southwards, and is widely distributed in Europe and Asia.

The stems of the hop always twine in one direction, i.e. to the right, termed dextrorse or clockwise. The Honeysuckle and twining Polygonum do likewise. Other plants twine in the reverse direction (counter-clockwise), an example being the Scarlet Runner.

ROCK ROSE 128

Helianthemum chamaecistus Mill. (× ½)

A low-spreading shrublet partial to limestone and chalky soils, with a short much-branched woody stem; branchlets produced annually up to a foot long, hairy; leaves opposite; shortly stalked, oblong-lanceolate to almost ovate, entire, green and glabrous or nearly so above, hoary or white beneath and hairy with branched hairs (A, ×20); stipules (B, ×¾) lanceolate, up to ¼ in. long; flowers in a terminal raceme, usually only one or two out at a time, the stalks deflected after flowering; sepals 5, three larger (C, ×½) with prominent ribs and two quite small; petals bright yellow or rarely white,

spreading, soon falling off; stamens (D, ×5) numerous; ovary (E, ×5) short, hairy, 1-locular with the ovules attached to the walls; style bent, rather long, with a head-like stigma; capsule (F, ×1¼) splitting into 3 valves with the seeds attached to the middle of each; (E, cross-section of ovary, ×8) (family *Cistaceae*).

There is no nectar in the flowers of this species, but insects visit them to collect the pollen, of which a large quantity is produced by the numerous stamens. These radiate away from the mature stigma, and cross-pollination is effected by insects alighting in the middle of the flower and carrying pollen from other blossoms. If these fail, automatic self-pollination takes place through the flowers closing at night or during wet weather.

When not in flower this species is easily detected because of the opposite stipulate entire leaves clothed with branched hairs. Such hairs are not very common amongst British plants, though they are very general in the *Malva* family (*Malvaceae*), and in some of the Crucifers (*Cruciferae*). Synonym *Helianthemum nummularium* Mill.

Helianthemum apenninum (L.) Mill. (× ⅓)

A low much-branched shrublet on limestone downs; older branches rough with the circular scars of the fallen leaves, the latter opposite, shortly stalked, oblong-oblanceolate, obtuse at the apex, about ¾ in. long, covered with stellate hairs on both surfaces, more densely so below, margins at length much rolled back; stipules linear, hairy; flowers in terminal racemes, white, stalked; sepals (A, × 1) 5, 3 larger and ovate, ribbed, 2 smaller and narrow;

petals (B, × 1) 5, broadly obovate; stamens (C, × 3) numerous, inserted below the ovary; ovary (D, × 2) globose, 1-locular, with 3 parietal placentas (E, × 2) and numerous ovules; style short and thick; capsule 3-valved, partly enclosed by the persistent sepals; seeds several, embryo curved amidst the endosperm (family *Cistaceae*).

Found only on limestone downs and cliffs in one or two southern counties; extends from west to central Europe.

An interesting feature of the flowers of the Rock Roses is that they follow the sun, facing the south-east in the early morning, the sun at noon, and the south-west in the afternoon; veritable nature clocks. Like the Poppies, the flowers of these plants last only a day or two, when the petals fall off. Synonym *Helianthemum polifolium* Mill.

One of our most lovely wild flowers and now very rare; one of the earliest shrublets to flower in woodlands as soon as frost and snow in January or February have gone or later if these persist; calyx petaloid, pink, one of the 4 lobes entirely embracing the others in bud (A, ×2); in the open flower (B, ×2) there are two outer and two inner lobes; stamens (C, ×4) 8, arranged in two rows in the tube, 4 opposite the lobes at the mouth, the other 4 alternating with the lobes and lower down in the tube; ovary (D, ×3) green and bottle-shaped, with a nearly sessile, slightly 2-lobed, fleshy, papillous stigma; ovule (E, ×2) solitary, pendulous; fruit (F, ×1) a round red berry (family *Thymelaeaceae*).

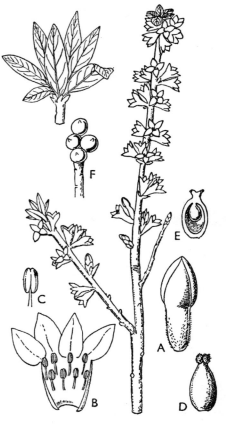

Occurs all over Europe through Asia Minor to Siberia; poisonous like the next species (*Daphne laureola*).

The fragrant flowers attract such bees as are abroad in the early part of the year. Nectar is secreted at the base of the ovary. In searching for it, the proboscis of an insect first brushes against the two rows of anthers without removing their pollen, and touches the stigma below them. When the proboscis is wetted with nectar, pollen adheres to it as it is withdrawn, and is transferred to another flower; self-pollination rarely occurs. The leaves appear after the flowers and are entire, without stipules.

SPURGE LAUREL
Daphne laureola L. ($\times\frac{1}{2}$)

Erect glabrous shrub sparingly branched; stems thick, marked with the scars of the fallen leaves; leaves evergreen, rather clustered, oblanceolate to obovate, up to 4 in. long and $1\frac{1}{2}$ in. broad, with rather obscure lateral nerves; no stipules; flowers (A, ×1) sweet-scented for a period,* in short, axillary bracteate racemes nestling among the leaves; perianth (B, ×2) green, composed of a tubular calyx (like a corolla), with tube nearly $\frac{1}{2}$ in. long and 4 ovate spreading lobes; stamens 8, inserted at different levels, the upper 4 slightly exserted; ovary (C, ×$2\frac{1}{2}$) free, ellipsoid, 1-locular,

with a very short style and broad rounded stigma; fruit (D, ×$1\frac{1}{2}$) an ellipsoid bluish-black berry (family *Thymelaeaceae*).

Grows in woods and is confined to the English counties, flowering in spring, found also in south-western Europe.

Nectar is secreted and concealed in the base of the perianth-tube, and is accessible to flies, bees, etc.

Like the previous species, all parts, especially the bark and berries, are acrid and poisonous. The berries are tempting to children, and deaths have occurred through eating them.

* Following Bentham's *British Flora*, I stated in my *British Flowering Plants* (1948) that the flowers were not scented.

Viola reichenbachiana Jord. ex Boreau. ($\times\frac{1}{3}$)

Perennial herb with spreading leafless stolons and short leafy shoots; stipules (A, $\times 2$) very conspicuous, linear-lanceolate, $\frac{1}{3}$ in. long, fringed with long comb-like teeth; leaves rounded-ovate, cordate at the base, rounded or slightly pointed to the apex, up to $1\frac{1}{2}$ in. long and 1 in. broad, minutely speckled but not hairy below, crenulate; stalks glabrous; flowers scentless, typically lilac or reddish-lilac, but varying to white (colour forms), on slender stalks longer than the leaves; bracts linear, borne well up towards the flower; sepals (B, $\times 1\frac{1}{2}$) 5, narrowly lanceolate, rounded at the

base; petals narrow and not overlapping, the spur (C, $\times 1\frac{1}{2}$) laterally compressed, nearly straight, darker than the limb; anthers (D, $\times 2\frac{1}{2}$) with a broad ovate appendage; style (E, $\times 2\frac{1}{2}$) slightly bent; fruit a glabrous angular capsule, produced to a limited degree by early opening flowers and in great quantity by later cleistogamous flowers (synonym *Viola silvestris* of various authors) (family *Violaceae*).

Found in open places in woods and on hedgebanks, March to May; several colour forms, **pallida**, pale bluish-mauve petals; **rosea**, deep pink petals; and **leucantha**, 'bone-white' petals. It hybridizes with *V. riviniana*.

Viola lutea Huds. ($\times\frac{1}{2}$)

Annual or perennial; stem often much branched; stipules deeply divided into several unequal slightly hairy lobes; leaves stalked,

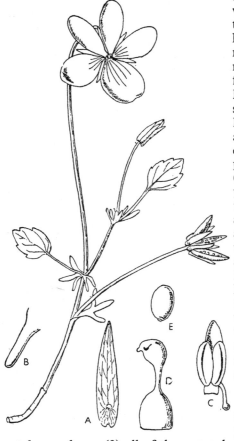

ovate, or ovate-elliptic, with 3 or 4 rather coarse teeth on each side, slightly hairy especially on the nerves and margin, 5-nerved from the base; flowers typically yellow. large (1 in. or more long); sepals (A, $\times$ 2) 5, narrowly lanceolate, prolonged at the base into a notched extension; lowermost petal the largest, spurred (B, $\times 2\frac{1}{2}$), the three lower petals with lines towards the base; 2 of the 5 anthers with long spurs at the base (C, $\times$ 5), all with an ovate terminal appendage; stigma swollen and much like the head of a Crane bird (D $\times$ 5); ovary 3-locular, with 3 placentas on the walls; fruits with 3 narrow valves and several straw-coloured obovoid seeds (E, $\times 1\frac{1}{2}$) (family *Violaceae*).

The flowers vary from (1) entirely yellow, (2) yellow with the two upper petals purple, or (3) all of them purple (var. **amoena**); var. **curtisii** grows in sands near the west coast and has rough angular stems.

The flowers of the genus *Viola* have an interesting structure, and are well adapted to particular groups of insects, for which the petals form a convenient landing-place. The front petal is spurred at the base, and into the spur projects a nectar-secreting appendage to each of the two lower stamens. The connective of all the anthers is produced at the apex into a

Viola canina L. ($\times\frac{1}{2}$)

Perennial with short rootstock girt here and there by the persistent leaf-bases; branches short; leaves long-stalked, ovate, cordate at the base, up to about 1 in. long and broad, minutely and thinly hairy on the upper surface, green or finely mottled below, crenulate; stipules linear, entire or toothed; flowers not scented, on longish stalks with a pair of linear bracts towards the top; sepals (A, $\times 1\frac{1}{2}$) lanceolate, entire, $\frac{1}{3}$ in. long, produced beyond the base into a rounded appendage; petals typically pale purplish-blue but sometimes white, prominently nerved; 2 of the 5 stamens (C, $\times 3$) produced into a large horn-like nectary on the back which protrudes into the spurred front petal (B,

$\times 3$); style (D, $\times 3$) slender, hook-like; ovary 1-locular, with 3 parietal placentas; fruit ovoid (family *Violaceae*).

Very common in various soils, flowering in spring and early summer; the flowers are without scent, and those without petals (cleistogamous) are produced all summer.

Mountain Pansy (*contd.*) :—

membranous appendage. These overlap one another at the sides and embrace the style below the stigma, forming a conical chamber into which the dry pollen falls. The stigma projects beyond this cone and closes the entrance so that an insect visiting the flower must first touch it and effect cross-pollination by the pollen collected from a flower previously visited. In many species additional cleistogamous flowers with vestiges of petals are produced, and these often develop into fruit and seed in abundance.

HAIRY VIOLET
Viola hirta L. (×⅓)

Perennial herb with rather slender often branched rootstock furnished with numerous much-branched fibrous roots; leaves on long softly hairy stalks, ovate, widely cordate at the base, rounded at the apex, up to 2½ in. long and 1½ in. broad, about 7-nerved from near the base, shallowly crenate (crenulate), thinly hairy all over; hairs on the leaf-stalks, spreading or somewhat reflexed; stipules narrowly lanceolate, toothed, ⅓ in. long; flowers few, nodding on slender stalks as long as or longer than the leaves, scentless; sepals (A, ×2) 5, oblong, obtuse, 3-nerved, ciliate towards the middle of the margins; corolla bluish-purple, the spur (B, ×1½)

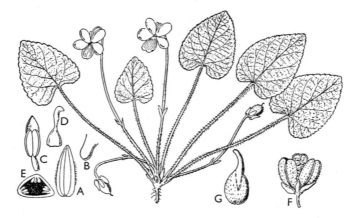

short, thick, and straight; anthers (C, × 2½) with a broad ovate appendage at the apex; stigma (D, ×2) hook-like; ovary (E, ×5) 1-locular, with 3 placentas on the walls; fruit (F, ×1½) a capsule opening by 3 valves, hairy; seeds (G, ×3) with a long appendage, slightly mottled or pale straw-coloured (family *Violaceae*).

Found chiefly in rocky places, open woods, and fields, mainly in limestone districts, flowering later than the Scented Violet, *Viola odorata* L.

The thirteen or so species found wild in Britain are not always easy to determine with certainty, and it is a favourite genus for both the 'lumper' and 'splitter' to exercise their skill.

Viola riviniana Reichb. ($\times \frac{2}{5}$)

Perennial, the slender rootstock covered with the persistent bases of the previous season's leaves; leaves broadly ovate, widely cordate at the base, crenulate, closely gland-dotted on both surfaces, long-stalked; stipules (A, $\times 1\frac{1}{2}$) conspicuous, narrowly lanceolate, with long comb-like teeth on the margin; flowers solitary in the upper leaf-axils, blue; stalks long, with a pair of narrow bracts about 1 in. below the flower; sepals (B, $\times 2\frac{1}{2}$) lanceolate, peltately attached at the base; petals obovate, veiny, the lowest produced into a large blunt grooved spur about $\frac{1}{3}$ in. long; anthers (C, $\times 2\frac{1}{2}$) sessile, the connective produced at the apex; ovary (D, $\times 2\frac{1}{2}$) with 3 placentas on the walls,

and a stout oblique style; capsule (E, $\times 1\frac{1}{4}$) splitting into 3 boat-shaped parts which spread horizontally and bear the rounded smooth seeds (F, $\times 3\frac{1}{2}$) in the middle (G, grooved spur, $\times \frac{1}{2}$).

The genus *Viola* belongs to the family *Violaceae*, which is mainly found in tropical regions. There it is chiefly represented by trees and shrubs, so that those who have only seen our British species can have a very poor idea of the family as a whole. That is the reason the family is included amongst the woody plants, *Viola* being a very highly evolved member of the family and largely herbaceous, though there are several woody exotic species.

SWEET VIOLET
Viola odorata L. ($\times \frac{1}{2}$)

Perennial with a short rootstock covered with the persistent bases of the old leaf-stalks and stipules, giving it a knotted appearance; runners (A) freely produced; leaves all borne on the main shoot (all radical) on long stalks, the latter covered with very short deflexed hairs; leaf-blade ovate to almost orbicular, widely cordate at the base, rounded or very bluntly triangular at the apex, averaging about $1\frac{1}{4}$–$1\frac{3}{4}$ in. long (sometimes up to 3 in. when growing in shade), crenate on the margin, very shortly pubescent on the upper surface and also below, but mainly on the nerves; stipules

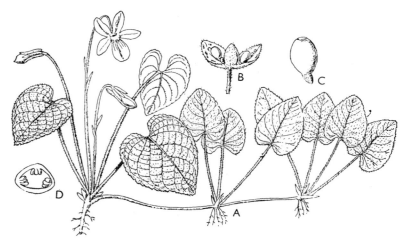

broadly lanceolate, finely toothed; flowers sweetly scented, axillary, on stalks mostly exceeding the leaves, the stalks with a pair of opposite bracts about half-way up (sometimes not quite opposite), glabrous or at most very slightly hairy; sepals oblong, obtuse, with narrow thinner margins; petals bluish-purple or sometimes white, the lowermost with a blunt round spur at the base; anthers forming a ring around the ovary, the connective produced at the apex; ovary 1-locular, with the ovules on 3 placentas on the walls; capsule (B, $\times 1\frac{1}{2}$) opening by 3 boat-shaped valves, thinly hairy; seeds (C, $\times 2\frac{1}{2}$) along the middle of the valves, smooth, attached by a short spongy stalk (D, cross-section of ovary) (family *Violaceae*).

The Sweet Violet is well known to most people, though there are several species closely related to it. It flowers in early spring.

A very variable species divided by some botanists into several; usually grows in cultivated ground or rarely in pastures or river shingles; distinguished from other native violets by the mixture in the flower colour, though this is not constant, and by the leafy much-divided stipules; leaves spoon-shaped or ovate-elliptic, on long stalks, crenate, very shortly pubescent; flowers axillary, the stalks longer than the leaves, usually a mixture of purple, white, and yellow, usually the upper petals tinged or tipped with purple; sepals oblong-lanceolate, about $\frac{1}{3}$ in. long, green; lower petal (A, $\times \frac{1}{2}$) spurred at the base; anthers (B, $\times 3$) with produced connective; ovary (D, $\times 4$) 1-locular, with ovules on the walls (E, $\times 6$);

capsule (F, $\times \frac{1}{2}$) $\frac{1}{3}$ in. long, smooth; seeds (G, $\times 2$) like little brown eggs (family *Violaceae*).

This species of *Viola* has usually large, brightly coloured flowers, the lower petal of which is produced at the base into a spur in which the nectar is secreted. The anther of each of the two lower stamens is provided with a nectar-secreting process which projects into the spur of the lower petal. An insect probing for the nectar touches the stigma and deposits on it pollen from another flower. In addition to the ordinary flowers, some species possess flowers which do not open and have only rudimentary petals, but which produce fertile seed. These are called cleistogamous flowers.

MARSH VIOLET
Viola palustris L. ($\times\frac{1}{2}$)

Perennial herb with a creeping rootstock covered with the remains of hard scale-like leaf-bases and a tangle of fine roots;
runners very short and few; leaves few in a bunch at the end of
the rootstock, on slender stalks, quite glabrous, the blade almost
orbicular except the deeply cordate base, averaging $1\frac{1}{2}$–2 in. diam.,
thin, very obscurely and distantly crenate on the margin, in a
dried state with minute brown markings on the lower surface;
stipules broadly lanceolate, acute, fringed with glands; flowers not
scented, on slender stalks longer than the leaves, the stalks bearing

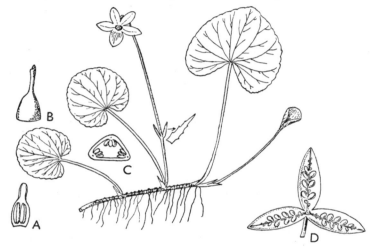

a pair of opposite or nearly opposite bracts below the middle;
sepals oblong, obtuse, glabrous; petals pale blue, with purple
streaks, the lowermost with a short and very broad spur; anthers
(A, ×6) forming a cone around the ovary (B, ×8), their tops
orange-coloured; ovary not hairy; capsule (D, ×3) also not hairy,
splitting into 3 boat-shaped parts with the seeds along the middle
of each (C, cross-section of ovary) (family *Violaceae*).

This species grows in a different habitat from that of the Sweet
Violet (see fig. 137), being partial to spongy bogs and swampy
places in woods. It is very widely distributed in northern latitudes
all around the northern hemisphere, and is common in Scotland
and Eire, but less so in England and Wales. Like the Sweet Violet,
it also produces flowers without petals and stamens (*cleistogamous* flowers), but both kinds bear fruits and seeds.

Frankenia laevis L. ($\times \frac{1}{2}$)

Woody perennial, prostrate, with purplish shoots up to 2 ft. long, rooting and bearing numerous narrow heather-like opposite leaves, these thick and broadly linear, with the margins much re-curved and often completely hiding the lower surface; no stipules; flowers (A, $\times 2$) sessile among the upper leaves, pink with a yellow eye; calyx tubular, with 4–5 teeth; petals (B, $\times 3$) long-clawed, limb spreading; stamens (C, $\times 6$) 6, alternating with the petals and often unequal in length; ovary (D, $\times 6$) 1-locular, with 3 parietal

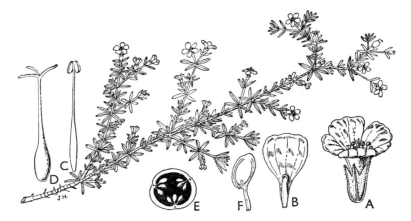

placentas (E, $\times 10$); capsule opening by valves with the very small seeds attached to their centre (family *Frankeniaceae*).

Found only on the coasts of the south-eastern counties from Lincolnshire to Hampshire; widely distributed into Asia. It grows at intervals along the Kent coast. I have myself seen a small stretch of this plant at Pegwell Bay, between Sandwich and Rams-gate, the pretty little pink flowers nestling at the top of the short crowded heath-like leaves.

Frankeniaceae is a very small family of 4 genera and about 70 species, most of which belong to *Frankenia*. It is usually placed next to *Caryophyllaceae*, but is probably most closely related to *Violaceae* and *Tamaricaceae*.

Although the petals with a scale attached to the claw recall those of some *Caryophyllaceae*, the ovary is very different, having the ovules arranged on the walls (parietal) instead of on the central axis as in *Caryophyllaceae*.

TAMARISK
Tamarix gallica L. ($\times\frac{1}{2}$)

Evergreen shrub or small tree up to about 12 ft. high found grow-ing naturally only at the seaside; branches slender, crimson or purplish; leaves very small and scale-like, sharply pointed, about $\frac{1}{12}$ in. long, overlapping; flowers (A, $\times$ 3) pink or white, very small and crowded in slender catkin-like racemes up to $1\frac{1}{2}$ in. long, these collected into panicles; flower-stalks short, each with a pointed bract at the base; sepals 5, narrow, glabrous; petals (B, $\times$ 5) 5, free, oblong; stamens (C, $\times$ 7) 5, free, the anthers with somewhat divergent lobes; ovary (D, $\times$ 10) slightly stalked, ovoid with 3 free

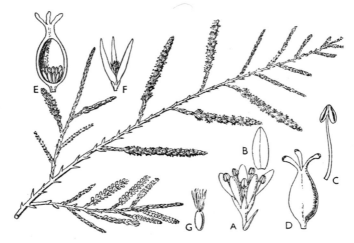

styles, 1-locular with 8–9 erect ovules attached at the base (E, $\times$ 10); fruit (F, $\times$ 5) a capsule opening by 3 valves; seeds (G, $\times$ 6) crowned by a tuft of cottony hairs (family *Tamaricaceae*).

A very common plant on sandy and marshy sea-coasts of the Mediterranean, extending up the Atlantic coast to Spain and France, but considered to be introduced around the south and south-eastern coasts of Britain; flowers in early summer, and is use-ful as a wind-break and sand-binder. It is very ornamental on many parts of our coasts with its rich deep verdure and its delicate red branches clothed in July with elegant spikes of pale rose-coloured flowers. It grows from cuttings as freely as those of the willow.

This family is also a small one of 4 genera and about 100 species. Most of these are found wild on steppes, deserts, and sea-shores of Mediterranean countries and central Asia.

Small perennial with tufted base, and numerous spreading or ascending branches up to 1 ft. long; leaves alternate, narrowly lanceolate to linear, entire, glabrous or nearly so; lower leaves shorter and broader; flowers in slender terminal racemes, with a small bract at the base of each stalk; sepals (A, ×2) 5, the two inner ('wings') much larger than the outer, obovate and veiny and resembling petals; petals (B, ×2½) united with the stamens, bright blue or pink, the lowermost tipped with a deeply lobed crest; stamens (B, ×2½) united into 2 bundles with 4 anthers in each and opening by a terminal pore; style (C, ×3) gaping at the top; fruit (D, ×3½) compressed, broadly obovate, margined with a narrow wing, notched at the top; seeds (E, ×6½) hairy, with a large caruncle (family *Polygalaceae*).

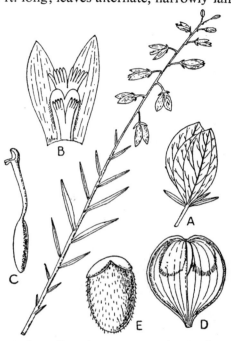

The flowers vary much in colour, and the chief means of attracting insects are the two large lateral petal-like sepals, the petals mainly serving to protect the stamens and pistil. Pollination mechanism is very interesting. The style has a spoon-shaped process near the stigma, which is a sticky hook-shaped protuberance. The anthers are so placed that when they shed their pollen it falls into this spoon, where it is stored while the stamens wither. An insect probing for nectar secreted at the base of the flower first encounters the pollen in the spoon and then the stigma, but it is not until the proboscis of the insect has been smeared with sticky matter from the stigma that the pollen adheres to it and is then carried to another flower.

WHITE BRYONY
Bryonia dioica Jacq. (×⅓)

Rootstock thick and tuberous, often branched; stems climbing over hedges and bushes, rather fleshy; tendrils arising by the side of the base of the leaf-stalk, usually unbranched, spirally twisted; leaves dotted on both sides with short sharp bulbous-based hairs, deeply divided into 5 or 7 lobes, these again angular-lobulate, widely cordate at the base, main nerves radiating from the top of the leaf-stalk, the latter shorter than the leaf; flowers unisexual,

the males (A, ×1¼) on one plant, the females on another (dioecious); males few in axillary stalked races, the females (D, ×⅖) 2–4 on a very short common stalk, smaller and less conspicuous than the male; male calyx-lobes 5, very small and narrow; corolla (B, ×⅘) yellowish green, 5-lobed, up to ¾ in. diam., with oblong nervose lobes; stamens 5, two pairs joined together, the fifth separate, anthers wavy; ovary (C, ×⅘) below the calyx; style 3-lobed; berries (E, ×⅖) red or orange, about ⅓ in. diam., with several flattish seeds (family *Cucurbitaceae*).

This plant is not found in Scotland and Eire. The fleshy tuberous rootstocks have caused poisoning to those who have eaten them in mistake for turnips or parsnips. The berries are poisonous.

Large handsome tree up to 120 ft. high; leaves alternate, stalked, rounded-ovate, pointed at the apex, heart-shaped at the base, sharply serrate, hairy below particularly in the axils of the nerves (A, $\times \frac{3}{4}$); flowers (B, $\times \frac{4}{5}$) few in an umbel, pendulous on a long stalk provided with a large narrow veiny bract and adnate to it in the lower half, sweet-scented and rich in nectar; sepals 5, not overlapping in bud; petals 5, greenish-white; stamens (C, $\times 3$) numerous, shortly united at the base into clusters; ovary (D, $\times 1\frac{1}{4}$) globose, hairy, with a long slender style and radiate stigmas; fruit a small globose nut with 1 or 2 seeds; pollination by honey-bees which cling to the stamens and stigmas (family *Tiliaceae*).

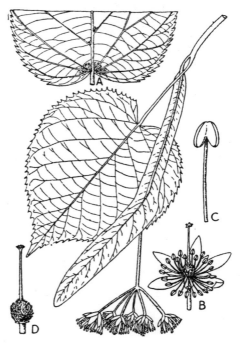

This tree is now known to be a hybrid between *T. cordata* Mill. and *T. platyphyllos* Scop., and it is probably the only hybrid upon which a genus has been founded. The wood has been extensively used for carving, turnery, toys, etc. *Tilia* is still included in the Pharmaceutical Codex, though it is now rarely used in medicine. The drug consists of the dried flowers of this and other species with their attached bracts, which are collected when fully expanded. These are stored in well-closed containers and protected from the light, and should not be used after more than twelve months from the date of collection. As a domestic remedy it is given in the form of a fresh infusion.

SMALL-LEAVED LIME
Tilia cordata Mill. ($\times\frac{1}{3}$)

Tree up to 100 ft. high and 20 ft. in girth; branches dark brown or purplish, zigzag; leaves long-petiolate, rounded-cordate, rather abruptly acuminate, usually about $2\frac{1}{2}$ in. long and broad, rather sharply serrate, dark green above, bluish or glaucous-green below, glabrous below except for tufts of orange-brown woolly hairs in the axils of the nerves, especially at the junction with the petiole (A, $\times\frac{1}{2}$); flowers (B, $\times 1$) 5–7 in a small erect umbel with a large veiny bract adnate to the stalk in the lower half; sepals 5, valvate, elliptic; petals (C, $\times 1\frac{1}{2}$) 5, free, oblanceolate, 3-nerved,

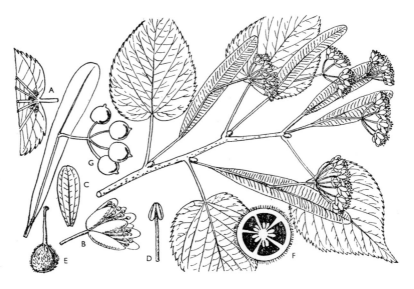

about twice as long as the sepals; stamens (D, $\times 2$) about 30; anther-loculi divergent from the apex; ovary (E, $\times 2$) 5-locular, stellate-tomentose, 5-locular (F, $\times 4$); style glabrous; fruit (G, $\times\frac{2}{3}$) subglobose, shortly beaked, $\frac{1}{3}$ in. diam. (family *Tiliaceae*).

Distributed through the greater part of Europe and in the Caucasus, extending north in Russia to lat. 62°.

A native of Britain, ranging from Cumberland southwards. It is supposed that Lyndhurst in the New Forest owes its name to the prevalence of this species there in ancient times, and Limehouse in London was originally called Limehurst, meaning a grove of trees in Saxon times.

DWARF MALLOW

146

Malva neglecta Wallr. ($\times \frac{2}{5}$)

Procumbent annual of roadsides and waste places; stems hairy; leaves on long stalks, orbicular, deeply cordate at the base, slightly 5–7-lobed, toothed (crenate); stipules conspicuous, lanceolate; flowers clustered in the leaf-axils, on slender hairy stalks, small, pale blue, about 1 in. diam.; sepals 5, lanceolate, with an epicalyx of small bracts; petals broadly notched, veiny; stamens (A, $\times 1\frac{1}{2}$) united into a tube, the anthers at first forming a cone over the stigmas and curving away from the latter on opening; stigmas emerging after the opening of the anthers and cross-pollinated by insects; if this fails they curl amongst the an-

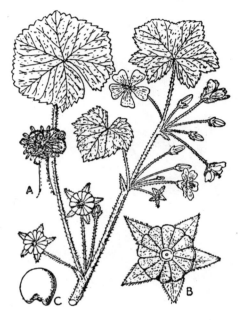

thers and may be self-pollinated; carpels (B, $\times 1\frac{2}{5}$), 10–15, hairy, forming a disk-like fruit with the persistent sepals like a rosette; seeds (C, $\times 5$) kidney-shaped; flowers spring to autumn (family *Malvaceae*) (synonym *Malva rotundifolia* L.).

The chief characters of the *Malva* family are that the calyx-lobes do not overlap each other in bud (valvate), and that the stamens are united into a single column around the styles (monadelphous). Another interesting feature is the 1-locular anthers, due to the splitting of the connective. Altogether it may be regarded as being a very highly evolved group, and some are of great commercial importance, such as Cotton, from the genus *Gossypium*. The stems of many *Malvaceae* are very fibrous, probably an indication that they have been evolved from arboreal ancestors, such as the Lime-tree family, *Tiliaceae*.

COMMON MALLOW
Malva sylvestris L. ($\times \frac{2}{5}$)

Biennial or perennial herb; stems, leaf-stalks and flower-stalks clothed with long spreading hairs with swollen bases; leaves alter-

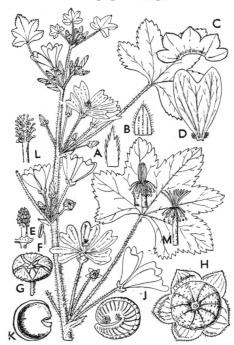

nate, on long stalks, 3–7-lobed but usually 3- or 5-lobed, widely heart-shaped (cordate) at the base, lobes rounded-ovate and crenate-dentate, hairy mainly on the nerves; nerves radiating from the base; stipules (A, $\times 1\frac{2}{3}$) large and pointed, fringed with long hairs; flowers several in a cluster, axillary, but only one or two in bloom at a time; calyx (C, $\times \frac{2}{3}$) of 5 lobes with 3 additional parts (bracteoles) below (B, $\times 1\frac{1}{3}$), all fringed with long hairs; petals (D, $\times 1$) 5, pale reddish-purple or blue, mark-

ed with darker circles, nearly 1 in. long, unequally 2-lobed; stamens united into a column (E, $\times \frac{2}{3}$), each filament bearing a 1-locular anther (F, $\times 2$); carpels about 10, united into a flat disk-like reticulate structure (G, $\times 1\frac{1}{2}$); style-branches the same number as the carpels; fruit (H, $\times 1\frac{2}{3}$) about $\frac{1}{3}$ in. diam.-grooved between the carpels (J, $\times 3$), strongly reticulate; seeds (K, $\times 4$) flattened and with a V-shaped slit on one side (family *Malvaceae*).

Mainly in waste places and by roadsides, flowering from about the middle of June. The petals are marked with darker circles, which serve as nectar-guides, the nectar being protected by hairs. At first the anthers are crowded in the middle of the flower and completely cover the still immature stigmas (E, $\times \frac{2}{3}$). After the anthers open they curve downwards (L, $\times 1\frac{1}{2}$), and their place is taken by the stigmas (M, $\times 1\frac{1}{2}$), which become receptive.

Perennial herb about 1½ ft. high; stems and leaf-stalks clothed with slender hairs with swollen bases; leaves alternate, on longish stalks, divided nearly to the base into several segments these again deeply and irregularly lobed, thinly hairy below or nearly glabrous; a form with nearly undivided (though toothed) leaves is called var. *heterophylla*; stipules (A, ×⅔) lanceolate, fringed with hairs; flowers in a bunch at the top of the stem and lateral shoots; stalks longer than the calyx, with long hairs; calyx (B, ×1) divided into 5 broad lobes, with 3 additional parts (bracteoles) towards the base of the tube, all clothed with long slender hairs; petals rose-coloured or rarely pure white, about 2 in. diam.; stamens united into a column (C, ×1), each

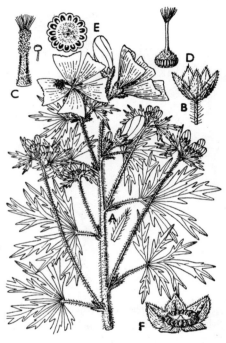

filament bearing a 1-locular anther; carpels (D, ×1) about 15, united and arranged in a circle; style branches as many as carpels; fruit (F, ×1¼) consisting of a low ring of about 15 united carpels with a hump in the middle, the carpels softly hairy (E, cross-section of ovary) (family *Malvaceae*).

The arrangement for cross-pollination in the flowers of this species is the same as for *M. sylvestris* (fig. 147). In most of the *Malva* family, *Malvaceae*, the stamens are united into a column in the middle of the flower, the anthers being peculiar in that they are 1-locular. This is due to the splitting of the connective and filament resulting in the separation of the 2 loculi. Another good spotting feature is shown by the calyx, the lobes of which are *valvate* in bud, i.e. they do not overlap one another.

Lavatera arborea L. ($\times\frac{1}{3}$)

Tall erect shrub up to about 5 ft. high; branches round in section, softly tomentose, becoming glabrous; leaves alternate, rounded

in outline, palmately 5–9-lobed, up to about 8 in. diam., lobes crenate, softly tomentose on both surfaces with star-shaped (stellate) hairs (A, ×4); leafstalks often longer than the blade; stipules ovate-lanceolate, rather large; flowers in fascicles in the upper leaf-axils collected into a long leafy inflorescence; bracteoles 3, forming an involucre below the calyx, ovate; calyx 5-lobed, tomentose; petals (B, ×1¼) 5, pink with crimson at the base, obovate, nerved with purple, pubescent at the base; stamens (C, ×7) numerous, united in a column; styles 5; fruit (D, ×1) surrounded by the three bracteoles and persistent calyx, depressed globose, composed of 7–8 reticulate carpels; seeds (E, ×2½) kidney-shaped, smooth (family *Malvaceae*).

A very local species chiefly on the south and west coasts of England and south Scotland and Eire, flowering in summer; distributed around the coasts of south-west Europe.

A second native species is *L. cretica* L., found near the coast in west Cornwall, the Scilly Isles, and Jersey, an annual or biennial more herbaceous than *L. arborea*, the epicalyx not enlarging in fruit and the carpels of the latter smooth or nearly so.

Perennial herb up to 3 ft. high, densely covered all over with soft stellate hairs (A, ×3); leaves alternate, stalked, ovate-pentagonal, lobulate and coarsely toothed, 3–4 in. long, and as much broad, strongly 5-(7-) nerved from the base, very densely hairy (tomentose) on both sides; stipules very narrow, nearly $\frac{1}{2}$ in. long, but soon falling off; flowers on short axillary branchlets forming a leafy oblong panicle; epicalyx of several (7–10) narrow bracteoles shorter than the 5-lobed calyx (B, ×1); petals pale pink, veiny, about 1 in. long; stamens (C, ×1) united in a column with the filaments free above; anthers 1-locular; ovary of 15–20 carpels, with a columnar style and as many stigmas; fruit (D, ×1) disk-like, about $\frac{1}{2}$ in. diam., with a 'hole' in the middle (family *Malvaceae*).

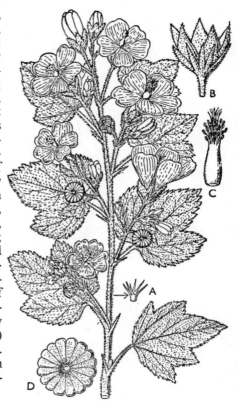

Grows in marshes, especially near the sea-coast, flowering in August and September; extends to western Asia and north Africa, introduced into North America.

Nectar is secreted between the bases of the petals and the bottom of the calyx, the flowers being protandrous. The nectar is protected from rain and small insects by hairs on the petals. Automatic self-pollination takes place if insect visits fail, the stigmas curving back among the anthers that have not yet lost all their pollen.

Linum bienne Mill. ($\times\frac{1}{3}$)

A biennial or perennial herb; stems 1–2 ft. long, slender, glabrous; leaves alternate, short and narrowly lanceolate, acute, glabrous;

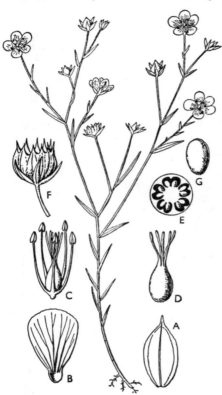

no stipules; flowers few in lax cymes with leaf-like bracts, the oldest in the middle of the forks and soon ripening into fruit; sepals (A, $\times 2\frac{1}{2}$) 5, elliptic, sharply and abruptly pointed, 3-nerved; petals (B, $\times 1\frac{1}{2}$) 5, pale blue or pale mauve, obovate, shortly clawed at the base, about $\frac{1}{2}$ in. long; stamens (C, $\times 2$) 5, the filaments united around the base of the ovary; anthers heart-shaped at the base; ovary (D, $\times 3$) ovoid, with 5 free undivided styles, 5-locular (E, $\times 5$), with the loculi partly divided into two; ovules 2 in each loculus; capsule (F, $\times 1$) 10-toothed at the top; seeds (G, $\times 3$) elliptic, $\frac{1}{8}$ in. long, shining (synonym *Linum angustifolium* Huds.) family *Linaceae*).

Mostly in limestone districts, but not found wild in Scotland; extends to southern Europe and western Asia.

The pointed sepals distinguish if from *L. perenne*, which is also a perennial, the remainder of the British species being annual.

Linaceae is a small family of about 150 species, about 90 of which belong to *Linum*. Only the two British genera (*Linum* and *Radiola*) and two others are herbs, the remainder being tropical trees, shrubs, and climbers.

These herbs, then, almost without doubt, have been derived from woody ancestors, though the same cannot be said of some other herbs such as Buttercups.

A small delicate erect or subdecumbent annual in meadows, pastures, and heaths especially on calcareous soils and sandy dunes; stems very slender, glabrous; leaves opposite, without stipules, the lowermost short and elliptic, the upper oblanceolate, pale glaucous-green, 1-nerved; flowers (A, $\times 2\frac{1}{2}$) very small, arranged in lax terminal cymes, each on a slender stalk; middle flowers maturing first, and already in fruit before upper ones bloom; sepals (B, $\times 3$) 5, with a few short gland-tipped hairs on the upper half of the margin; petals (C, $\times 3$) 5, white; stamens (E, $\times 5$) 5, united in the lower part into a cupular tube around the base of the ovary;

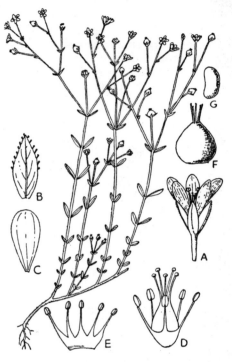

styles 5, free, with head-like stigmas; capsule (F, $\times 5$) with the 5 cells divided by a membranous partition, each with a single seed (G, $\times 4$); related to the flax-plant, *Linum usitatissimum* L., but differing from this and other native species by the opposite leaves and tiny white flowers (family *Linaceae*).

The staminal tube secretes on its outer side five drops of nectar from five small flat pits situated in the middle of the filaments. The five petals are inserted a little above the nectar pits, giving access to the nectar. The anthers are at the same level as the stigmas but at first remote from them, so that cross-pollination may take place. Failing this self-pollination is brought about by the flowers closing in the evening and pressing the anthers against the stigma.

Radiola linoides Roth. ($\times \frac{3}{5}$)

A diminutive annual, much branched from the base, the branches repeatedly forked and thread-like, glabrous; leaves opposite, sessile, very small (at most $\frac{1}{8}$ in. long), ovate; in the middle of each fork a single older flower on a short slender stalk; remainder of the flowers (A, $\times 3$) bunched together into a cyme at the top of the branches, very small; sepals 4, with 2–4 small teeth; petals (B, $\times 6$) 4, soon falling off; stamens 4, alternate with the petals; anthers 2-locular, opening by slits lengthwise; ovary of 4 rather loosely united carpels (C, $\times 6$), with 4 free styles; capsule (D, $\times 5$)

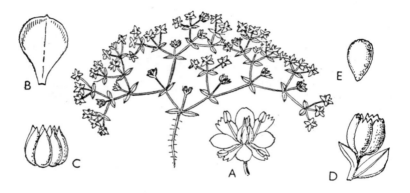

opening at the top, without any central column, each carpel opening on the inner side by a longitudinal slit and with 2 seeds, the latter (E, $\times 6$) obovoid, pale brown, shining (family *Linaceae*).

One of the smallest of British annual plants, growing in damp sandy and gravelly places, flowering from July to August. It may easily be mistaken for a small member of the *Caryophyllaceae*, but can be recognized especially by the 4-locular ovary (in *Caryophyllaceae* the ovary is 1-locular), and the seeds have no reserve food material (endosperm).

The genus *Radiola* is monotypic, i.e. it is represented by only one species, though it is very widely distributed. It ranges from northern Europe to the island of Madeira, and is even found in the mountains of tropical Africa, and eastward into Asia. The correct name according to international rules is used here, but in most British botanical books it is called *Radiola millegrana* Sm. Bentham remarked that *R. linoides* was an earlier name, 'but very inapplicable'!

Mercurialis perennis L. (female plant, $\times \frac{2}{5}$)

Rootstock slender, creeping, the roots covered with fine hairs; stems unbranched, erect, up to about 15 in. high, covered with short stiff spreading hairs; leaves stalked, opposite, each with a pair of stipules at the base of the stalk, elliptic to oblong - lanceolate, more or less acute at the apex, rounded at the base, toothed (crenate) on the margin, thinly hairy on both surfaces; flowers unisexual, the male and female on separate plants (dioecious), arranged on slender axillary common stalks as long as or longer than the leaves; male flowers (A, $\times 5$) small and green, in clusters on the stalk; calyx 2-3-lobed; no petals; stamens 9-12, radiating from the middle of the flower; anthers rounded;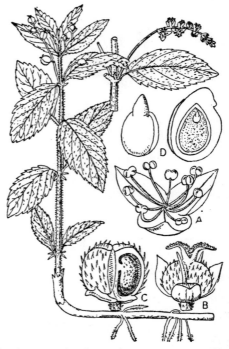
female flowers (B, $\times 5$) single or paired on the common stalk; calyx as in the male; no petals; ovary 2-lobed, covered with stiff bristly hairs, with 2 spreading stigmas; fruit (C, $\times 5$) a 2-lobed capsule, bristly hairy, each lobe with a single pendulous warted seed (D, $\times 8$) (family *Euphorbiaceae*).

This grows in woods and shady places, flowering in early spring before the leaves of other plants are fully developed; a second native species is *M. annua* L. (fig.155), an annual, with branched stems, and the female flowers sessile or shortly stalked in the axils of the leaves. As in the nettle, the pollen from the male flowers is carried to the female by the wind. The anthers are at first yellow, but afterwards the cells diverge and scatter their pollen and become a beautiful indigo blue colour. Dog's Mercury is poisonous to stock.

Mercurialis annua L. ($\times\frac{1}{3}$)

Annual and mostly as a weed in cultivated or waste ground; stems glabrous, with a thick rib running between the nodes and

between the leaf-stalks; leaves opposite, stalked, each with a pair of stipules, lanceolate, rather irregularly crenate, glabrous; stalk with a pair of minute glands at the top (A, $\times\frac{3}{4}$); flowers unisexual, mostly each sex on a different plant (dioecious), sometimes the two sexes mixed; male flowers (B, $\times 2$) numerous, clustered on long-stalked axillary spikes; sepals 4, ovate; no petals; stamens (C, $\times 6$) several, with 2 divergent rounded loculi; female flowers sessile or shortly stalked, axillary, solitary or 2 or 3 together on separate stalks; sepals as in the male; no petals; ovary 2-locular, covered on the shoulders by conical warts, each tipped by a hair; fruit (D, $\times 2$) slightly 2-lobed, tuberculate; seeds brown, reticulate (family *Euphorbiaceae*).

Though rather a troublesome weed, this plant has an interesting structure, the flowers being of one sex only and usually confined to different plants, and the leaf-stalks have a pair of glands (extra floral nectaries) at the apex.

A characteristic feature of the stem is the thick rib which traverses the internode between each pair of leaves. The two halves of the anther (loculi) are quite separate on the filament, and open by a slit across the top. The pollen discharged from them is conveyed from the male to the female by the wind (anemophilous).

KEY TO BRITISH SPECIES OF EUPHORBIA

(those marked with an * not native) '

A. Glands of involucre rounded on the outer margin: B. Prostrate maritime plant with opposite unequal leaves with minute stipules; seeds smooth . . . *peplis*.   BB. More or less erect stems, the lower leaves alternate; no stipules: C. Leaves not toothed: D. Leaves very narrow and sharply pointed, quite glabrous, willow-like; fruits with long horn-like tubercles, seeds smooth . . . *ceratocarpa**.   DD. Leaves more or less oblong and rounded at the apex, rounded or narrowed to the base, often pilose: E. Ovary and fruit densely pilose, the latter not warted; seeds smooth . . . *coralloides**.   EE. Ovary and fruit warted but not pilose; seeds smooth: F. Leaves narrowed to the base (oblanceolate); glands green, at length purple . . . *dulcis**.   FF. Leaves broad and rounded at the base (oblong): G. Fruit shortly warted or nearly smooth . . . *villosa* GG. Fruit densely clothed with cylindric warts; glands yellowish, at length brown . . . *hyberna*.   CC. Leaves toothed: H. Leaves more or less obovate; fruits smooth, seeds pitted . . . *helioscopia*. HH. Leaves oblong, often pointed, fruits more or less warted; seeds smooth: J. Fruits subglobose, with hemispherical warts . . . *platyphyllos*.   JJ. Fruits 3-sided; warts cylindrical or conical . . . *stricta*.   AA. Glands of involucre crescent-shaped, with the points turned outwards (like a new moon): K. Floral leaves not united to each other: L. Umbel of 5 or more rays: M. Umbel of 5–6 rays: N. Umbel very compact; seeds smooth or slightly warted . . . *paralais*.   NN. Umbel spreading: O. Leaves entire; seeds pitted . . . *segetalis**.   OO. Leaves toothed at the top . . . *portlandica*.   MM. Umbel of 6–8 or more rays; seeds not pitted: P. Leaves broader above the middle, narrowed to the base . . . *esula*.   PP. Leaves broader below or about the middle, broadish at the base . . . *virgata**.   PPP. Leaves acicular . . . *cyparissias**.   LL. Umbel of 3–4 rays: Q. Tall very glaucous biennial with large fruits; seeds wrinkled . . . *lathyrus*.   QQ. Low green annuals: R. Stem-leaves broadly obovate, petiolate; seeds pitted; fruits triangular, the angles with a double ridge . . . *peplus*.   RR. Stem leaves linear, seeds at most slightly wrinkled . . . *exigua*.   KK. Floral leaves of each pair more or less united; seeds smooth; fruit at most finely pustulate . . . *amygdaloides*.

HAIRY SPURGE
Euphorbia villosa Waldst. & Kit. ($\frac{1}{2}$)

Perennial herb up to 1$\frac{1}{2}$ ft. high, softly hairy all over; leaves (A, ×1) alternate, sessile, oblong-lanceolate, about 2–2$\frac{1}{2}$ in. long and $\frac{1}{2}$ in. broad, with several lateral nerves; no stipules; leaves below the umbel forming a whorl sometimes shorter than the stem leaves; umbel usually of 5 rays with a few axillary branches below it; peduncles about 1$\frac{1}{2}$–2 in. long; involucre (B, ×4) glabrous or hairy, margined with 4 transversely elliptic entire glands; male flowers (C, ×10) few; female flower a single glandular-warted ovary (D, ×4); capsule glandular-warted to almost smooth; seeds (E, ×5) smooth (family *Euphorbiaceae*).

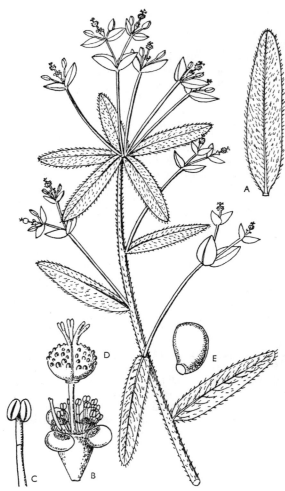

In damp woods and amongst bushes on shady banks, only in Somerset, in early summer, rare; distributed east to Siberia and south to Algeria.
Synonym *Euphorbia pilosa* L.

Euphorbia helioscopia L. ($\times\frac{1}{3}$)

Annual up to about 1½ ft. high, with milky juice; stems unbranched or with 2 weaker branches at the base, rounded, with a few weak spreading hairs in the upper part; leaves spirally arranged, few and scattered, broadly spoon-shaped (spathulate), glaucous-green, shortly and rather unequally toothed only in the upper half, about 1 in. long; upper 5 leaves in a whorl and forming ring of bracts similar to the leaves but broader and rounded at the base, toothed only in the upper half; stalks of flower-clusters 5, opposite the bract-leaves, with a few slender spreading hairs, bearing at the

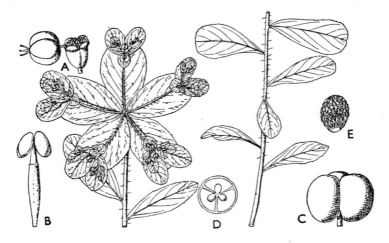

top 3 leaf-like bracts, one smaller than the other two; secondary branches repeat the above description but with smaller bract-leaves and surrounding the flower-clusters (inflorescences) (A, ×2); glands of the involucre broadly elliptic, green; male flowers (B, ×6) several; female solitary in the middle of the males but sharply bent away from them; ovary green, 3-lobed and 3-locular (D, ×2), smooth; fruits (C, ×5) 3-lobed; seeds (E, ×8) broadly obovoid, closely reticulate (family *Euphorbiaceae*).

    Grows in fields and waste places, frequently as a garden-weed; it is widely distributed in the northern hemisphere and is introduced into North America; one of the most easily recognized of the Spurges, the involucre of leafy bracts forming a pretty pattern with an equal number of rays, the whole ensemble glowing with yellowish-green.

Euphorbia lathyrus L. (× ⅓)

A tall very clean-looking annual or biennial full of milky juice, with a simple upright main hollow stem covered with 'bloom' like that of a grape which readily rubs off, often crimson towards the base; leaves opposite, sessile, increasing in size upwards, the lower soon becoming reflexed, about 1 in. long, the uppermost pair spreading and about 4 in. long and 1 in. broad, pale below, darker green above, with numerous faint looped lateral nerves; topmost leaves forming a whorl of 4, each with a flowering shoot in its axil; flowering shoots 4, one usually shorter than the others, each with a pair of broadly lanceolate leafy sessile bracts in the middle of which is an involucre, with a pair of lateral shoots, which in turn have a pair of shoots bearing pairs of bracts with an early matured involucre in the middle; involucre (A, ×3) sessile, bell-shaped, the lobes with jagged tips; glands (B, ×8) outside and between the lobes almost erect, broadly Y-shaped with rounded tops, fleshy; male (C, ×8) flowers (each consisting of one stamen) numerous (25–30), with cream-yellow anthers; female flower (a single ovary) stalked and carried above the males; ovary (D, ×5) 6-lobed, with a purple line between each lobe, 3-locular; styles 3, free, rather deeply 2-lobed; ovule solitary and pendulous in each loculus; fruit (E, ×⅔) a large 3-lobed wrinkled capsule; seeds (F, ×3) broadly ellipsoid, with a crenulate caruncle, wrinkled when ripe (family *Euphorbiaceae*).

A native of woodlands, where it is rare, but sometimes found on waste ground and in or near gardens, as far north as southern Scotland. The fruits (capsules) have been used as a substitute for capers (real capers are the flower buds of *Capparis spinosa* L.), but they are very bitter. It flowers in early summer and is the only British species of the genus, besides *E. peplis*, with opposite leaves.

This is the tallest of the British species of *Euphorbia*, sometimes growing to about 4 ft. in height and easily recognized because of its deep sea-green foliage here and there tinged with purple. Its green flowers are produced in June and July and are sufficiently large to enable the student to understand the structure of the individual inflorescences of this remarkable genus, notes on which will be found at the end of the description of fig. 160.

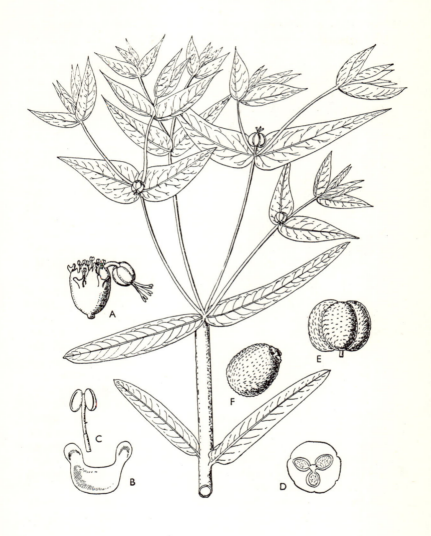

PETTY SPURGE
Euphorbia peplus L. ($\times \frac{2}{5}$)

Annual, erect or ascending, usually branched from the base, up to about 1 ft. high, glabrous in all its parts; stem leafy, the leaves in-

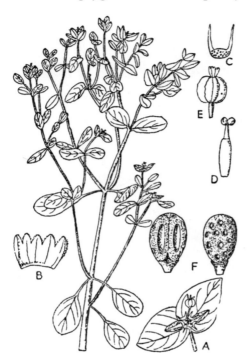

creasing in size upwards, alternate, obovate, with slender stalks, the upper ones becoming opposite, sessile; flowers (A, $\times 2\frac{1}{2}$) very small, surrounded and almost hidden by the broad upper leaves; each apparent flower consists of a cup-like involucre (B, $\times 3$) of united bracts bearing conspicuous crescent-shaped glands (C, $\times 3\frac{1}{2}$) on the margin, each gland with a long tail at each end; male flowers (D, $\times 7$) consisting of a single stamen jointed in the middle, with 2 rounded anther-lobes opening across the middle; female flower (E, $\times 7$) composed of a single ovary supported on a stalk in the middle of the male flowers; ovary deeply 3-lobed, with 3 short bifid styles, 3-locular, with 1 ovule in each compartment; fruit a 3-lobed capsule, splitting into 3 lobes, each lobe containing a single grey seed (F, $\times 4\frac{1}{2}$) deeply pitted on the back and with two large elongated cavities on the inner face (family *Euphorbiaceae*).

The glands of the involucre secrete a shallow layer of exposed nectar; pollination mainly by flies, bettles, and wasps; a common weed in cultivated and waste places, seeding very rapidly; it flowers during the whole summer and autumn; a tincture and a liquid extract of the whole plant have been recommended for asthma and bronchial catarrh.

Small glabrous annual with a slender taproot and erect or ascending stem often branched from the base, mostly in cultivated and waste places, and flowering nearly the whole year; leaves alternate, sessile, gradually increasing in size upwards, linear to linear-lanceolate, the upper ones more rounded at the base than the others and forming whorls of 3–5 at the base of the flowering branchlets; apparent flowers (A, ×5) consisting of a short top-shaped cup margined by fleshy elliptic glands (B, ×8) between

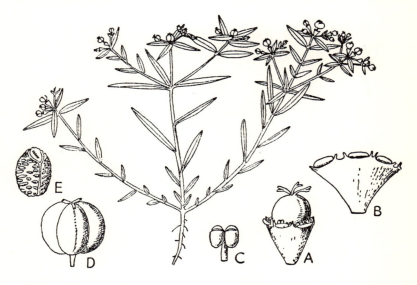

which are two short awl-shaped lobes; stamens very few, short, each representing a male flower; anthers rounded, opening across the top (C, ×5); ovary shortly stalked within the cup and representing the female flower; styles 3, spreading, 2-lobed; fruit (D, ×4) 3-lobed, opening into the 3-loculi, each of which contains a single transversely warted seed (E, ×4) (family *Euphorbiaceae*).

There are several species of this genus in our islands, interesting because the apparent flower is really an aggregation of several males and one female, girt by an involucre of bracts margined by glands. Good characters for distinguishing the species are to be found in the shape of these glands and in the seeds, some of which are warted or wrinkled, or deeply pitted.

Euphorbia cyparissias L. ($\times \frac{1}{2}$)

Perennial with rather woody stems, bushy with densely leafy lateral branchlets and full of milk-like juice; leaves rather like those of a pine tree (acicular), $\frac{3}{4}$–1 in. long, very narrow and glaucous-green, with a single mid-nerve; no stipules; main stem ending in an umbel-like inflorescence below which younger bunches of flowers develop later; 'flowers' (A, $\times 3$) consisting of a pair of ovate, pointed bracts, within these a cupular involucre bearing on its margin 4 young-moon-shaped yellow glands (A, $\times 3$); male flowers each consisting of one stamen jointed in the

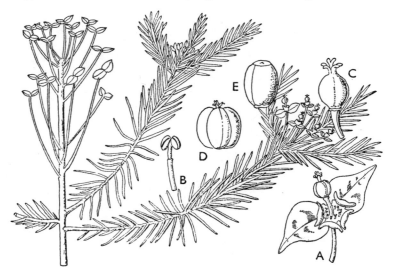

middle (B, $\times 3\frac{1}{2}$), and two rounded anther-lobes; female flower in the middle, shortly stalked, and reduced to an ovary (C, $\times 4$) with 3 loculi and 3 shortly 2-lobed styles; fruit (D, $\times 2\frac{1}{2}$) 3-lobed, each lobe containing a single seed (E, $\times 3\frac{1}{2}$), with a caruncle at the base (family *Euphorbiaceae*).

Regarded as an introduced species from the continent of Europe, but well established among the native vegetation in dry, hilly pastures in many localities.

The seeds of our native species of *Euphorbia* are interesting, and afford very distinctive specific characters.

A dwarf perennial with many spreading branches, the latter rough below with the leaf scars; leaves (A, B, $\times 2\frac{1}{2}$) alternate, narrowly oblanceolate to obovate, toothed near the top, less than 1 in. long; bracts below the main umbel ovate-cordate; glands on the involucre (C, $\times 2\frac{1}{2}$) 4, half-moon-shaped; male flowers (D, $\times 6$) few; female flower stalked, the ovary and capsule finely

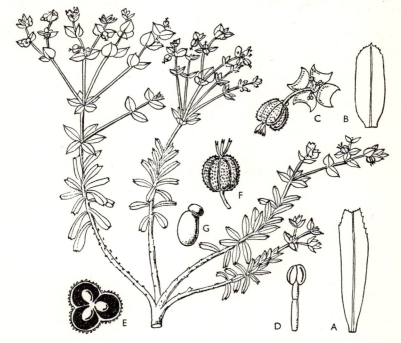

warted (E, F, $\times 2\frac{1}{2}$); seeds (G, $\times 5$) with a large ellipsoid caruncle, smooth (family *Euphorbiaceae*).

A coastal species extending north as far as Ayr in Scotland; local in sandy and rocky places; found also in France, Spain, and Portugal.

The plant used for the first description of a species is called by botanists the *type specimen*, and the locality in which it was found is known as the *classical locality* (*locus classicus*). Very few species of flowering plants, however, were founded on specimens collected in Britain, because most of our wild flowers were first described from specimens collected on the continent of Europe. (*Contd. on p.* 212.)

WOOD SPURGE

Euphorbia amygdaloides L. (×½)

Perennial, rather woody at the base, up to about 2 ft. high, often with several sterile shorter shoots at the base; stems green to crimson, exuding a milk-like juice when cut or bruised, softly hairy (pilose); leaves (A, × 1) crowded towards the upper part of the flowering stem, gradually merged into smaller broader bracts, narrowly oblanceolate and rather similar to those of a peach tree, about 3 in. long and ½ in. broad, softly hairy below and on the margin; main stem terminated by an umbel of 5–6 rays bearing successive pairs of yellowish green involucres (B, × 2½) composed of 2 united bracts, below the terminal umbel single peduncles in each leafy bract, each main involucre with 2 smaller stalked involucres; cyathium pilose within, bearing on the margin 4 crescent-shaped glands with convergent horns; male flowers (C, × 10) (each consisting of a single stamen) few; ovary (D, × 5) (female flower) stalked; capsule (E, × 2) 3-lobed, finely pustulate; seeds (F, × 6) smooth, grey (family *Euphorbiaceae*).

In shady woods and hedges, flowering in spring; locally somewhat common throughout England and Wales, but rare in Eire and not found in Scotland; extends to the Caucasus and south to Algeria.

Portland Spurge (*contd.*):—

Euphorbia portlandica has the distinction of having been first collected on Portland Bill in Dorset. It was originally named by the famous English botanist John Ray, who called it 'Tithymalus maritimus minor, Portlandicus', and he stated that it was 'found in 1711 by the Reverend Mr. Stonestreet in the narrow neck of Land which joyns Portland to Devonshire'.

In his celebrated *Species Plantarum* (Species of Plants), the Swedish botanist Linnaeus in 1753 reduced the name to two words, *Euphorbia portlandica*, after the custom which he did so much to establish, and his description reads as follows:

'Euphorbia * umbella quinquefida: dichotoma, involucellis cordatis, foliis lineari-lanceolatis obtusiusculis acuminatis reflexis.' – 'Habitat in Angliae Devonschire', giving a sign that indicated the plant is a perennial.

* Translation for very young readers: 'Euphorbia with a five-rayed umbel; branches in pairs; little involucres cordate; leaves linear-lanceolate, rather obtuse, acuminate, reflexed'.

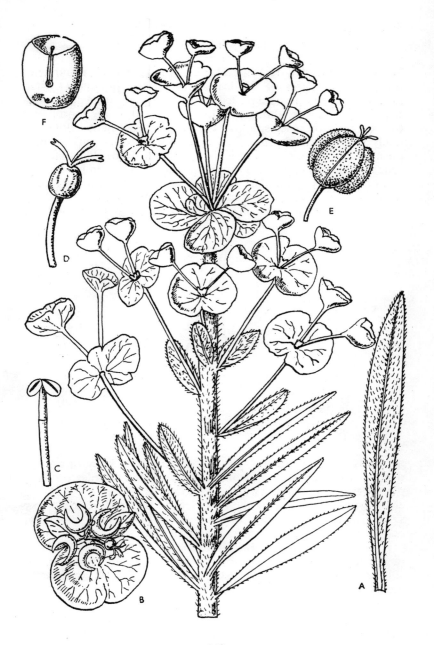

Small wiry shrublet, densely leafy; lower part of stems rough with the persistent bases of the leaf-stalks; young branchlets often purplish, shortly glandular; leaves (A, ×2) very crowded, alternate, shortly linear, about $\frac{1}{2}$ in. long, 1-nerved, finely toothed on the margin, otherwise smooth, the midrib prominent below and finely rugose, the short petiole persistent; flowers pink to purplish blue, clustered in the leaf-axils in an umbel-like inflorescence; pedicels slender, 1–1$\frac{1}{2}$ in. long, reaching 2 in. in fruit, crimson and shortly glandular; calyx (B, ×2) deeply 5-lobed, lobes glandular-hairy outside; stamens (C, ×3$\frac{1}{2}$) 10, free from the bell-shaped 5-toothed corolla; filaments nearly glabrous; anthers

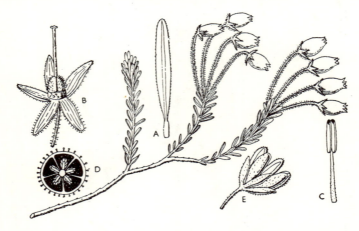

narrowly oblong, opening by 2 terminal pores, without appendages; ovary (D, ×7) 5-locular, with numerous ovules on axile placentas; style columnar, stigma lobulate; fruit (E, ×2$\frac{1}{2}$) an erect capsule opening by the partitions (septicidally); seeds very small, margined (family *Ericaceae*). – Synonyms *Bryanthus caeruleus* (L.) Dippel; *Menziesia caerulea* Sm.

A very rare species, in Britain found only on mountain heaths in Perthshire, Scotland, at about 2400 ft. altitude, flowering in July and August; widely distributed through Arctic Europe, northern Asia, and in North America.

Phyllodoce is a small genus of 6 or 7 species distributed in North America, northern Europe, and northern Asia, all being low evergreens with heath-like foliage and attractive flowers.

Andromeda polifolia L. ($\times\frac{1}{2}$)

A low shrublet up to 1 ft. high; old branches dark coloured with split bark; young branches glabrous; leaves evergreen, alternate, nearly sessile, oblanceolate, mucronate, up to $1\frac{1}{4}$ in. long and $\frac{1}{3}$ in. broad, dark green and shining above, very glaucous below and densely papillous, lateral nerves spreading, the margins strongly recurved; flowers in a bunch at the end of the shoot, drooping, each stalk with a large ovate leathery bract at the base; no bracteoles on the stalks; calyx (A, $\times\frac{1}{2}$) deeply 5-lobed, lobes triangular; corolla pale pink, ovoid-globular, $\frac{1}{4}$ in. long with 5 short recurved lobes, glabrous; stamens (B, $\times7$) 10, included in the tube, filaments hairy, anthers with 2 long curved horns on the back at the top; ovary (C, $\times5$) 5-locular with several ovules in each loculus on an axile placenta; style undivided, persistent in fruit; capsule (D, $\times3$) opening by 5 slits down the middle of the chambers (E, $\times3$); seeds (F, $\times9$) several, brown, smooth (family *Ericaceae*).

Grows in peat-bogs in central England, southern Scotland, and in Eire, flowering during summer; widely distributed around the northern hemisphere; recognized by the very glaucous lower surface of the leaves, the bunched pink flowers, and by the fruit, which opens by slits into the loculi (loculicidal dehiscence).

The genus *Andromeda* is named after the mythical daughter of Cepheus and Cassiopeia, who, when bound to a rock and exposed to a sea-monster, was delivered by Perseus. It embraces only two species, the one here shown, and *A. glaucophylla* Link, which grows wild in the eastern United States of North America. Its leaves are white-tomentose beneath and the pedicels are shorter.

ST DABEOC'S HEATH

Dabeocia cantabrica (Huds.) (×3)

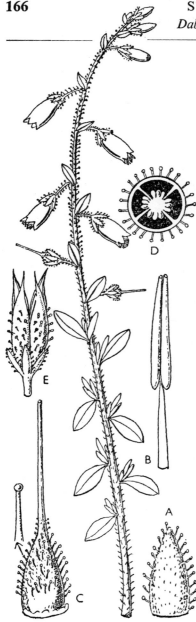

Low shrublet; branches with gland-tipped hairs; leaves alternate, elliptic to oblong-lanceolate, green and with a few gland-tipped hairs on the upper surface, covered with white, later yellowish, woolly hairs below; flowers pendulous in a slender terminal raceme, densely covered with sticky gland-tipped hairs; bracts linear, half as long as the pedicel; pedicels and calyx-lobes (A, ×5) covered with long gland-tipped hairs; corolla deep pink or crimson or sometimes white, ovoid, nearly ½ in. long, contracted below the 4 short recurved lobes; stamens (B, ×4) 8, anthers brown-purple, opening by pores at the top; ovary (C, ×3) 4-locular, with numerous ovules on axile placentas (D, ×4); fruit (E, ×2) opening by the partitions (septicidal); seeds minute (synonyms *Dabeocia (Daboecia) polifolia* and *Menziesia polifolia* Sm.) (family *Ericaceae*).

This is an interesting representative of the Lusitanian flora in Britain. It is found in Eire (in the counties of Galway and Mayo). A very closely related plant * (regarded until recently by botanists as the same species) is found in the Azores Islands.

* *Dabeocia azorica* Tutin and Warburg.

A small shrublet sometimes up to 2 ft. or so high, but usually dwarfer, much branched; branches softly hairy with very short hairs; leaves opposite, arranged in 4 rows on the young shoots, very small, produced at the base below the point of insertion, softly hairy or at length glabrous; flowers (A, ×3) arranged in leafy racemes, small, each subtended by a few triangular bracts fringed with hairs; sepals 4, coloured pink like the corolla or very rarely white, dry and scarious; corolla (B, ×3) deeply 4-lobed, much shorter than the calyx; stamens 8; anthers (C, ×4) with 2 tails at the base, opening by a long pore-like slit; ovary (D, ×4) depressed - globose, hairy; style stout, protruding beyond the calyx; fruit a small capsule opening by slits between the loculi; often dominant on moors with acid soils, and very common in Scotland; flowers from July to early September (family *Ericaceae*).

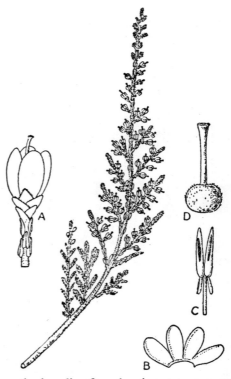

The Scotch Heather is a very valuable bee-plant, heather honey being greatly preferred by some people. Beehives are a familiar sight on heather moors, to which they are transported before the heather flowers open in late summer. Nectar is secreted by eight little swellings between the stamens at the base of the flower.

Erica tetralix, L. ($\times \frac{2}{3}$)

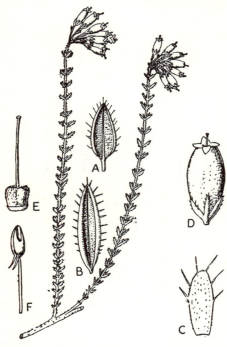

A low shrublet branched from the base; branches pubescent; leaves (A, ×4) in whorls of 4, rather densely arranged, shortly stalked, rather variable in width from narrow with the margins recurved to the midrib to broader and markedly papillous below (B, ×5), furnished also with rather long stiff hairs; flowers drooping in a terminal umbel-like cluster; stalks bearing a leafy bract, sepals (C, ×4) oblong, finely hairy and with a few bristly hairs; corolla (D, ×1¾) tubular but narrowed to each end, shortly 4-lobed; stamens 8, the anthers (F, ×2¼) with 2 long appendages at the base; ovary (E, ×2) truncate at the top, pubescent; style a little longer than the corolla; fruit with a very thin shell; often grows with the common heather but much less abundant; flowers in late summer (family *Ericaceae*).

Pollination is by bees. The flowers are nodding or pendulous and the nectar is secreted in a blackish annular ring around the base of the ovary. As the blackish sticky stigma occupies the mouth of the corolla or beyond it, an insect visitor hanging on to the corolla and probing for the nectar must first touch this, some of the sticky substance adhering to the proboscis. When it probes into the flower the anthers are shaken by the insect touching the horn-like processes at their base and the pollen falls on its head, adhering to the part made sticky. It is thus carried to another flower, when the process is repeated. As the proboscis of the honey-bee is rather short it commits burglary by using the hole made by other bees.

Erica cinerea L. ($\times \frac{2}{5}$)

A low woody undershrub, much branched from the base; stems very shortly hairy; leaves (A, $\times 1\frac{3}{5}$) usually 3 in a whorl, often with short shoots in their axils, very shortly stalk-ed, short and needle-like, acute, the margins re-curved and meeting to-gether on the lower sur-face; flowers (B, $\times 1\frac{3}{5}$) in interrupted clusters in the upper part of the shoot and borne on short shoots; sepals linear-lanceolate, acute, keel-ed, with narrow mem-branous margins; corolla reddish purple, ovoid in outline, about $\frac{1}{8}$ in. long, gaping at the mouth and with 4 very small lobes; stamens (C, $\times 5$) 8, inserted below the ovary and free from the corolla; anthers included in the corolla - tube, opening by pores, with two toothed appendages at the base; ovary (D,

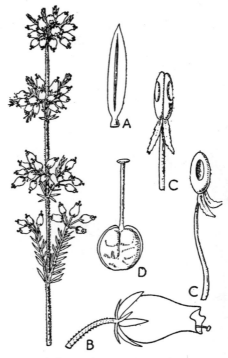

$\times 5$) globose, style shortly exserted from the corolla, with a term-inal head-like (capitate) stigma; capsule enclosed in the corolla-tube, with numerous minute seeds (family *Ericaceae*).

This species flowers in summer and autumn, and covers large tracts of moorland country often in company with *E. tetralix* L. (fig. 168) and the common heather, *Calluna vulgaris* (L.) Hull (fig. 167).

The nectar is secreted around the base of the ovary and the flowers are pollinated by insects as described under *Erica tetralix* (fig. 168), the bells being often perforated by humble-bees.

170 TRAILING LOISELEURIA OR 'AZALEA'
Loiseleuria procumbens (L.) Desv. (×½)

Much-branched shrublet with procumbent stems and branches, the older parts rough with the scars of fallen leaves; leaves (A, ×4) evergreen, opposite, numerous, and crowded on the younger crimson-tinged glabrous shoots, oblanceolate and tapered to a thick stalk, with a grooved midrib above, and a very prominent thick midrib below, with the margins thick and strongly recurved, pubescent between the midrib and margins; flowers (B, ×4) about 3 at the ends of the short branchlets; stalks with 2–3 leafy bracts at the base; calyx (D, ×2) deeply 5-lobed, lobes ovate-lanceolate, glabrous; corolla rose-pink, campanulate, 5-lobed to the middle;

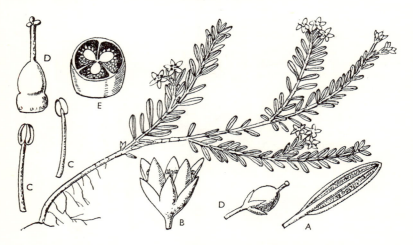

stamens (C, ×7) 5, inserted on the disk surrounding the bottom of the ovary; anthers opening by slits lengthwise; ovary (D, ×2) 2–3-locular, with numerous ovules on large axile placentas (E, ×12); style with a disk-like 3-lobed stigma; fruit a dry capsule, red, valves shortly split at the top, calyx persistent (family *Ericaceae*). – Synonym *Azalea procumbens* L.

Often forming a dense carpet in moorland and rocky places up to nearly 4,000 ft. in Scotland, to which it is confined in Britain; in Europe south to the Pyrenees.

This is the only species of the genus which Linnaeus first assigned to *Azalea*, the latter now merged in *Rhododendron*. *Loiseleuria* differs from *Rhododendron* by the opposite leaves and the anthers opening by slits lengthwise and not by pores.

Arbutus unedo L. ($\times\frac{1}{2}$)

Evergreen small tree or shrub with greenish-crimson branches finely puberulous when young; leaves alternate, shortly stalked, ovate-elliptic to oblong, more or less toothed, 2–3 in. long, thick, shining above; flowers in drooping terminal panicles; bracts small and thick, ovate; sepals 5, overlapping, ovate, thick, slightly hairy on the margin; corolla (B, $\times1\frac{1}{2}$) greenish-white or tinged with pink, ovoid, shortly 5-lobed, about $\frac{1}{3}$ in. long; stamens (A, $\times2\frac{1}{2}$) 10, free from but included in the corolla; anthers (C, $\times4$) opening by terminal pores and with two horn-like appendages at the back;

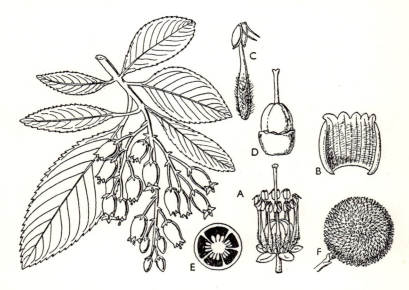

ovary (D, $\times2\frac{1}{2}$) seated on a thick disk, 5-locular, with several ovules in each loculus (E, $\times3$); fruit (F, $\times\frac{1}{2}$) a red berry, globular and densely warted all over, somewhat resembling a strawberry, hence the common name (family *Ericaceae*).

This tree is found wild only in south-west Eire, where it flowers in autumn. It is of great interest to botanists, being one of a number of plants which grow naturally only in the south-western parts of our islands as well as in Portugal or Spain. They represent the 'Lusitanian element' in our flora. The Strawberry tree occurs right around the Mediterranean as far east as Asia Minor, and it is also found in Morocco.

RED BEARBERRY

Arctostaphylos uva-ursi L. ($\times\frac{1}{2}$)

Low shrub with procumbent branches and ascending branchlets; branches covered with blackish flakey bark, branchlets shining, brownish green; winter-bud-scales more or less persistent; leaves (A, $\times 1\frac{1}{2}$) evergreen, crowded, oblanceolate, rounded at the apex, about 1 in. long, thick and leathery, shining on both surfaces and finely reticulate, the margins covered with short hairs when young; flowers (C, $\times 2\frac{1}{2}$) drooping in short racemes at the ends of the branchlets; bracts ovate, thick, about as long as the thick flower-stalks; sepals (B, $\times 2\frac{1}{2}$) 5, overlapping, rounded, fringed with very short hairs; corolla ovoid, about $\frac{1}{5}$ in. long, contracted below the 5 broad lobes; stamens (D, $\times 7$) 10, concealed in the corolla, filaments slightly hairy; anthers opening by terminal pores and with 2 slender curved shortly hairy appendages hanging from behind the apex; ovary (E, $\times 1\frac{1}{2}$) free from the calyx and surrounded by a thick lobulate disk, 5-locular, with 1 ovule in each loculus; style shorter than the corolla, undivided; fruit (F, $\times 1\frac{1}{2}$) a red shining berry about $\frac{1}{3}$ in. diam. (family *Ericaceae*).

Flowers in spring and is found only in moorland country in the north of England, Scotland, and Eire.

Elsewhere it is widely distributed around the cooler parts of the northern hemisphere reaching as far south as New Mexico and northern California in North America.

The berries of this plant are small and round, but they are mealy and too dry to be really pleasant, though they provide common food for moorland birds.

Evergreen shrub naturalized in woodlands, forming a dense mass of stems and spreading by underground suckers; young branches reddish and bristly with gland-tipped hairs; leaves alternate, ovate-rounded, rounded or slightly cordate at the base, abruptly and shortly pointed, up to 3½ in. long and 2½ in. broad, closely crenulate, reticulate, with about 4–5 pairs of lateral nerves, glabrous; flowers (A, ×1¼) in terminal often paired racemes with a cluster of bud-scales at the base; bracts ovate-elliptic, persistent; pedicels about ⅕ in. long, glandular-hairy; calyx (B, ×2½) white, 5-lobed, glandular outside; corolla pinkish-white, ovoid, about

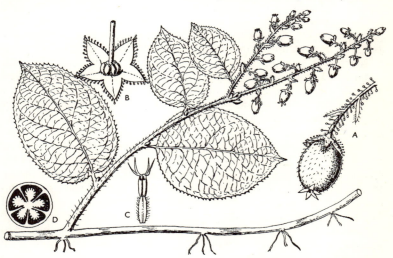

½ in. long, finely bristly with gland-tipped hairs, shortly 5-lobed; stamens (C, ×2) 10, slightly attached to the base of the corolla; filaments flattened, ciliate; anthers opening by terminal pores, with 2 deeply divided bristles behind the apex; ovary (D, ×5) 5-lobed and 5-locular, with numerous ovules on large axile placentas; style slightly 5-fid; fruit a juicy top-shaped berry enclosed by the persistent hairy calyx, dark purple, becoming black, with numerous minute seeds (family *Ericaceae*).

A native of western North America, naturalized in moist shady woods, and useful among Rhododendrons, etc., as a cover for game; it appears as if wild in the New Forest, Leith Hill in Surrey, and other places.

MARSH LEDUM
Ledum palustre L. (×½)

Small erect shrub; branches densely covered with rust-coloured hairs; leaves (A, ×1½) alternate, crowded, broadly and shortly linear, loosely covered with small sessile glands on the upper surface when young and very green, the margins much recurved and between them the lower surface densely rusty-hairy; stalk short, hairy; flowers white, arranged in a terminal umbel-like raceme from a winter bud as in Rhododendron; bracts large, obovate, rusty-hairy, and glandular; pedicels slender, ¾ in. long, rusty-pubescent; calyx very small; petals (B, ×2½) 5, free, obovate-elliptic, veiny; stamens (C, ×2½) 10, free from the petals; filaments slightly pilose near the base; anthers oblong, opening by 2 rounded pores at the top; ovary (D, ×4) superior, 5-locular (E, ×7), glandular; ovules numerous on axile placentas; style nearly twice as long as the ovary; stigma capitate, lobulate; fruit (F, ×3) a septicidal capsule opening from below upwards; style persistent; seeds (G, ×5) numerous, linear, with a tail at each end (family *Ericaceae*).

Doubtfully native and probably naturalized in peat bogs and boggy swamps in Scotland; circumpolar distribution in the northern hemisphere.

Ledum is a genus of three species which grow wild in the colder regions of the northern hemisphere. *Ledon* is the Greek name for *Cistus* (Rock Roses). *L. palustre* was introduced into cultivation in this country as long ago as 1762. Another species, *L. groenlandicum* Oeder, is known as Labrador Tea, and is a native of North America and Greenland. It is a very hardy and pretty shrub with white flowers and is the most commonly cultivated species in gardens in this country, flowering from the end of April until June. The third species, *L. glandulosum* Nutt., is confined to the western United States, and has failed to establish itself in cultivation in Britain.

The genus is quite closely related to *Rhododendron*, but is a more primitive type of the family *Ericaceae* because the petals are free and not united into a tube as in *Rhododendron*.

The family *Ericaceae* is related to the Tea family, *Theaceae*, through a smaller family *Clethraceae*, formerly included in the *Ericaceae*. In *Clethraceae*, however, the petals are free and not united into a tube as in most of the *Ericaceae*, a feature they have in common with *Theaceae*. In all of them the stamens are inserted below the ovary (hypogynous) and are not attached to the corolla.

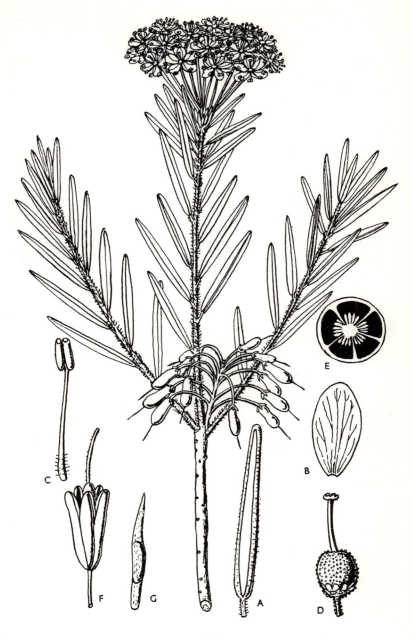

175 BILBERRY, BLUEBERRY, WHORTLEBERRY
Vaccinium myrtillus L. ($\times\frac{2}{5}$)

Small much branched erect glabrous shrublet up to about 1 ft. high; branchlets somewhat flattened but distinctly angular or almost winged; leaves deciduous, alternate, ovate-elliptic, very shortly stalked, minutely toothed (crenulate); flowers (A, $\times 1\frac{1}{4}$) solitary in the leaf-axils, shortly stalked, pendulous; calyx combined with the inferior ovary, not lobed; corolla greenish and tinged with red, with a globose tube and short lobes; stamens (B, $\times 1\frac{1}{4}$) twice as many as corolla-lobes, free from the corolla; anthers (C, $\times 3$) with two longish horns at the back; ovary inferior; style stout, undivided; fruit (D, $\times 1\frac{1}{4}$) formed of the ovary and calyx united together, a globose berry, blue-black

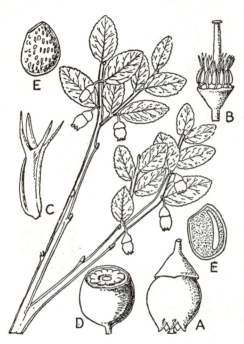

and covered with a glaucous bloom like that of a black grape; seeds (E, $\times 4$) with a long slender embryo (family *Vacciniaceae*).

Grows on mountain and hilly heaths and woods often with heather; berries an important food for grouse and used locally for tarts and jam. The flowers are without odour, but are rich in nectar. This is secreted around the base of the style. The corolla hangs more or less downwards and only bees with a proboscis long enough to reach to its base are able to act as pollinating agents. When a bee inserts its proboscis into the corolla it strikes against the horns on the back of the anthers, causing the pollen to fall out on to the visitor's head. When visiting another flower this is likely to be brushed against the stigma, which projects beyond the mouth of the corolla.

A shrublet with wiry procumbent stems rooting towards the base, younger parts minutely hairy; leaves evergreen, alternate, shortly stalked, obovate to narrowly elliptic, rounded to slightly tapered to the base, rounded at the top, averaging about 1 in. long and $\frac{1}{2}$ in. broad, rather thick, slightly dentate, with 3–4 pairs of lateral nerves, glabrous above, sparingly but minutely setulose below; flowers (A, $\times 1\frac{1}{2}$) in a short terminal curved or drooping bracteate raceme; bracts broad and boat-shaped, $\frac{1}{6}$ in. long; calyx (B, $\times 3$) of 4 ovate sepals borne on top of the inferior ovary; corolla white or pale rose,

broadly tubular, 4-lobed, about $\frac{1}{5}$ in. long; lobes ovate, spreading; disk large and encircling the base of the style; stamens (C, $\times 6$) 8; filaments hairy; anthers prolonged into long tubes at the apex with a hole at the top; ovary (D, $\times 5$) inferior, 4-locular; style unbranched, exserted; berries about the size of red-currants but much darker in colour (family *Vacciniaceae*).

Found on moors and heaths in the northern parts of Britain and Eire, flowering in early summer; widely distributed across the northern hemisphere; in some parts valued for its edible berries. The curious specific name refers to Mount Ida, a celebrated mountain in Anatolia, Asia Minor. The dark red berries make an excellent jelly, considered to be far superior to that of red currants for eating with game or venison. In Sweden they are much used with roast meat.

The family *Vacciniaceae*, to which *Vaccinium* gives its name, is very closely related to *Ericaceae*, from which it differs mainly in the inferior ovary, i.e. the ovary is below instead of above the calyx. The family is very numerous in South America.

177   CRANBERRY
Oxycoccus quadripetalus Gilib. ($\times\frac{1}{2}$)

Tiny much-branched shrublet with very slender wiry creeping branches and very fine roots; leaves (D, $\times1\frac{1}{2}$) alternate, shortly

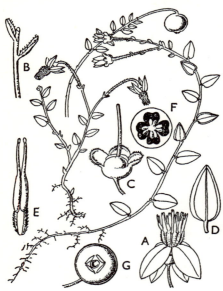

stalked, ovate, rounded at the base, about $\frac{1}{2}$ in. long, thick, shining above, paler and glaucous below, with markedly recurved margins; flowers (A, $\times1\frac{1}{2}$) solitary or often paired or up to 4 at the ends of the branchlets, on slender shortly hairy stalks about 1 in. long and bearing a pair of bracteoles (B, $\times5$) just below the middle; sepals (C, $\times1\frac{1}{2}$) 4, broader than long, fringed with very short hairs; corolla deeply divided into 4 reflexed lobes, pink, ovate-triangular; stamens (E, $\times5$) 8, erect around the slender undivided style; filaments thick, setulose on the margins; anthers with two long terminal tails and opening by holes (pores) at the top; ovary (F, $\times3$) below the calyx (inferior), 4-locular, with about 3 ovules in each loculus, ascending from the base; fruit (G, $\times2\frac{1}{2}$) globose or pear-shaped, at first pale green, soon becoming red or speckled with brown, 4-locular (synonym *Vaccinium oxycoccus* L.) (family *Vacciniaceae*).

Grows in bogs and marshes on moors, often creeping amongst Sphagnum moss, in Scotland, the English Lake District, and Wales, becoming rarer farther south; also in Eire.

Oxycoccus is usually included as a subgenus of *Vaccinium*. There are only three species, one of which, *O. microcarpus* Turcz., is found in bogs in Scotland from Perth to Inverness and widely distributed like *O. quadripetalus*; the third is *O. macrocarpus* (Ait.) Pers., which is introduced and naturalized here and there.

Rootstock perennial, decumbent, bearing long narrow chaffy scales amongst the leaf-stalks; leaves crowded towards the base of the stem, long-stalked, broadly elliptic to nearly orbicular, minutely tooth-ed on the margin, glabrous, very laxly veiny and with 4–6 pairs of divided lateral nerves; flowers in a short-stalked raceme; bracts as long as the pedicels; calyx deeply 5-lobed; petals 5, white or pale pink, quite free, rounded; stamens (A, $\times 4$) 10, not on the corolla; anthers opening by pores; ovary (B, $\times 1\frac{1}{2}$) depressed-globose, 5-locu-lar, with numerous ovules on axile placentas; style short, straight, with a 5-lobed stigma; fruit (C, D, $\times 1\frac{1}{4}$) a 5-lobed cap-

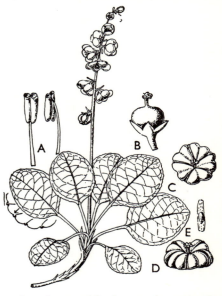

sule, opening by slits into the chambers, with the persistent style much shorter than the fruit; seeds (E, enlarged) numerous, very minute, shortly tailed at each end (family *Pyrolaceae*).

Distinguished from other species by the style, which is shorter than the corolla and much shorter than the capsule (fruit); in woods and moist shady places mostly in Scotland and northern England; rare in Eire; flowers during summer.

Some species of *Pyrola* do not secrete nectar, and this is one of them. Instead, however, the 5 stigmatic lobes exude a sticky fluid which appears to be licked by insects before they search for pollen and thereby bring about cross-pollination.

The family *Pyrolaceae* was formerly often included in *Ericaceae*, but is now generally regarded as distinct. As in *Ericaceae*, the anthers open by pores, and the pollen-grains are in tetrads. A striking feature of the fruit of *Pyrola* is that the margins of the valves are connected by web-like threads.

Pyrola rotundifolia L. ($\times\frac{1}{2}$)

Perennial herb with a very slender creeping rootstock; stems un-branched, up to 1 ft. high; leaves towards the base of the stem long-stalked, shaped like broad spoons, elliptic-or-bicular, entire or slightly toothed, 1–2 in. long and nearly as much broad, with 3–4 pairs of branch-ed lateral nerves, gla-brous; bracts narrow; flowers drooping; sepals 5, linear, about $\frac{1}{2}$ as long as the white corolla-lobes, the latter 5, greenish-white, free nearly to the base; stamens (A, ×8) 10, anthers opening by ter-minal pores; ovary (B, ×8) 5-locular, with nu-merous ovules on axile placentas; fruit (C, ×3) a 5-locular capsule, opening by slits lengthwise into the chambers, the persistent style longer than the fruit; seeds (D, ×3) numerous, minute, shortly tailed at each end (family *Pyro-laceae*).

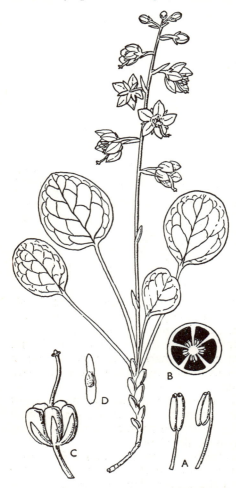

A less common species than *P. minor* L. (fig. 178), and at once distin-guished from it by the style being longer than the corolla and longer than the fruit. The flowers, though slightly scented, are devoid of nectar. The style is at first directed downwards, so that the line of fall of the pollen from the porous anthers is well in front of the stigma; later the style bends upwards, so that auto-matic pollination may take place.

Perennial herb with slender creeping rootstock; leaves in whorls of 3 or 4, stalked, rounded but very spoon-shaped together with the winged stalk, at most about $\frac{3}{4}$ in. diam., finely crenate, glabrous; flowers about $\frac{3}{4}$ in. diam., solitary, (very rarely 2) on a long stalk (up to 4 in. long), drooping, with a single elliptic bract towards the top (above the middle); sepals (A., $\times$2) 5, rounded, closely denticulate; petals 5, white, slightly united at the base, broadly obovate, veiny; stamens (B, $\times$3) 10, with large anthers, each lobe of which is broadly produced at the apex and ends in a circular pore; ovary 5-locular; style thick, with a thick deeply lobed stigma; capsule depressed-globose, opening by slits down the middle of the 5 loculi; seeds (D, $\times$12) elongated, reticulate (family *Pyrolaceae*). – Synonym *Pyrola uniflora* L.

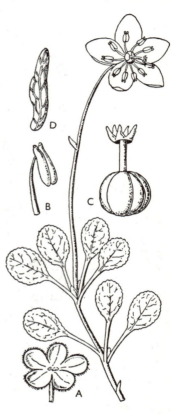

A very rare plant, in Britain found only in Scotland, flowering in June and July; circumpolar in distribution.

The family *Pyrolaceae* was formerly included in *Ericaceae*, but is now generally treated as distinct. There are about eleven genera and about forty species, all in the boreal and temperate regions of the northern hemisphere. They are herbs or low shrublets, sometimes parasitic and without chlorophyll, and are more advanced than, but clearly derived from the same stock as, the *Ericaceae*.

When the flowers of this plant are visited by insects, owing to their drooping position, they brush first against the stigma and directly afterwards against the anthers, which sprinkle the visitor with pollen and which they carry to another flower. If cross-pollination fails, however, self-pollination takes place when the flower becomes less pendant.

A saprophyte associated with mycorhiza on the roots of certain trees, chiefly beech, pines, and willows; stem simple, 6–9 in. high, covered with large slightly overlapping yellowish scales about $\frac{1}{2}$ in. long, glabrous or slightly hairy, especially in the upper parts; no proper leaves; flowers pale yellow, arranged in a terminal bracteate nodding raceme 2–3 in. long; bracts (A, ×2) boat-shaped, toothed on the margin; sepals (B, ×2) and petals in the terminal flower 5 each, in the lateral flowers only 4 of each; petals (C, ×2) erect, pouched at the base and dentate at the top; stamens (D, ×4) as many as the petals; anthers opening outwards by a transverse slit, the lower half disk-like; ovary (E, ×6) deeply 4- or 5-lobed; style as long as the ovary, lobulate; fruit (G, ×2) a capsule opening by slits lengthwise in the middle of the chambers; seeds (H, ×10) tailed at each end, reticulate (family *Monotropaceae*).

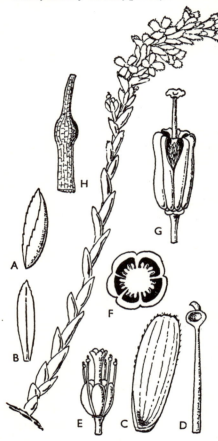

This family, represented by a single species in our flora, which is widely distributed in the north temperate zone, was formerly included in the Heath family, *Ericaceae*, to which it is no doubt related through *Pyrolaceae*. Nectar is secreted at the base of the ovary and lodged in the fleshy base of the petals, which are shallowly pouched. Insect visitors first touch the stigma, making their head or proboscis sticky with stigmatic fluid to which pollen adheres and is carried to another flower.

Densely tufted woody perennial forming small clumps; leaves thick and leathery, crowded along the short shoots and often forming rosettes, spathulate, ⅓–½ in. long, 1-nerved above, glabrous, becoming recurved; flowers single in the middle of each rosette of leaves, stalked, the stalk with 1 or 2 large bracts with thin margins and usually 3 similar bracts below the calyx; sepals (A, ×2) 5, free to the base or nearly so, greenish yellow, broadly oblong, slightly jagged across the top, about ¼ in. long; corolla (B, ×1) white, widely tubular, longer than the sepals, 5-lobed nearly to the middle, lobes rounded; stamens 5, inserted below and between the corolla-lobes; filaments wide and flat; anthers cordate, exserted; ovary (C, ×2) superior, 3-locular (D, ×3½); style stout, slightly 3-lobed; ovules numerous on axile placentas;

fruit a capsule (E, ×1¼), opening into the loculi (loculicidal); seeds (F, ×6) several, obliquely quadrangular (family *Diapensiaceae*).

Occurs in arctic and alpine subarctic regions of the northern hemisphere, but not in the mountains of central Europe; unknown in this country (except under cultivation) until July 1951, when it was discovered at about 2,500 ft. in the mountains of Inverness, Scotland, growing amongst stones and gravel, in flower in June and July.* If truly native, and so far there is no evidence to the contrary, this remarkable discovery added a family not hitherto represented in the flora of Britain.

* Students will find an account of this discovery by Blakelock (*Kew Bulletin* 1951: 325), and by Grant Roger (*Trans. & Proceed. Bot. Soc. Edinb.* 36: 34, with map and figure (1952). – Note: On no account should this plant be collected.

183   ST JOHN'S WORT
Hypericum perforatum L. ($\times \frac{2}{5}$)

Perennial with short runners and erect glabrous 2-ridged stems up to 1½ ft.; leaves opposite, sessile, ovate-oblong, 3-nerved from

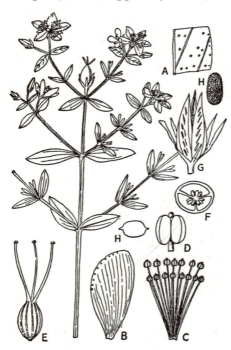

the base, entire, marked with transparent dots and sometimes a few black spots below (A, ×3); flowers in a terminal leafy cyme, the oldest flower terminating the main and lateral shoots; sepals 5, lanceolate, entire, marked with a few gland-dots or glandular lines; petals (B, ×2), twice as long as the sepals, free, many-nerved and margined with glands; stamens (C, ×2½) numerous, shortly united into 3 bundles; anthers (D, ×7) rounded, tipped by a globular gland; ovary superior (E, ×3), with 3 slender free styles, 3-locular, with numerous ovules attached to the central axis (F); fruit (G, ×2) divided into 3 segments, marked with glandular globules outside; seeds (H, ×3) finely reticulate; flowers in summer and autumn; (H, cross-section of stem showing ridges) (family *Hypericaceae*).

St John's Wort is easily recognized by the opposite, entire (not toothed) leaves, which if held up to the light show a number of small transparent dots, and by the stamens being united into bundles or phalanges as they are called. There are no stipules. There are many handsome garden plants among the numerous species of this widely spread genus. The 3 spreading styles are placed between the bundles of stamens and the anthers do not touch the stigmas, so that cross- and self-pollination depend on insect visitors.

234

Hypericum pulchrum L. ($\times\frac{1}{2}$)

Perennial with slender erect glabrous rounded stems; leaves (A, $\times 1\frac{1}{2}$) opposite, sessile, ovate, cordate at the base, rounded at the apex, $\frac{1}{2}-\frac{3}{4}$ in. long, those on the lateral shoots much smaller, with transparent glands towards the margins; flowers rather few in a loose oblong cyme, the lower stalks the longest, usually 3-flowered; sepals (B, $\times 1$) 5, obovate, fringed with sessile black glands; petals (C, $\times 1\frac{1}{2}$) yellow, narrowly obovate, about $\frac{1}{2}$ in. long, margined with sessile black glands; stamens (D, $\times 2$) shortly united into bundles; anthers red; ovary (E, $\times 2\frac{1}{2}$) glabrous, 3-locular, with 3 slender styles nearly as long as the stamens; fruit a capsule wrapped in the persistent petals; seeds (F, $\times 7$) narrowly oblong, finely pitted (family *Hypericaceae*).

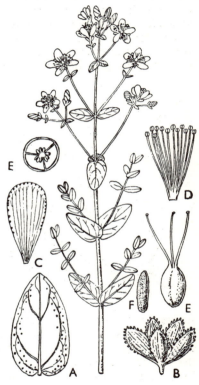

This species favours dry woods, and open heaths and waste land, flowering in summer; it is widely dispersed over Europe.

Different theories are held by botanists as to whether the bundles of stamens so common in this family are due to fusion or to branching. In most British textbooks they are described as being fused, thus implying that their ancestral types had free stamens. This view is held by the present author, because the fusion of stamens is a common tendency in many families, and he sees no reason for an exception to be made for the family *Hypericaceae*.

Hypericum humifusum L. (×½)

Low decumbent, much-branched herb, sometimes forming dense spreading tufts; rootstock perennial, but sometimes flowering in the seedling stage; stems slender, green or suffused with dull crimson, rounded and without ridges, glabrous; leaves (A, ×2) sessile, opposite, broadly elliptic, rounded at each end, pale glaucous-green, glabrous, with about 3 pairs of transparent nerves and with numerous transparent dots, besides a few black glands below along the margin; flowers in short, loose, leafy cymes; pedicels

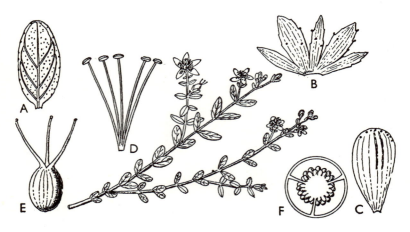

suffused with crimson; a pair of small leaf-like bracts below each flower; sepals (B, ×3) 5, shortly united at the base, unequal-sized, 2 larger than the others, all slightly toothed and with here and there a small black gland; petals (C, ×4) 5, free, rich cream-yellow, with streaks of red outside, about 5 mm. long, with a few small black glands on the margin; stamens (D, ×5) about 15, in 3 bundles; ovary (E, ×5, F, ×7) 3-locular; styles 3, between the bundles of stamens; fruit a capsule wrapped in the dry persistent petals and by the sepals (family *Hypericaceae*).

This pretty little plant grows in a variety of places, stony heaths, and bogs, fields, and waste places, sometimes on lawns; it flowers from early summer until the autumn. The flowers do not open in unfavourable weather, and automatic self-pollination then takes place.

Hypericum androsaemum L. ($\times\frac{1}{2}$)

A glabrous shrub; stems and branches pale green and often tinged with crimson, with 2 narrow wings running down between the insertion of the leaves; leaves opposite, spreading, sessile, ovate, not pointed, rounded at the base, averaging about 3 in. long and 2 in. broad, green above, paler below, the margin sometimes tinged with crimson, nerves running parallel with the margin; flowers few in terminal cymes, the middle one opening first, usually 3 on each branch; sepals in bud tinged with crimson, 5, unequal-sized, usually 2 smaller than the others, gland-dotted, not toothed; petals

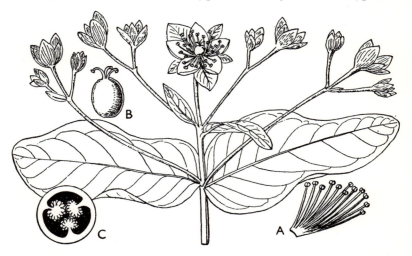

5, forming a fruit-like body in bud, at length spreading, yellow; stamens (A, $\times 1\frac{1}{2}$) numerous, united into 5 bundles; ovary (B, $\times 1\frac{1}{2}$) globose, with 3 free recurved styles; ovules numerous on 3 placentas on the walls of the ovary (C, $\times 3$); fruit a black berry, globose, partially 3-locular (family *Hypericaceae*).

Found in woodlands and hedges in the south of England and the west of Scotland, local and rather rare, flowering in summer. A useful plant for shady places in the garden.

The curious name, Tutsan, is a corruption of *toute-saine* (heal-all) and refers to the many curative properties the plant was once supposed to possess.

Hypericum maculatum Crantz (× ⅓)

Perennial herb with erect 4-angled stems (A) up to 2 ft. high; leaves opposite, sessile, elliptic, or oblong-elliptic, rounded at the base, 1–1½ in. long and up to 1 in. broad, glabrous except for a few black dots around the margin (B, ×⅔), the main nerves mostly ascending from the base; flowers numerous in a terminal leafy corymb; bracts leafy; sepals (C, ×2) 5, oblong, a little toothed towards the apex, nerved lengthwise and minutely dotted; petals (D, ×1) 5, yellow, narrowly obovate, veiny and with a few unequally long resinous lines here and there; stamens (E, ×3) numerous in 3 bundles; anthers (F, ×9) with a large black gland behind the apex; ovary (G, ×1⅓) 3-lobed, 3-locular, with 3 free styles and numerous ovules on axile placentas (H, ×2); fruit a 3-valved capsule, streaked with glandular lines (family *Hypericaceae*). Synonym *H. dubium* Leers.

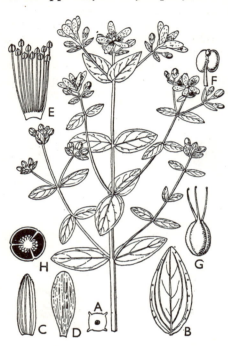

Recognized from the rather similar *H. perforatum* L. (fig. 183) by the 4-angled stems, and from *H. quadrangulum* L. by the blunter sepals; flowers in summer and autumn.

Generally spread over England, southern Scotland, and Eire, but not so common as *H. perforatum*.

Hypericum is the ancient Greek name of obscure meaning. There are over two hundred species, mostly in temperate and subtropical regions of the northern hemisphere. All have opposite or whorled leaves without stipules, and often dotted with transparent glands; a feature of the flowers are the stamens united at the base into bundles.

Erect, narrowly branched perennial herb up to about 2 ft. high, softly hairy all over, especially the stems, the latter not angular;

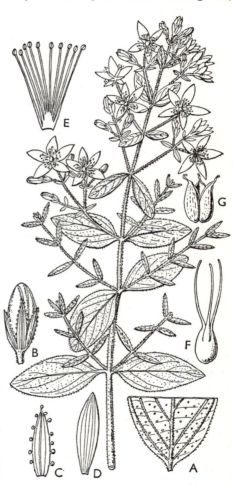

leaves (A, ×1) opposite, sessile or nearly so, connected by a crimson line at the base across the stem, ovate-lanceolate, rounded at the apex, the largest about 2 in. long and 1 in. broad, very shortly and thinly hairy on both surfaces, with a few ascending nerves, gland-dotted (glands seen best if held up to a bright light); flowers in a leafy terminal panicle; bracts and the 5 sepals similar and margined with large black glands (B, ×2), the sepals (C, ×1½) ribbed; petals (D, ×1) 5, pale yellow, more than twice as long as the sepals; stamens (E, ×4) in bundles of about 10 each; ovary (F, ×2½) glabrous; styles 3, slender; fruit (G, ×2) splitting into 3 parts; seeds numerous, very small (family *Hypericaceae*).

Flowers in summer in woods, and is locally abundant; distributed from Europe to western Asia.

Hypericum elodes L. ($\times \frac{1}{2}$)

Aquatic or semi-aquatic perennial herb with often unbranched leafy shoots up to about 1 ft. long; stems softly pubescent; leaves

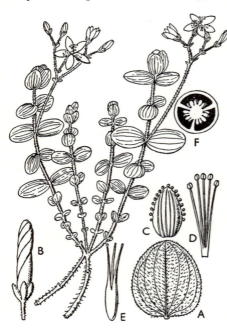

(A, $\times 1$) opposite, gradually increasing in size upwards, sessile, rounded, or broadly elliptic, entire, averaging about 1 in. diam., about 7-nerved from the base, softly pubescent on both surfaces; flowers few, arranged in an axillary cyme towards the top of the shoots, the petals spirally twisted in bud (B, $\times 2$); bracts small, margined with glandular teeth; sepals (C, $\times 3$) 5, narrowly ovate, margined with shortly stalked glands; petals 5, yellow, nearly 3 times as long as the sepals, finely nerved; stamens (D, $\times 4$) united into 3 separate bundles; ovary (E, $\times 4$) 3-locular, with 3 free styles and numerous ovules on axile placents (F, $\times 10$) (family *Hypericaceae*).

Flowers in summer in bogs, ditches, and pools on wet moors; locally common; widely distributed in Europe. The flowers have a very strong and disagreeable odour, especially noticeable in hot weather.

The species is easily recognized by the shaggy downy hairs on the stem and leaves, and from the fact that it grows in swampy places.

The base of the yellow petals bears a split scale which probably secretes nectar, and above these scales, between the bundles of stamens, there are small tongue-like bifid glands, probably modified stamens, which may also secrete nectar. In the bud stage the petals are spirally twisted, as shown in fig. B.

Ilex aquifolium L. ($\times \frac{2}{5}$)

An erect much-branched evergreen tree or large bush; stem smooth, dark green; leaves alternate, shortly stalked, ovate or elliptic in outline, but often rather deeply lobed, the lobes ending in a sharp prickle, often the upper leaves of a tree quite entire, leathery in texture and dark green; flowers (A, $\times 1\frac{1}{2}$) in small axillary clusters, shortly stalked, sometimes unisexual; calyx of small short lobes; petals white, obovate, united at the base into a very short tube (B, $\times 1\frac{1}{2}$); stamens as many as the petals and inserted between them on the inside of the tube; no disk; ovary 4-locular, with one pendulous ovule in each division;

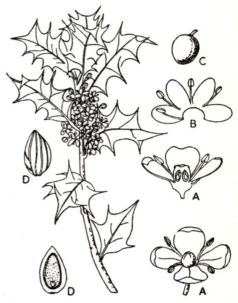

stigmas 4, forming a disk-like plate on the top of the ovary; fruit (C, $\times \frac{4}{5}$) a red berry enclosing 4 little stones each containing a seed (C, $\times 2\frac{1}{2}$) (family *Aquifoliaceae*).

The common Holly should be the least troublesome tree to identify, as it is so well known in connexion with Christmas festivities. Few people, however, are familiar with the flowers, which are produced in spring. The wood of the holly is very hard and is the lightest in colour of our native timbers. It is therefore valuable in marquetry work. Bird-lime may also be made from holly bark. Holly is much used as a hedge plant for it bears cutting extremely well, and there are many beautiful holly hedges in Britain. I have myself found the branches very effective in removing soot from the chimneys of my bungalow. The well-known Maté or Paraguay tea is obtained from a South American species of this genus, *Ilex paraguensis* St Hil.

CROWBERRY
Empetrum nigrum L. ($\times \frac{1}{2}$)

A low decumbent much-branched shrublet; older branches rough with the persistent bases of the leaves; leaves (A, $\times 3$) crowded on

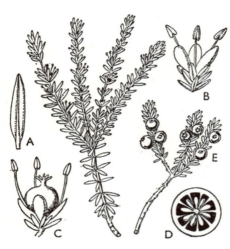

the shoots, evergreen, thick, scarcely $\frac{1}{4}$ in. long, flat on top, the edges rolled back and exposing only the midrib below; flowers (B, C, $\times 3$) polygamous, axillary, sessile; sepals 3, free, narrowly oblong; petals 3, free, oblong-obovate, glabrous; stamens 3–4, alternate with the petals; anthers extrorse; ovary superior, globose, 3–9-locular (D, $\times 5$); stigmas 6 or more, radiating; ovule solitary in each loculus, erect; fruit (E, $\times \frac{1}{2}$) a small black berry-like drupe, containing several 1-seeded stones; seeds with a narrow embryo and copious endosperm (family *Empetraceae*).

Common on mountain heaths and in bogs, especially in northern Britain; generally distributed in the colder parts of the northern hemisphere.

The genus is characterized by its heather-like (ericoid) habit and by its rolled leaves, which show a deep furrow on the lower surface. The margins are rolled back so closely that they nearly touch, and they are locked together by numerous hairs. The actual lower surface of the leaf is thus quite hidden and is clothed with glandular hairs.

The flowers of this species have as a rule been described as *polygamous*, i.e. bisexual and unisexual flowers on the same or on different individuals of the same species. There are many such plants scattered through several families in different parts of the world which have this characteristic. J. Lange in 1880 called the plants with purely bisexual flowers *E. nigrum* forma *hermaphrodita*. This seemed sufficient, but Hagerup in 1926 raised this form to specific rank and called it *E. hermaphroditum*, and he has been followed in the latest *Flora*.

A shrub up to about 6 ft. high, much branched, with short twiggy branchlets; leaves deciduous, opposite, rather small at flowering time, but increasing in fruit to about 3 in. long and $1\frac{1}{2}$ in. broad, elliptic, acutely and gradually pointed, closely but obscurely toothed (crenulate), glabrous, lateral nerves about 7–8 pairs, looped and branched within the margin; flowers in little axillary cymes, about 3 flowers on each common stalk, the middle flower (B, × $1\frac{1}{4}$) opening first, yellowish green; sepals 4, green, rounded;

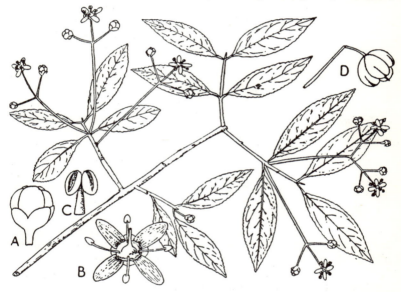

petals 4, oblong, overlapping in bud (A, ×2); stamens (C, ×3) 4, inserted on a thick disk; anthers facing outwards; ovary hidden in the disk, with a short undivided style; fruits (D, × $\frac{1}{2}$) usually 4-lobed, red to pink, opening into the lobes, the seeds covered by a yellow fleshy aril (family *Celastraceae*).

The Spindle Tree is poisonous in all its parts. The wood is hard and used for making butchers' skewers, and it makes excellent artists' charcoal. In addition to the flowers shown, unisexual ones also occur, with vestiges of the opposite sex. Cross-pollination is effected by insects, the anthers, which face outwards, opening before the stigmas are receptive. Nectar is secreted in the fleshy disk surrounding the base of the style.

Shrublet parasitic on various trees; stems woody, repeatedly forked like a catapult, very brittle and easily broken at the joints; leaves

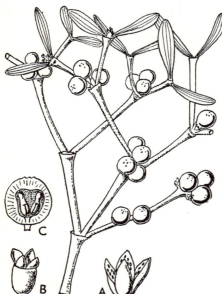

opposite, rather obliquely oblanceolate, rounded at the apex, narrowed to the base, about 1½–2 in. long, and up to 1 in. broad, thick, 3–5-nerved lengthwise; flowers very small and inconspicuous, unisexual, the males (A, ×3) on one plant, the females (B, ×3) on another (dioecious), almost sessile in the forks of the branches; males few together in a cup-shaped fleshy bract; calyx not evident; petals 4, each with an anther attached to its face, the anthers opening by several small pores; female flowers with the calyx united to the ovary and not apparent; petals very small; stigma sessile; fruit (C, ×1) a white semi-transparent globose berry containing a single seed (family *Loranthaceae*).

Common in southern and western England but becoming rare further north; fruits ripe at Christmas; widely distributed into Asia.

Clusters of Mistletoe, with their forked branches, pale yellow green leaves and clear white berries may often be observed in winter-time perched on deciduous trees, especially in the southern counties of England, often on Poplar and Lime trees. The small yellow flowers appear from March to May. At no time in its life is the Mistletoe nourished by the soil, but derives all its food from the tree on which it grows. It is therefore truly parasitic and not just epiphytic.

Thesium humifusum DC. ($\times\frac{1}{2}$)

A perennial herb with a woody rootstock; stems annual, procumbent or ascending, ribbed, glabrous, up to 1 ft. long; leaves alternate, linear, 1-nerved, up to 1 in. long, glabrous; flowers (A, $\times5$) small, in terminal sometimes 1-sided racemes; stalks about $\frac{1}{4}$ in. long, with 3 leaf-like bracts at the top; calyx above the ovary (superior), of 5 ovate-triangular greenish-yellow sepals not overlapping in bud, each with a pair of inflexed lobes towards the base; no petals; stamens 5, opposite the sepals; ovary inferior (below the calyx), 1-locular, with 2 pendulous ovules on a long basal placenta (B, $\times6$); fruit (C, $\times4$) a small green nut crowned by the calyx, reticulately nerved; seed (D, $\times3$) solitary (family *Santalaceae*).

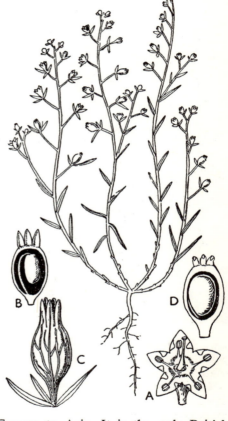

Found in chalky meadows and pastures in the southern counties of England, growing on the roots of various other plants and not easy to detect; flowers all the summer; widely distributed from Europe to Asia. It is the only British representative of an otherwise mostly tropical and subtropical family, very abundant in southern Africa.

This plant bears a great superficial resemblance to *Scleranthus*, a genus belonging to the family *Illecebraceae*. In the latter, however, the leaves are opposite and the ovary is free from the calyx.

Frangula alnus Mill. ($\times \frac{2}{5}$)

A shrub; branches alternate, without thorns, hairy when young; winter buds not covered with scales; leaves broadly elliptic to obovate, rounded at the base triangular at the apex, $1\frac{1}{2}$–2 in. long, entire, glabrous above, pubescent on the nerves below when young, lateral nerves about 7 pairs, fine, looped within the margin and with fine cross nerves; stipules soon falling off; flowers (B, $\times 1\frac{1}{2}$) bisexual, several in each leaf-axil; stalks hairy; buds (A) angular; sepals 5, united in the lower half, ovate, valvate in bud; petals 5, small and narrow, embracing the 5 stamens, one opposite each petal; anthers 2-locular, facing and curved inwards; ovary (C, $\times 2$) in the base of the calyx and surrounded by nectar, 3-locular; style undivided; fruit (D, $\times 1\frac{1}{2}$) globose, black when ripe, about $\frac{1}{4}$ in. diam. (synonym *Rhamnus frangula* L.) (family *Rhamnaceae*).

Compared with the drawing of *Rhamnus cathartica* L., shown in fig. 196, it will be seen that the species described above differs in having bisexual flowers, with 5 sepals, 5 petals, and 5 stamens. On account of these differences the Alder Buckthorn is now often referred to a separate genus, *Frangula*.

The anthers are ripe before the stigma of the same flower is receptive, so that cross-pollination is effected when insects visit to suck the nectar, which is secreted within the base of the calyx and around the ovary.

Rhamnus cathartica L. (male flowering shoot, $\times \frac{2}{5}$)

Shrub with numerous spreading branches, the branchlets often ending in a short stiff thorn; leaves deciduous, elliptic or ovate-elliptic, increasing in size when the fruits develop (A, $\times \frac{4}{5}$), pubescent on the nerves below to glabrous or nearly so, shortly toothed (serrulate) on the margin; flowers green, unisexual, dioecious, borne in clusters at the base of the young shoots, the males (B, $\times 2\frac{1}{2}$) on slender stalks (pedicels); sepals 4, united into a tube at the base, lanceolate, 3-nerved; petals (C, $\times 3\frac{1}{2}$) 4, very

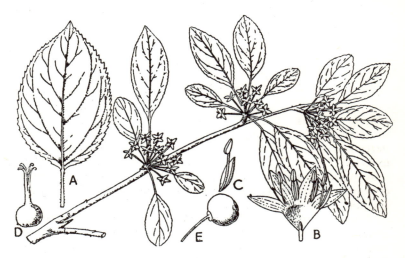

small and narrow, inserted at the mouth of the calyx-tube, each with a stamen opposite; stamens longer than the petals; anthers facing inwards (introrse); rudimentary ovary at the base of the calyx-tube; female flowers with rudiments of stamens and smaller petals; ovary (D, $\times 3$), with a 3–4-lobed style and 1 erect ovule in each loculus; fruit (E, $\times \frac{4}{5}$) black, about the size of a pea (family *Rhamnaceae*).

Owing to the two sexes being separate, cross-pollination by insects is essential; the fact that each sex possesses rudiments of the other shows that the ancestral stock of this species had bisexual flowers, as are found in the related genus *Frangula* (fig. 195). The wood makes excellent gunpowder and charcoal, and the berries, which are poisonous, produce sap green for water colours.

Hippophaë rhamnoides L. ($\times\frac{1}{3}$)

A shrub or small tree rather like a willow but covered all over with silvery scales (lepidote); axillary shoots mostly ending in a stout

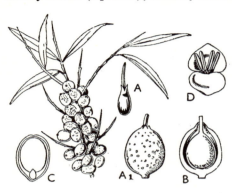

spine; leaves alternate, linear or linear-lanceolate, entire, glabrous or thinly scaly above, densely so below; flowers dioecious (male and female on separate plants), the males (D, ×2) in axillary clusters resembling catkins, the female (A, ×2) solitary; male flowers very small, consisting of a calyx of 2 small segments and 4 stamens with oblong anthers; female flowers crowded, the tubular calyx minutely 2-lobed at the top becoming juicy, brown or yellow, berry-like (A$_1$, ×2) around the true fruit (B, ×2); style short, exserted (family *Elaeagnaceae*). – C, vertical section of seed, ×3.

A maritime plant confined to the coasts of some of the eastern counties, flowering in spring; extends into Russian Asia and in Europe as far north as the Baltic.

When growing wild on sea cliffs and sand hills, this species is usually a small thorny-branched shrub. But when cultivated it sometimes becomes a tree with a thick woody trunk up to 20 ft. high with numerous irregular branches.

Most members of the *Elaeagnus* family, to which the Sea-Buckthorn belongs, are clothed with peltate and star-shaped hairs. The peltate hairs consist of a large number of narrow ray-cells spreading from a central core or shield.

The roots of the Sea-Buckthorn are long and straggling and assist in binding the loose sea-sand in which it flourishes. The leaves resemble those of some willows and are silvery white which makes the bush very ornamental. Though the flowers are small and inconspicuous the fruits are of a bright orange colour when ripe and remain on the bush most of the winter. In parts of Europe they are used to make jelly, though in some districts they are considered to be poisonous.

Acer campestre L. ($\times \frac{2}{5}$)

Tree with a rounded head with dense dark green foliage, often in hedges and then sometimes bushy; leaves opposite, the base of the stalks meeting around the branchlets; stalk slender; blade cordate at the base, divided nearly to the middle into 5 (rarely 3 or 7) lobes, lobes entire or slightly lobulate, pubescent beneath especially at the base of the radiating main nerves; flowers in cymes terminating short lateral branchlets, greenish, the lateral male (A, ×2), the terminal flower female (B, ×2); sepals usually 5, narrow, and not very different from the petals and inserted around a fleshy ring-

like disk; stamens about 8, inserted within the disk which is covered with minute drops of nectar; ovary rudimentary in the male flower, spreading within the disk in the female and 2-locular; styles 2, divergent; fruit (C, ×$\frac{3}{5}$) separated when ripe into 2 parts, spreading horizontally, each produced into a large veiny thin wing ('key'); seeds 1 or 2 in each part; found wild as far north as the Tyne, extending in Europe eastwards as far as the Caucasus; the wood is beautifully marked and, when available, is employed for furniture and veneers, and turned into bowls, cups, etc.; a second species, *A. pseudo-platanus* L., the Sycamore or Plane Tree (fig. 199), is introduced, and reaches a height of about 100 ft., has more toothed leaf-segments, slender pendulous racemes, and the 'keys' of the fruit are less spreading; the timber is valuable (D, cross-section of ovary, ×4) (family *Aceraceae*).

Acer pseudoplatanus L. ($\times\frac{1}{2}$)

A tree with a thick stem up to 100 ft. high and 20 ft. in circumference; bark fissuring and scaling off in large strips from old trunks; leaves opposite, 5-lobed, with as many nerves radiating from the base, lobes toothed on the margins; no stipules; flowers (A, $\times 2$) small in loose oblong pendulous racemes; sepals 5, overlapping in bud; petals 5, as long as the sepals; stamens (B, $\times 2$) about 8, inserted on a large fleshy disk below the ovary; anthers rounded; ovary (C, $\times 2$) with 2 lateral humps, 2-locular, each loculus with 2 ovules suspended from the inner angles; style 2-lobed, lobes spreading; carpels (D, $\times 1$) winged, the two wings more or less forming a right angle and separating when ripe into two parts ('keys'); seeds 1 or 2 in each carpel, without endosperm (family *Aceraceae*).

Not a native tree but extensively planted and an often conspicuous feature of the landscape; grows wild from the Pyrenees east to the Caspian Sea. The wood is light in colour and moderately hard, and the timber is valuable, especially as a veneer. It has been used for making large rollers for cotton-dyeing and washing machines, dairy utensils, mangles, brushes, toys and turnery, and for bobbins and many other articles. It reaches its greatest size in the more hilly parts of England and Scotland, and is not affected by frost.

· It is often found in hedges and frequently planted near houses, affording during summer a broad and pleasant shade with its spreading leafy boughs; gales usually leave it unharmed, even near the sea.

The tree is very attractive when in young leaf in early spring with the green foliage emerging from the small pink scales which have protected them during the winter. In autumn the reddish winged seed-vessels and the fading leaves give colour to many a landscape.

In a wild state the Sycamore is remarkably constant in foliage, only one well-marked geographical form being known, var. *villosa*, with leaves pubescent all over the lower surface and the fruits more or less densely hairy with broader wings. Elwes and Henry, authors of those great books, *The Trees of Great Britain and Ireland*, describe no less than 19 varieties which occur in cultivation.

In some parts of Britain this tree attains a very great size, some over 100 ft. high and as much as $17\frac{1}{2}$ ft. in girth, with a clear bole of some 30 ft.

A C B

D

251

Ligustrum vulgare L. ($\times \frac{1}{2}$)

A much-branched shrub with slender whip-like branchlets; leaves opposite or nearly so, shortly stalked, lanceolate to oblong-elliptic, rounded or tapered to an acute point, more or less acute at the base, entire, glabrous and with very obscure nerves; no stipules; flowers (A, $\times 2$) scented, crowded in pyramidal panicles at the ends of the branchlets; lower bracts somewhat leafy, upper small and awl-shaped (subulate); calyx cupular, minutely toothed;

corolla white, shortly tubular with 4 or rarely 5 obovate lobes; stamens (B, $\times 3$) 2 or rarely 3, inserted in the corolla-tube but protruding from it; ovary (C, $\times 3$) superior, 2-locular, with 2 pendulous ovules (D, $\times 5$) in each loculus; style undivided, with an oblong stigma; fruit a purple-black globose berry (E, $\times \frac{2}{3}$) about $\frac{1}{3}$ in. diam., 2-locular, loculi 1–2-seeded (family *Oleaceae*).

Grows in hedges and woods, especially on chalk downs, extending into western Asia, often employed as a hedge.

Nectar is secreted by the ovary and stored in the base of the corolla-tube.

Fraxinus excelsior L. ($\times \frac{2}{5}$)

A tall handsome tree with elegant deciduous foliage; branches opposite; leaves opposite, pinnate, with 3–5 pairs of opposite leaflets, these lanceolate or ovate-lanceolate, acute or pointed, toothed (serrate), and with an odd terminal leaflet rather larger than the others; no stipules; flowers bisexual or unisexual, opening in spring before the leaves, arranged in opposite clusters (A, $\times \frac{2}{5}$) in the axils of the leaves fallen from the previous year's shoot; clusters surrounded by a few woolly scales; flower ⸗ stalks very short but elongating in fruit; no sepals and no petals; male flowers (C, $\times 3$) with 2 stamens; anthers elliptic; ovary 2-locular, with a short thick style and 2-lobed stigma and often with 2 abortive stamens; fruit (D, $\times \frac{4}{5}$) a capsule produced at the top into a wing, in all about $1\frac{1}{2}$ in. long (E, vertical section of seed, $\times 2$) (family *Oleaceae*).

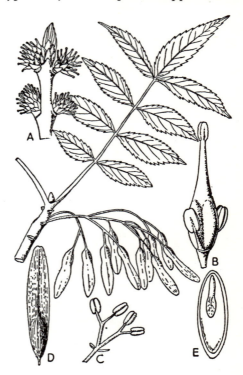

The flowers of the common Ash are pollinated by the wind and the large fleshy stigmas mature a few days before the anthers. The pollen is mealy and freely blows about. The wood of the Ash is a valuable, very tough timber, and used for many purposes. The branches, when split and steamed, are easily bent into various shapes and are employed in conjunction with willow, etc., for making the handles and framework of trug-baskets for the garden and farm. The Olive, *Olea europa* L., from which Olive oil is obtained, belongs to this family, as also the Lilac (*Syringa*).

Perennial with creeping rootstock and trailing glabrous shoots rooting at the lower nodes; leaves opposite, stalked, the stalks

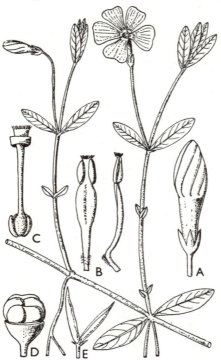

connected at the base by a rim, ovate or ovate-elliptic, rounded at the base and apex, with 5–6 pairs of spreading looped nerves less prominent below, glabrous and shining; stalks flattened above and minutely hairy on the margins; flowers about 1 to each shoot, axillary; stalks 1 in. or more long; calyx (A, $\times 1\frac{1}{2}$) deeply 5-lobed, lobes not overlapping, oblong; corolla blue, tubular, limb about $1\frac{1}{4}$ in. diam., divided into 5 obliquely obovate lobes with a narrow rim at the base, the lobes (A, $\times 1\frac{1}{2}$) twisted to the left in bud, the tube inside behind the stamens covered with downwardly directed white hairs; stamens (B, $\times 3$) 5, on the corolla, and alternate with the lobes; anthers with hairy tips, and 2 separate loculi; ovary (D, $\times 3$) laterally 2-lobed; style (C, $\times 3$) widened at the top into a broad rim, crowned by a dense tuft of white hairs; fruit (E, $\times 1$) composed of two divergent parts (family *Apocynaceae*).

The 'Periwinkle' is of strong sentimental interest to the writer, and was one of the earliest of which he learned both the common and Latin names. It rhymed with that favourite 'bedtime story' in the peaceful days of Queen Victoria, which was chanted into the ears of children by devoted mothers; 'Twinkle, twinkle, little star'! If for no other reason, then, it finds a place in this book.

Note: the corolla-lobes are twisted to the left and not to the right as shown in fig. A.

Asperula odorata L. ($\times\frac{4}{5}$)

Perennial with a slender creeping rootstock growing mainly among dead leaves under the shade of trees; stems erect, unbranched, angular, smooth; leaves in whorls of 8 (rarely fewer or more, composed of indistinguishable leaves and leafy stipules), oblanceolate, up to about $1\frac{1}{2}$ in. long, mucronate at the apex, a few very short stiff hairs on the margin and below; below the whorls a ring of very minute bristles; flowers (A, $\times 3\frac{1}{2}$) in a terminal loose cyme, white; calyx very minute, above the inferior ovary (B, $\times 6$); corolla soon falling off, 4-lobed, about $\frac{1}{4}$ in. long; stamens 4, alternate with lobes; fruit (C, $\times 3$) globular, covered with fine hooked bristles (family *Rubiaceae*).

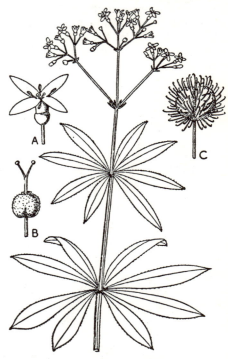

The whole plant has a sweet hay-like scent; not likely to be confused with *A. cynanchica* L., which grows in dry pastures, warm banks, and stony or sandy places, and which has only 2 or 4 much narrower leaves to each whorl, and smooth fruits. The Woodruff is intolerant of strong light and dies out immediately the tree-canopy is removed.

The abundant nectar is concealed at the bottom of the corolla-tube and insects searching for it brush against the anthers above the entrance, transferring pollen from one flower to the stigmas of another. As in Cleavers (fig. 208), the fruits readily adhere to the fur or skin of animals and are transported from place to place. Even considerable parts of the plants may be dragged by means of the rough margins of the leaves.

FIELD MADDER

Sherardia arvensis L. ($\times\frac{1}{2}$)

A small annual, very much branched from the base; branches bristly with stiff short hairs; leaves usually 6 in a whorl, sessile, lanceolate, entire, acute, shortly bristly on both surfaces, especially on the nerves below and on the margin; flowers (D, ×4) in a cluster (B, ×2) at the end of the shoots and surrounded by an involucre (A, ×1) composed of the upper leaves more or less united at the base; calyx shortly 4-lobed, adnate to the ovary,

the lobes becoming more distinct in fruit; corolla violet or pink, on top of the ovary, tubular, 4-lobed, lobes valvate in bud (C, × 4); stamens 4, exserted, inserted between the base of the lobes; ovary inferior; style surrounded by a fleshy disk; fruit (E, vertical section) crowned by the leafy calyx-lobes (family *Rubiaceae*).

This is a typical cornfield weed, and is seldom found elsewhere. The flowers are gynodioecious, the bisexual being somewhat larger than the females. In the former the stigmas are often receptive at the same time as the anthers open at the same level, when automatic self-pollination takes place. The nectar is secreted by a fleshy disk surrounding the base of the style.

Galium uliginosum L. (×½)

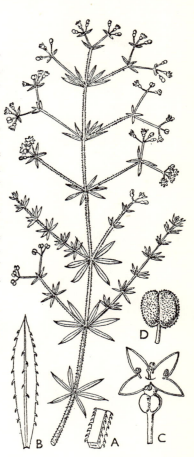

Perennial herb with very slender quadrangular stems and branches loosely covered with minute recurved prickles (A); leaves (B, ×4) 6–8 in a whorl, narrowly oblanceolate, acute, about ½ in. long, with a prominent midrib and small recurved prickles on the margin; flowers (C, ×3½) few in small axillary cymes; ovary inferior, 2-lobed; calyx obsolete; corolla white, 4-lobed, with a very short tube; lobes triangular; stamens 4, alternate with the lobes; style with 2 rounded stigmas; fruit (D, ×4) 2-lobed, finely granular all over the surface (family *Rubiaceae*).

To be looked for in marshes, where it is locally common; widely distributed in north and central Europe and Asia; flowers in summer.

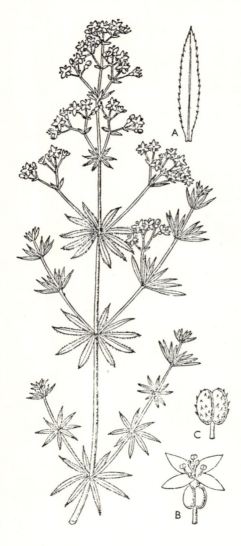

Perennial herb with erect or suberect (not trailing) stems, usually quite smooth; leaves (A, ×2) in distant whorls of 6–9, broadly linear to narrowly oblong, about $\frac{3}{4}$–1 in. long, sharply pointed and with very small forwardly directed teeth on the margin; midrib without teeth; flowers (B, ×2½) in short axillary cymes, these forming narrow oblong panicles with whorled leaves gradually reduced in size; ovary inferior, 2-locular; styles 2, united at the base; calyx obsolete; corolla with a very short tube and 4 spreading ovate triangular lobes; stamens 4, exserted; fruit (C, ×2) 2-lobed, with very few prickles (family *Rubiaceae*).

Grows in pastures and in waste places, widely distributed in western Asia and north Africa.

Perennial; stems up to about 4 ft. high, erect or trailing, obtusely 4-angled, smooth or rather softly hairy; leaves usually 8 in a whorl (half really stipules), narrowly oblanceolate, rounded to a very sharp tip, minutely bristly on the margin, otherwise glabrous; flowers numerous in leafy cymes, the ultimate branches of the cymes bearing 1 or a pair of leafy bracts; pedicels about as long as the bract; calyx reduced to a mere line on top of the ovary; corolla white, 4-lobed, lobes spreading from the base, ovate-lanceolate, acute; stamens 4, inserted between the corolla lobes; a nectariferous ring around the base of the two styles, these with rounded stigmas; fruit small and smooth or nearly so (family *Rubiaceae*).

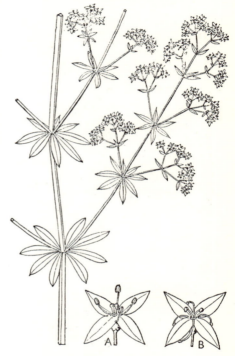

Unlike the Cleavers or Goosegrass, *Galium aparine* L., described in fig. 208, this is a perennial, and the stems are not, as in that species, provided by hook-like hairs. It grows in hedges and woods, and has a wide range into western Asia.

The anthers are mature before the stigmas are receptive. At first the stamens are erect, while the 2 head-like stigmas are close together, as shown in fig. A ($\times 3$). After the anthers have shed their pollen, the filaments bend away between the lobes of the corolla, as shown in fig. B ($\times 3$), when the styles diverge into the position previously held by the anthers. Thus cross-pollination is easily brought about by visiting insects.

A slender scrambling annual several feet long, clinging to bushes and hedges by means of short recurved hook-like hairs on the

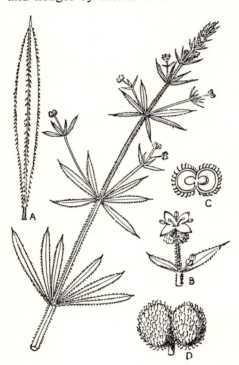

angles of the stems, the margins and midrib of the leaves; leaves (A, $\times \frac{4}{5}$) and stipules 6–8 in a whorl, indistinguishable from one another, linear or linear-oblanceolate, tapered to the base, up to 2 in. or so long, ending in a long slender sharp point, midrib and margins covered with short, sharp hard recurved prickle-like hairs; flowers (B, $\times 1\frac{1}{4}$) very small, borne in small leafy clusters (cymes) in the axils of the upper leaves, soon developing into fruit; calyx completely reduced; corolla very short, with 4 spreading lobes which do not overlap in bud; stamens 4, inserted between the corolla-lobes, anthers small, on rather short filaments; ovary inferior, 2-locular and 2-lobed, covered with hooked hairs, each lobe (C, $\times 2\frac{1}{2}$) with a single ovule attached to the central axis; styles 2, free to the base, each with a single rounded stigma; fruits (D, $\times 2$) divided into 2 rounded lobes, each densely covered with hooked bristly hairs; seeds solitary in each half.

The common name Cleavers alludes to the persistence with which the plant clings by means of the small hook-like hairs on the stems and leaves and bristly fruits. The family *Rubiaceae*, to which this plant belongs, is mainly found in tropical regions; it includes the quinine-producing *Cinchona*, and the Coffee plant.

Galium verum L. ($\times \frac{4}{5}$)

Rootstock woody, short and creeping; stems slender, ascending, often much branched from the base, up to about 15 in. high, covered with minute reflexed hairs; leaves in whorls of 6 to 8 (half of them stipules and half leaves, but these indistinguishable), linear or needle-like, acute, with recurved slightly rough margins, often with a short leafy shoot in their axils; flowers (A, ×5) numerous in an oblong panicle, each cluster in the axils of a whorl of small leaves, and each ultimate cluster has a whorl of small leafy bracts; flower-stalks smooth; calyx very minute on top of the inferior ovary; corolla yellow, 4-lobed, the lobes spreading from the extremely short tube; stamens 4, inserted between the corolla-lobes; anthers oblong; at the mouth of the tube 2 fleshy disk-like bodies; ovary inferior, 2-lobed and 2-locular, with 1 ovule in each lobe; style with 2 branches and a head-like stigma to each; fruits (B, × 10) slightly 2-lobed, smooth (family *Rubiaceae*).

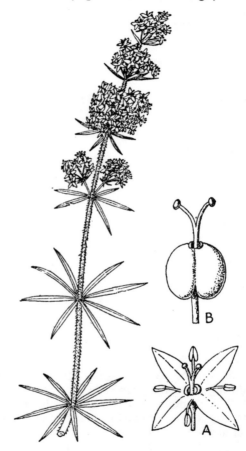

This species flowers more or less the whole summer in clumps on banks, dunes, and pastures; the flowers smell strongly of cumarin and pollination is brought about mainly by the feet of insects crawling among the flowers.

Perennial with weak stems slightly rough on the angles; leaves (including the similar stipules) often 6 in a whorl, sometimes 4,

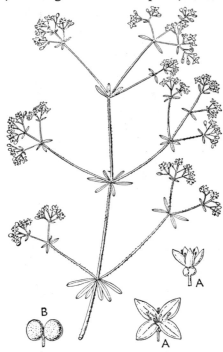

narrowly oblanceolate, narrowed to the base, blunt at the apex, about ¾ in. long, glabrous except the slightly rough margins, 1-nerved; flowers (A, ×5) in lax leafy straggly panicles, each final cluster with a pair of leafy bracts at the base; stalks thread-like; ovary below the corolla (inferior), 2-locular; calyx completely reduced (really encircling the ovary); corolla white, very short, 4-lobed, lobes ovate, not overlapping in bud; stamens 4, alternate with the lobes; styles 2, with a rounded stigma; fruit (B, ×2) deeply 2-lobed, lobes rounded, almost smooth (family *Rubiaceae*).

As implied by the specific name, this plant usually grows in marshy and wet places, sometimes quite in the water; it flowers during the summer months.

The student who has seen only the British examples of the family *Rubiaceae* can have only a very imperfect idea of the family as a whole. Among many others it includes the *Gardenia*, the Coffee plant, Ipecacuanha, and the Quinine tree (*Cinchona*). All the British genera belong to the tribe *Galieae*, distinguished from the others by the stipules being leaf-like and not distinct from the true leaves. The leaves of *Rubiaceae* are never lobed, not even toothed, and the stipules are between (inter-) or within (intra-) the leaf-stalks.

Galium cruciata (L.) Scop. ($\times\frac{1}{2}$)

Perennial with creeping rootstock; stems weak and slender, up to 2 ft. long, trailing, quadrangular, angles rounded, loosely covered with long bristly white hairs, green but tinged with crimson just above the leaves; leaves (A, ×1) in whorls of 4, 2 being real leaves and 2 leafy stipules exactly similar, elliptic-lanceolate, narrowed to the base, not pointed, 3-nerved from the base, bristly hairy on both surfaces; flowers (B, ×2) few in a 3-forked cluster from each real leaf with 2 or 3 leafy erect bracts on the top side at the base of the flower-stalks, the outer flowers bisexual (C, ×4), the inner male (D, ×4); calyx not evident; corolla yellow, of 4 petals united at the base, spreading; stamens 4, between the corolla-lobes; ovary below the corolla (inferior),

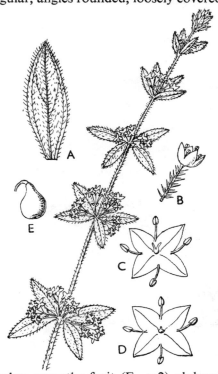

with a 2-lobed style, 2-locular, smooth; fruit (E, ×2) globose, the stalk soon deflexed (family *Rubiaceae*).

Grows in woods and hedges, but rare in Eire; extends to Siberia. It is not easy to explain in simple words the rather complicated and quite fascinating morphology of this species. For botanical examination purposes it is as well to know that only 2 of the leaves in each whorl are real, the others being leafy stipules resembling them in every respect except that they have no buds in their axils such as the real leaves have. And the flowers are of 2 sexes, the outer being bisexual and producing the fruit, which is soon deflexed, the inner males and soon falling off. They smell like honey, and are pollinated mainly by means of the feet of insect visitors crawling about amongst them.

MADDER
Rubia peregrina L. (×⅓)

A straggling perennial herb often trailing over other bushes and hedges, armed on the angles of the stems and leaf-margins with

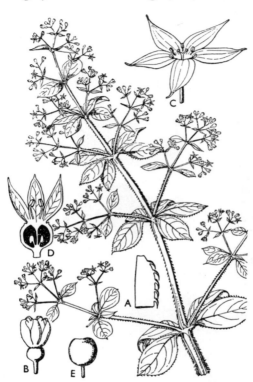

very sharp recurved teeth (A, ×3); stems sharply angled or almost winged; leaves (including precisely similar stipules) 4 or 6 in a whorl, very shortly stalked, lanceolate to elliptic, narrowed to each end, 1–2 in. long and about ½ as much broad, with numerous recurved teeth on the margins and midrib, not visibly nerved below; flowers (C, ×5) greenish, numerous, small, in loose axillary cymes with very small awl-shaped bracts; calyx (B, ×5) completely reduced; corolla usually 5-lobed, the lobes much longer than the very short tube, sharply pointed, the points inflexed in bud (B, ×5); stamens 5, inserted on the corolla and exserted; ovary inferior, 2-locular (D, ×4); style 2-armed; ovule 1 in each loculus, erect; fruit (E, ×1) a small black slightly 2-lobed berry (family *Rubiaceae*).

Flowers during summer and confined to the southern counties of England, Wales, and Eire, mostly near the coast; south to north Africa. A particularly interesting feature is that the leaves and stipules are indistinguishable from each other, except that the leaves may have a bud or an inflorescence in their axils. – Drawn by Olive Tait.

Verbena officinalis L. ($\times\frac{1}{2}$)

Perennial with a woody rootstock; stems 4-angled, sparingly clothed with very short bulbous-based hairs; leaves opposite, connected at the base by a slight ridge, oblanceolate in outline but deeply pinnately lobed and coarsely toothed, shortly hairy on both surfaces and with almost sessile glands; flowers (A, $\times 2\frac{1}{2}$) arranged in axillary and terminal glandular spikes; bracts lanceolate, pointed; calyx with 5 narrow lobes, pubescent; corolla (B, $\times 3\frac{1}{2}$) pale violet, tube slightly wider above the middle, with white hairs at the mouth; lobes 5, spreading; stamens 4, included in the tube below the hairs; anthers rounded; disk fleshy below the ovary; ovary (C, $\times 5$) superior, 4-locular (D, $\times 7$), each chamber with 1 erect ovule; fruit of 4 granular nutlets (family *Verbenaceae*).

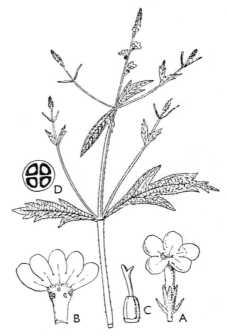

This is the only representative in the British flora of this large and mainly tropical family, which is here regarded as a parallel group with the Dead Nettle family, *Labiatae*. Nectar is secreted below the ovary, and protection against unbidden guests is provided by a ring of white hairs at the mouth of the corolla-tube. Either cross- or self-pollination may take place.

To the *Verbena* family belongs one of the hardest-wooded and most valuable trees in the world. This is the Teak tree, *Tectona grandis*, which grows wild in the forests of Burma and provides one of the major industries in that country.

CORAL PAEONY
Paeonia mascula (L.) Mill. ($\times\frac{1}{3}$)

Perennial herb with tuberous rootstock and fleshy roots; lower leaves twice divided into three (biternate), leaflets ovate to elliptic, shortly pointed, up to about 5 in. long and 3 in. broad, laxly reticulate below; flowers solitary on a stout stalk up to about 4 in. long; sepals 5, partly leaf-like and unequal in size, glabrous; petals 6–8, free, spreading to about 4 in. across the whole flower, bright red, obovate to nearly rounded, with wavy margins;

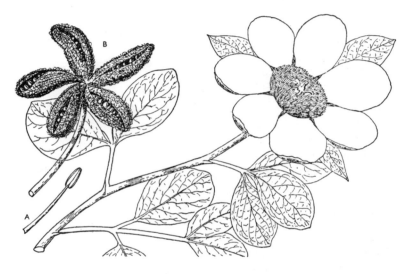

stamens (A, $\times 1\frac{1}{4}$) very numerous, with oblong anthers opening at the side; carpels 3–5, free, very densely woolly, spreading in fruit (B, $\times\frac{1}{3}$); seeds black, at first enclosed in a scarlet aril (family *Paeoniaceae*). – Synonym *Paeonia corallina* Retz..

This species was supposed to have been introduced and to have become naturalized on the island of Steep Holm in the Severn Estuary, where it is now very rare; a native of south Europe from Spain as far as the Near East. *Paeonia* is regarded by some modern botanists as a separate family from *Ranunculaceae*. The segregation of some large, unwieldy and unnatural families into smaller units has often much to recommend it, but it can be carried to excess, sometimes leading to the *declassification* of a genus or group of genera from their close relatives.

Perennial herb up to about 2 ft. high; lower leaves long-stalked, pedately divided into about 10 narrowly lanceolate lobes, these serrate except towards the base; leaf-stalks gradually broadened at the base; flowers globose, drooping, green tipped with purple, several in a terminal panicle with large leafy 3-lobed to entire bracts; flower-stalks mealy-pubescent; sepals broadly obovate, remaining connivent (erect) until the fruiting stage; petals (A, $\times 3$) small and hidden by the sepals, tubular, with a jagged top; stamens (B, $\times 1\frac{1}{4}$) numerous, free; anthers ellipsoid, opening at

the side; carpels (C, $\times 1\frac{1}{4}$) usually 3, free, each with a longish curved style and several ovules; fruits dehiscent, obliquely oblong, opening by the inner (adaxial) margin; seeds (D, $\times 2$) obovoid, with a basal aril (family *Helleboraceae*).

Found in stony places, mainly in woods in chalky districts, flowering in early spring. The second native British species, *H. viridis*, occurs in similar situations, and differs by its fewer flowers with widely spreading sepals.

The Christmas Rose of our gardens is *Helleborus niger* L., which opens its large nodding white flowers in the depth of winter. The conspicuous part of the flower is the calyx, which is white to attract the few insects about during the winter, the real petals being modified into tubular nectaries.

WINTER ACONITE
Eranthis hyemalis Salisbury (×¾)

Perennial herb with a short underground rootstock; leaves (E, ×¾) appearing after flowering, long-stalked, circular in outline,

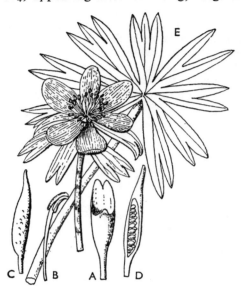

deeply divided into numerous oblong segments, glabrous; flowers appearing before the leaves in very early spring, solitary on a longish stalk, closely subtended by a leaf-like involucre deeply cut into oblong segments; this functions as a calyx and protects the flower on emerging from the soil, often through the snow; sepals yellow, resembling petals, ¾–1 in. long, marked with numerous nerves; petals (A, ×2) green horn-like structures much shorter than the sepals; stamens (B, ×2) numerous; carpels (C, D, ×2) about 5, free, becoming stalked in fruit and splitting on the upper side, transversely nerved, with several seeds (family *Helleboraceae*).

Naturalized in some parts; native of western Europe; of great interest, the leaf-like involucre functioning as a calyx, the sepals resembling petals.

The actual petals are scarcely recognizable as such, being reduced to horn-like structures (see fig. A) with an oblique mouth in which nectar is secreted. The carpels also are much reduced in number compared with many other members of the family, being usually only five.

The flowers close in dull weather and open in sunshine, their stamens and carpels maturing at the same time, so that insects effect cross-pollination. In cloudy weather self-pollination may take place in the closed flower.

Trollius europaeus L. (×½)

Perennial up to about 2 ft. high; basal leaves on very long hollow stalks broadly sheathing at the base; blade palmately divided into about 5 main segments, these in turn deeply lobed and coarsely toothed, glabrous, main nerves parallel and lighter green (almost translucent), upper leaves nearly sessile, with a broad almost membranous base; flowers solitary, terminal, 1–1½ in. diam.; sepals (A, ×1) 10–15, overlapping and crowding together into a depressed-globose mass, rich cream-yellow, the outer tinged with green and toothed on the margin; petals (B, ×2) almost hidden among the

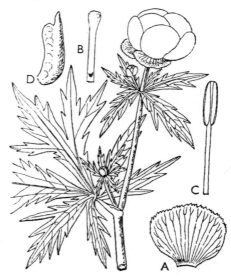

stamens, linear, with a nectary above the base; stamens (C, ×2) numerous, anthers with a distinct connective; carpels (D, ×4) numerous, beaked on the ventral (anterior) side, with about a dozen ovules; seeds several, angular (family *Helleboraceae*).

This is a very lovely wild flower which should not be picked (see p. xiii); wild flowers are much more pretty growing in their native habitat, and few last for any length of time in a vase; there are plenty of garden flowers for home decoration!

In the Globe-flower it is not the petals but the large rich cream-yellow sepals which serve as the means of attraction to insects. They are folded together into a sphere, and hide the small narrow petals, which bear an unprotected nectariferous pit near the base (fig. B). If cross-pollination is not effected by insects, automatic self-pollination is inevitable, as the outer of the numerous stamens lie above the stigmas.

Trollius is more frequently seen in gardens (often double forms) than in the landscape, though it is not uncommon in mountainous places in the north of England, as well as in Wales and Scotland, flowering in June and July.

Actaea spicata L. ($\times\frac{1}{3}$)

Perennial herb up to 2 ft. high, with leaves like some of the family *Umbelliferae*, these triternate or triternate-pinnate (see drawing),

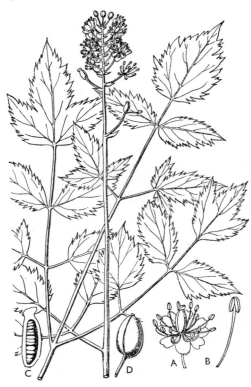

leaflets rounded to broadly wedge-shaped at the base, ovate to rounded-elliptic, very coarsely and sharply toothed, thin and nearly glabrous except on the nerves; flowers (A, ×1) white, tipped with violet, in a terminal raceme, often with a small extra raceme at the base of the main peduncle; bracts spreading, oblong-lanceolate, acute; pedicels at length curved, $\frac{1}{3}$ in. long; sepals 4–6, imbricate, free, obovate; petals 4–6, spathulate, clawed, as long as the sepals; stamens (B, ×1$\frac{1}{2}$) about 15, very conspicuous in flower, filaments broader towards the apex; carpel (C, ×2) 1, green, sessile, with a broad sessile stigma; fruits (D, ×2) ellipsoid, berry-like and blue-black, with several brown seeds in 2 rows (family *Helleboraceae*).

In ash-woods on limestone in only two or three of the northern counties of England; extends eastward to Siberia and China.

There are no nectaries, the flowers providing pollen for insects attracted by the whitish sepals, petals, and stamens.

The rhizome of this species was formerly official and known to pharmacists as *Radix Christophorianae*. It was used for skin diseases and asthma.

Aquilegia vulgaris L. ($\times \frac{1}{3}$)

Perennial herb up to about 2 ft. high; basal leaves on long stalks, the stalk broadly sheathing at the base and very strongly nerved, softly hairy; blade divided into 3 separate leaflets (ternate), the leaflets again deeply 3-lobed, the lobes with 2 or more rounded teeth, glaucous-green and softly pubescent below; flowers (A, section, $\times 1$) few in a terminal panicle, the first-opened flower soon fruiting; sepals 5, coloured; petals 5, blue or dull purple, each extended at the base into a curved horn-like spur; stamens (B, $\times 6$) numerous, anther fixed at the base; staminodes (C, $\times 6$) several within the fertile stamens, membranous, as long as the body of the carpels, the latter 5, free, with several ovules; styles 5, free; carpels in fruit (D, $\times 2$) recurving on opening; seed (E, F, $\times 5$) with a small embryo and rich in endosperm (family *Helleboraceae*).

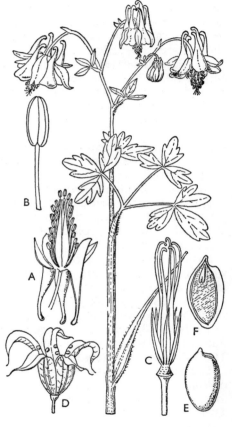

Local in open woodlands and usually in calcareous soil, but in some places escaped from gardens. It is distributed from the Atlantic Islands east to Siberia, and is naturalized in North America, where it is known as Blue-bells, Lady's-shoes, Capon's-tail, Cock's-foot, and Snapdragon.

MARSH MARIGOLD
Caltha palustris L. ($\times\frac{1}{2}$)

Perennial, often forming extensive tufts; rootstock thick and tuber-like, growing in marshy places by the side of brooks and streams; leaves (A, $\times\frac{1}{2}$) mostly from the rootstock, on long stout stalks, suborbicular, deeply cordate at the base, with radiating nerves, crenate on the margin, glabrous; stem leaves becoming sessile upwards and clasping the stem; flowers (B, $\times\frac{1}{2}$) large and showy; sepals 5–6, bright yellow and petal-like; no petals; stamens (C, $\times 5$) numerous, in several series; anthers rather large; carpels (D, $\times 2$; E, $\times 3$) several (about 6–10), free, laterally compressed, narrowed to the small stigma; seeds (F, $\times 4$) constricted in the middle (family *Helleboraceae*).

As there are no petals the sepals serve to attract insects which visit the flower for the nectar. This is secreted in a shallow depression on each side near the base of the carpels, and it is interesting that it should be found in this position because in the related Buttercups (*Ranunculus*) it is concealed in a small pit at the base of the petals. It often happens that when an organ has been modified, reduced, or dispensed with during the course of evolution another is modified to function in its stead. The plant is injurious to stock, which usually avoid it, especially at flowering time during spring and early summer.

Easily mistaken for a buttercup, but recognized by the single whorl of petal-like sepals, and by the numerous ovules (and seeds) in each carpel; the stems, if cut across, will be found to be hollow.

In the large egg-yolk yellow flowers – which spread out in the sunshine to about 2 in. across – nectar is so abundant that the drops from adjacent nectaries run together. The anthers dehisce outwardly, favouring cross-pollination. In France and the Tyrol stocks with purely male flowers have been observed.

The name *Caltha* was first employed by Tournefort for a species of *Calendula* (*Compositae*), but later it was used by Linnaeus for the Marsh Marigold, which was the only species known to him. There are now about 40 species of the genus, scattered throughout the cooler parts of the world, but mostly in the Southern Hemisphere, especially New Zealand and in the Andes of South America, where some very peculiar and distinctive kinds are found.

Nigella damascena L. ($\times\frac{1}{2}$)

Annual up to $1\frac{1}{2}$ ft. high with a long straight taproot; stems erect, strongly ribbed, glabrous; leaves alternate, the lowermost crowded

and stalked, bi-pinnately divided with linear acute lobes, the upper ones sessile and gradually small-er, forming a 'misty' whorl around the flow-er; sepals 5, large and like petals, blue and veiny, with a white claw; petals (A, $\times 3$) 8, much modified into nectaries and clawed, 2-lipped, inner lip with a flap, outer with 2 lobes with an eye-like process at the base of each, the mar-gins with long slender hairs; stamens (B, $\times 3$) fairly numerous, anthers oblong, greenish yellow; carpels (C, $\times 3$) united, with free spreading styles, each loculus with several ovules; fruit (D, $\times\frac{2}{3}$) bladder-like, broadly oblong-ellip-soid to subglobose, gaping by slits at the top; seeds black and transversely ribbed (family *Helleboraceae*).

An escape from gardens in waste places or in cornfields. The flowers are pollinated by bees, the large brightly coloured sepals serving to attract them.

Erect annual herb up to 2½ ft. high, with a deep straight taproot; leaves alternate, shortly stalked or sessile, deeply divided to the base into long narrow segments, very softly and shortly hairy; flowers blue and white or reddish, in a terminal raceme or panicle with leaf-like bracts; pedicels softly hairy, usually shorter than the flowers; bracts gradually reduced upwards to short subulate structures; sepals (B, ×2) 5, terminating below in a long curved hollow spur; petals (A, ×2) 2, united into 1, produced into a spur within the calyx; stamens (C, ×2) about 15, with thin flattened filaments and elliptic anthers opening at the side; carpel (D, ×2) 1, softly pilose, with numerous ovules in 2 rows; style short and glabrous; fruit (E, ×1) a follicle

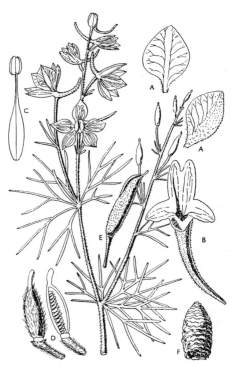

splitting down one side containing several seeds transversely plaited (family *Helleboraceae*).

A native of the eastern Mediterranean region and long cultivated in Europe and often a common weed in cornfields, flowering with the corn and later.

In Delphinium nectar is secreted at the bottom of the long spur and is concealed so deeply that it can only be reached by humble-bees with a long proboscis. The sepals take the place of the petals as the chief means of attracting insects.

MOUSETAIL
Myosurus minimus (L. ($\times \frac{1}{2}$))

A small inconspicuous annual with a short bare taproot and a bunch of side roots; leaves all basal, linear but widest towards the

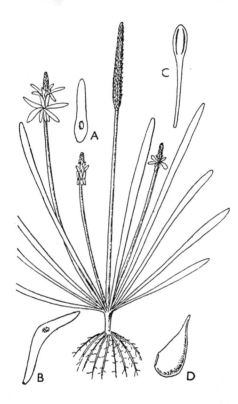

top, up to 3 in. long, glabrous, 1-nerved; flowerstalks about as long as the leaves, usually several to each plant, becoming hollow in the upper part; sepals (A, $\times 1\frac{1}{2}$) 5, oblong, prolonged downwards from the base into a spur; petals (B, $\times 1\frac{1}{2}$) 5, greenish-yellow, very narrow, with tubular claws and spreading limb; stamens (C, $\times 1\frac{1}{2}$) few, anther clubshaped; carpels (D, $\times 3$) very numerous on a long slender axis up to 2 in. long in fruit, crowded and spirally arranged (family *Ranunculaceae*).

In moist, sandy or gravelly places, flowering in spring; widely distributed; nectar is secreted on the small greenish-yellow petals; either cross- or self-pollination may occur, the visitors being minute flies or midges.

Students should compare the floral structure of this tiny herb with that of a *Magnolia* flower. The general arrangement of the parts is very similar, but, in the present writer's opinion, this is not an indication of close relationship, but due to parallel evolution from remote and separate ancestral stocks.

Owing to the shape of the floral axis in the fruiting stage, it is commonly called in France *Queue de Souris*, and by country folk in Germany, *Das Mäuseschwanzchen*, by the Spaniards, *Cola de Raton*, and by the Italians, *Cora di Sorcio*.

Ranunculus bulbosus L. ($\times \frac{2}{5}$)

Stem swollen at the base like a small corm (A); whole plant hairy; basal leaves on long stalks, broad and deeply lobed, lobes again lobulate or coarsely toothed (dentate); stem leaves scarcely stalked, deeply and more regularly divided into narrow lobes; flowers solitary on long, grooved stalks (pedicels); sepals 5, green, reflexed in the open flower; petals (B, $\times \frac{4}{5}$) 5, bright yellow and shining, broadly obovate, with a nectar - secreting scale above the base; stamens (C, $\times 2\frac{1}{2}$) numerous, inserted below the numerous free carpels (D, $\times 6$), each of which is tipped by a small stigma, spirally arranged on a cone-like axis; each ripe carpel (E, $\times 3$) contains a single seed.

As in most other buttercups, the petals have a shining surface, which acts as a looking-glass to insects visiting the flowers to gather the nectar stored in a pit at their base.

These plants belong to the family *Ranunculaceae*, named after the largest genus *Ranunculus*, all herbs (except some species of *Clematis*), and regarded as representing a primitive group of flowering plants, in which all the parts of the flower are free among themselves and from one another. Two other buttercups are very common; both differ from the one illustrated in having spreading (not reflexed) sepals; the Meadow Buttercup, *R. acris* L., produces no runners, is sometimes as much as 3 ft. high, and has a rounded (not grooved) flower-stalk, whilst the Creeping Buttercup, *R. repens* L., gives off runners which root at the nodes and develop into new plants, and the flower-stalk is grooved.

MEADOW CROWFOOT
Ranunculus acris L. (×⅓)

Perennial with very short rootstock; basal leaves on long stalks with sheathing hairy bases, more or less orbicular in outline,

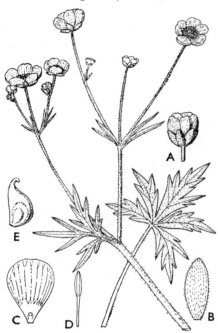

usually 5-lobed nearly to the base, the lobes again deeply divided and lobulate with rather narrow acute divisions, softly hairy on both surfaces, finely mealy below; stem leaves gradually merging into bracts and becoming stalkless (sessile) and divided into 2 or 3 segments; flowers about 1 in. diam., on long stalks forming a lax panicle; stalks not grooved, but covered with very short appressed hairs; sepals (B, ×2) 5, spreading in the open flower but not becoming reflexed (as in *R. bulbosus*), yellowish-green, covered with rather long hairs; petals (C, ×¾) 5, broadly clawed, shining except for a large patch at the base, with a scale in front of the nectary and hiding 2 dark spots (C, ×¾); stamens (D, ×¾) numerous; carpels (E, ×3) numerous, with recurved stigma; fruit a bunch of achenes, not hairy (glabrous) (A, flower bud) (family *Ranunculaceae*).

Rather like *R. bulbosus* (fig. 224), but the stem not swollen at the base and the sepals are spreading and not reflexed as in that species.

The bright-yellow very glossy petals are very conspicuous, and attract hover flies, small bees, and other insects, which collect the nectar protected by a scale at the base. As the stigmas mature before any of the anthers open, they are easily brushed with pollen from older flowers, and by the time the anthers are open the carpels are already swollen and the stigmas shrivelled.

Ranunculus flammula L. ($\times \frac{2}{5}$)

Perennial of short duration or annual growing in marshes and wet
fields and beside lakes and ponds; stems decumbent at the base
and then erect, up to
about 1½ ft. high, with
few ascending bran-
ches, glabrous and
closely ribbed; radi-
cal leaves on long
stalks with broad
sheaths at the base,
elliptic-lanceolate,
rather blunt, slightly
dentate with very
distant teeth on the
margin, with 3–5 as-
cending subparallel
nerves; stem-leaves
becoming sessile on
the broad membran-
ous sheathing base,
lanceolate to almost
linear, becoming en-
tire as they merge
into bracts, nerves
parallel to the mid-
rib; flowers few, and
forming lax corymbs,
the older flowers in

the middle of each fork; sepals remaining erect, rounded with a
few minute hairs outside; petals (A, ×1¼) bright yellow, shining,
obovate, with a nectariferous pit just above the base; stamens
numerous (about 35); carpels (B, ×3) numerous and free, with a
very short stigma, in fruit forming a globose head, each carpel
with a short hook-like point and a flat membranous margin on
one side (family *Ranunculaceae*).

A few of our British buttercups have undivided leaves which at
most are very slightly toothed, and with more or less parallel
nerves as in some Monocotyledons, such as in the *Alisma* family,
Alismataceae (see figs. 714–717). Indeed they are quite closely related to the family mentioned, which forms a link between the
Dicotyledons and Monocotyledons.

GREAT SPEARWORT
Ranunculus lingua L. ($\times\frac{1}{2}$)

Perennial in marshes and ditches; leaves all borne on the rather thick quite hollow green stems, linear-lanceolate, with faint nerves running parallel with the entire margins, closely covered above with minute grey spots, minutely hairy below with short appressed hairs, tip blunt and pore-like; base of leaves sheathing and almost circling the stem, sheaths membranous on the margin; flowers very handsome, about 2 in. diam., few in a loose panicle; middle flower the oldest, long-stalked; sepals 5, forming a 5-lobed depressed mass in bud (A, $\times$1), spreading, deeply and widely pouched in the middle (B, $\times$1$\frac{1}{2}$), yellow tinged with green, scarcely hairy; petals (C, $\times$1) rich cream-yellow, widely obovate, 1 in. long, with a nectariferous pit at the base, very glossy all over; stamens (D, $\times$4) numerous, anthers opening at the side; carpels free, very numerous, forming a globose mass and arranged on an oblong receptacle (E, $\times$6), not hairy; ovule 1 (G, $\times$10), ascending; fruitlets (achenes) (F, $\times$10) glabrous (family *Ranunculaceae*).

This is one of the most beautiful species of Buttercup in the British flora, the rich cream-yellow flowers being quite 2 in. diameter. The flower-buds are very distinctive, the rounded pouched sepals giving a lobed or angular appearance, with here and there the tip of a petal emerging from the tight flower-pack. In the bud stage the wonderful gloss on the petals is scarcely noticeable. The stigmas are receptive before the anthers open, cross-pollination being effected by flies, which usually alight on the stigmas, dusting them with pollen from another flower.

Flower-lovers in numerous countries can enjoy the sight of this lovely plant, which has a wide range from Eire eastward into temperate Asia and as far south as the Himalayas.

This is the most handsome of our native buttercups, with flowers as much as 2 in. in diam. It is a local plant of marshes and fens from Caithness southwards, and in Eire and the Channel Islands. A broad-leaved form of *R. flammula* may easily be mistaken for it, but this has much smaller flowers.

The student should note the great similarity of this species and *R. flammula* and members of the *Alismataceae*, figured and described in volume II (figs. 714–717). They seem to be connecting links between the Dicotyledons and Monocotyledons, as pointed out under fig. 226.

281

CELERY-LEAVED BUTTERCUP
Ranunculus sceleratus L. ($\times\frac{1}{2}$)

Annual up to about 2 ft. high or more, in wet places and ditches, resembling Celery; roots fibrous; stems thick, hollow, ribbed, much branched; lower leaves variously 3-lobed to the middle or to the base, long-stalked, upper leaves gradually becoming sessile and finally unlobed and bract-like but green; leaves rather fleshy and bright green and glossy; flowers (A, ×1) in bud very shortly stalked, together forming a lax leafy panicle; buds globose, slightly hairy; pedicels at length up to about 1 in. long, slightly grooved on one side, thinly hairy; sepals (B, ×4) 5, soon reflexed and falling off, oblong, yellowish-green; petals (C, ×4) 5, yellow, spreading horizontally, broadly elliptic, about $\frac{1}{4}$ in. long, shortly clawed at the base, and with a circular pit-like nectary, glossy except at the base; stamens (D, ×6) about 20; carpels (E, ×1$\frac{1}{2}$) very numerous, arranged on a conical axis which elongates in fruit up to about 1 in. long and bearing the little fruits (F, ×7) (achenes) each containing a single seed (family *Ranunculaceae*).

Highly poisonous, and especially dangerous to cattle; even if not fatal it causes a falling off in the milk supply. Among its French names are *Mort aux Vaches* and *Herbe sardonique*. All parts are acrid, blistering the mouth and skin, and it has been used by beggars to induce sores. In the United States, where it is introduced, it is called 'Cursed Crowfoot'!

The flowers are relatively small, but numerous on each plant, collectively forming a leafy panicle, the stalks of those with ripening carpels elongating considerably. The stigmas are receptive in advance of the ripening anthers in the same flower, so that cross-pollination is brought about by many short-tongued insects, which seek the nectar secreted in an open pit at the base of each petal. As the anthers open, their stalks bend away from the carpels, but should cross-pollination not take place the pollen of fading anthers may reach the stigmas.

It flowers in June and is one of the most acrid of the Crowfoots. In former times it was in frequent use as a blister. Carrying it by hand may cause inflammation and it should not be brought into contact with tender parts of the skin. Considering the size of the plant, the flowers are relatively very small.

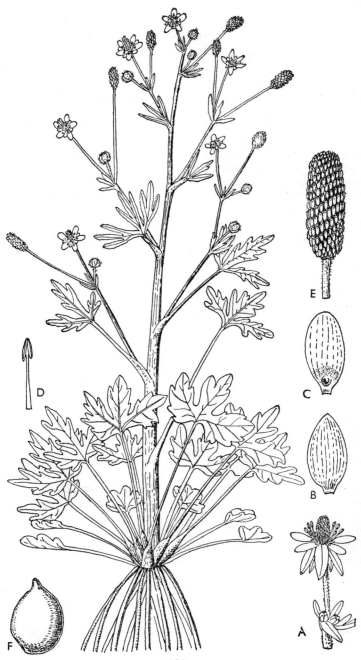

283

CREEPING BUTTERCUP
Ranunculus repens L. ($\times\frac{1}{3}$)

Perennial with numerous long rather stilt-like roots; stem decumbent at the base, giving off long runners which root at the nodes and produce new plants (vegetative reproduction); basal leaves with broad membranous sheathing stalks, the latter covered with long fine hairs; blades divided into 3 distinct parts, each part stalked and again divided nearly to the midrib, each division very coarsely toothed, teeth with hardened tips; stem-leaves also with membranous sheathing bases, but smaller in size, sparingly covered with rather bristly hairs; flowers 2–4 to each shoot, the open

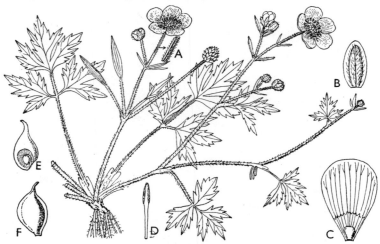

flower on a longer furrowed stalk (A, $\times 1$) than those in bud, about 1 in. diam.; sepals (B, $\times 1\frac{1}{4}$) 5, soon falling off, elliptic, with long hairs on the back; petals (C, $\times 1\frac{1}{4}$) 5, golden-yellow, shining above except a broad patch at the base, and with a large wedge-shaped scale covering the nectar; stamens (D, $\times 2$) numerous, facing outwards; carpels (E, $\times 4$) numerous, free, arranged in a globose mass, with curled stigmas; ovule solitary, attached at the base; fruiting carpels (F, $\times 2$) not hairy, sharply beaked (family *Ranunculaceae*).

Grows in waste ground and by roadsides, flowering from late May until August; readily recognized by the shape of the basal leaves, the early deciduous (falling off) sepals, and the grooved flower-stalk. The nectar at the base of the petal is hidden by a scale (C, $\times 1\frac{1}{4}$), and the stigmas are mature before the anthers open.

Ranunculus auricomus L. ($\times \frac{2}{5}$)

Perennial; basal leaves very variable, long-stalked, kidney-shaped and irregularly and coarsely toothed, or deeply 3-lobed; stem-leaves sessile, cut nearly to the base into 5 segments, the lowermost with narrowly wedge-shaped stalked segments, the upper with linear irregularly lobed segments, bright green, glabrous below but very minutely pubescent above; flowers terminal and axillary, on slender stalks; sepals 5, or sometimes 4 where only 1 petal, mixed with green and yellow, more green when there are all 5 petals; petals (C, $\times 1\frac{1}{4}$) 5, or sometimes fewer or absent, and then the sepals more yellow, shining on the upper

surface, with a nectariferous pit at the base; stamens (D, $\times 3\frac{1}{2}$) numerous; carpels (E, $\times 3\frac{1}{2}$) shortly stalked, numerous, conspicuously beaked, shortly pubescent (family *Ranunculaceae*).

This is very variable with regard to the presence or absence of petals; sometimes there is only one petal (A, $\times \frac{2}{5}$), and then the sepals are more or less half green and half yellow. In a large batch growing in the grass at Kew I found only a very occasional flower with a petal, all the others being without petals (apetalous) (B, $\times \frac{2}{5}$), and then the sepals nearly completely yellow. The apetalous condition therefore approaches very near to *Anemone*, which is also without petals, the function of these being carried out by the sepals. Goldilocks seems to represent an intermediate and indeterminate stage between the two genera *Ranunculus* and *Anemone*, and shows clearly how the latter genus has been evolved.

Ranunculus sardous Crantz ($\times \frac{2}{5}$)

An erect annual, but mostly much branched from the base and resembling a perennial, softly hairy all over, though less hairy states occur; basal leaves (A, $\times \frac{2}{5}$) with a broadly sheathing stalk, the sheath fringed with long hairs; stalks also fringed with hairs; blade divided into 3 separate parts, each part again very coarsely toothed or lobulate to about the middle, softly hairy all over; stem-leaves gradually becoming sessile upwards and forming leafy bracts, deeply divided; flowers numerous, the first opening soon fruiting whilst the remainder are still in bloom; stalks scarcely grooved; sepals 5, clothed with very long slender hairs in bud (B, $\times 1\frac{1}{4}$), becoming sharply reflexed as the flower opens (C, $\times \frac{4}{5}$); petals (D, $\times 1$) pale yellow, glossy, the nectary at the base covered with a rounded scale; stamens (E, $\times 2$) about 25–30; carpels numerous, in fruit (F, $\times 2$) compressed and rounded, with a row or 2 of small tubercles within the margin (family *Ranunculaceae*).

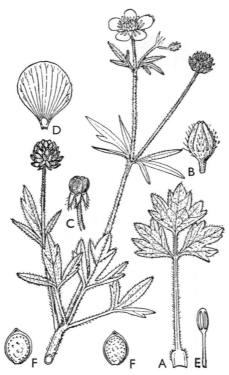

This species may easily be mistaken for the more common *Ranunculus bulbosus* L., having, like that species, reflexed sepals, but it is an annual and the carpels are flattened with 1 or 2 rows of small tubercles within the margin. In *R. bulbosus* the carpels have no tubercles.

Biennial with spreading basal leaves and several more or less decumbent branches, thinly covered with long fine hairs; stalks of basal leaves long and sheathing at the base, 1–1½ in. broad, lobed to about the middle, the lobes with few coarse teeth; nerves radiating from the base; flowers rather few, the upper ones opposite the leaves on stalks reaching 1 in. in fruit; sepals (A, $\times 2\frac{1}{2}$) 5, narrowly elliptic, hairy; petals (B, $\times 4$) yellow, with a nectary at the base, variable in number, mostly 2, sometimes 5 or fewer, occasionally absent; stamens (C, $\times 4$) 8–1, often 5; carpels (D, $\times 3$) numerous, soon developing into fruit and then compressed with a broad margin and the two surfaces covered with hooked tubercles (family *Ranunculaceae*).

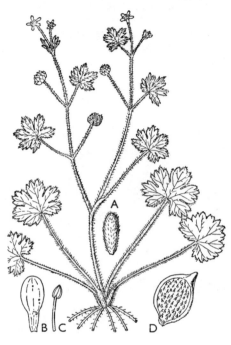

This is a very interesting species, the morphology and ecology of which have been studied in detail.* The species seems to represent an advanced type in which the petals tend to be reduced from the normal number five (in the genus) to one, or they may be absent altogether. The normal flowering period of this species extends from April to June. An interesting feature is that each of the flowers is borne on the main axis opposite to a leaf. The number of stamens varies from 8 to 1; when the number of petals is high the number of stamens tends to be low.

* E. J. Salisbury, *Annals of Botany* 45: 539–578 (1931).

Ranunculus arvensis L. ($\times \frac{1}{3}$)

An erect annual with rather thick roots; stems up to $1\frac{1}{2}$ ft. high, branched in the upper part, and very slightly hairy in the upper part; basal leaves deeply pinnately lobed, the lobes broader than those of the stem leaves, with a few rounded teeth; stem leaves with narrow linear segments; flowers small, the lower developing into fruit before the others have faded; stalks clothed with reflexed hairs; sepals (A, $\times 3$) 5, spreading, hairy; petals (B, $\times 3$) 5, pale

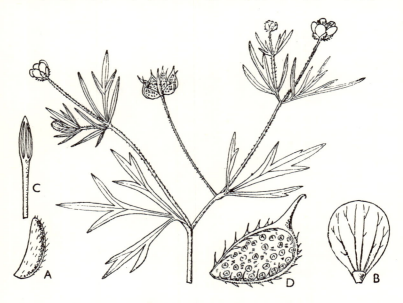

yellow, with a wedge-shaped scale over the nectary at the base; stamens (C, $\times 5$) rather few; carpels (D, $\times 2\frac{1}{2}$) few, free, in fruit compressed and covered with sharp-pointed warts and with bristly margins (family *Ranunculaceae*).

A common weed, and often abundant in neglected cornfields, flowering and ripening its seed with the corn. It is a regular companion of Fool's Parsley, Venus' Comb, and other similar followers of the plough, and it often appears in stackyards. It proves a pest to farmers because it gets bound up with the straw in harvesting, being tall when growing in the shelter of the corn. The prickly fruits are unique among our native buttercups, and are readily spread by means of the hooked tubercles.

In muddy places in ditches or floating in water; stems rooting at the nodes; leaves opposite or alternate, kidney-shaped, shallowly 5–7-lobed, widely heart-shaped at the base, on long stalks, rather fleshy and glabrous green, with a half-moon-shaped darker patch; stalks expanded at the base into a broad membranous sheath; flowers (A, $\times1\frac{1}{2}$) solitary from near the axil of the leaf-stalk, about $\frac{1}{4}$–$\frac{1}{3}$ in. diam., rather long-stalked, but the stalks shorter than those of the leaves and recurving in fruit; sepals 5, green,

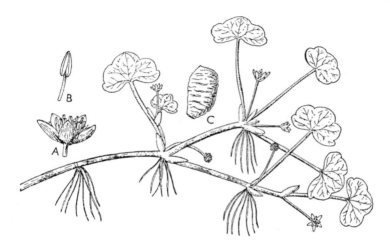

shorter than the petals; petals 5, white, 3–5-nerved; stamens (B, $\times 6$) few (about 10); carpels free from one another, several, blunt and becoming transversely reticulated in fruit (C, $\times 10$) (family *Ranunculaceae*).

This species is rather intermediate between the Field and the Water Buttercups, but the leaves are never finely divided, as in the latter. It also shows some relationship with the Lesser Celandine, *Ficaria verna* Huds. (fig. 236).

The anthers of the 8–10 stamens shed their pollen on the stigmas when the flower opens, and self-pollination is effective; afterwards the stamens move outwards. Nectar is sparingly secreted in a pit at the base of the petals.

Ranunculus lenormandii Schultz ($\times\frac{1}{2}$)

Aquatic floating herb or creeping in the mud with soft fleshy branches giving off numerous fine roots at the nodes, each node with a large rounded membranous stipule and with an extra-axillary pedicel; leaves long-stalked, rounded or kidney-shaped in outline, cordate at the base, 3–5-lobed, $\frac{1}{2}$–1 in. diam., lobes rounded and often emarginate, glabrous; stipules very conspicu-

ous; pedicels about 1–1$\frac{1}{2}$ in. long, recurved in fruit; sepals (A, ×2) 5, oblong, erect; petals (B, ×2) 5, much longer than the sepals, white, 5-nerved, without a scale at the base; stamens (C, ×2) 10–8; receptacle glabrous; carpels (D, ×3) numerous, in fruit transversely wrinkled (E, ×6) and with a nearly central curved beak (family *Ranunculaceae*).

Sometimes locally common in streams from central Scotland southwards, and in Eire; extends south to northern Spain and Portugal.

Though it grows both in the water and in the mud, there are no dissected leaves as in other water buttercups, all of which have white flowers. It shares this leaf-character with *R. lutarius* and *R. hederaceus*.

Known to nearly every country child, and often used as a test of the liking for butter by the amount of reflection from the shining petals on the skin below the chin; one of the first spring flowers (February–May) and frequently included with the true buttercups in the genus *Ranunculus*, but recognized here as a separate genus because of the apparently opposite unequal-sized leaves, only 3 (instead of 5) sepals, and more than 5 petals; remarkable in the family by the fact that the young plantlet (embryo) has only 1 seed-

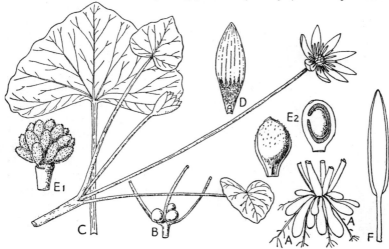

leaf (cotyledon); the short perennial rootstock bears numerous finger-like tubers (A, × ⅖); frequently small rounded bulbils (B, × ⅖) in the axils of the leaves, especially in plants growing in very shady places; lowest leaves (C, × ½) long-stalked, glossy, broadly-triangular, all with wavy margins; flowers star-like, solitary, axillary, closing in bad or dull weather; petals (D, × 1¾) about 8 or more, an outer whorl of 3 alternate with the sepals, an inner whorl of 5, if more than these within the 5, broadly lanceolate, bright yellow and shining, with a dull deeper-coloured nectar-secreting base, bleaching with age, stamens numerous; anthers (F, × 4) opening at the sides; carpels about 20–25 (E1, × 1¼), free, with a subterminal sessile stigma not receptive until most of the anthers have shed their pollen, each carpel containing a single ovule attached at the side (E2, × 2) (family *Ranunculaceae*) (synonym *Ranunculus ficaria* L.).

PHEASANT'S EYE
Adonis annua L. ($\times \frac{1}{3}$)

Erect annual herb up to $1\frac{1}{2}$ ft. high; stem little-branched, glabrous or nearly so; leaves alternate, the lower stalked, the upper sessile,

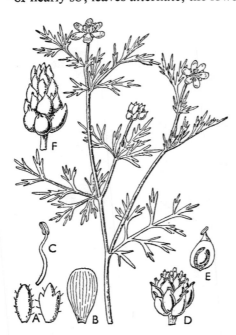

all deeply 2–3 times pinnate into narrow sharply-pointed segments, glabrous; flowers solitary at the ends of the stem or shoots, stalked; sepals (A, $\times 2$), free, purplish, rather unequal, some 3-toothed; petals (B, $\times 2$) 6, free, deep red, with a purple mark at the base, obovate, closely nerved; stamens (C, $\times 3$) 10–15, free; carpels (D, $\times 2$) numerous, free, with a short oblique stigma and 1 pendulous ovule (E, $\times 4$); fruiting carpels (F, $\times 1$) loose on the elongated up to about 1 in. long axis, wrinkled-reticulate when dry (synonym *Adonis autumnalis* L.) (family *Ranunculaceae*).

A very beautiful flower in late summer with vivid red petals which serve to attract insects, though there is no nectar. Either cross- or self-pollination takes place. It grows in cornfields and gardens or on waste ground. Named after Adonis, a youth beloved of Venus, who at his death was changed into a flower.

The genus *Adonis* is closely related to the Buttercups (*Ranunculus*), the absence of a nectary from the claw of the petals being the chief difference. This may seem trifling, though it is of great biological importance in connexion with the visits of insects.

It is a genus of nearly 40 species, mostly European, but some in eastern Asia south to the Himalayas and in North Africa. Only a few are in cultivation, a striking species being *A. amurensis* from Manchuria and Japan, with large golden yellow, rose or bright red-striped flowers about 2 in. across.

Herb up to 3 ft. high, with a perennial rootstock; stem stout, hollow, furrowed; leaves alternate, twice pinnate, expanded into a large toothed stipule at the base and embracing the stem; leaflets about 2–3 pairs and a terminal one, shaped more or less like a narrow spade and deeply 3-lobed in the upper half, the lobes ascending, nerves radiating from the base, prominent below and reticulate; flowers (B, $\times 8$) in a terminal dense panicle with leafy bracts gradually reduced in size upwards; pedicels erect in flower; sepals (A, $\times 6$) 5, -yellow, free, veiny; petals absent; stamens (C, $\times 12$) several, yellow, with slender free filaments and narrow anthers with a rather broad connective; carpels several, sessile,

obliquely ovoid, with a large sessile stigma; ovule 1; fruiting carpels (D, $\times 6$) about 3–5 with several abortive ones between, ovoid, strongly ribbed (E, $\times 7$) and tipped by the persistent stigma (family *Ranunculaceae*).

In moist meadows and along ditches in Europe and north Asia, flowering in summer.

PASQUE FLOWER
Anemone pulsatilla L. ($\times\frac{1}{2}$)

Perennial herb with thick rootstock covered in the upper part with the fibrous remains of the leaf-stalks; old flower-stalk (A) usually persisting during the next season's growth, erect; leaves in bunches on the rootstock, stalked, deeply divided to the third degree into narrow acute segments and finely pilose with long weak hairs; stalk sheathing towards the base and closely nerved; flowers appearing with the leaves, at first inverted, at length spreading or erect, single on each stalk which bears below the middle a much divided sessile leafy bract covered with long silky hairs; sepals (B, $\times\frac{1}{2}$) mostly 6, blue-violet, ovate-lanceolate, $1\frac{1}{4}$–$1\frac{1}{2}$ in. long, covered with long hairs on the outside; no petals; stamens (C, $\times 8$) numerous, the outermost very short and transformed into globular gland-like nectaries (D, $\times 4$); carpels (E, $\times 8$) numerous, free, silky, with slender thread-like styles; fruiting carpels (bunch of achenes) (F, $\times 1$) much like those of the 'Traveller's Joy' (*Clematis vitalba* L.) with long persistent silky hairy styles (synonym *Pulsatilla vulgaris* Miller) (family *Ranunculaceae*).

This species, and others which are not found wild in Britain, are regarded by some botanists as a distinct genus, *Pulsatilla*, chiefly because the outer stamens are transformed into stalked gland-like nectaries. In *Anemone* proper there are no nectaries.

The large, coloured sepals attract insects, mainly nectar-sucking and pollen-collecting bees, which serve as pollinators, while ants steal the nectar. In the first flowering stage the stigmas are already receptive, and they remain in this condition for 2–4 days, during which the numerous stamens are opening and shedding their pollen. Nectar is secreted by the outermost stamens which are converted into stalked head-like structures. As the stigmas project far above the longest stamens, insects first come into contact with them and effect pollination if they have already visited another flower.

One of our most lovely native plants, and a glorious sight when in full flower in chalky pastures and downs fully exposed to the sun; confined to England, but frequently grown in gardens from continental stock; widely distributed from Europe to Siberia.

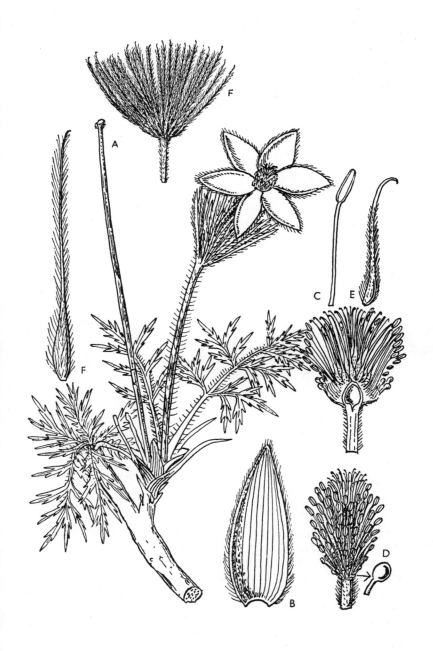

295

WOOD ANEMONE
Anemone nemorosa L. ($\times\frac{2}{5}$)

Perennial with slender black rootstock, flowering in and near woods in early spring before the trees become leafy; leaves 2–3

from the rootstock, long-stalked, divided to the base into three parts, each part narrowed to the base and deeply lobed and coarsely toothed; flowering stem solitary, bearing a single terminal flower · (A, $\times\frac{4}{5}$) and a whorl of 3 leaves towards the top like the root leaves but smaller and shortly stalked; sepals usually 6, glabrous, petal-like and white or mauvish pink to purple-blue; no petals; stamens (B, $\times2\frac{1}{2}$) numerous; filaments slender; anthers fixed át the base, short; carpels (C, $\times1\frac{3}{4}$) free, hairy, beaked; seed solitary in each carpel; easily distinguished from the much rarer *A. pulsatilla* L. (Pasque flower), which has silky-hairy sepals and the carpels ending in feathery beaks like *Clematis* (family *Ranunculaceae*).

There are no nectaries in the Wood Anemone, but insects of many kinds visit it for the sake of its pollen. The absence of petals is perhaps best explained by assuming that they have been dispensed with during the course of evolution and their function, that of attracting insects, has been taken over by the sepals. These, in addition, protect the pollen by the flower bending over at night and during wet weather, so that they do double work.

Clematis vitalba L. (×⅔)

Large slender climber, spreading over trees, shrubs, and hedges by means of the twisted leaf-stalks; branches softly pubescent, tough; leaves opposite, without stipules, pinnate, leaflets usually 5, ovate or ovate-lanceolate, 3-nerved from the base, entire or with a few coarse teeth, hairy on the nerves; flowers with a hawthorn-like odour, in loose axillary panicles, at the end of short axillary branchlets; sepals 4, not overlapping in bud (valvate) white or greenish white, softly hairy outside; no petals; stamens numerous, outer opening first and bending away from stigmas; carpels numerous, on a short axis, free, very conspicuous in fruit, forming a dense white mass with long silky hairs,  the style elongated into a thread-like tail; seed solitary (family *Ranunculaceae*).

There is no nectar, but the pollen provides food for insect visitors. This species may cause injury to stock if eaten in quantity; the branches are useful for making light baskets. It is usually very common on calcareous soil, particularly on the North and South Downs in the south of England, flowers during summer, and is easily distinguished from other wild British plants by its climbing habit, opposite pinnate leaves, loose axillary panicles of flowers with a coloured calyx but no petals, and the bunch of hairy long-tailed fruits. It is widely distributed in central and southern Europe as far east as the Caucasus.

WHITE WATER-LILY
Nymphaea alba L. ($\times\frac{1}{3}$)

Aquatic perennial with thick fleshy rootstock; leaf-stalks rounded, with 4 large and several smaller intercellular spaces with inter-
nal hairs (K, $\times 1\frac{1}{2}$); leaf-blade floating on the water, rounded,
deeply cordate, with several radiating nerves; flowers on long
stalks, lying on the surface of the water, white, not scented, 3–4
in. diam.; sepals (A, $\times\frac{1}{3}$) 4, greenish-white; petals (B, C, $\times\frac{3}{4}$)
numerous, white or tinged with pink downwards, the outer broad-
ly lanceolate and gradually transformed into stamens (D–G, $\times\frac{3}{4}$);

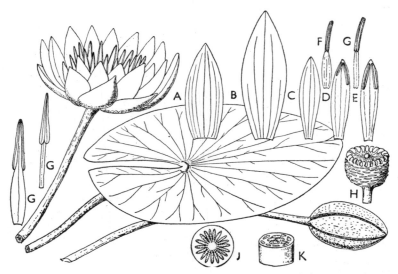

carpels about 20, united into an ovary with spreading united yellow stigmas, each ending in an incurved rich cream-yellow appendix; ovary (H, $\times\frac{1}{2}$) with as many loculi as stigmas, with numerous
ovules on the walls (J, $\times\frac{1}{2}$); fruit a pulpy berry, ripening under
water (family *Nymphaeaceae*).

In lakes, ponds, and backwaters, flowering from June to September; widely distributed in the temperate northern hemisphere.

Although clearly related to the Buttercup family (*Ranunculaceae*), the Water-lily family, *Nymphaeaceae*, shows a considerable advance in some parts of its floral structure. Its more primitive features are the scarcely perceptible difference between the
sepals and petals; the latter are numerous and grade into the also
numerous stamens.

Nuphar lutea (L.) Sm. ($\times\frac{1}{3}$)

In lakes, ponds, and ditches; rhizome creeping; submerged leaves on rather short stalks, very thin, floating leaves rather leathery, deeply 2-lobed at the base, lobes contiguous, blade in outline broadly obovate, with a wide midrib and many slender side-nerves; leaf-stalk thick and fleshy, flattish on the upper surface; flowers shortly exserted from the water on long stalks, broadly cup-shaped, 2–2½ in. diam.; sepals 5, green and yellow outside, yellow inside, thick and fleshy; petals (A, ×1) 12–15, broadly obovate-wedge-shaped, about ½ in. long and broad, closely and strongly nerved;

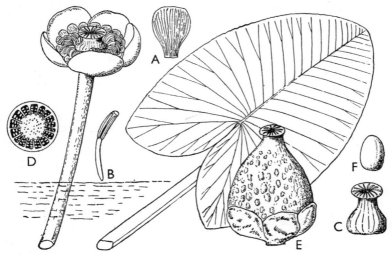

stamens (B, ×1) numerous, in about 6 rows, facing inwards (introrse), curving outwards as they ripen; anther-lobes separate, connective produced and very blunt (truncate); ovary (C, ×⅓) ovoid, style short, thick, top composed of about 15 united stigmas radiating from the middle; fruit (E, ×⅔) ovoid, with numerous seeds (F, ×1) (D, cross-section of ovary, ×½) (family *Nymphaeaceae*).

The name 'Brandy Bottle' is given to this plant probably in reference to the shape of the fruit (E, ×½), and not because of the flower-scent. The radiating stigmas recall those of the poppy capsule.

Epimedium alpinum L. ($\times \frac{1}{3}$)

Perennial herb up to about 1 ft. high with slender creeping root-stock covered with loose brown bark; leaves often single, erect on

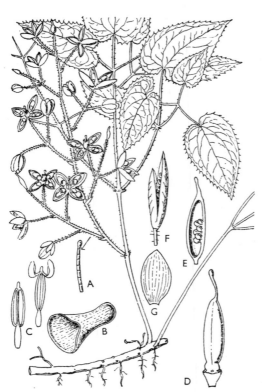

wiry stalks, thrice divided, each division with three leaflets or sometimes up to 7 leaflets, these ovate, cordate at the base, acute at the apex, with 5 main nerves ascending from the base, sharply toothed on the margin, paler below and almost glaucous; joints of the stalk swollen and bearing a few slender hairs; flowers in a slender open panicle borne on the stem below the leaf; axis and branches with long gland-tipped hairs (A, $\times 3$); bracts ovate - lánceolate, short; pedicels slender, glandular; sepals (G, $\times 3$) 4, greenish red, half as long as the 4 red boat-shaped petals, opposite each of which a yellow tubular nectary (B, $\times 3$); stamens (C, $\times 3$) 4, rather shorter than the petals; anthers opening by valves, with produced connective; ovary (D, $\times 4$) of 1 carpel, with about 6 ovules in 2 series up the middle (E, $\times 4$); fruit (F, $\times 1\frac{1}{4}$) a follicle with 2 unequal valves (family *Podophyllaceae*).

A native of southern Europe, introduced and found in damp places in woods, flowering from March to May. The blood-red petals serve to attract insects, the broadly tubular yellow nectaries secreting the nectar. The anthers open by valves which are characteristic of the family.

Shrub up to 6 ft. high, without spines except on the margins of the leaves; leaves leathery, clustered at the ends of the shoots, pinnate with an odd terminal stalked leaflet and 3–4 pairs of leaflets, these opposite, sessile, ovate to rounded acute, with numerous very sharply pointed deltoid teeth; lateral nerves much branched and forming a fine network with the veins; flowers (A, $\times 2$) in racemes clustered at the ends of the shoots, with ovate bud-scales at the base; bracts ovate, acute; pedicels longer than the bracts; sepals (B, $\times 3$) and petals (C, $\times 3$) yellow, the latter distinguished by a pair of nectaries towards the base; stamens (D, $\times 5$) 6, facing inwards, the anthers opening by flaps (valves) the filament with

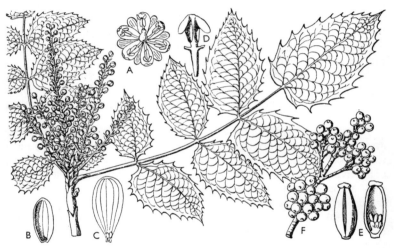

a large tooth on each side near the top; ovary of 1 carpel (E, $\times 3$) with about 6 ovules on the wall near the base; fruit (F, $\times\frac{1}{3}$) a dark-blue 1-seeded berry like a small grape and with a similar 'bloom' (family *Berberidaceae*). – Synonym *Berberis aquifolium* Pursh.

A native of western North America, from Vancouver Island southwards, and much planted as an ornamental shrub in British gardens, often found as an escape in woodlands, flowering in early spring. The stamens are sensitive to touch and move towards the stigma, striking the head of the visiting insect during the process, and depositing a load of pollen which they carry to another flower. The anthers open by valves or flaps (see fig. D), a character common to the family as a whole.

BARBERRY
Berberis vulgaris L. ($\times \frac{2}{3}$)

A shrub up to several feet high in hedges and copses; wood yellowish in section; branches of two kinds, of long and short shoots, the long shoots ribbed and bearing 3-forked, prickle-like, modified leaves (A, $\times 1\frac{1}{2}$); short shoots in the axils of these bearing a tuft of normal leaves, and with the persistent stalks of the previous years' leaves at the base; leaves spoon-shaped-obovate, stalked, very veiny, and with fine sharp teeth on the margin; flowers (B, $\times 4$) in pedulous racemes, each raceme apparently terminating each short shoot; bracts very small; stalks as long or longer than the flowers; sepals usually 9, scarcely distinguishable from the 6 petals in 2 rows, but the latter with a pair of nectaries near the base (C, $\times 10$); stamens 6, moving towards the middle when touched; anthers opening by flaps (D, $\times 6$), as in the Laurel family; ovary (E, $\times 12$) with a few basal ovules; fruit (F, $\times \frac{1}{2}$) an orange-red oblong-elliptic berry, with a broad blackish stigma (G, section of seed) (family *Berberidaceae*).

This bush fell into great disfavour when it was discovered that it was a host for the aecidiospores of the Rust of wheat, *Puccinia graminis*, and for that reason the species is not nearly so common as formerly.

The make-up (morphology) of the Barberry is of great interest, and can be best understood when compared with the Oregon Grape, *Mahonia* (fig. 245). In the latter genus, which is the more primitive, the leaves are pinnate with an odd terminal leaflet, and they are evergreen, whilst the flower-clusters (inflorescence) arise from the axil of a scale of the winter-bud which terminates the long shoot. In *Berberis*, however, the leaves are always simple and usually deciduous, but they are jointed at the base, which shows that they are really a compound leaf like *Mahonia*, but reduced to a single leaflet; and the inflorescence is at the apex of a short shoot, which arises in the axil of a leaf-thorn.

Honey is produced in abundance in swellings on the petals and is eagerly sought by bees. As soon as they touch the lower part of the stamen, the latter moves towards it, and showers the pollen on the head of the insect, which transfers it to the stigma of another flower. The movement of the stamens may be observed by touching the anther of a newly opened flower with the tip of a pencil.

Asarum europaeum L. (× ⅓)

Perennial herb with slender creeping rootstock and a very short
stem clothed with long many-celled hairs; leaves few, usually 2
(or 4) paired
on each stem,
long-stalked,
kidney-shaped
or rounded,
deeply cordate
at the base and
5-nerved, en-
tire, slightly
hairy on the
nerves; stalks
clothed with
long hairs as on
the stem; flower
terminal and
single to each
stem between
the leaf-pairs,
stalked; calyx
persistent, bell-
shaped, tubu-
lar, deeply 3-

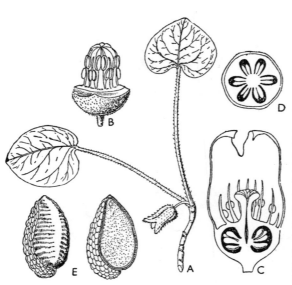

lobed, ⅔–¾ in. long, brownish and hairy outside, dark-purple inside; no petals; stamens (B, ×4) 12, in 2 rows, the filaments prolonged into a point above the anther; ovary (C, ×6) inferior, 6-
locular (D, ×6); style with a 6-lobed stigma; ovules numerous on
axile placentas; fruit rather leathery, bursting irregularly, hairy;
seeds (E, ×8) with a warted caruncle up one side, and minute embryo in abundant endosperm (family *Aristolochiaceae*).

A rather rare plant in Britain and found in shady places in
woods and on hedgebanks, flowering in May; distributed in south
and central Europe to Asia Minor and east to Siberia.

Most members of the family occur in tropical and subtropical
regions.

The calyx (perianth) of *Asarum europaeum* at first opens by
fissures between the three lobes, and these serve as entrances for
the small flies seeking access to the interior of the flower. The
stigmas are close below these three fissures and the insects pass
over them and deposit pollen from previously visited flowers.

Aristolochia clematitis L. ($\times \frac{1}{3}$)

Perennial herb with erect ribbed zigzag stems; leaves alternate, stalked, very broadly ovate, deeply cordate at the base, slightly notched at the apex, up to 5 in. long and broad but usually about $2\frac{1}{2}$ in., entire, glabrous, more or less glaucous below; no stipules; flowers usually 3 or 4 in each leaf-axil, stalked; bud (A, $\times \frac{3}{4}$) acute; calyx modified into a corolla-like tubular structure with a globular base, narrow tube and an ovate oblique notched limb, pale greenish-yellow; stamens (C, $\times 2$) 6, the anthers adnate to the short columnar style below the 6-lobed stigma; ovary (D, $\times 4$) inferior, 6-locular; fruit (E, $\times 1$) a globose, 6-locular capsule about 1 in. diam., seed (F, $\times \frac{1}{2}$) triangular, flat (family *Aristolochiaceae*).

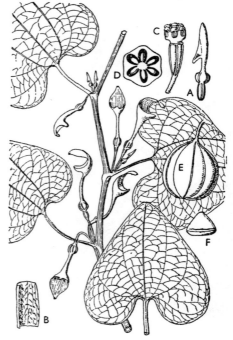

An escape from gardens found here and there amongst old ruins in the south and east of England; native of southern Europe.

The flower is a trap for small insects. It is at first upright and the tube is furnished with downwardly-directed hairs (B, $\times 1$) on the inside, which allow tiny flies and gnats to enter but prevent them from creeping out again. The stigmas are ripe before the anthers of the same flower so that if insects have visited an older flower in which the anthers have opened they effect cross-pollination. The anthers then dehisce and the flower, until now upright, bends downwards, and the hairs closing the tube shrivel so that the exit is no longer barred to the little prisoners. Completely covered with pollen, they emerge and transfer it to a newly opening flower.

Annual, erect, up to about 2 ft. high, clothed with stiff spreading bristly hairs; lower leaves deeply pinnately divided, the divisions

again deeply cut or coarsely toothed (serrate); flowers solitary on long stalks, nodding in bud and covered by two bristly hairy sepals which fall off as the flower opens (A, $\times \frac{1}{2}$); petals 4, overlapping and crumpled in bud, rich scarlet with a black eye at the base; stamens numerous, with slender filaments; ovary really 1-locular, but the placentas (B, $\times 1\frac{1}{2}$) extending from the walls nearly to the middle, broadly top-shaped with a disk-like top from the middle of which radiate the 8–12 sessile stigmas; capsule (C, $\times \frac{3}{4}$) more or less globose, crowned by the disk-like stigmas and opening beneath them by as many pores; seeds (D, $\times 8$) numerous, kidney-shaped, reticulate. (E, vertical section of seed, $\times 8$) (family *Papaveraceae*).

The common Poppy flowers all summer and is often very abundant in cornfields, frequently colouring the landscape. It is poisonous to stock in a green condition. There are no nectaries. Although the stamens are already mature in the bud stage and pollen from them falls on the already receptive stigmas, this self-pollination is ineffective, and later on cross-pollination is brought about by insects visiting the flowers for the pollen itself, as there are no nectaries in the flowers of the whole family.

Another feature of the family is the very fugitive nature of the sepals in many species, which usually fall off as the petals expand. The petals are usually crumpled in bud.

Papaver argemone L. ($\times\frac{1}{2}$)

Annual herb up to about 1 ft. high, usually branched from the base, covered all over with erect bristly hairs; leaves twice deeply divided into narrow lobes, the hairs on the surfaces long and weak; flowers, several on each branch, on long slender stalks; bud (A, ×1) obovoid, of 2 sepals which soon fall off, sparingly bristly outside; petals 4, about 1 in. long, obovate, pale red, often with a large dark blotch at the base; stamens (B, ×4) numerous, the filaments dark crimson and dilated above the middle; ovary bristly-hairy; capsule (C, ×1¼) narrowly oblong, ¾ in. long, crowned by 5 sessile stigmas with a window-like opening below each of them; seeds (D, ×7) curved, ellipsoid, reticulate (family *Papaveraceae*).

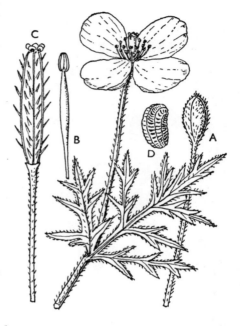

A cornfield weed much less common than the Field Poppy (*Papaver rhoeas* L., fig. 249), and readily distinguished from that species by the swollen filaments of the stamens and the very narrow bristly fruit with only 5 stigmas.

It is the smallest of the British poppies. Poppy capsules are interesting, as they open by little holes near the top through which the seeds escape when blown about by the wind. A similar mode of opening is found in the genus *Campanula* (see figs. 494–504).

Four of the poppies which grow wild or naturalized in Britain are shown in this book. There are other two, *P. dubium* L., the Long-headed Poppy, and *P. lecoqii* Lamotte, known as Babington's Poppy, both of them with glabrous (hairless) capsules, those of the former gradually narrowed from near the top, the latter suddenly narrowed only near the base.

Papaver dubium L. ($\times\frac{2}{3}$)

Annual with a narrow carrot-like root, up to about $1\frac{1}{2}$ ft. high; leaves (A, $\times\frac{2}{3}$) up to 1 ft. long, pinnately divided almost to the

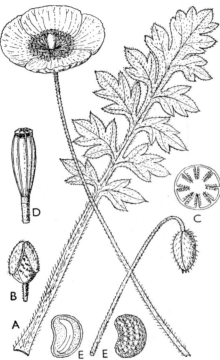

midrib, the lobes again deeply cut into oblong segments, loosely covered with long bristle - like hairs; stems leafy in the lower part, also bristly-hairy; flowers salmon-red, $1\frac{1}{2}$–2 in. diam., on long slender stalks; sepals 2, falling off as the flower opens (B, $\times\frac{2}{3}$), egg-shaped, $\frac{3}{4}$ in. long, loosely covered with long bristle-like hairs; petals 4, veiny; stamens numerous, their stalks and anthers dark purple; no nectary; ovary longer and narrower than in the Field Poppy (fig. 251), narrowed to the base, smooth, 1-locular with 6–12 intruding placentas (C, $\times3$) and numerous ovules; stigmas about 6–12 radiating on the flat top of the ovary; fruit (D, $\times\frac{2}{3}$) tapered to the base (narrowly obconic), capped by the radiating stigmas and opening by 'windows' between each rib; seeds (E, $\times8$) numerous, deeply pitted (family *Papaveraceae*).

Grows in old quarries, in fields, and amongst rubbish-dumps. Like the Field Poppy, it is poisonous to stock, and remains so if mixed with hay. It is readily recognized, especially by its fruit, which is long and narrowed to the base, with fewer stigmatic rays (usually about 8) than in the Field Poppy. As in the latter, there are no nectaries in the flower, insects visiting them to collect the pollen for food.

Erect annual up to 3 ft. high, glabrous except for the bristles on
the flower-stalks; lower leaves oblanceolate in outline and narrowed to the
base, gradually
becoming sessile
upwards and
cordate-auricu-
late, all pin-
nately lobulate
and coarsely
toothed, very
thin; flowers
large, bluish-
white, the petals
with a large
purple blotch at
the base; sepals
2, glabrous or
with a few bristly
hairs at the top,
soon falling off;
petals rounded-
obovate with
crinkly margins;
stamens (A, $\times 3$)
n u m e r o u s;
ovary globose,
shortly stipitate,
1-locular, 9–10
intrusive placen-
tas bearing nu-
merous ovules;
capsule shortly
stipitate, glo-
bose, smooth,
capped by a

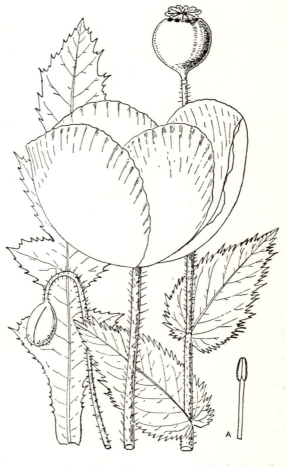

plate-like 9–10-rayed stigmatic disk, with as many holes below the
disk from which the small pitted seeds escape (family *Papaveraceae*).

Flowers from July onwards; a native of southern Europe and
much cultivated; naturalized, especially in maritime districts and
in the Fens of East Anglia.

Perennial herb with yellow sap; rootstock stout, branched; stems slender, up to about $1\frac{1}{2}$ ft. high, glabrous or with a few slender

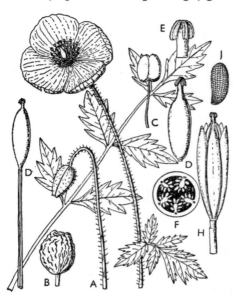

bristles; basal leaves pinnately divided, long-stalked, segments lanceolate, narrowed to the base, coarsely toothed, glabrous or nearly so; stem-leaves becoming nearly sessile upwards, also pinnately divided; flowers terminal, solitary on long slender stalks, nodding in bud (A, $\times \frac{2}{5}$); buds ovoid, thinly bristly-hairy; sepals 2, soon falling off; petals 4, much crumpled in bud (B, $\times \frac{2}{5}$), orange-coloured on opening, changing to chrome-yellow, whole flower nearly 2 in, in diam.; stamens (C, $\times 6$) numerous; anthers small, yellow; ovary (D, $\times 1\frac{1}{4}$) narrowly ellipsoid, green, glabrous, 1-locular with 5 placentas on the walls (F, $\times 3$); ovules numerous; style short, thick, with 5 grooved reflexed stigmas (E, $\times 3$); fruit (H, $\times 1\frac{1}{4}$) a capsule opening by short valves below the persistent style; seeds (J, $\times 8$) small, rugose (family *Papaveraceae*).

A very interesting plant because of its Atlantic distribution, being found only in the western mountainous parts of our islands, growing in moist shady glens from Devon northwards through Wales to Westmorland, up to 2,000 ft. altitude; it is also wild in Eire and is naturalized in some parts of Scotland. On the whole it favours calcareous soil. Elsewhere it occurs in Atlantic Europe, as far south as the central Pyrenees.

This species is the type of the genus *Meconopsis*, and the first specimens (from Wales) were described by Linnaeus, who called them *Papaver cambricum*.

A strong-growing annual on sandy or pebbly sea-shores, very glaucous; basal leaves (A, $\times \frac{2}{5}$) thick, stalked, up to 1 ft. long, deeply

pinnately lobed, the
lobes increasing in size
upwards, these again
coarsely toothed, loose-
ly covered below when
young with short hairs;
stem - leaves sessile,
ovate, less deeply lob-
ed; flowers shortly
stalked, the lower ones
forming well-developed
fruits whilst the upper
are still open; sepals
2, falling off early,
with a few crisped hairs
outside; petals 4, yel-
low, about $1\frac{1}{2}$ in. long;
stamens numerous;
ovary linear, with 2
sessile stigmas; fruit
elongated and slender,
curved, up to 1 ft. long;
the large petals fall off
the second day after
opening, and the stig-
mas develop before the
anthers open and project beyond them, thus preventing self-
pollination; there are no nectaries (synonym *Glaucium luteum*
Scop.) (family *Papaveraceae*).

Although this plant belongs to the same family as the Field
Poppy (fig. 249), to which its flowers bear some general resemblance, though they are yellow, its fruits are quite different, and
are more like those of some of the Crucifer family (*Cruciferae*).
Indeed, the elongated fruits are the most conspicuous feature of
the plant and mature very early. There are several connecting
links between the Poppy and the Crucifer families, the latter being
a more recent or highly evolved group.

VIOLET HORNED POPPY
Roemeria hybrida (L.) DC. ($\times\frac{1}{3}$)

Annual herb up to about 1 ft. high; branches few, sparingly setose-pilose; basal leaves soon withering, stalked, the stalks expanded and ciliate at the base, the blades twice deeply divided into narrow bluntish 1-nerved lobes tipped by a slender bristle; upper leaves sessile but divided like the lowermost; flowers single at the ends of long pedicels, violet-purple with a large deeper coloured basal blotch; buds (A, $\times\frac{1}{3}$) nodding, setose; sepals 2, falling off on opening; petals 4, crumpled in bud; stamens (B, $\times2$) numerous, with purple filaments; ovary 1-locular, with numerous ovules on nerve-like parietal placentas; stigma (C, $\times2$) sessile, 2–4-lobed; fruit a linear capsule, opening by as many valves as stigma-lobes, thinly setose; seeds (D, $\times6$) broadly kidney-shaped, pitted-reticulate (family *Papaveraceae*).

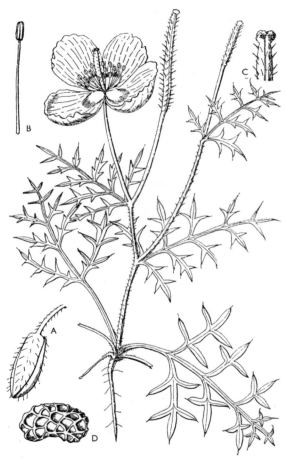

Formerly more common in cornfields in eastern England, but now a rare weed; a native of central and south Europe.

Chelidonium majus L. ($\times\frac{2}{3}$)

Perennial; rootstock thick, fleshy, full of yellow juice which turns reddish when broken; leaves glaucous below, irregularly pinnate, the segments elliptic or obovate, coarsely toothed and often lobulate at the base on one side and resembling stipules; flowers in a loose umbel on a long common stalk (peduncle) opposite the leaf (leaf-opposed); calyx minute; petals 4, yellow, soon falling; stamens (A, $\times 1\frac{2}{3}$) several; ovary linear, with a very short style and small head-like stigma; fruit (B, $\times\frac{4}{5}$) cylindrical, smooth, up to about 2 in. long; seeds (C, $\times 2\frac{1}{4}$) with a large crest on one side; flowers all summer and grows on roadsides and in waste places often near houses and occasionally in neglected gardens; flowers re-

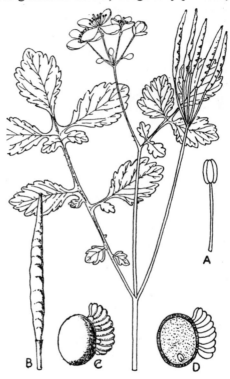

main closed during dull weather, and the anthers then open in bud and effect self-pollination; open flowers are pollinated by bees collecting pollen; no nectaries; juice of root reputed to cure warts; injurious to stock.

This species is rather different from other members of the Poppy family (*Papaveraceae*) to which it belongs, but is not likely to be confused with any other in the British flora because of the position of the flower cluster (inflorescence), whose stalk is placed opposite to a leaf. Only one or two other common herbs share this striking feature, namely the Fumitory (*Fumariaceae*) (fig. 258) and *Coronopus didymus* (*Cruciferae*) (fig. 307). The fruits are similar to those of some *Cruciferae*.

A very delicate slender herbaceous annual climber; leaves twice pinnate; leaflets borne on a slender common stalk which ends in a branched tendril, narrowly elliptic, very thin, narrowed to the base, rounded to a sharp point at the apex, about $\frac{1}{2}$ in. long, finely lined with nerves parallel with the midrib and margin; flowers (A, $\times 2$) whitish, with a dark lilac hood, few, borne on a slender common stalk opposite the leaves (leaf-opposed), white or tinged with yellow; bracts (B, $\times 3$) small, broadly oblong or ovate; flower-stalks very short; petals 4 in 2 pairs, 1 of the outer petals with a short round spur at the base; stamens (D, $\times 2$) in 2 bundles,

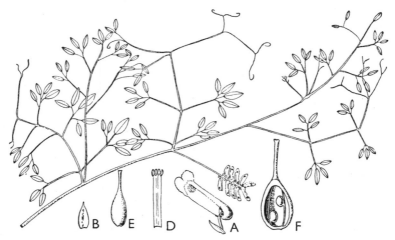

the middle anther 2-locular, the side anthers 1-locular; ovary (E, $\times 4$, F, $\times 7$) with 2 ovules on the placenta on the walls (parietal); style single; fruits few, oblong, beaked, slightly constricted between the seeds, about $\frac{1}{4}$ in. diam., black and shining, with a small crest at the point of attachment (family *Fumariaceae*).

Widely distributed but rarely common, in hilly districts; rare in Eire; flowers in summer, and easily recognized by the climbing habit with tendrils, and the leaf-opposed common flower-stalk (peduncle).

The stamens are at first shorter than the style, the stigma being concealed in the dark lilac hood of the inner upper petal. Into this hood the pollen is discharged and self-pollination may take place.

FUMITORY

258

Fumaria officinalis L. ($\times \frac{2}{3}$)

Annual, glabrous all over, pale green, often forming a dense spreading tuft up to a foot or two in diameter; leaves bipinnate,

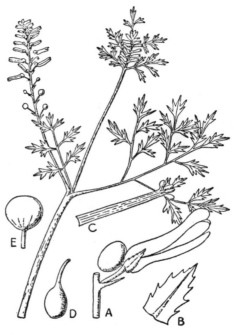

the ultimate segments often coarsely 3-tooth-ed or lobed; flowers (A, ×2) in slender ra-cemes opposite the leaves (leaf - opposed) or terminal, the lower often developed into fruits before the upper have finished; stalks short, in the axil of a small bract; sepals (B, × 4) 2, white or colour-ed, toothed; petals, 4, dull purple, with dark coloured tips, in two pairs, the outer two united at the base, ·the upper with a large pouch at the base; fila-ments (C, ×2½) united into a sheath; ovary (D, ×2½) 1-locular, with two placentas and two ovules on the walls; fruit (E, ×2) a 1-seeded nut, nearly globose (family *Fumariaceae*).

This plant is not likely to be confused with any other except species of the same genus, which are very difficult to distinguish among themselves. The genus may be at once recognized by the position of the common stalk of the flowers (peduncle) which is placed opposite to a leaf (leaf-opposed). Attention is also drawn to this same character in the Greater Celandine (fig. 256) in the Poppy family, and *Coronopus didymus* (fig. 307) in the Crucifer family. Although nectar is secreted in the pouch of the upper petal, the flowers are self-pollinated.

Matthiola incana R. Br. ($\times\frac{1}{3}$)

Hoary herb covered all over with short soft star-shaped whitish hairs (A, ×5); leaves narrowly oblanceolate, the lowermost up to 6 in. long and 1 in. broad, slightly notched at the apex, faintly nerved; flowers mauve, fading to purple or red, few in a terminal raceme; sepals 4, tomentose; petals (B, ×1) 4, with a long claw and broad obovate limb; stamens (C, ×1) 6, 4 long and 2 shorter; anthers cordate at the base; ovary linear with numerous ovules; stigma U-shaped, sessile; fruit (D, ×$\frac{1}{3}$) 4–5 in. long, compressed, shortly hairy; seeds (E, ×3) numerous, compressed, orbicular, with a narrow white wing (family *Cruciferae*).

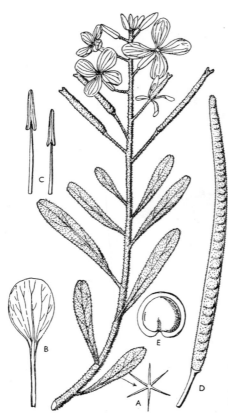

Rare on sea cliffs in southern England and Wales; extends from the Canary Islands to Asia Minor.

The flowers are sweetly scented like cloves. The long narrow claws of the petals are closely clasped by the sepals forming a tube sometimes half filled with nectar which arises from swellings at the base of the shorter stamens.

The anthers of the four long stamens are situated just below the opening of the flower and open by slits which face inwards; they are nearest the stigmas and serve for self-pollination. The anthers of the shorter stamens serve for cross-pollination for the proboscis of an insect trying to reach the nectaries will be dusted by their pollen and transferred to another flower.

Malcolmia maritima (L.) R. Br. (×⅓)

Annual herb up to about 1 ft. high, but sometimes spreading and much branched from the base, covered all over with adpressed stellate 4-armed or 2-armed hairs; leaves grey-green, alternate, spathulate to oblanceolate, the lowermost sometimes with 1–2 teeth on each margin, remainder mostly entire, very thin and loosely covered with 4–2-armed hairs (A, ×4); flowers few in terminal racemes; sepals (B, ×1) 4, two with broader hyaline tips, all covered with adpressed medifixed hairs; petals (C, ×1¼) 4, long-clawed, bilobed, mauve with darker veins, claws greenish; stamens (D, ×2) 6, 4 longer and 2 shorter; anthers rounded to sagittate at the base, produced at the apex; ovary (E, ×2) linear,

with several ovules, closely beset with medifixed hairs; style long; fruits (F, ×½) linear, about 2 in. long, with a slender sharp beak, not flattened, covered with closely adpressed hairs (G, ×3) (family *Cruciferae*).

A favourite garden annual, native of the sea-coasts of southern Europe, sometimes found on shingle beaches.

An interesting feature about the flowers of this species is that the erect stiff pointed rows of bristles on the ovary prevent an insect from probing for nectar concealed around the base of the ovary except in such a way that its proboscis and head touch the pollen-covered anthers and the stigma. The flowers are also said to be self-fertile.

DAME'S VIOLET
Hesperis matronalis L. ($\times \frac{1}{3}$)

Erect annual herb up to 3 ft. high, with simple or slightly branched thinly setose-pilose stems; basal leaves more or less forming a

rosette, soon withering, petiolate, oblanceolate, very slightly toothed and thinly setulose; stem-leaves shortly stalked, lanceolate to oblanceo-late, distinctly dentate, those towards the flowers about 3 in. long and 1 in. broad, thinly pubescent with mostly 2-forked hairs; flowers fragrant in the evening, violet-purple; pedicels about as long as the flower, shortly setulose; outer of the 4 sepals pouched at the base (A, ×2); petals (B, ×2) 4, more than twice as long as the sepals, with a tooth on each side to-wards the base, veiny; sta-mens 6, 4 long and 2 shorter; anthers very large (C, ×2); ovary (D, ×2) elongated, with a ses-sile slightly bilobed stig-ma; fruit (E, ×$\frac{1}{3}$) about 3 in. long, torulose, opening by 2 nerved valves and shortly beaked; seeds (F, ×3) compressed, narrowly elliptic, dark brown (family *Cruciferae*).

A native of central and southern Europe and northern Asia; in Britain only as a garden escape and sometimes found in waste places and by roadsides, flowering in early summer. The large violet-purple flowers give off a strong odour of violets, especially in the evening. Two large green fleshy nectaries surround the bases of the shorter stamens, the nectar collecting on each side of the flower between the insertion of the filaments and the base of the ovary.

Alliaria officinalis Andrz. (flowers and leaves, $\times \frac{2}{5}$;   fruits $\times \frac{4}{5}$)

Erect annual or biennial up to about 3 ft. high, often crowded together, and when rubbed giving off a strong smell of garlic; stems and leaves glabrous or nearly so; lower leaves on very long stalks, these decreasing in length upwards; leaves broadly ovate-triangular, very widely cordate at the base, triangular-pointed at the apex, very coarsely toothed (dentate); main nerves 3–5 from the base; flowers small and white, in terminal and lateral racemes though at first forming a close cluster-like corymb; sepals (A, $\times 2$) soon falling off, green, oblong, rounded at the apex, 4–5-nerved; petals (B, $\times 1\frac{3}{5}$) narrowly obovate, white; sta-

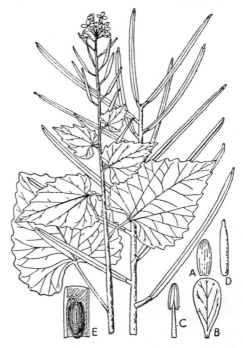

mens (C, $\times 4$) 6, 4 long and 2 short; ovary (D, $\times 3$) with a very short bifid style and several ovules; fruits on very short stout spreading stalks, about 2 in. long, nearly cylindrical, very narrow and with a prominent middle nerve on each valve; seeds (E, $\times 2$) with a broad curved stalk, black, oblong-ellipsoid, flattened on one side, lined (striate) lengthwise (synonym *Sisymbrium alliaria* Scop.) (family *Cruciferae*).

This plant grows in colonies under hedges and in shady waste and cultivated places, flowering in spring; easily recognized by the distinctive shape of the leaves, the very short and stout fruit stalks and the striate seeds. The nectaries are placed at the base of the two short stamens, secreting on their inner sides, and filling the space between the filaments and ovary.

Arabis hirsuta (L.) Scop. ($\times \frac{2}{5}$)

Stiff, erect biennial or annual with an unbranched stem or rarely with one or two weaker stems in addition, up to about 1 ft. high;

basal leaves forming a rosette, spreading, spoon-shaped or ob-lanceolate, narrowed to a broad-based stalk entire or with a few teeth, clothed with rather stiff forked hairs (A, ×15); stem-leaves sessile and half encircling the stem oblong-lanceolate, rather coarsely toothed only in the lower half or entire; flowers small in a small terminal umbel-like cluster but the axis elongating in fruit; sepals (B, ×4) 3-nerved; petals (C, ×4) white, nearly twice as long as the sepals; stamens (D, ×6) 6, 4 long and 2 shorter; ovary (E, ×4) elongated, with numerous ovules and a sessile slightly 2-lobed stigma; fruits (F, ×⅔) very narrow, erect, with numerous flattened seeds (G, ×3); flowers in summer and grows on walls, banks, and rocks (family *Cruciferae*).

Nectar is secreted only on the inside of the bases of the two short stamens. If cross-pollination is not brought about by insects, self-pollination takes place from the anthers of the longer stamens, which are on the same level or above the stigma. A good spotting feature for this plant is the hairy covering of the leaves which is composed of stiff forked hairs. Similar hairs are found in *Erophila* (fig. 296), and star-shaped hairs in *Capsella* (fig. 300), whilst in the wild Wallflower (fig. 271) they are T-shaped.

ALPINE ROCKCRESS 264
Arabis alpina L. (×⅓)

Low-spreading perennial with decumbent slender knotted stem; leafy branches short, softly hairy; leaves (A, ×1) spoon-shaped, coarsely toothed, about 1¼ in. long, rather thick, densely covered on both surfaces with stalked branched (stellate) hairs (B, × 10), flowering-stem-leaves eared (auriculate) at the base, sessile, oblong, coarsely toothed, hairy like the others; flowers in a lax, simple or a little branched raceme, the lower fruits well developed while the uppermost flowers are still in bloom; stalks

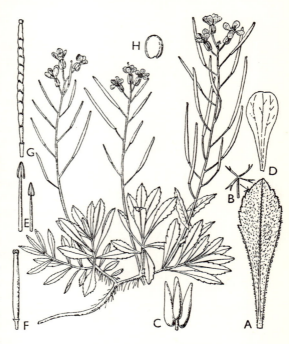

spreading at an angle of 45°, ½ in. long, glistening green and not hairy (glabrous); sepals (C, ×1½) 4, the outer pair larger and deeply pouched at the base, greenish-yellow; petals (D, ×1½) white, spoon-shaped, with a broad claw; stamens (E, ×1½) 6, 4 long and 2 shorter; ovary (F, ×1½) narrow, soon elongating into the slender undulate fruit (G, ×⅘); seeds (H, ×2) rounded, smooth (family *Cruciferae*).

In Britain found only in the Isle of Skye, on the west coast of Scotland, where it should not be disturbed; otherwise distributed in the alps and arctic regions of Europe, Asia, and North America.

The hairy covering (*indumentum*) of the leaves of this plant is very distinctive, being composed of densely packed hairs which are stalked and branched at the top like a star as shown in fig. B.

TOWER MUSTARD
Turritis glabra L. ($\times\frac{1}{3}$)

Erect biennial herb with unbranched stem and basal rosette of leaves, the latter withering during the fruiting period; stem some-

times tinged with violet, slightly hairy towards the base with simple or 2-forked hairs; basal leaves like those of a Dandelion with scattered forked hairs (F, $\times 10$) on both surfaces; stem-leaves sessile, lanceolate, auriculate at the base, entire, glabrous, or very slightly hairy; flowers in a terminal raceme; stalks slightly longer than the flowers; sepals (A, $\times 2$) half as long as the petals, glabrous; petals (B, $\times 2$) yellowish or greenish white; stamens (C, $\times 5$) 6, 4 long and 2 short, the longer as long as the petals; nectaries 6, forming a closed ring around the filaments; stigma disk-like, subsessile; fruit (D, $\times\frac{1}{3}$) up to $2\frac{1}{2}$ in. long, linear, erect, on stalks $\frac{1}{2}$ in. long, opening by valves from the base with a very distinct nerve up the middle; seeds (E, $\times 4$) in 2 rows, compressed, with angular margins (family *Cruciferae*). – Synonym *Arabis perfoliata* Lam.

A very distinctive plant flowering from May to June; widely distributed around the north temperate zone.

There are four nectaries in this flower and they may unite to form a ring. The anthers of the four long stamens touch the stigma with their lower ends, while those of the shorter stamens do the same with their tips, so that automatic self-pollination is effected by either.

Perennial with very short rootstock, often bearing small fleshy scales or tubers; stem erect, up to about 1 ft. high; leaves pinnate,

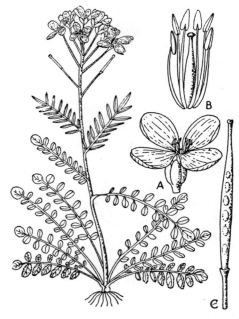

the basal with broader leaflets than those further up the stem; leaflets of basal leaves in 5–7 pairs, elliptic to obovate, the end one larger and more rounded, those of the stem-leaves becoming linear in the uppermost leaves; flowers (A, ×1) corymbose but cluster slightly, elongating as the lower ones grow into fruits; sepals 4; petals 4, white to mauve; stamens (B, ×2) 6, 4 long and 2 short, the anthers rather large and attached at the back near the base; ovary elongated, with a short style and head-like stigma; fruit (C, ×1½) about 1 in. long, divided into two by a thin partition; seeds in a single row in each loculus (family *Cruciferae*).

This delightful little plant is always a great favourite because it is one of the first to flower in spring, soon following the Primrose. It usually grows in little colonies in moist meadows and by the sides of small streams and brooks. Although little used it may be eaten as a salad in the same way as the ordinary Watercress (fig. 273). There are four nectaries, two larger at the base of the short stamens, and one smaller outside each pair of long stamens. The nectar collects in the pouched bases of the sepals, and the pouches of those opposite the two short stamens with the larger nectaries, are proportionately larger than the other two.

Cardamine flexuosa With. ($\times \frac{2}{3}$)

Annual, sometimes much branched at the base, glabrous or with a few scattered stiff hairs on the stems and some of the leaves;

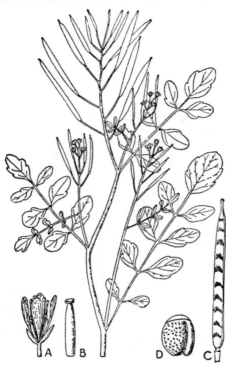

basal leaves forming more or less a rosette, pinnately lobed into separate pairs of leaflets, these more or less obovate and oblique at the base, the terminal one larger and rounded - obovate; flowers (A, $\times 4$) very small, in slender axillary and terminal racemes; sepals lanceolate; petals narrow and erect, white; stamens 6, 4 long and 2 short, the longest as long as the petals; anthers small and rounded; ovary (B, $\times 6$) cylindric, as long as the petals, with a nearly sessile disk-like stigma; fruits (C, $\times 1\frac{1}{2}$) erect, in a slender raceme with a zigzag (flexuous) axis, $\frac{3}{4}$–1 in. long, undulate with the impression of about a dozen seeds on each face, without nerves; seeds (D, $\times 8$) compressed, brown, slightly reticulate, with a distinct radical on one side (family *Cruciferae*).

This plant is scarcely recognizable as being related to the much more handsome **Cuckoo** flower or Lady's Smock, *Cardamine pratensis* L., shown in fig. 266. It is a much more delicate plant and grows on moist or shady banks, and in waste and cultivated places, and is very widely spread in temperate regions. The name of the species refers to the flexuous or zigzag growth of the stem and the axis of the raceme, especially when it is in the fruiting stage.

Cardamine hirsuta L. ($\times\frac{1}{2}$)

A rather dark green annual, on moist or shady banks, and in waste and cultivated places throughout temperate regions, usually about 6 in. but some-times nearly a foot high, glabrous (in spite of the specific name) or very slightly hairy; lower leaves form-ing a loose rosette, pinnate, with a few rounded stalked lateral leaf-lets and a broader rounded or kid-ney-shaped end leaflet; a few stem leaves with rather narrower and smaller leaflets; flowers very small, white, few, in ter-minal racemes, soon developing into fruit (A, $\times\frac{1}{2}$); petals about twice as long as the sepals; stamens often only 4; ovary linear, with a sessile stigma; fruits (B, $\times2$) on

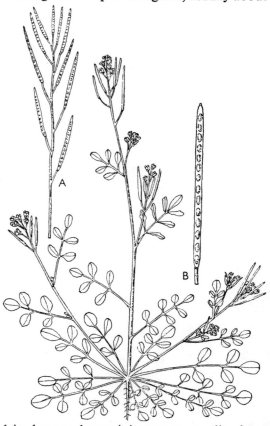

slender stalks up to $\frac{1}{2}$ in. long and remaining erect, usually about 1 in. long, the valves not keeled; seeds brown, compressed, almost square in outline, smooth (family *Cruciferae*).

This species has a very unsuitable specific name, for it is only slightly hairy and certainly not *hirsute*, which means covered with hairs. When botanists were free to choose what they considered to be the most suitable name, this one would have been objected to, especially by R. A. Salisbury, who gained notoriety in this prac-tice early last century.

Cardamine amara L. ($\times \frac{1}{2}$)

Perennial herb with slender rootstock, and with creeping offshoots rooting at the nodes; stems and leaves glabrous; leaves borne on

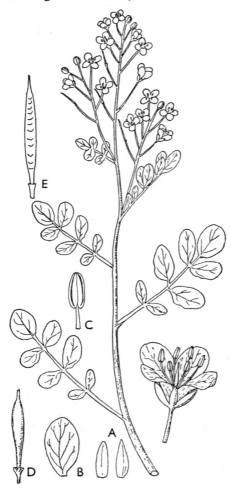

the flowering stems, pinnate, with usually 3 pairs of leaflets and a large terminal leaflet, all these more or less elliptic or rounded, with wavy or very obscurely toothed margins, the lateral leaflets sessile or nearly so, the end one shortly stalked; flowers in terminal and axillary racemes; sepals (A, $\times 2\frac{1}{2}$) oblong, with thin margins; petals (B, $\times 2\frac{1}{2}$) 4, somewhat spreading, typically white but sometimes pink (var. **erubescens**), veiny; stamens (C, $\times 6$) 6, nearly equal in length, the anthers purple-red; ovary (D, $\times 3$) shortly stalked, with several ovules on 2 parietal placentas; style short; fruit (E, $\times 1\frac{1}{4}$) linear, flat, crowned by the persistent style, the valves without a nerve up the middle; seeds in a single row in each partition (family *Cruciferae*).

Grows in wet meadows and along brooks and streams, flowering in spring and early summer.

Recognized from the more common *Cardamine pratensis* L. (fig. 266) by the slender rootstock throwing off creeping offshoots, weaker zigzag stems, fewer leaflets, and usually pure white petals with purple-red anthers.

Perennial herb with a very pale (nearly white) creeping rootstock (R) bearing a few thick ovate scales toothed at the top; stem erect but weak, up to 2 ft. high; leaves alternate, scattered, usually with a dark violet bulbil (A) in the axil, the lower stem-leaves fern-like and pinnate with 2–3 pairs of leaflets and an odd terminal one, gradually becoming reduced to a single leafy bract; leaflets narrowly and obliquely oblong, the terminal oblanceolate, all slightly toothed, very minutely hairy on the margin, bright green above, paler below; flowers (B, $\times1\frac{1}{4}$) few, mauve, in a short raceme; sepals 4, rounded at the base, purplish or greenish; petals (C, $\times1\frac{1}{4}$) 4, lilac or almost white;

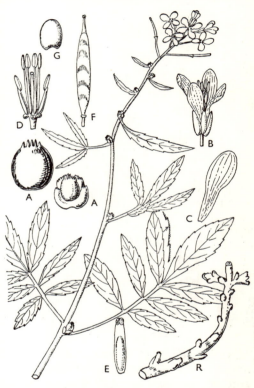

stamens (D, $\times2\frac{1}{2}$) 6, 4 longer and 2 shorter, the longer with a pair of small green nectaries between them at the base, the shorter with a larger single nectary opposite the base; ovary oblong (E, $\times2$); style short; fruit (F, $\times\frac{1}{2}$) rarely if ever produced in Britain, compressed, about $1\frac{1}{2}$ in. long, 3–4-seeded, beaked by the persistent style; seeds (G, $\times2$) broadly oblong, smooth (family *Cruciferae*). – Synonym *Dentaria bulbifera* (L.).

One of the most interesting plants in the British flora and confined to Bucks, Herts, west Middlesex, Kent and north Sussex; otherwise distributed from south Norway and Denmark east to Petrograd and south to the Caucasus, Persia, and Italy.

271   WALLFLOWER
Cheiranthus cheiri L. ($\times \frac{2}{5}$)

Perennial with woody stems and several branches, more or less covered on these and the leaves with 2-armed appressed hairs

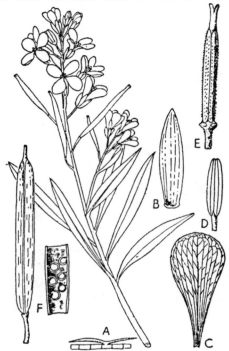

(A, $\times 5$); leaves lanceolate to linear, narrowed to each end, entire; flowers sweet-scented in a lax terminal and sometimes axillary raceme, the lowermost forming fruits whilst the uppermost are still in bud; sepals (B, $\times 2$) 4, narrowly lanceolate; petals (C, $\times 2$) 4, pale yellow to deep red, spoon-shaped, gradually narrowed to the base, veiny; stamens 6, 4 long and 2 short; anthers (D, $\times 1\frac{1}{4}$) rather large, fixed at the base; ovary (E, $\times 3$) covered with short reflexed hairs, with a short stout style, and 2 divergent stigmas; fruit (F, $\times \frac{4}{5}$) narrow, flattened, divided by a thin partition, about $1\frac{1}{2}$–$2\frac{1}{2}$ in. long; grows freely on old walls or rocky railway cuttings, and near houses, either wild or escaped from cultivation; flowers in spring (family *Cruciferae*).

A good spotting feature for this plant when not in flower is the character of the hairy covering on all parts. This is composed of 2-armed hairs with a very short stalk in the middle, the two tips of the arms being free. These peculiar hairs have thus the appearance of lying flat on the surface. There are only two nectaries in the flower, one at the base of each of the two short stamens. The anthers completely close the entrance to the flower. The four upper anthers touch the stigma with their lower ends, while the two lower ones do so with their tips. Either cross-pollination or self-pollination is possible.

328

Erect annual up to 2½ ft. high, more or less branched in the upper part; stem angular, loosely clothed with minute appressed medi-fixed hairs (A, ×3); leaves lanceolate, thin, slightly and distantly toothed, finely pubescent with 3-armed hairs (A1, ×3) on both surfaces; flowers numerous in racemes which soon elongate and the lower develop into fruit; stalks longer than the flowers but shorter than the fruit; 2 of the 4 sepals (C, ×2½) with hooded apex showing particularly in bud (B, ×2), pubescent; petals (D, ×2½) pale yellow, claw equal to the elliptic limb; stamens (E, ×3) 6, 4 long and 2 shorter; ovary (F, ×2) angular, with 2 nearly sessile stigmas; fruits (G, ×1) ribbed-angular, ¾ in. long, with a very short beak; seeds (H, ×6) smooth, brown (family *Cruciferae*).

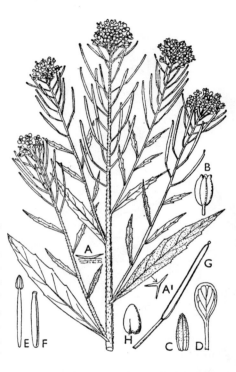

Found chiefly in cultivated and waste ground; probably introduced from Europe, from which it ranges to eastern Asia; introduced into North America.

Other names for this species are 'Wormseed Mustard' and 'Wallflower Mustard'. According to Syme the seeds of this plant were at one time given to children as a vermifuge, and were said to be very effective. The plant formed an ingredient in the so-called Venice treacle and many rustic medicines.

Stem much branched, creeping in mud or floating in shallow water; leaves alternate, pinnate, the end leaflet largest and ovate

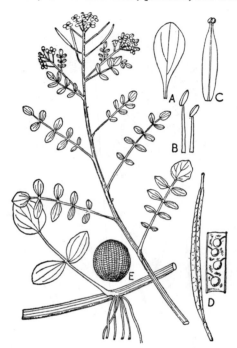

to orbicular and slightly toothed, the other leaflets gradually smaller downwards, glabrous; flowers small, forming a corymb in the upper part, those of the main shoot maturing first and of the lateral shoots later; sepals 4; petals (A, $\times 3$) 4, white, broadly spoon-shaped, entire; stamens (B, $\times 3\frac{1}{2}$) 6, 4 long and 2 short; anthers attached near the base; ovary (C, $\times 4$) soon elongating into fruit, with a short style and 2 stigmas; fruits (D, $\times 1\frac{1}{4}$) nearly 1 in. long; seeds (E, $\times 7$) globose and finely pitted, the embryonic root lying against the edge of the seed-leaves (cotyledons) (family *Cruciferae*).

Howard and Manton (Ann. Bot. n. ser. 10: 1 (1946)) have shown that two distinct species were confused under the name 'Nasturtium officinale R. Br.', the true one, a diploid with short fruits and seeds in a double row, and the other, to be called *N. microphyllum* (see Airy-Shaw, Kew Bull., 1947, 39), a tetraploid with longer fruits and seeds in a single row. My drawing represents the latter.

CREEPING YELLOW CRESS 274
Rorippa sylvestris (L.) Besser ($\times\frac{1}{3}$)

Perennial herb up to 1½ ft. high with rather weak zigzag angular and ribbed stems clothed with minute reflexed hairs; rootstock thick and nearly white, creeping; leaves alternate, pinnate, with about 4 pairs of leaflets and a terminal leaflet, these more or less lobed or coarsely toothed (dentate), bright green and not hairy; flowers (A, ×2) in terminal racemes, at first rather crowded but the main axis soon elongating in fruit; stalks ½ in. long (in fruit); buds glabrous; sepals (B, ×4) 4, green, elliptic; petals (C, ×2) 4, rich cream-yellow, clawed, twice as long as the calyx; stamens (D, ×2) 6, 4 long and 2 a little shorter; nectaries 4, separate, very deep green; ovary (E, ×2) cylindric, stigma slightly 2-lobed; ovules numerous; fruit (F, ×1) curved, spreading, narrow, ½ in. long; seeds (G, ×8) brown and very minutely pitted

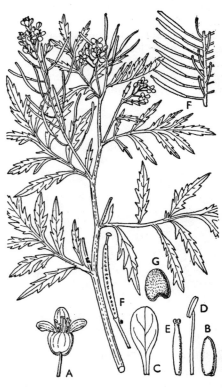

(synonym *Nasturtium sylvestre* R. Br.) (family *Cruciferae*).

Found usually in moist ground by streams and brooks, but sometimes in neglected gardens, flowering in July and August. Widely distributed from Europe to eastern Asia, and introduced into North America.

Other names are Water Rocket and Wild Nasturtium. *Rorippa* is usually classified as a section of the Watercress genus *Nasturtium*, mainly because of its yellow flowers and relatively shorter pods. Genera of the family *Cruciferae* are mostly very similar to one another and separated by slight differences, which in other families would be considered to be not more than specific.

331

ICELAND WATERCRESS
Rorippa islandica (Geder) Borbás (×½)

Perennial growing in muddy places by ditches, etc.; basal leaves withering as the plant develops; stem-leaves auriculate at the base, lyrately-pinnately lobed almost to the midrib, lobes rather unequal, the top 3 more or less merged together into one, all the lobes coarsely toothed, glabrous; flowers numerous on axillary and terminal leafy shoots, very soon producing fruits whilst a few at the top are still in bloom; stalks slender, as long as the fruit; sepals (A, ×6), elliptic, rounded at the apex; petals (B, ×6) 4, white, narrowly obovate, clawed; stamens (C, ×6) 6, 4 long and

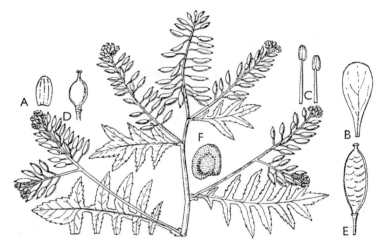

2 short; anthers elliptic; ovary (D, ×4) ellipsoid, with a short style and 2-lobed stigma; fruit (E, ×1½) narrowly oblong, almost round in section, containing numerous small pale brown closely beaded seeds (F, ×6) (synonym *Nasturtium* palustre (Leyss.) DC.) (family *Cruciferae*).

This is quite a common plant which is described in most *Floras* and lists under the name *Nasturtium palustre* DC. The latest classification, however, assigns it to a separate genus, *Rorippa*. It has also been called *Radicula*, and if it could speak it might modify this word a little to abuse the botanists who have changed its name so often.

Barbarea vulgaris R. Br. ($\times \frac{2}{3}$)

Perennial, with stiff erect stems up to 2½ ft. high, branched in the upper part; lower stem leaves deeply pinnately divided, the terminal lobe much the largest and more or less obovate or elliptic, the other lobes quite small; stem leaves sessile and markedly eared (auriculate) at the base, more or less deeply lobed or toothed; racemes forming a panicle, the branches of which elongate in fruit; flower-buds (A, ×4) with two short horns at the apex, glabrous; sepals B, ×3) 4, oblong, obtuse, faintly 3-nerved; petals (C, ×3) 4, narrowly oblanceolate; stamens (D, ×7) 6, 4 long and 2 short; ovary elongated, with a short style; fruits (E, ×1¼) very narrow, wavy, more or less erect, about

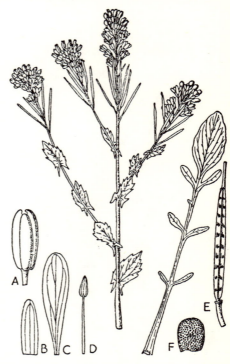

1 in. long, beaked by the persistent style; seeds (F, ×4) several, very finely and closely pitted (family *Cruciferae*).

Grows on roadsides, in hedgebanks, and by canals, flowering in spring and summer; a very closely related but less common species is *B. stricta* Andrz., distinguished by its hairy buds.

Wintercress was formerly called Herb St Barbara, hence the Latin name of the genus. In Sweden it is boiled and eaten.

There is a small fleshy green nectary on each side of the short stamens, and these are often united into a semicircular ridge. There is also a larger elongated tooth-like nectary outside and between the bases of each pair of long stamens and corresponding to the short stamens which have disappeared. The latter secrete much less nectar than those at the base of the short stamens.

FRENCH ERUCASTRUM
Erucastrum gallicum (Willd.) O. E. Schulz ($\times \frac{1}{3}$)

Annual or biennial herb; stems erect, more or less hairy with downwardly directed hairs; leaves alternate, petiolate, half clasp-

ing the stem at the base, deeply and rather irregularly pinnately lobed, lobes with rounded lobules, with very scattered bulbous-based hairs on both sides; flowers in a terminal corymb-like raceme soon elongating when in fruit, a few of the lower pedicels sub-tended by a reduced leaf; pedicels longer than the flowers; se-pals 4, erect, with a few slender hairs on the upper part; petals (A, $\times 2\frac{1}{2}$) 4, obovate, long-clawed; sta-mens (B, $\times 3$) 6, 4 longer and 2 shorter, anthers attached above the base; ovary (C, $\times 2$) linear, with a short style and broad capitate stigma; fruits (D, $\times \frac{2}{3}$) 1½ in. long, ascending on stalks about ½ in. long, 2-valved, the valves with a distinct median nerve; seeds (E, $\times 5$) numerous, compressed, elliptic, brown, minutely pitted-reticulate (family *Cruciferae*). – Synonyms *Sisymbrium erucastrum* Poll.; *S. gallicum* Willd.

In waste ground especially near ports; a native of west and central Europe. A second introduced species occurs in similar places, with bright-yellow petals and the fruit distinctly stalked (stipitate) above the scar of the fallen calyx, and of which the sepals are spreading and not erect as in *Eruscatrum gallicum.*

HEDGE MUSTARD   **278**
Sisymbrium officinale (L.) Scop. ($\times\frac{1}{2}$)

Erect tough annual up to about $1\frac{1}{2}$ ft. high, with green stems sometimes tinged with crimson, clothed with very short hairs, becom-

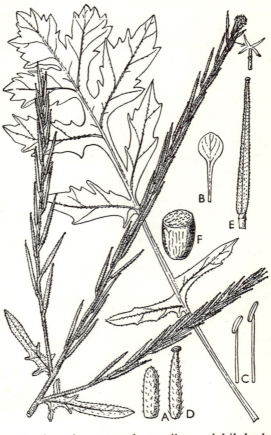

ing rather zigzag
with age; lower
leaves deeply and
very irregularly
pinnately lobed,
the lobes rather
unequally toothed
or lobulate, thinly
and very shortly
bristly hairy on
both surfaces;
flowers very small,
yellow, in short
racemes terminat-
ing the branches,
which elongate
greatly in fruit,
forming a leafy
panicle; pedicels
very short; sepals
(A, ×6) 4, ob-
long, thinly hairy;
petals (B, ×6)
spoon-shaped,
with a long slen-
der claw; stamens
(C, ×8) 6, 4 long
and 2 shorter;
anthers attached
in the middle;
ovary (D, ×10)
very narrow, pubescent, the stigma nearly sessile, and bilobed;
fruits (E, ×2) remaining parallel with and close to the elongated
axis of the inflorescence, about $\frac{1}{2}$ in. long, sharply pointed, pubescent or at length glabrous; valves with a prominent keel-like midrib; seeds (F, ×8) rounded but with a flat top (family *Cruciferae*).

A weed in waste places and by the roadside, widely distributed
into Russian Asia; flowers in summer; readily recognized by its
elongated spreading branches.

335

Sisymbrium altissimum L. ($\times \frac{1}{2}$)

Erect annual, up to about $1\frac{1}{2}$–2 ft. high; basal leaves pinnately divided to the midrib, lobes opposite, spreading, lanceolate in outline, coarsely and irregularly toothed, with a larger lobe on the lower margin near the base, loosely clothed with long stiff hairs on the midrib and nerves, especially below; upper leaves among the flowers also deeply divided into narrow entire segments, glabrous or nearly so; flowers in panicles, fruits being developed before the upper flowers have opened; buds (A, $\times 1\frac{1}{2}$) ellipsoid, with a pair of humps (like a purse) at the top; sepals (B, $\times 3$) narrowly oblong, the outer 2 horned below the apex; petals (C, $\times 3$) 4, white, veiny; stamens (D, $\times 3$) 6, 4 long and 2 short; anthers (D, $\times 3$) long, sagittate at the base; ovary (E, $\times 3$) elongated, cylindric, stigma sessile; fruits (F, $\times \frac{1}{2}$) long and very slender, cylindric, glabrous (synonym *Sisymbrium pannonicum* Jacq.) (family *Cruciferae*).

This is an alien in the British flora, and is a native of the continent of Europe and Asia. After the First World War it became very abundant in the battlefields of France and Belgium, and is spreading rapidly in Britain.

The family *Cruciferae* is one of the most homogeneous or natural and very easily recognized. This is because the members of the family are all herbs with radical or alternate leaves, without stipules, there are 4 sepals and 4 petals, and associated with them, with a very few exceptions, 6 stamens, 4 of which are always longer than the other 2. This condition is described in botanical language as *tetradynamous* – a rather formidable word to which some readers might take exception, and which I have not employed in the descriptions.

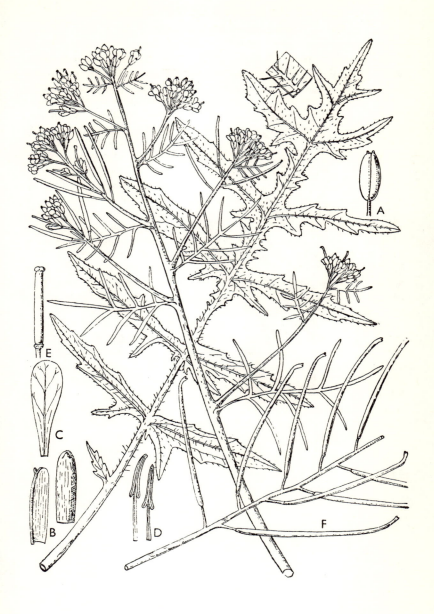

337

FLIXWEED
Sisymbrium sophia L. (×½)

Erect annual up to 2½ ft. high; stems minutely hairy with stellate hairs, flexuous; leaves 2–3 times pinnate from the base, up to about 3 in. long, segments lanceolate or narrowly oblong, glabrous or very finely pubescent with woolly stellate hairs; flowers very small in terminal racemes, these elongating to about 1 ft. long in fruit, many of the latter ripe before the upper flowers are finished; sepals (A, ×5) 4, oblong-lanceolate, glabrous; petals (B, ×10) 4, yellow, spoon-shaped, much shorter than the sepals; stamens (C, ×8) 6, 4 long and 2 shorter; ovary (D, ×6) narrow, with 2 sessile stigmas; fruit (E, ×2) ¾ in. long, slightly curved and a little torulose, with a distinct midrib down the middle of the valves; seeds (F, ×10) ellipsoid, brown, smooth (synonym *Descurainia sophia* (L.) Prantl) (family *Cruciferae*).

Found in waste places and sandy fields, chiefly in eastern Britain; flowers in summer.

Arabidopsis thaliana (L.) Heynh. ($\times \frac{2}{3}$)

Slender erect annual sometimes branched from the base; leaves in a basal rosette, petiolate, oblanceolate, dentate especially in the lower half, sprinkled on both surfaces with stiff simple or 2–3-armed hairs (A, ×8); stem-leaves very few and sessile; branches ending in a bunch of flowers, the main axis elongating as the fruits soon ripen; sepals 4, elliptic; petals (B, ×4) 4, white, narrowly obovate, clawed, faintly nerved; stamens (C, ×4) 6, 4 long and 2 short; anthers ovoid, short; ovary (D, ×4) elongated, with numerous ovules, and a nearly sessile stigma; fruits (E, ×1½) about ¾ in. long, on spreading stalks, 1-nerved; seeds (F, ×4) numerous and very small, rounded, smooth, brownish (synonym *Sisymbrium thalianum* (L.) Gay) (family *Cruciferae*).

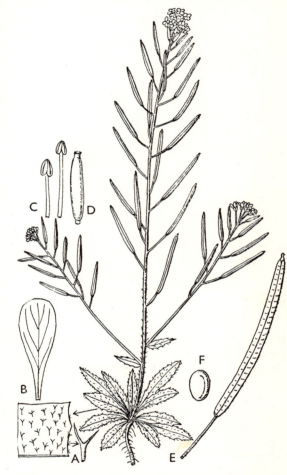

This species is locally abundant, and is found in light sandy fields, on walls and rocks. It is widely distributed.

282 BLACK MUSTARD

Brassica nigra (L.) Koch. ($\times\frac{1}{3}$)

Annual up to about 4 ft. high, glaucous-green all over, especially the branches, not hairy (glabrous); leaves alternate, lower stalked,

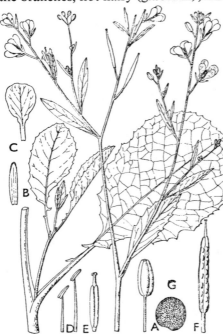

more or less obovate or broadly elliptic, with one or two much smaller or very small extra lobes on the edge of the deeply channelled stalk, wavy-toothed on the margin, paler below; leaves smaller upwards and entire as they become bracts at the base of the branches bearing the flowers; these few in racemes; buds (A, $\times 1$) 4-humped at the top; sepals (B, $\times 1\frac{1}{2}$) spreading in flower, a little longer than the claws of the lemon-yellow petals (C, $\times 1$); stamens (D, $\times 1\frac{1}{2}$) 6, 4 long and 2 short; anthers becoming curved, arrow-shaped at the base; ovary (E, $\times 1\frac{1}{2}$) narrow, containing several ovules inserted on the walls; fruits (F, $\times 1$) parallel with the flower-axis, about $\frac{1}{2}$ in. long, beaked by the persistent style, 4-angled by the 4 ribs, a rib up the middle of each valve; seeds (G, $\times 4$) dark brown, closely and minutely pitted (family *Cruciferae*).

To be found in hedges and waste places, sometimes on sea-cliffs; frequently an escape from cultivation; it has the appearance of a maritime plant because of the clean glaucous-green colour of the stems. The bright-yellow flowers of this species have a strong odour of coumarin. There are 4 green nectaries, of which 2 are on the inner side of the short stamens, and the others between the insertions of the long stamens. Insects effect cross-pollination. Self-pollination may also be brought about when the flowers are bent by the wind, as the anthers of the long stamens are at the same level and close to the stigma.

Sinapis alba L. ($\times\frac{1}{3}$)

Annual, up to about 3 ft. high; stems bright green, with a narrow hollow centre lined with a layer of white, ribbed, and with a few short reflxed bristles; leaves alternate, stalked, lyrately and pinnately divided to the stalk, the lobes increasing in size upwards, the upper much the largest and 3-lobed to about the middle, margins coarsely and irregularly toothed, bright green, glabrous except for short bristle-hairs here and there on the nerves; flowers numerous in slender racemes, the oldest at the base and well into fruit before the uppermost have opened; no bracts; sepals (A, $\times 1$) · 4, half-spreading, very narrow, yellowish-green, $\frac{1}{4}$ in. long;

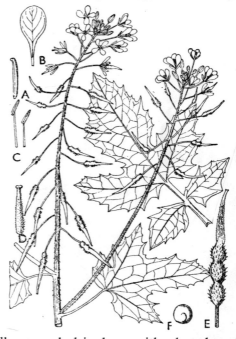

petals (B, $\times 1$) lemon-yellow, nearly $\frac{1}{2}$ in. long, with a long broad claw; stamens (C, $\times 1$) 6, 4 long and 2 short; ovary (D, $\times 1$) elongated, covered with bristly white hairs; stigma large and fleshy, bifid; fruits (E, $\times 1$) scattered along the elongated axis, stalks spreading, about $\frac{1}{3}$ in. long; lower part 3–6- or rarely 1–2-seeded, bristly, the upper part prolonged into a flat beak about $\frac{3}{4}$ in. long; seeds (F, $\times 2$) rounded, straw-coloured, the size of a very small pea (family *Cruciferae*).

The golden-yellow flowers, which exhale an odour like that of vanilla, are very similar to those of the Black Mustard (*Brassica nigra*) (fig. 282), and there are 4 nectaries. Automatic self-pollination is prevented, however, for the anthers of the long stamens turn their pollen-covered sides outwards away from the stigma. The anthers of the shorter stamens face inwards. Honey-bees and hover-flies visit the flowers.

A coarse-growing annual weed up to 2 ft. high, often spread amongst corn in great quantity; stems clothed with a few stiff whitish hairs, lower leaves shortly stalked, upper sessile, obovate-elliptic, coarsely toothed or lobulate and toothed, with several spreading forked lateral nerves, with a few stiff hairs mainly on the nerves; flowers yellow, showy, at first in a congested raceme which soon elongates as the fruits develop, some of which are nearly ripe by the time the topmost flowers open; flower-stalks very short; sepals 4, spreading and soon falling off; petals (A, $\times 1\frac{1}{4}$) spoon-shaped with slender claws; stamens 6, 4 long and 2 short; anthers rather large, arrow-shaped at the base; ovary smooth or hairy; fruits (B, $\times \frac{4}{3}$) about $1\frac{1}{2}$ in. long, the upper part

composed of a stout beak, the lower part smooth or hispid with reflexed hairs, containing about 10–12 seeds, the latter black and finely pitted-reticulate (family *Cruciferae*).

A common cornfield weed which when in flower in any quantity gives quite a colour to the landscape. The sepals spread horizontally so that the nectar is exposed, but the flowers are so crowded that insects find it more convenient to reach it in the ordinary way by thrusting their proboscis between the stamens. If cross-pollination is not attained, self-pollination is effected by the stigma pushing up between the anthers.

Perennial herb up to $1\frac{1}{2}$ ft. high; basal leaves glabrous or hairy, lyrately pinnate, the end lobe obovate and often 3-lobed, dentate or subentire, up to 9 in. long, the stem leaves becoming smaller and bract-like; flowers yellow in lax panicles of racemes, the branches much elongating in fruit with the fruits more or less parallel and close to the branch; sepals (A, $\times 2$) oblong, obtuse, glabrous; petals (B, $\times 2$) spathulate, long-clawed; stamens (C, $\times 2$) 6, 4 long and 2 short; ovary (D, $\times 2$) linear, with 2 sessile papillous stigmas; fruits (E, $\times 2$) terminated by a 1-seeded beak;

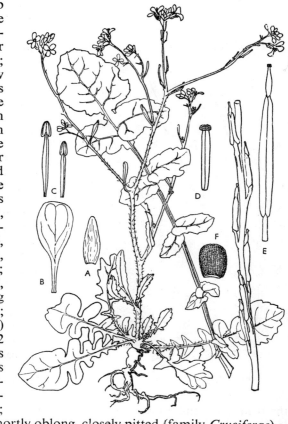

seeds (F, $\times 4$) shortly oblong, closely pitted (family *Cruciferae*). – Synonyms *Brassica adpressa* Boiss.; *Sinapis incana* L.

In waste places often around docks and near the sea, flowering during summer, producing mature fruits whilst still in flower; extends to southern Europe. – Drawn by Olive Tait.

Rhynchosinapis erucastrum (L.) Dandy ($\times\frac{1}{3}$)

Annual or biennial herb about 1 ft. high, with a narrow taproot, the stem often with a few bulbous-based bristles towards the base;

basal leaves up to about 6 in. long, pinnately divided, the lobes irregularly dentate, glabrous except for long slender bristly hairs on the midrib below and on the petiole; stem leaves smaller, with narrow sometimes entire segments; flowers in branched racemes, rather large; sepals 4, longer than the pedicels, with thicker tips; petals pale yellow, long-clawed with a broad veiny limb; stamens 6, 4 longer and 2 shorter; anthers large, yellow; ovary glabrous; style half as long as the ovary; fruits spreading, 2½–3 in. long, valves ribbed on the back, with a thick acute beak (A, $\times\frac{2}{3}$) about ¼ as long as the fruit body and containing 1–3 seeds; fruit-stalks about ½ in. long; seeds (B, $\times4$) numerous, dark, rounded, deeply pitted-reticulate (family *Cruciferae*). – Synonyms *Brassicella erucastrum* (L.) O. E. Schultz; *Brassica cheiranthus* Vill.

An introduced plant in waste places in south and eastern England and in south Wales; native of south-west and central Europe as far east as Italy.

Diplotaxis muralis (L.) DC. ($\times\frac{1}{3}$)

Annual herb with a dense basal rosette of spreading leaves, aromatic when bruised; leaves spoon-shaped-oblanceolate in outline, up to about 6 in. long, deeply pinnately lobed, the lobes with wavy or slightly toothed margins, glabrous or with a few stiff hairs; flowering stems up to about 9 in. high, few-flowered, the main stalk with a few bulbous-based reflexed stiff hairs (A, ×3); sepals (B, ×2) 4, 2 of them hooded at the apex, not hairy; petals (C, ×2) 4, yellow or tinged with crimson (when dry), obovate-spoon-shaped, veiny; stamens (D, ×2) 6, 4 longer and 2 shorter; ovary

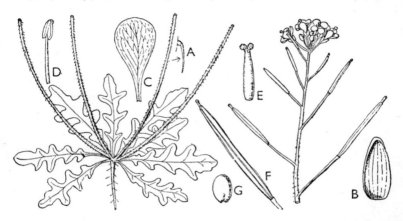

(E, ×2) glabrous, with 2 almost sessile rounded stigmas; fruit (F, ×$\frac{2}{3}$) developed while the upper flowers are still opening, 1$\frac{1}{4}$–1$\frac{1}{2}$ in. long, with a distinct midrib up the middle of the valves; seeds (G, ×5) numerous, rounded, smooth, greenish-brown (synonym *Brassica muralis* (L.) Boiss.) (family *Cruciferae*).

Grows in fields and in cultivated and waste places, flowering all the summer; common in southern and central Europe.

This plant has a disagreeable smell when rubbed. It is distinguished by the fruits with numerous seeds and the stems clothed with a few bulbous-based hairs, which are directed downwards.

AWLWORT
Subularia aquatica L. ($\times\frac{1}{2}$)

Tiny aquatic or terrestrial annual or biennial herb up to about 3 in. high, with white fibrous roots; leaves small and sedge-like,

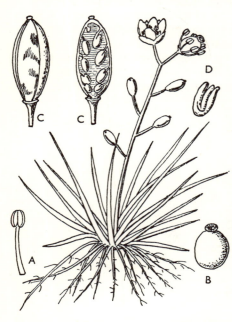

somewhat fleshy, erect, linear-subulate, entire, glabrous; stem leafless, 2–8-flowered; pedicels longer than the very small flowers; sepals 4, elliptic, erect, green, margined with white, all equal and not pouched at the base; petals 4, white, oblong, boat-shaped to narrowly obovate, about twice as long as the calyx; stamens (A, ×4) 6, with about equally long filaments and ellipsoid anthers; nectar stored in an annular ring below the ovary; ovary (B, ×4) globose-ellipsoid, the base immersed in the receptacle; stigma sessile, disk-like and with a ring-like margin; fruits (C, ×3) oblong-elliptic, about $\frac{1}{4}$ in. long, valves with a faint middle nerve; seeds 2–7 in each partition, pendulous, elliptic, brown, punctate (family *Cruciferae*). – D, embryo (×4).

A genus with a single species circumpolar in the northern hemisphere, south to the eastern Pyrenees; in Britain only from north Wales northward, in lakes and pools or near them, flowering in late summer and autumn.

When under water the flowers do not open (cleistogamous), and more seeds are set in the fruits than in the chasmogamous form living on the shore. In the submerged flowers there are large papillae on the stigma which receives the pollen directly from the anthers near by.

Cochlearia officinalis L. ($\times\frac{1}{2}$)

A fleshy annual or biennial up to about 1 ft. high; lower leaves on long stalks, rounded-ovate, widely cordate at the base, about 2 in. wide, sometimes larger and more or less pentagonal, 3–5 nerved from the base, with undulate or crenate margins; stem-leaves sessile and eared (auriculate) at the base; flowers (K, $\times2$) in short corymb-like racemes collected into a leafy panicle; sepals (A, $\times2$) 4, oblong-elliptic; petals (B, $\times4$) white, oblong, broadly clawed; stamens (C, $\times5$) 6, 4 long and 2 shorter; anthers (D, E, $\times7$) attached at the back above the base; ovary (F, $\times3$) broadly ovoid, with a short thick style and capitate stigma; fruit (G, H, long-section, $\times2$) broadly ellipsoid, $\frac{1}{4}$ in. long, openly reticulate, beaked by the short persistent

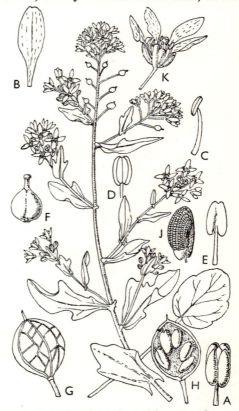

style, the valves falling away and leaving the white membrane-like false septum; seeds (J, $\times8$) few, much curved, with a caruncle, and closely pitted all over (family *Cruciferae*).

Scurvy Grass is common on many muddy sea-shores and on damp maritime cliffs, especially where water trickles down. The flowers open from May to July, and are followed by the short, nearly globular fruits. The common name is derived from its former antiscorbutic use, and it was well known to the early voyagers as a remedy for the disease which in olden days decimated ship's crews on long voyages.

Cochlearia anglica L. (×⅓)

A low, rather fleshy annual or biennial, with semi-decumbent or ascending stems, glabrous all over; basal leaves on long stalks winged upwards towards the wedge-shaped base, the blade more or less rhomboid and with a few coarse teeth or lobules on each margin, the 2 or 3 pairs of lateral nerves much branched and looped well within the margin; stem-leaves gradually smaller and becoming more sessile upwards; flowers white, in slender terminal racemes, fruiting towards the base before the upper flowers have finished; sepals (A, ×2) 4, narrowly obovate; petals (B, ×2) ladle-shaped, with a truncate top and short claw; stamens (C, ×2) 6, 4 long and 2 shorter; anthers attached in the middle; ovary ovoid, with a short style and a head-like stigma; fruits (D, ×1½) on spreading stalks about ½ in. long, broadly ovoid, ½ in. long, reticulate, beaked by the short persistent style; seeds rounded, brown, minutely warted all over (family *Cruciferae*).

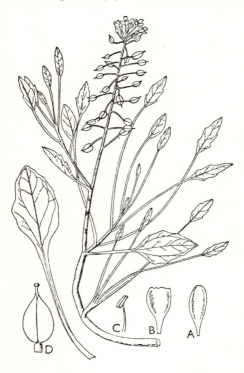

Grows in muddy salt marshes and amongst stones of embankments by the sea and by the shores of tidal rivers, flowering in spring and early summer.

Cochlearia is a genus of about 25 species distributed in Europe, Asia and North America; 6 species are found in Britain, the two included here and four others, mostly growing in mountainous districts.

Amoracia lapathifolia Gilib. ($\times\frac{1}{2}$)

Perennial with a stout parsnip-like rootstock, very sharp to the taste; basal (radical) leaves large, on long stalks, the base of the stalk embracing the stem; blade more or less elliptic, rounded at the apex, some decurrent at the base, usually bluntly and irregularly crenate, but sometimes deeply and very irregularly divided; stem leaves gradually sessile, linear and only obscurely toothed; racemes on long axillary peduncles and all forming an oblong leafy panicle, the flowers at first closely bunched together, the lower stalks long and very slender; flower-buds broadly ellipsoid, glabrous; sepals 4 (A, $\times 5$) unequal, ovate-elliptic, green; petals 4 (B, $\times 2\frac{1}{2}$) white, ovate-lanceolate; stamens 6 (C, $\times 5$), 4 long and 2 short; anthers ovoid; ovary (D, $\times 6$) ellipsoid, crowned by a fat sessile stigma; fruits (E, $\times\frac{1}{2}$) not ripening in Britain (synonym *Cochlearia armoracia* L.) (family *Cruciferae*).

Horse Radish is always associated with the roast beef of Old England, and its roots find a place in nearly every kitchen garden. It is also naturalized in many places.

292 SMALL ALISON

Alyssum alyssoides L. ($\times\frac{1}{3}$)

Annual herb branched from the base, covered all over with whitish
stellate hairs (B, ×8); taproot with numerous thread-like root-
lets; lower part of stems leafless; leaves (A, ×1) alternate, linear-oblanceolate, without visible nerves except for the midrib; flowers (C, ×3) in terminal racemes; sepals boat-shaped, covered with stellate and fine simple hairs; petals (D, ×5) yellow, linear, contracted above the middle and slightly bi-lobed at the apex, about $1\frac{1}{2}$ times as long as the sepals; stamens (E, ×5) 6, the shorter filaments with 2 long setae at the base; anthers very small and cordate; ovary

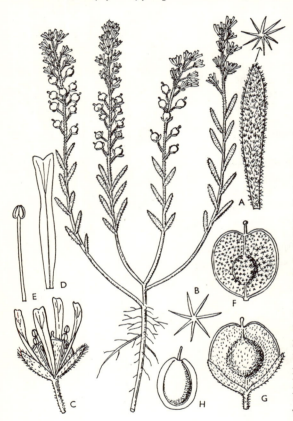

(F, ×5) orbicular, compressed, with 2 ovules in each partition;
style very short in the *V*-shaped groove at the apex; fruit (G, ×3)
with persistent sepals at the base, compressed, orbicular, covered
with short stellate hairs and with 2 seeds in each division bulging
out the middle; seeds (H, ×4) with a narrow hyaline wing (family
Cruciferae). – Synonym *Alyssum calycinum* L.

An introduced plant in fields and arable land; native of Europe
and western Asia.

Berteroa incana (L.) DC. ($\times\frac{1}{2}$)

Erect annual herb with rather woody stems crimson towards the base, clothed all over with stellate hairs mostly with unequal-lengthed rays; stem-leaves sessile, narrowly lanceolate, grey-green, entire, about 2 in. long, covered with stellate hairs (A, $\times 15$); flowers racemose-corymbose; pedicels longer than the flowers, covered with stalked stellate hairs with one arm longer than the others (B, $\times 12$); sepals 4, half as long as the petals, pilose with stellate hairs; petals (C, $\times 4$) 4, white, deeply bilobed and clawed; stamens (D, $\times 4$) 6, 4 longer and 2 shorter, the filaments of the shorter with a large tooth on one side; anthers ellipsoid; ovary (E, $\times 5$) ellipsoid, densely stellately hairy; style as long as the ovary; ovules several; fruit (F, $\times 2\frac{1}{2}$) oblong-ellipsoid, tipped 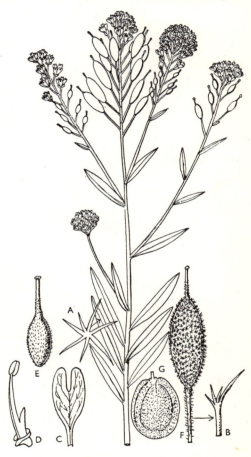 by the persistent longish style, compressed, covered with very short stellate hairs; seeds (G, $\times 6$) compressed, rounded, very minutely warted (family *Cruciferae*). – Synonym *Alyssum incanum* L.

A native of dry places in central and southern Europe and north Asia; often found in Britain along railways and roadsides.

SWEET ALYSSUM
Lobularia maritima (L.) Desv. (×½)

Dwarf herbaceous to rather woody perennial plant up to about 1 ft. high, covered all over with grey adpressed hairs attached by

their middle (bifurcate) (A, ×8); leaves (B, ×2) scattered, linear to narrowly linear-oblanceolate, entire, up to 2 in. long, covered, especially when young, by grey hairs as described above; flowers (C, ×5) white, scented like honey, in slender terminal racemes, the lower flowers soon developing into fruit; pedicels ⅓ in. long; sepals (D, ×7) 4, spreading, elliptic, hairy outside; petals (E, ×7) 4, more or less orbicular and clawed; stamens (F, ×7) 6, 4 longer and 2 shorter; anthers rounded; style short; fruit (G, ×4) compressed, dehiscent, orbicular-elliptic, slightly hairy, with 1 compressed seed (H, ×4) in each loculus (family *Cruciferae*). – Synonym *Alyssum maritimum* (L.) Lam.

Naturalized on walls and waste places near the sea; much grown in gardens as an edging; very abundant around the Mediterranean and in the Atlantic Islands.

A favourite garden plant, best known under its common name of Sweet Alyssum.

Draba incana L. ($\times\frac{1}{2}$)

Perennial or biennial herb growing amongst rocks on mountains; annual rosette of leaves spreading, oblanceolate, about $\frac{3}{4}$ in. long, slightly toothed, all the stems and leaves covered with simple and stellate hairs; stem-leaves crowded and overlapping, sessile, oblong-lanceolate, up to 1 in. long, with 2–4 spreading teeth on the margins, densely covered with hairs; flowers small and white in a terminal cluster which soon elongates in the fruiting stage; sepals (A, $\times\frac{1}{2}$) oblong, 3-nerved, slightly hairy; petals (B, $\times3\frac{1}{2}$) oblong-spoon-shaped, shortly clawed; stamens (C, $\times5$) 6, 4 long and 2 shorter; ovary (D, $\times3\frac{1}{2}$) with sessile stigmas; fruit (E, $\times\frac{1}{2}$) oblong, about $\frac{1}{3}$ in. long, glabrous, valves flat, becoming slightly twisted after opening (family *Cruciferae*).

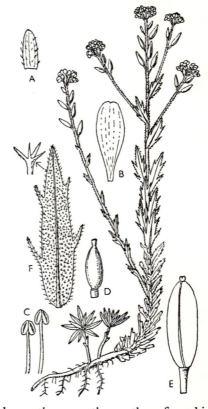

Found only in the hills and mountains of northern England, north Wales, Scotland, and in Eire.

Besides the species shown above, there are three others found in Britain:. *D. aizoides* L., the Yellow Whitlow Grass, with glabrous leaves except on the margin, *D. rupestris* R. Br., the Rock Whitlow Grass, with hairy leaves and the flowering stem leafless or nearly so, and *D. muralis* L., the Wall Whitlow Grass, leaves densely hairy below and broadly ovate and clasping the stem.

Erophila verna (L.) E. Mey. ($\times\frac{2}{3}$)

Dwarf annual flowering in early spring and lasting only a few weeks; leaves all in a dense rosette and spreading on the ground, oblanceolate to ovate or oblong, slightly toothed, clothed with stalked star-shaped hairs (A, ×10); flowering stalks (peduncles) several from the leaf-axils, leafless, up to a few inches high, the lower flowers developed into fruits before the uppermost open; flowers very small; sepals (B, ×10) 4; petals (C, ×4) 4, white, deeply divided into 2 parts; stamens (D, ×8) 6, 4 long and 2 short; anthers attached near the base; ovary (E, ×5) ellipsoid,

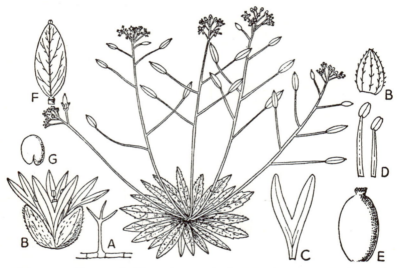

with a sessile comb-like stigma; fruits, on long slender stalks, about ¼ in. long, compressed, divided by a thin partition, containing numerous minute seeds (G, ×10) on stalks of varying length (family *Cruciferae*). (In many botanical books this plant is called *Draba verna* L.)

The observer will notice that in this plant and several others nearby the stamens are described as being '4 long and 2 short'; this arrangement is called tetradynamous, and is characteristic of all the Wallflower family *Cruciferae*; other constant features are the four sepals and four petals arranged in the form of a cross, hence the Latin name of the family.

Biennial or perennial herb forming clumps; stems simple, erect or ascending, up to 9 in. high in fruit; basal leaves (A, ×2) long-petiolate, spathulate-obovate, the blade about 1 in. long, glabrous, with very faint nerves; stem-leaves few, sessile and sub-cordate at the base, ovate to lanceolate; flowers (B, ×4) numerous, the lower opening first and soon developing into fruit, the upper ones when still in bloom forming a small close corymb; pedicels

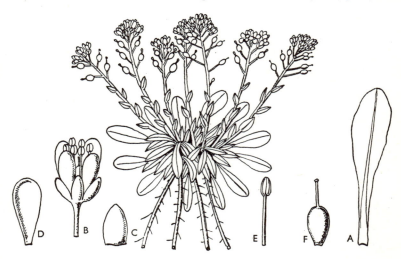

$\frac{1}{2}$ in. long in fruit; sepals (C, ×4) erect; petals (D, ×5) white or pinkish, oblanceolate-spathulate; stamens (E, ×5) 6, 4 long and 2 short; anthers drying black; ovary (F, ×5) compressed, the style distinct but shorter than the ovary; fruits spreading about $\frac{1}{4}$ in. long, winged at the top, the wings forming a wide notch, style persistent, the valves falling away from the partition; seeds 6–8 in each loculus, brown, smooth (family *Cruciferae*).

In mountain pastures in limestone districts, flowering during summer; extends to southern Sweden and south to the Himalayas.

Besides this species and the Field Penny Cress shown in fig. 298, there is one other species, *T. perfoliatum* L., much less common and confined to limestone soils from Oxford to Gloucester and Worcester. It is an annual with ovate-cordate amplexicaul leaves and yellow anthers.

Thlaspi arvense L. ($\times \frac{1}{2}$)

Erect glabrous annual up to about 1 ft. or 15 in. high, each branch ending in a raceme of small flowers, most of these becoming almost mature fruit whilst the uppermost are still in bud; lower leaves narrowed to the base but soon withering; upper leaves gradually becoming sessile and ear-shaped (auriculate) at the base, from oblanceolate (lower ones) to oblong (upper ones), rather irregularly and distantly toothed (obtusely dentate); flowers more

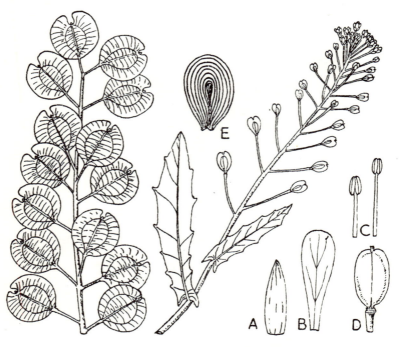

or less corymbose at the top, the axis bearing young fruits soon elongating; sepals (A, $\times 6$) 4, green and faintly 3-nerved; petals (B, $\times 6$) white; stamens (C, $\times 7$) 6, 4 long and 2 a little shorter; ovary (D, $\times 5$) compressed, slightly winged, elliptic, notched at the top and with a very short style; fruits orbicular, thin and flattened contrary to the thin partition between the two halves, not quite the size of a farthing, deeply notched at the top and broadly winged; seeds (E, $\times 7$) 5 or 6 in each loculus, obovoid, dark brown, surrounded by several ribs (family *Cruciferae*).

Usually a tiny and neat annual with a rather long taproot, but sometimes up to $1\frac{1}{2}$ ft.; leaves spreading in a rosette forming a circle 2–3 in. diam., deeply pinnately lobed, the largest lobes towards the end, the terminal lobe broad and rounded, glabrous or nearly so, except the stalks; flowers very small in a dense cluster at the end of a long common stalk (peduncle) from one to several to each plant; sepals (A, ×6) 4, triangular, green with white tips; petals (B, ×6) 4, white, narrowly oblong-oblanceolate, outer longer than the inner; stamens (C, ×7) 6, 4 long and 2 shorter; filaments with a very white scale at the base; anthers ellipsoid; ovary (D, ×6) nearly orbicular, glabrous, with a sessile stigma; 2 ovules in each loculus (E, ×9); fruits (F, ×3) rather compressed,

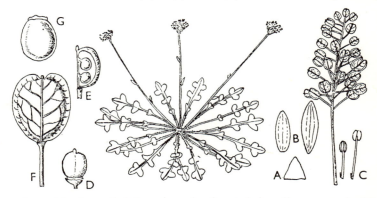

nearly orbicular, slightly winged, about $\frac{1}{6}$ in. diam.; seeds (G, × 10) 2 in each half, rounded, with a narrow crest at the base (family *Cruciferae*).

At first the raceme of tiny flowers is congested, but it lengthens as the fruits develop, and in vigorous specimens is 2 in. or so, excluding the stalk; it grows in sandy and gravelly places and flowers from April to June.

The outer petals are larger than the others, as in some *Umbelliferae*, and the inflorescence at first resembles that of the same family. As the outer flowers fade in turn, however, the axis of the inflorescence lengthens out into a raceme. There are 4 nectaries, and, failing cross-pollination, self-pollination is effected by the long stamens.

Capsella bursa-pastoris (L.) Medik. (×⅖)

Annual, common weed in cultivated and waste places, flowering nearly all the year round, clothed with star-like hairs (A, ×10);

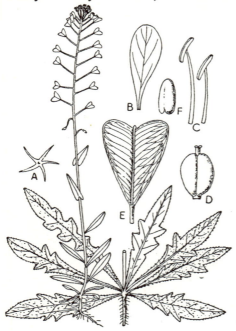

taproot slender; radical leaves in a rosette, pinnately lobed or entire, tapered to the base; lower stem-leaves oblanceolate, entire or toothed, upper ones clasping the stem with ear-like base; flowers very small, in a slender terminal raceme which elongates during flowering; lower flowers already fruiting whilst the uppermost are still in bud; sepals 4; petals (B, ×6) 4, white, spoon-shaped; stamens (C, ×6) 6, 4 long and 2 short, anthers attached in the middle; ovary (D, ×8) ellipsoid; style short with 2 stigmas; fruit very characteristic (E, ×2), narrowly obtriangular, shortly 2-lobed at the top, wedge-shaped to the base; seeds (F, ×5) several in each of the two divisions (family *Cruciferae*).

For our purposes we may regard the Shepherd's Purse as consisting of one rather variable species, though critical students of the British flora are able to recognize more than one. A good spotting character is the star-shaped hairs. It is noteworthy in this highly evolved and most successful type of plant that either cross-pollination or self-pollination may occur, and that the latter is effective. Cultural experiments made in England showed that there was no appreciable difference in the size of plants grown from seed produced by crossing compared with those from self-pollinated stock.

A small annual herb up to about 4 in. high, branched from near the base; stem and branches very minutely hairy, with star-shaped hairs; leaves pinnate, mostly basal, shorter than the racemes, with several narrowly obovate side-lobes and a slightly larger terminal lobe, glabrous; flowers numerous in short slender racemes, white; sepals 4, nearly erect, equal at the base; petals (A, ×10) very small, equal, entire; stamens (B, ×10) 6, with slender

filaments and rounded anthers; filaments with a small nectary on each side of the two shorter stamens; fruits (C, ×5) broadly elliptic, about $\frac{1}{10}$ in. long, compressed at right angles to the partition, purplish, reticulate; seeds (D, ×10) 2 in each half of the fruit, compressed, not margined or winged (family *Cruciferae*). – Synonym *Hutchinsia petraea* (L.) R. Br.

A rare species found amongst limestone rocks in western Britain; extends to Asia Minor and north Africa; now excluded from the genus *Hutchinsia* because of the presence of mucilage in the seeds.

BITTER CANDYTUFT
Iberis amara L. ($\times\frac{1}{3}$)

Annual herb, up to about 9 in. high, with spreading branches; stem slightly ribbed, the ribs with very short hairs; leaves scattered along the stem and branches, sessile but very much narrowed to the base, narrowly oblanceolate, up to $2\frac{1}{2}$ in. long, with up to three short blunt lobes on each side, glabrous or very slightly hairy; flowers (A, $\times 2$) white, tinged with pink or purple, nearly $\frac{1}{2}$ in. in diam., arranged in corymbs; sepals 4, rounded; petals (B, $\times 3\frac{1}{2}$) 4, unequal in size, the two towards the outside of the cluster much larger than the inner two, making the flower 'irregular', entire, with short claws; stamens (C, $\times 3\frac{1}{2}$) 6, 4 long and 2 shorter; fruits (D, $\times 3$) compressed at right angles to the partition, appearing winged, reticulate, produced beyond the actual tip into short triangular points, style persistent; seeds (E, $\times 2\frac{1}{4}$) solitary in each half of the fruit, rather compressed and slightly winged around one side (family *Cruciferae*).

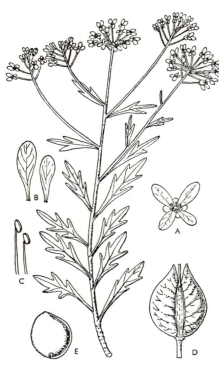

Sometimes fairly common on chalky soils of hills and in cornfields, especially in the southern counties of England.

Lepidium heterophyllum Benth. ($\frac{1}{2}$)

Perennial herb branching from the base, up to nearly 2 ft. high in fruit; stems and leaves softly pubescent all over with short hairs; basal leaves (A, $\times\frac{1}{2}$) on long stalks, oblanceolate, entire or slightly toothed, up to 6 in. long including the stalk; stem leaves numerous and often closely set, sessile, eared (auriculate) at the base, lanceolate, somewhat acute, 1–1$\frac{1}{2}$ in. long, varying from nearly entire to rather sharply toothed; flowers crowded in oblong terminal racemes which in fruit elongate to about 4 in.; axis, flower-stalks, and sepals hairy; petals (B, $\times$2) white, clawed; stamens (C, $\times$2) 6, the filaments without appendages; anthers violet; fruit (D, $\times$3) short and elliptic, $\frac{1}{4}$–$\frac{1}{3}$ in. long, compressed laterally (i.e. in the opposite plane to the partition), the sides winged upwards and forming a notch with the persistent style overtopping the notch; seed solitary in each partition (family *Cruciferae*).

Grows in pastures and waste places and by roadsides, flowering in spring and summer; confined to western Europe. Synonym *Lepidium smithii* Hook.

Lepidium campestre (L.) R. Br. ($\times\frac{1}{2}$)

Annual or biennial up to about 15 in. high, with a long slender taproot, softly and very shortly hairy all over; lower leaves form-

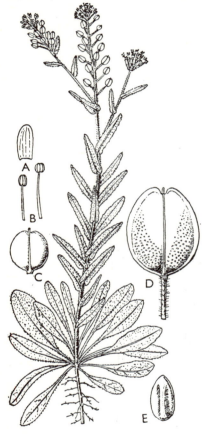

ing a loose rosette, withering away in fruit, spathulate-ob-lanceolate, entire to pinnati-fid; stem-leaves narrowly ob-long-lanceolate, sessile and eared (auriculate) at the base; racemes few, forming a panicle at the top of the plant, at first short and dense, soon elongat-ing, with the fruits maturing in the lower part whilst the top is still in flower; pedicels spreading; sepals (A, ×5) oblong, rounded at the top; petals absent; anthers (B, × 6) yellow; ovary (C, ×6) broadly elliptic, notched at the top and with a very short style; fruits (D, ×2) numer-ous, somewhat compressed, ovate in outline, with a wing on each side from near the base upwards, minutely flaky; seeds (E, ×3) oblong-ellipsoid (family *Cruciferae*).

The fruits are very charac-teristic, and with their stalks resemble a small ladle-spoon.

In some books this plant is called 'Mithridate Pepper-wort'. In old pharmacy the term mithridate was used for a composition of many ingredients which were regarded as a universal antidote or preservative against poison and infectious disease. It grows in hilly fields and in cul-tivated and waste ground.

Cardaria draba (L.) Desv. ($\times \frac{1}{2}$)

Perennial; stems simple, up to about 1 ft. high or more, with prominent angles, not hairy (glabrous), or very slightly so;

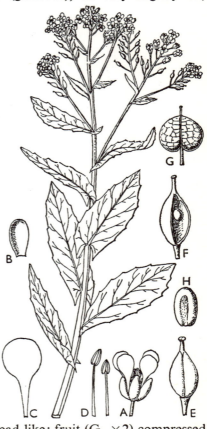

leaves alternate, sessile, oblong or oblong-elliptic, deeply eared (auriculate) at the base, rather rounded to the subacute apex, very minutely hairy on both surfaces, with short unbranched hairs, pale green and slightly shining, remotely and shortly toothed; flowers (A, ×3) in racemes bunched together in the axils of the upper leaves and forming a corymb; leaves gradually reduced to bracts at the base of each raceme; pedicels slender, spreading, up to $\frac{1}{2}$ in. long; sepals (B, ×5) 4, almost equal-sized, not pouched at the base, pale green with white margins; petals (C, ×5) 4, white, spoon-shaped, $\frac{1}{6}$ in. long, with a long slender claw; stamens (D, ×5) 6, 4 long and 2 short; anthers ellipsoid; ovary (E, ×5) narrowly ovate, compressed, with 1 ovule in each loculus (F, ×5); style short, stigma head-like; fruit (G, ×2) compressed at right angles to the partition, broadly ovate, reticulate, not winged; seed (H, ×3) solitary in each loculus, flattened, elliptic, smooth, brown (synonym *Lepidium draba* L.) (family *Cruciferae*).

Grows in waste places and by roadsides, and widely distributed in central and south Europe, and into Russian Asia; it flowers during spring and early summer.

WOAD
Isatis tinctoria L. ($\times\frac{1}{3}$)

Tall erect herb; stems clothed here and there with a few long weak spreading hairs; basal leaves long-stalked, oblong-elliptic, gradu-

ally narrow to the base, the blade about 4–5 in. long and up to 2 in. broad, undulate on the margin, bristly hairy especially on the stalk; stem-leaves gradually becoming sessile upwards and ear-shaped (auriculate) at the base, oblong-lanceolate, glaucous; flowers (A, ×2) small and numerous in a terminal panicle with leaf-like ear-shaped bracts; sepals (B, ×3) 4, elliptic; petals (C, ×3) yellow, narrowly obovate, broadly clawed; stamens (D, ×3) 6, 4 longer and 2 shorter; anthers elliptic; ovary (E, ×5) obovoid, compressed, with a sessile stigma; fruit (F, ×1) pendulous on slender stalks, compressed, oblong-oblanceolate, emarginate at the apex, not opening, containing a single seed (G, ×3) (family *Cruciferae*).

On cliffs in chalk pits and in cornfields, flowering in summer; widely distributed in the northern hemisphere.

This plant is of interest because it was used by the natives of Britain to colour their bodies when the country was invaded by the Romans. Until recent times it was much cultivated in Lincolnshire for dyeing cloth. Easily recognized, especially by the fruit which does not open but is broadly winged, notched at the apex and usually with only a single seed, although there are two ovules, one of which fails to develop.

Coronopus didymus (L.) Smith ($\times \frac{4}{5}$)

Annual with numerous spreading or ascending branches, often sprinkled with a few slender hairs; leaves deeply pinnately divided into 3–5 pairs of narrow entire or slightly toothed lobes, glabrous or nearly so; flowers (A, $\times 5$) very minute, white, arranged in loose leaf-opposed racemes which at first are contracted, but soon elongate in the fruiting stage; stalks slender and soon spreading; sepals 4, boat-shaped; no petals; stamens 2, between the two lobes of the ovary; anthers rounded; ovary (B, $\times 6$) 2-lobed, with a sessile minutely 2-lobed stigma in the middle; fruit (C, $\times 4$) divided

into 2 rounded coarsely reticulate lobes readily separating from the central axis (synonym *Senebiera didyma* (L.) Pers.) (family *Cruciferae*).

This is doubtfully native, but is very common in waste and cultivated ground and spreads rapidly; remarkable in the family in having only 2 stamens instead of the usual 6 with 4 long and 2 short. The second species found in this country, *C. procumbens* Gilib., is really native, and is a coarser plant with shorter racemes of fruits which are not notched at the top, and is coarsely wrinkled and warted, even horned; a sketch of the fruit (D, $\times 4$) of this species is inset at the top left-hand corner of the figure.

Crambe maritima L. ($\times\frac{1}{3}$)

A maritime plant on sandy and shingly coasts; perennial, with
fleshy rootstock; branches spreading from the root; leaves few,
large and fleshy, up to nearly 1 ft. long, ovate-triangular in outline
but with wavy and irregularly toothed margins, very glaucous;
flowers (A, ×2) arranged in a panicle of racemes; flower-stalks
(pedicels) up to $1\frac{1}{2}$ in. long in fruit; sepals (B, ×2) 4, soon falling
off; petals (C, ×$1\frac{1}{3}$) white, rounded, shortly stalked (clawed),
spreading, the 'stalk' at first yellowish-green, then violet-red,
stamens 6, 4 longer and 2 shorter, the longer stalks (filaments)
with a tooth near the middle (D, ×2); ovary (E, ×2) with a
sessile 2-fid stigma; fruit (F, ×1) composed of a lower very short

stalk-like portion, and an upper broadly ellipsoid reticulate part
containing a single globose seed (family *Cruciferae*).

Well known to gardeners, who force it in the dark in green-
houses in early spring; the etiolated growths are eaten as a deli-
cacy. It was at one time an object of special regard in the dwellings
of south coast fishermen, who climbed the cliffs or hung by
means of ropes in order to collect the tender shoots as they
emerged from the sand and shingle in spring.

The flowers smell like honey, and at the base of each pair of
longer stamens is a large green nectary, to which a drop of nectar
clings. The stigma is already mature in the bud before the anthers
open, and occupies the middle of the newly-opened flower.

Raphanus raphanistrum L. ($\times \frac{2}{5}$)

Annual or biennial up to 2 ft. high; stems with stiff bristly spreading hairs; leaves deeply pinnately lobed, the terminal lobe much the largest, obovate rounded, irregularly dentate, often with darker tipped teeth, remainder of lobes smaller and spreading, oblong or lanceolate, all loosely clothed with bristly hairs; upper stem-leaves becoming narrow and entire or nearly so; flowers few, in a terminal raceme, large and showy; sepals (A, $\times 1\frac{3}{5}$) 4, about $\frac{1}{3}$ in. long, with a few bristles towards the apex; petals (B, $\times 1\frac{1}{4}$) large, $\frac{3}{4}$ in. long, broadly spathulate, either white with coloured veins or pale yellow or lilac; stamens 4 long and 2 short; anthers (C, $\times 4$) large, attached above the base; ovary glabrous; style

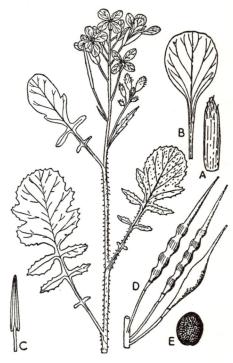

very short; fruit (D, $\times 1$) with a long beak, not opening, contracted between the few (4–7) seeds (sometimes only 1–2-seeded and then not jointed), the latter (E, $\times \frac{3}{5}$) rounded and finely reticulate (family *Cruciferae*).

A common weed of cultivation and waste places, flowering in summer and autumn.

There are four nectaries in the flower, two on the inner side of the short stamens, the other two between the long stamens. Automatic pollination takes place, but is ineffective, the long stamens projecting beyond the stigmas, and the shorter on the same level, the anthers turning their opened sides towards the stigma.

SEA ROCKET
Cakile maritima Scop. ($\times\frac{1}{3}$)

A fleshy annual much-branched from the base, branches slightly angular; leaves alternate, half clasping the stem, fleshy, deeply lobed, lobes narrow and mostly obscurely toothed, slighty paler beneath; flowers (B, $\times1\frac{1}{4}$) in terminal and leaf-opposed racemes which elongate in fruit; stalks shorter than the flowers; buds (A, $\times2$) crowded together, their tips covered when young with weak hairs which fall off; sepals 4, nearly equal, green; petals (C, $\times2$) 4, very pale mauve, veiny, the blade about $\frac{1}{4}$ in. long; stamens (D, $\times2$) 6, 4 longer and 2 shorter; ovary (E, $\times1\frac{1}{4}$) green, with a sessile

slightly 2-lobed stigma; fruit (F, $\times\frac{2}{3}$) with a short thick stalk, at first narrow and entire, when ripe separating transversely into 2 parts, the upper half falling away and containing 1 erect seed, the lower half persistent and with 1 ovule which rarely ripens into a seed (family *Cruciferae*).

Common in maritime sands and salt marshes all around Britain, and in Europe generally and western Asia; flowers from June to the autumn.

Cakile is a small genus of four species, three of which inhabit maritime shores, the fourth being found only in the deserts of central Arabia. The fruits of this genus are very distinctive, being composed of two unequal 1-seeded joints.

Annual or biennial herb; stem erect, up to 2 ft. high, full of soft white pith, slightly ribbed, sparingly clothed with short down-wardly directed setose hairs; lower leaves with a large ovate blade and with auricles on the petiole, wavy-toothed, upper leaves becoming unlobed and narrow but toothed, all with a few simple short hairs or nearly glabrous; flowers in lax panicles of ra-cemes, soon developing fruits along the branches with the terminal part still in bloom; pedicels a little shorter than the flowers; sepals 4, glab-rous; petals (A, ×3) 4, citron-yellow with darker veins paling to white, long-clawed, blade obovate; stamens (B, ×3) 6, 4 longer and 2 shorter; ovary (C, ×3) shortly stalked, shortly hairy; fruit (D, ×2½) more or less parallel

with the axis, composed of 2 joints, lower joint stalk-like, upper part ovoid, ribbed and setose-pilose (family *Cruciferae*).

An introduced weed of arable and waste land, native of the Mediterranean region but widely spread in many countries.

Two of the four nectaries in the flower are situated on the inner side of the bases of the shorter stamens, and their nectar collects in the pouched bases of the sepals. The other two nectaries are smaller and like papillae, and they lie outside and between each pair of the longer stamens and secrete very little nectar.

Coringia orientalis (L.) Dumort. (×⅓)

Annual or semibiennial up to 2½ ft. high; taproot whitish; stem erect, unbranched or nearly so, terete, glabrous; basal leaves few;

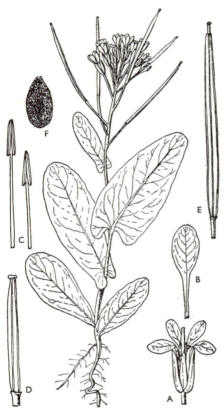

stem-leaves glaucous-green, sessile, amplexicaul and obtusely cordate-auriculate at the base, oblong, rounded at the apex, up to 4 in. long and 2 in. broad, about 7-nerved at the base, entire, decreasing in size upwards; flowers (A, ×1¼) few in terminal corymb-like racemes, these soon elongating during the fruiting stage with the uppermost flowers still in bloom; pedicels nearly as long as the flowers; sepals 4, narrowly oblong to broadly linear, the outer shortly pouched at the base; petals (B, ×2½) 4, about ½ in. long, long-clawed, yellowish or greenish-white; stamens (C, ×2½) 6, 4 longer and 2 shorter; anthers cordate at the base; ovary (D, ×2) linear, with very short thick style and capitate stigma; fruits (E, ×½) erect, about 3 in. long, 4-angled and 4-ribbed, glabrous; seeds (F, ×3) ovoid, closely pitted, dark brown (family *Cruciferae*). – Synonyms *Erysimum orientale* Crantz; *E. perfoliatum* Crantz.

On waste ground and on cliffs by the sea or by railways, introduced; native of southern Europe, north Africa, and western Asia.

An entirely hairless plant with very distinctive stem-leaves which are clasping and cordate at the base.

370

Herb, usually biennial, up to 4 ft. high; root carrot-shaped; stem erect, often purple at the base, branched above, with scattered subsessile glands and when young with slender white hairs; basal leaves (A, and B, $\times\frac{1}{3}$) lyrately lobed and with remotely toothed margins, lobes spreading or slightly reflexed, with scattered stellate hairs on both surfaces, upper leaves gradually becoming sessile, lanceolate, and less lobed to merely toothed with scattered glands on the margins; flowers in corymb-like panicles, bright yellow, the branches subtended by narrow leaf-like bracts; pedicels twice as long as the flowers; sepals (C, $\times3$) 4, narrowly oblong, glabrous; petals (D, $\times3$) $1\frac{1}{2}$ times as long as the sepals, veiny; sta-

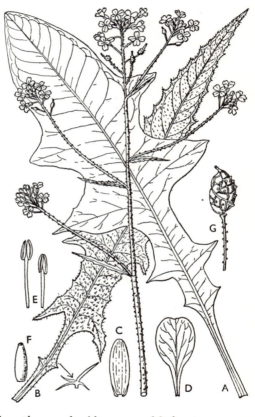

mens (E, $\times3$) shorter than the sepals, 4 longer and 2 shorter; ovary (F, $\times1\frac{1}{4}$) oblong, with 2 ovules; style subsessile; fruit (G, $\times1\frac{1}{4}$) ovoid, sometimes with an oblique constriction in the middle, beaked by the persistent style, veiny and glandular (family *Cruciferae*).

Native of continental Europe; a casual in arable land and on river banks in Britain, spreading into grasslands on downs.

Another species of this small genus occurs in Britain, also introduced; this is *Bunias erucago* L., distinguished by its fruits, which have four crested wings and a much longer persistent style.

Erect annual herb up to $2\frac{1}{2}$ ft. high, sometimes branched from the base; stem thinly covered with Y-shaped hairs, becoming glabrous upwards; lower leaves (A, $\times\frac{1}{3}$) oblanceolate, remotely dentate; lower stem leaves narrowly oblanceolate, narrowed to the base, upper leaves becoming narrower but with distinct ears (auriculate) at the base, all thinly covered with star-shaped or Y-shaped hairs (B); flowers small, yellow, in a terminal raceme, often the fruits fully developed before the top flowers open; pedicels slender, nearly 1 in. long in fruit; sepals (C, $\times 3$) 4, elliptic, with thin margins; petals (D, $\times 3$) 4, spoon-shaped, clawed; stamens (E, $\times 3$) 6, 4 long and 2 shorter; anthers cordate at the base;

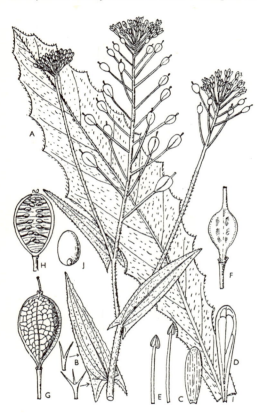

ovary (F, $\times 3$) shortly stipitate, glabrous; style nearly as long as the ovary, stigma terminal; fruit (G, $\times 2\frac{1}{2}$) obovate, slightly compressed parallel to the thin membranous partition (H, $\times 2\frac{1}{2}$), valves hard and rather brittle, with a distinct median nerve; seeds (J, $\times 6$) elliptic, compressed, brownish (family *Cruciferae*).

Introduced and sometimes found as a weed amongst farm and garden crops; native of eastern Europe and western Asia.

Reseda luteola L. (×⅖)

Biennial or annual, with a hard stiff often unbranched stem; leaves linear to lanceolate, entire but with rather wavy margins, glabrous, pale green or almost glaucous; no stipules; flowers (A, × 2) yellowish green, arranged in stiff terminal spike-like racemes, numerous; bracts narrowly lanceolate, shorter than the flowers but conspicuous in the bud stage; sepals 4, small; petals 4 or 5; very unequal, the upper ones (B, ×5) divided into 3 or 5 lobes and with a 2-lobed scale at the base, the others narrower, 2-lobed or entire (C, ×5); stamens (D, × 4) several, inserted below the ovary on a glandular disk; ovary of 3 carpels, early gaping at the top and exposing the ovules arranged on the walls; fruit (E, ×4) wide open

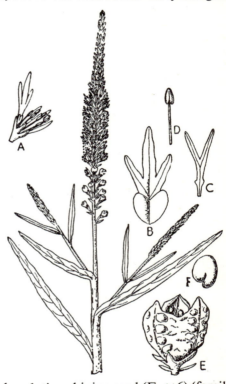

at the top, lobulate around each tiny shining seed (F, ×6) (family *Resedaceae*).

A peculiarity of the genus *Reseda* is that the capsular fruit opens at the top long before the seeds are mature. Even the flower itself is not closed in the bud stage, and it quickly withers. Nectar is secreted at the back of the broad erect disk behind the ovary and the expanded claws of the posterior and middle petals protect it from rain and unwelcome visitors. The plant is common in waste places and grows up to 3 ft. high; employed as a yellow and green dye-plant for cotton and woollen fabrics; similar to and closely related to the Sweet Mignonette of gardens, *Reseda odorata* L.

WATERWORT
Elatine hexandra (Lapierre) DC. ($\times\frac{1}{2}$)

Very small glabrous aquatic or semiaquatic annual, the semi-aquatic form with smaller more spoon-shaped leaves than the aquatic form shown in the drawing; leaves opposite, entire, about $\frac{1}{3}$ in. long, nerveless; stipules very minute; flowers (A, $\times$5) axillary, solitary, very distinctly stalked; sepals 3, ovate, spreading; petals 3, rose-coloured, obovate, a little longer than the sepals; stamens 6, with short filaments and 2-locular anthers; ovary superior, depressed-globose, 3-locular; styles 3, free and spread-

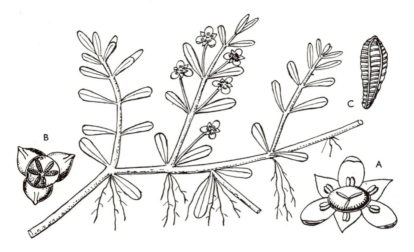

ing; ovules numerous on axile placentas; fruit (B, $\times$8) a 3-valved capsule, with several grub-like slightly curved seeds (C, $\times$20) beautifully ribbed and transversely striated (family *Elatinaceae*).

Widely distributed in Europe (including the Azores), in ponds and muddy places, flowering in summer. A second species, *E. hydropiper* L., much less frequent, is also found in Britain; this differs from the one here described by its sessile flowers, 4 petals, 8 stamens, and 4 styles, and fewer seeds in each loculus of the fruit.

The anthers open inwardly and shed their pollen directly on to the three stigmas which spread over the wide surface of the ovary.

Sagina nodosa (L.) Fenzl. ($\times \frac{3}{4}$)

A small tufted perennial, often flowering the first year; stems slender, decumbent to erect, thin and wiry, sometimes scarcely branched, glabrous; leaves opposite, the lower linear or needle-like, acute, the upper ones much smaller and mostly with a little cluster of smaller ones in their axils; no stipules; flowers (A, $\times 1\frac{1}{2}$)

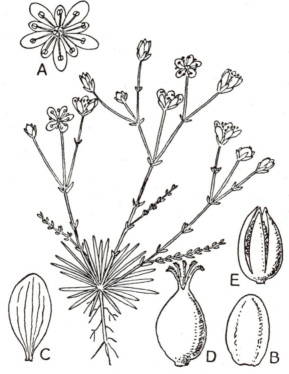

few, sometimes only one open at the end of each branch or stem; stalks slender; sepals (B, $\times 6$) 5, broadly elliptic, rounded at the apex, shorter than the 5 narrowly obovate white petals (C, $\times 4\frac{1}{2}$); stamens 10; anthers short and rounded; ovary (D, $\times 7$) smooth, with 5 rather large styles and papillous stigmas, 1-locular with the ovules attached to the central axis; fruit splitting into 5 parts; seeds very minute (family *Caryophyllaceae*).

PROCUMBENT PEARLWORT
Sagina procumbens L. (×¾)

A tiny tufted perennial, flowering from the seedling stage; stems short and slender, spreading; leaves in a dense rosette, linear or

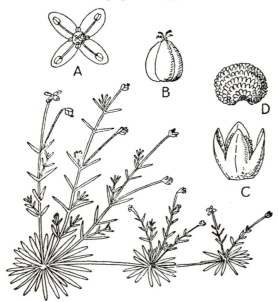

needle-like, with a very sharp point, smooth or minutely hairy on the margin, the stem leaves opposite and connected by a membranous sheath at the base; no stipules; flowers (A, × 3) few, axillary and solitary, and terminal, soon developing into fruit; stalks slender, several times longer than the leaves; sepals 4, broadly elliptic, sometimes tinged with crimson on the margin; petals 4, very small, or absent; stamens 4, opposite the sepals; ovary (B, ×8) ovoid, with 4 short hairy styles, 1-locular, with the ovules attached to the central axis; fruit (C, ×4½) splitting into 4 parts; seeds (D, ×20) very minute (¼ mm.), kidney-shaped, brown, closely pitted; flowers from spring to autumn (family *Caryophyllaceae*).

This little plant has become very much reduced both in stature and in its petals, which are either completely absent or are very minute. Their function has been assumed by the sepals, which are sometimes tinged with crimson on the margin, thus rendering the flower a little more conspicuous. As mentioned under *Anemone*, when one set of organs becomes reduced or dispensed with, another is adapted to perform its function.

There are four small nectaries at the base of the filaments. The stamens are mature at the same time as the stigmas, and automatic self-pollination takes place. The flowers remain closed in dull weather.

A tiny annual with numerous branches from the base, forming a flat tuft; branches almost thread-like (filiform), glabrous; leaves opposite, awl-shaped (subulate), very acute, with membranous margins united at the base and fringed with hairs like a comb; flowers (A, B, $\times 6$) usually 2 or 3 at the top of each shoot, on very slender thread-like stalks; sepals 4, free, green, ovate-elliptic; petals none or very minute; stamens (C, $\times 12$) 4, opposite the

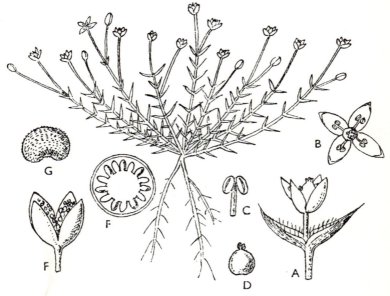

sepals; anthers rounded, the loculi separate; ovary (D, $\times 10$) sessile, ovoid, glabrous, crowned by 4 short stigmas, 1-locular, with numerous ovules on a central placenta (F, $\times 20$); seeds (G, $\times 16$) minute, closely warted (family *Caryophyllaceae*).

It needs a strong lens to examine the very small flowers of this tiny plant, which might be mistaken for *Linum catharticum* L. (fig. 152) or *Radiola linoides* Roth. (fig. 153), both of which have petals, however, and belong to quite another family, *Linaceae*; in *Radiola* the sepals are also 4, but they are united in the lower half.

FRINGED PEARLWORT
Sagina ciliata Fries (×⅔)

A very small and exceedingly delicate matted annual 2–3 in. high with slender thread-like stems sparingly clothed with short gland-tipped hairs; leaves opposite, connected at the base by a thin sheath fringed with long hairs (A, ×2), linear, with a very sharp point (awned); flowers (B, ×3) terminal and axillary, very numerous, on thread-like stalks clothed more or less with short gland-tipped hairs; sepals 4, oblong-elliptic, hooded, with a few gland-tipped hairs outside; petals absent; stamens 4, with thread-

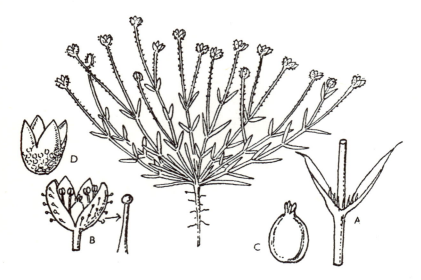

like filaments and rounded anther-lobes; ovary (C, ×3) with 4 very short styles and a free-central placenta bearing numerous ovules; capsule (D, ×3) a little longer than the sepals, opening by 4 valves; seeds numerous, minute, brownish (family *Caryophyllaceae*).

Grows in dry places on sandy heaths, found more or less throughout the British Isles, in Europe generally and in north Africa.

Closely related to *S. apetala* L., from which it differs by its sepals appressed to the ripe fruit and not spreading horizontally.

Sagina maritima Don ($\times\frac{1}{2}$)

A very small densely matted annual herb up to 3 in. high; stems ascending, thread-like, glabrous; leaves opposite, connected at the base, shortly linear, blunt at the apex, rather fleshy, entire, glabrous; flowers (A, $\times4$) terminal and axillary, very numerous, on thread-like stalks; sepals 4, elliptic, with membranous margins;

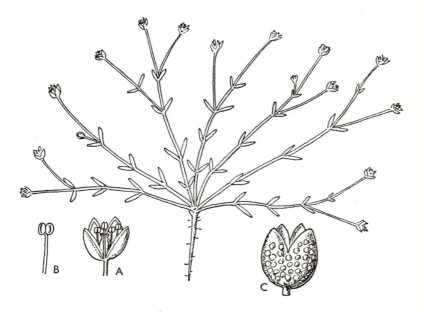

petals very short or absent; stamens (B, $\times4$) 4; ovary with 4 short styles and a free-central placenta bearing numerous ovules; capsule (C, $\times5$) broadly ovoid, about as long as the sepals, which persist and spread slightly, opening by 4 valves at the top; seeds very small, brownish (family *Caryophyllaceae*).

Widely distributed on the sea-coast, and on the coasts of Europe and northern Africa. Related to *S. ciliata*, shown in fig. 320, but with the leaves blunt at the apex and not tipped with a bristle-like point.

HEATH PEARLWORT
Sagina subulata Presl (×½)

Perennial densely tufted herb with leaves in dense clusters; leaves (A, ×2) linear, with a very sharp point, connected a t the base and

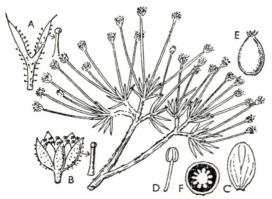

there margined with short gland-tipped hairs; flowers (B, ×3) solitary at the top of the short leafy branches, on long very slender thread-like stalks, which towards the top and like the sepals bear a few short gland-tipped hairs; sepals 5, elliptic; petals (C, ×3) 5, white, obovate, usually a little longer than the sepals; stamens (D, ×3) 10; ovary (E, F, ×4) ovoid with 5 short styles; capsule ovoid, sessile (family *Caryophyllaceae*).

Grows in dry gravelly and sandy places; recognized from several closely-related species by its having glandular hairs on the leaf margins and flower-stalks, and 5 sepals and petals, 10 stamens, and 5 styles; the flowers are single on each little branch.

About nine species of this genus occur in Britain, which are difficult to determine because of the minute characters by which they are classified.

Arenaria trinervia L. (×⁴⁄₃)

A delicate, much-branched, decumbent or spreading annual up to about 1 ft. long, much resembling the common Chickweed (fig. 326); stems and branches very slender, with short recurved hairs mainly on one side; leaves opposite, their short stalks connected at the base across the branchlets, ovate or ovate-elliptic, rather abruptly narrowed to the winged stalks, rounded to the shortly acute apex, with 3(–5) distinct parallel nerves from the base to the apex, very minutely hairy on the nerves and margin; flowers (A, × 2) usually only one from the axil of each pair of leaves, on slen-

der thread-like stalks exceeding the latter in length, minutely hairy with reflexed hairs; sepals 5, narrow, very acute, with a green minutely hairy keel and white membranous margins; petals white, shorter than the sepals; stamens (B, ×3) 10, with very slender thread-like filaments, and minute rounded anthers; ovary (C, ×3) globose, with 3 slender minutely hairy styles, 1-locular, with numerous ovules attached to the central axis (D, ×5); fruit (E, ×6) a 6-valved capsule; seeds (F, ×12) very small (about ¹⁄₂₄ in.), rounded, rich brown, minutely and transversely grooved, with a white frill-like appendage at the base (family *Caryophyllaceae*).

Arenaria serpyllifolia L. ($\times \frac{2}{3}$)

A very small annual with branched stems up to a few inches long, covered with minute reflexed scabrid hairs (A, $\times 2\frac{1}{2}$); leaves opposite, connected at the base around the stem but no stipules, ovate, acute, loosely covered with very short rough hairs (scabrid) 3–5-nerved from the base; flowers (B, $\times 1\frac{1}{2}$) in the upper leaf-axils, shortly stalked, very small; sepals 5, larger than the petals, hairy on the nerves; petals (C, $\times 3$) white, smaller than the sepals but rather variable in size, obovate; stamens usually 10, anthers (D, $\times 6$) rounded; ovary (E, $\times 6$) ovoid, smooth, with 3 twisted styles,

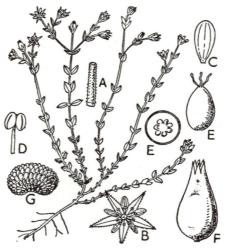

1-locular with the ovules arranged around the central axis (E, $\times 8$); fruit (F, $\times 3$) opening by 6 short teeth at the top; seeds (G, $\times 6$) kidney-shaped, closely covered with bead-like warts in transverse rows; often grows on dry walls and in dry sandy waste places; flowers in summer (family *Caryophyllaceae*).

In this species the stamens and stigmas mature simultaneously, and in bright sunny weather drops of nectar can be seen in the base of the flower. Sometimes some of the flowers are entirely female, and even in bisexual flowers the stamens are often reduced in number. Automatic self-pollination by contact of stigmas and anthers takes place.

Perennial with creeping rootstock; stems usually much branched, rather fleshy, glabrous; leaves (A, $\times1$) opposite, in four rows, sessile, ovate-elliptic or elliptic, thick and fleshy, green, with thin and slightly frilled margins; flowers (B, $\times2$) solitary in the forks and in the upper leaf-axils, stalked; sepals 5, green and fleshy; petals (C, $\times2$) white, very small, spoon-shaped (spathulate); stamens usually 10; anthers short and rounded; ovary (D, $\times3$) ovoid, with 3–5 short styles; fruit (F, $\times1\frac{1}{2}$) a capsule opening by 3–5 valves; seeds (G, $\times2\frac{1}{2}$) obovoid, minutely tuberculate (E, ovules $\times4$) (family *Caryophyllaceae*).

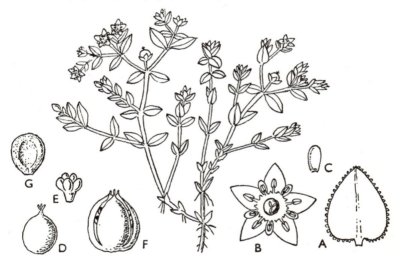

A very widely spread maritime plant growing in sandy places and sometimes amongst shingle; rather outstanding, and different in general appearance from other species of *Arenaria*; the petals are very small. In habit it somewhat resembles the Sea Milkwort (*Glaux maritima* L.) (see fig. 374), but the latter grows on muddy shores. The rootstock is long and slender and creeps in the sand or amongst the pebbles. In Yorkshire the plant was formerly much used as a pickle and accredited with a pleasant pungent taste.

The species is sometimes regarded as representing a genus distinct from *Arenaria*, and is then called *Honckenya peploides* (L.) Ehrh.

Stellaria media Vill. ($\times \frac{4}{5}$)

Annual with succulent smooth stems and branches, except for a line of reflexed hairs along one side; the hairs (F, ×5) consist of

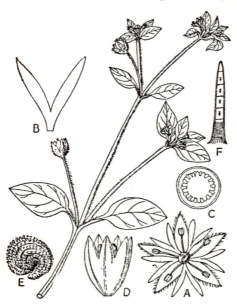

one row of several cells; leaves ovate, the lower hairy on the short stalks; flowers (A, ×3) scarcely stalked when young, but the stalk elongating in fruit; sepals free and hairy, with a narrow thin border; petals (B, ×5) shorter than the sepals, deeply 2-lobed, white, usually only one stamen between each, though sometimes the stamens reduced to 3 or 2; anthers pink when young; ovary with 3 styles; fruit (capsule) (D, ×2½) opening by 6 short teeth; seeds (E, ×6) several, closely warted, and curved (family *Caryophyllaceae*).

Chickweed is one of the most troublesome weeds in gardens and on farms, and it flowers and produces seed in a very short time. Nevertheless it is of considerable economic and biological interest, representing a high stage of evolution. The seeds provide food for small birds nearly all the year round. There is great economy in the number of the stamens, which are sometimes reduced to 2. A good spotting feature is the line of hairs down one side of the stem, and on the leaf-stalks, and these hairs carry out a special function. They are readily wetted by rain and dew and retain a considerable amount of water. This is conducted down to the leaf-stalks, where some of it is absorbed by the lower cells of the hairs, and any surplus is passed further down to the next pair of leaves and so on; the same process being repeated in each case. One of these hairs is shown enlarged in the figure (F), the three lower cells being absorbent.

Stellaria graminea L. ($\times\frac{1}{2}$)

Perennial; stems very slender and straggling, sharply 4-angled, not hairy; leaves opposite, united and slightly hairy on the margin at the base, very narrowly lanceolate, acute at the tip, up to about $1\frac{1}{2}$ in. long, with a strong midrib and faint parallel nerves below; flowers many, but very laxly arranged, with the oldest in the forks, $\frac{1}{2}$–$\frac{2}{3}$ in. diam.; stalks up to $1\frac{1}{2}$ in. long, slender; buds acute and ribbed; sepals (A, $\times1$) 5, slightly united at the base, with 3 prominent green nerves and pale membranous margins, the outermost one without, but the others with short hairs on the margin; petals (B, $\times2$) 5, but appearing like 10, being deeply divided almost to the base, white, spreading, not twice as long as sepals; stamens (C, $\times2$) with small brown anthers attached in the middle; ovary

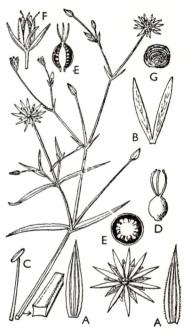

(D, $\times2$) 1-locular with several ovules attached to the central axis (E, $\times4$); styles 3, with slightly swollen tips; fruit (F, $\times1$) a capsule, a little longer than the sepals; seeds (G, $\times4$) orbicular, verrucose (family *Caryophyllaceae*).

Grows in dry pastures, hedgebanks, and at the base of crumbling walls, flowering from May to August. It is not always easy to distinguish this from the very similar *S. palustris* Ehrh., which grows in wetter places; the latter is glaucous (more greyish), and has petals very much longer than the sepals, and its sepals are not hairy on the margin. In *S. graminea* the petals are usually not much longer than the sepals.

There is a nectary at the base of each of the outer stamens. When the flower opens these bend inwards and open, the 5 inner ones not yet being ripe and curved outwards, and the stigmas are not receptive.

Stellaria holostea L. ($\times \frac{2}{3}$)

A perennial with weak stems in hedges and amongst bushes; stems quadrangular, glabrous; leaves sessile, lanceolate to almost

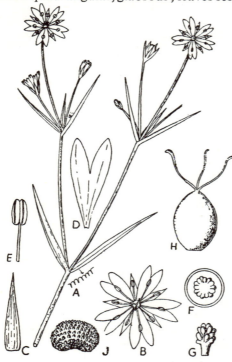

linear, tapered to a sharp point, up to about $2\frac{1}{2}$ in. long, with minute comb-like teeth on the margin (A, $\times 3$); no stipules; flowers (B, $\times \frac{4}{5}$) large, in leafy panicles; stalks slender; sepals (C, $\times 1\frac{1}{2}$) 5, lanceolate, sharply pointed, faintly nerved; petals (D, $\times \frac{4}{5}$) nearly twice as long as the sepals, narrowly wedge-shaped, divided nearly to the middle into 2 divergent lobes; stamens (E, $\times 2$) 10, nearly as long as the sepals; anthers broadly oblong; ovary (F, $\times 5$) 1-locular, with the ovules attached to the middle (G, $\times 4$), ovoid-globose, glabrous, topped by 3 slender styles; fruit a capsule opening by 3 valves; seeds (J, $\times 3$) kidney-shaped, with transverse lines of warts (family *Caryophyllaceae*).

Compared with the Chickweed (fig. 326) this plant has narrow sessile leaves, much larger and more showy flowers and ten stamens; and the stems have not the line of hairs so characteristic of the Chickweed. Three other species of this genus in Britain have the petals considerably longer than the sepals, and only one of these, *S. palustris* Ehrh., is at all common. This has very narrow leaves and the sepals are distinctly 3-nerved.

Stellaria aquatica (L.) Scop. ($\times \frac{1}{3}$)

Perennial with weak straggly angular stems glabrous in the lower parts but thinly hairy upwards; leaves opposite, sessile, ovate, rounded to subcordate at the base, acutely and gradually acuminate, up to $2\frac{1}{2}$ in. long, and $1\frac{1}{3}$ in. broad, not hairy, but becoming pustulate in the dried state; flowers about $\frac{1}{2}$ in. diam., axillary but often forming terminal lax leafy cymes, with the oldest flower in the middle of each pair of branchlets; stalks hairy; sepals 5, ovate-elliptic, pointed, about $\frac{1}{4}$ in. long; petals (A, $\times 1\frac{1}{4}$) 5, white,

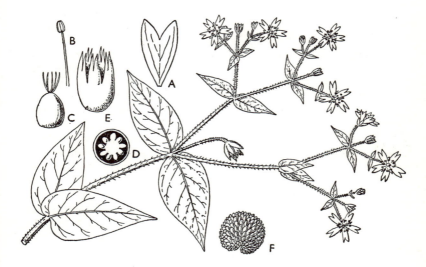

obovate and deeply notched with divergent lobes; stamens (B, $\times 2$) usually 10; ovary (C, $\times 2$) ovoid, 1-locular, with numerous ovules on a free central placenta (D, $\times 3$); styles 5, rarely 3, free; capsule (E, $\times 3$) bell-shaped, opening by 5 valves, each valve deeply bifid; seeds (F, $\times 3$) rounded-kidney-shaped, densely tubercled (synonyms *Myosoton aquaticum* (L.) Moench, and *Malachium aquaticum* (L.) Fr. (family *Caryophyllaceae*).

Grows in wet places along ditches and streams, distributed into central Asia; introduced into North America; flowers during summer.

Cerastium vulgatum L. ($\times \frac{2}{5}$)

Slender annual; stems with a line of denser hairs down one side; basal leaves stalked, upper opposite, narrowed to the base, nar-

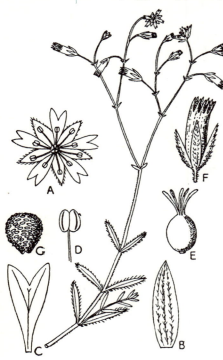

rowly oblanceolate, rather blunt, clothed with rather long hairs, 1-nerved; flowers (A, $\times 1\frac{3}{5}$) in lax cymes, the middle flower already well into fruit, whilst the upper are still open-ing; pedicels slender; sepals (B, $\times 4$) 5, green with membranous mar-gins, hairy outside; pe-tals (C, $\times 3$) usually longer than the calyx but sometimes shorter or even absent, notched at the apex, white; sta-mens 10 or 5 or fewer; anthers (D, $\times 4$) round-ed; ovary (E, $\times 6$) smooth, with 5 free styles; fruit a shining cylindric capsule (F, $\times 1\frac{3}{5}$) opening by 10 sharp narrow teeth, up to twice as long as the calyx; seeds (G, $\times 6$) loosely warted, very variable and sometimes divided by critical botanists into several species; flowers the whole season, usually in cultivated and waste places, etc. (family *Caryo-phyllaceae*).

Flowers of the Chickweed type of this family have much the same means of pollination. They are usually quite small and in-conspicuous and rarely crowded enough to attract much attention. The petals spread out in the sunshine, the nectar secreted at the base of the flower at the same time becoming visible and access-ible to insects with a very short proboscis. Flies and the less specialized kinds of bees are the visitors, but automatic self-pollination is usually possible during bad weather.

Cerastium arvense L. ($\times \frac{2}{3}$)

Perennial herb much branched from the base, often much matted together and prostrate, the flowering branches ascending to about 6 in. high, leafy to the top and covered all around with deflexed hairs; leaves opposite, linear, entire, the bases touching round the stem, obtuse or only half acute at the apex, $\frac{1}{2}$–$\frac{3}{4}$ in. long, more or less hairy all over, but especially on the margin; no stipules; flowers about 3–5 (rarely more) together in a cyme at the end of each shoot, rather large and conspicuous; sepals 5, $\frac{1}{4}$ in. long, oblong-elliptic, green with a narrow membranous margin, softly pubescent; petals twice as long as the sepals, deeply 2-lobed; stamens (A, $\times 4$; B, $\times 8$) usually 10; ovary (C, $\times 4$) globose, 1-locular, with numerous ovules on a

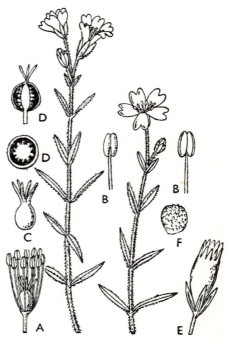

free central placenta (D, $\times 6$); styles 5, free; capsule (E, $\times 2$) oblique, a little longer than the sepals, opening at the top by 10 teeth; seeds rounded-obovoid, warted all over (F, $\times 3$) (family *Caryophyllaceae*).

Grows in sandy fields and waste ground, flowering from spring to early summer, and found in many parts of the world.

Holosteum umbellatum L. ($\times \frac{1}{2}$)

Annual herb usually much branched from the base; branches glandular-hairy (A, ×6) only towards the nodes from below, bearing only 2–3 pairs of opposite oblanceolate glabrous leaves narrowed to the base and there forming a very short tube around the branch; no stipules; flowers few in terminal umbels, bisexual or sometimes female; pedicels slender, with membranous bracts at their base; sepals 5, ovate, with very narrow membranous mar-

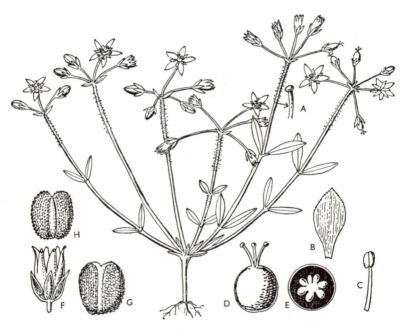

gins; petals (B, ×3) 5, white, free, ovate and broadly clawed; stamens (C, ×2) 5–3 or rarely 2, free, with a green fleshy nectary at the base of each filament; ovary (D, ×2) ovoid-globose, 1-locular, with several ovules on a free central placenta (E, ×2); styles 3, free; fruit (F, ×2) a 6-lobed capsule, surrounded by the persistent calyx; seeds (G, ×12) broadly ellipsoid, closely warted (family *Caryophyllaceae*).

A rare plant in Britain and now found wild only in Surrey, but formerly in Norfolk and Suffolk; grows on walls, thatched roofs, and more rarely in sandy soil; extends into Asia.

A slender annual weed, branching from the base into erect or
ascending stems, the latter glabrous or very slightly hairy; leaves
in clusters at the nodes
and appearing in
whorls, almost needle-
like, i.e. very narrow,
like those of a pine tree,
up to about 1 in. long,
very slightly hairy;
stipules very small and
dry; flowers numerous
in terminal forked cy-
mes, the slender stalks
turning downwards as
the flowers mature; se-
pals 5, ovate-elliptic,
slightly pubescent out-
side; petals (A, ×2) 5,
white, broadly oblong-
elliptic, shortly con-
tracted at the base,
usually shorter than the
sepals, not divided;
stamens (B, ×3) 10 or
5 on the same plant;

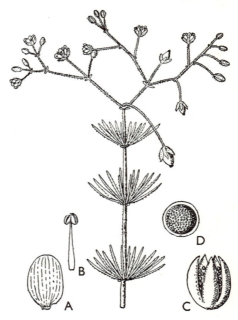

anthers rounded; ovary rounded, 1-locular; styles 5; capsule (C,
× 3) ellipsoid, opening from the top into 5 entire parts; seeds (D,
× 4) flattened, orbicular, papillous, and with a narrow membranous margin (family *Caryophyllaceae*).

Spurry is a common weed in moist fields on light soils, but in
some parts of Europe it is grown for fodder. Sheep are very fond
of it, and cows fed on it are said to give good milk. The leaves and
seeds are also eaten by poultry. Formerly in Scandinavia a kind
of bread was made of the seeds in times of scarcity.

Though a favourite plant with farmers on the Continent, it is
usually regarded as a troublesome weed in this country. On this
account in Norfolk it is called 'Pickpurse' and is considered by
farmers to merit the name.

Spergularia bocconii (Scheele) Asch. & Grab ($\times \frac{3}{4}$)

Small annual or biennial with numerous stems branching from the base and forming flat tufts; stipules (A, $\times 4\frac{1}{2}$) very conspicuous, ovate-lanceolate, membranous and white; leaves opposite, linear, with a sharp tip; pedicels and sepals clothed with short gland-tipped hairs (B, $\times 6$); sepals with a membranous margin, lanceolate; petals (C, $\times 4\frac{1}{2}$) usually shorter than the sepals, usually pink, rarely almost white; stamens (D, $\times 9$) usually 10, as long as the petals; anthers (E, $\times 9$) attached in the middle; filaments flat and broad; style with 3–5 very short lobes; ovary (F, $\times 10$) oblong, 1-locular, with the ovules attached to the central axis; fruit (G, $\times 4$) opening in as many valves as styles (3–5); seeds (H, $\times 15$) with the rootlet (radicle) conspicuous on one side, minutely warted (family *Caryophyllaceae*). Synonym *Spergularia campestris* Archers.

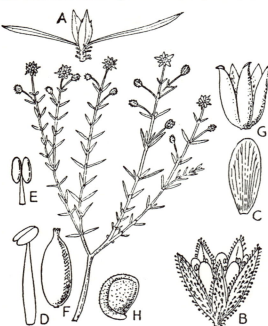

Grows in sandy or gravelly heaths and waste places, and very widely distributed in the northern hemisphere and even in Australia. A coastal form is often treated as a species, *Spergularia sabina* Presl (synonym *S. marina* Griseb.). This, as is often the case with maritime forms of species, has thicker more fleshy leaves.

Frequently only three stamens are developed. Nectar is secreted by a fleshy ring inside the base of the stamens. In bad weather the flowers remain closed and automatic self-pollination then takes place.

A low very much branched annual herb, often forming small car-
pets on beaches and old walls; stem and branches glabrous, the
latter repeatedly forked; leaves in whorls of four or opposite in
pairs, obovate, narrowed to the base, up to $\frac{1}{2}$ in. long, entire,
glabrous, very obscurely nerved; stipules (A, $\times 1\frac{1}{2}$) conspicuous,
triangular-lanceolate, with slender points, thin and whitish;
flowers (B, $\times 5$) numerous, in terminal cymes; bracts like the
stipules, membranous; sepals (C, $\times 4$) 5, free, green margined
with white, with a dorsal point at the top; petals 5, free, narrowly

obovate, white; stamens (D, $\times 10$) 5, free; anthers ellipsoid; ovary
ovoid, with 3 free styles and capitate stigmas; capsule (E, $\times 4$)
splitting from the top into 3 valves; seeds (F, $\times 10$) obliquely obovoid, very small, finely reticulate (family *Caryophyllaceae*).

A rare and local plant in sandy waste places from Dorset to
Cornwall, but widely spread in many other parts of the world.

The genera of the family *Caryophyllaceae* are divisable into two
groups, those with *free* sepals and those with the sepals *united
into a tube*. Typical of the latter group are *Dianthus* (Pinks) and
Catchflies (*Lychnis* and *Silene*). *Polycarpon* belongs to the first
group, which is closely related to another small family *Illecebraceae*, united by some botanists with *Caryophyllaceae*.

336 WHITE CAMPION
Lychnis alba Mill. ($\times\frac{1}{3}$)

Strong-growing biennial up to 3 ft. high; stem hollow, branches loosely covered with long pale several-celled hairs; leaves opposite

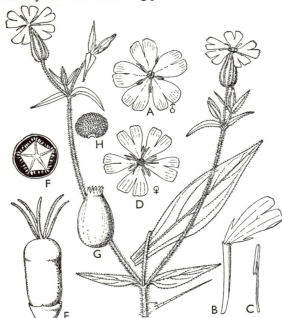

bases connected by a narrow hairy rim, oblanceolate, narrowed to the apex, softly hairy on the nerves, not toothed; flowers dioecious (males (A, $\times\frac{2}{3}$) on one, females (D, $\times\frac{2}{3}$) on another plant), opening in the evening (hence one synonymous specific name, *vespertina*), sweetly scented; calyx green, ovoid, 10-ribbed, pubescent, narrowly 5-lobed; petals (B, $\times0$) 5, white, with a long claw and a 2-lobed limb with a sharp tooth-like lobe on each side near the base; at the junction of the claw and limb a 4-toothed corona; stamens (in the male) (C, $\times0$) 10; anthers attached nearly in the middle; disk fleshy, 5-toothed; ovary (E, $\times2$) bright green, bottle-shaped, smooth; styles 5; ovules numerous on a central pentagonal placenta (F, $\times2\frac{1}{4}$); fruit (G, $\times0$) ovoid, opening by 10 teeth; seeds (H, $\times4$) kidney-shaped, closely warted (synonym *Melandrium album* (Mill.) Garcke) (family *Caryophyllaceae*).

Flowers in the early summer in fields and hedgerows, the blooms opening in the evening and giving off a sweet scent. When females are found growing remote from the males, the flowers, not being pollinated, drop off very readily.

Lychnis dioica L. ($\times \frac{2}{3}$)

Biennial up to 2 ft. high; stems covered with long spreading and shorter slightly reflexed hairs, not sticky; leaves opposite, sub-sessile, ovate, rounded to an acute apex, pubescent with short stiff hairs above and on the nerves beneath, more or less 3-nerved from above the base, the younger ones often tinged with dull crimson; no stipules; flowers unisexual (dioecious), the males on one, the

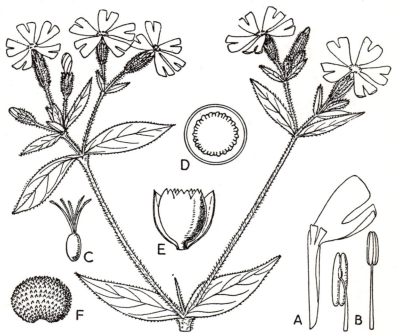

females on another plant, few together; stalks about $\frac{1}{2}$ in. long; calyx tubular, about $\frac{3}{4}$ in. long, 5-toothed at the apex, prominently 5-ribbed, and with 5 less prominent ribs, pubescent, crimson-green; petals (A, $\times 1\frac{3}{4}$) 5, deep pink, 2-lobed with a long pale claw and 2 toothed white outgrowths at the top; stamens (B, $\times 2\frac{1}{2}$) 10, the longest opening first; anthers large, dull white; ovary (C, $\times 3$) ellipsoid, 1-locular, with numerous ovules on the central placenta (D, $\times 8$); styles 5; fruit (E, $\times 2$) contained in the bladder-like expanded calyx, campanulate, opening at the top by 10 short teeth; seeds (F, $\times 10$) numerous, kidney-shaped, closely warted (family *Caryophyllaceae*).

Perennial with erect rather weak stems and long internodes; leaves opposite, narrowly linear-oblanceolate, fringed with hairs

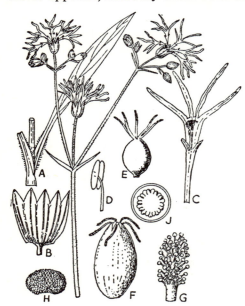

towards the base (A, ×⅘); flowers in loose terminal clusters (cymes) the middle flower the oldest and often forming the fruit whilst the others are still open or in bud; calyx (B, ×1¼) shortly 5-lobed and with 10 conspicuous ribs; petals (C, ×1¼) 5, red, deeply cut into 4 linear lobes, the middle pair longest, the claw with two appendages near the middle; stamens (D, ×3) 10, the 5 outer maturing first and then curving outwards, making room for the 5 inner;

the 5 styles mature last of all, their ends being spirally twisted; pollination by insects, the nectar secreted at the base of the stamens; ovary (E, ×2) 1-locular, with the ovules on the central axis; capsule (F, ×2) ellipsoid, opening by 5 teeth, the styles often remaining; seeds (G, ×1½) stalked on the axis, kidney-shaped, closely warted (H, ×3) (J, cross-section of ovary, ×2½) (family *Caryophyllaceae*).

In this species nectar is secreted at the base of the stamens, which open before the stigmas are receptive to pollen. The five outer stamens are mature first, and their anthers as they open occupy the middle of the flower; after their pollen is shed, their filaments elongate and curve outwards, making room for the inner five stamens, which in turn follow the same procedure. Then the five styles develop and occupy the same position in the middle of the flower.

Lychnis alpina L. ($\times \frac{1}{2}$)

Perennial herb with a dense rosette of shortly linear or narrowly spathulate leaves about 1–1½ in. long with membranous sheath-

ing bases; flowering stems single to several in each rosette, 6–9 in. high, cloth-ed with 2–4 pairs of linear-lanceolate leaves; flowers several in a ter-minal cluster; calyx cam-panulate, shortly 5-lobed, lobes triangular, becom-ing membranous; petals (A, $\times 2\frac{1}{2}$) 5, pink, long-clawed, the limb deeply bilobed and with a bifid appendage at the base; stamens (B, $\times 2\frac{1}{2}$) 10; ovary (C, $\times 2\frac{1}{2}$) stipitate; styles 5, free; capsule (D, $\times 3$) 5-lobed to about ⅓ of its length, lobes re-curved at the tip, inside the capsule 5 short pro-truding partitions; seeds (E, $\times 15$) kidney-shaped, closely warted (family *Caryophyllaceae*).

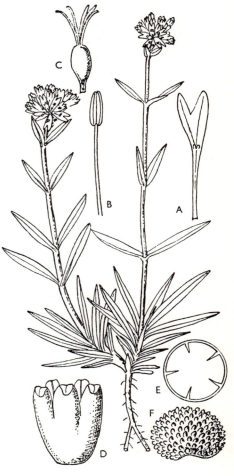

A very rare British plant found only in a re-stricted area in Scotland and the Lake District of north-west England; a species of the Alps and Pyrenees and in the sub-arctic regions of Europe, western Asia, and North America, including Greenland. Some botanists split off this species together with another British one, *Lychnis viscaria* L., from *Lychnis*, but by very slender characters.

Lychnis githago (L.) Scop. ($\times \frac{1}{2}$)

A tall coarse annual clothed all over with long silky hairs and scabrid below these; leaves opposite, linear, sessile, with a pro-

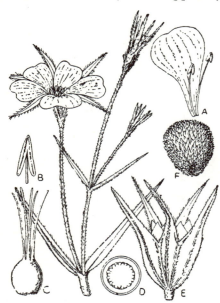

minent midrib; flowers scentless, solitary on long nude stalks thickening towards the top; calyx-lobes longer than the petals, the tube strongly ribbed outside; petals (A, $\times \frac{4}{5}$) spreading, red, widely notched at the apex; stamens 10, in two series; anthers (B, $\times 1\frac{1}{2}$) arrow-shaped; styles 5, free to the base; ovary (C, $\times 1$) 1-locular, with the ovules attached to the middle; capsule (E, $\times \frac{4}{5}$) opening by 5 teeth at the top, surrounded by the enlarged calyx; seeds (F, $\times 3$) obovoid, closely warted (D, cross-section of ovary, $\times 1\frac{2}{5}$) (family *Caryophyllaceae*).

Some botanists on the continent of Europe treat this cornfield weed as a separate genus, *Agrostemma*. The differences are not very pronounced, however, though this is a very striking plant with its long pointed calyx-lobes. The stamens and stigmas mature in turn, and pollination is by butterflies. The flowers appear in July and August, and remain open at night and during bad weather.

The roughness of the seed-coat serves to fix it in the soil. The seeds are poisonous and dangerous if mixed with cereals. They give a disagreeable odour to bread and render it unfit for human consumption.

Anne Pratt says of this plant, 'This showy Cockle unfolds its rich purple blossom at the period when the corn fields are looking very beautiful, when the nodding grain is daily becoming more golden in hue, as the sunshine of July is ripening it for the sickle'.

Annual up to about 2 ft. high; stem and branches very sticky with gland-tipped hairs (A); leaves opposite, lower tapered to the base, upper sessile and connected at the base by a rim, lanceolate, rounded at the base, tapered to the apex, up to 5 or 6 in. long, entire, shortly and softly hairy on both surfaces; lateral nerves few and inconspicuous; flowers few and collected in an open leafy cyme, the oldest flower in the middle of each fork and soon maturing into fruit; calyx clothed with short gland-tipped hairs and longer several-celled non-glandular hairs (H, $\times 5$), tubular, 5-lobed, with 10 green ribs; petals (B, $\times 1$) pale pink or nearly white, narrow, 2-lobed, with a corona inside the bend; stamens 10; ovary (C, $\times 2$) cylindric, 1-locular, with numerous ovules on

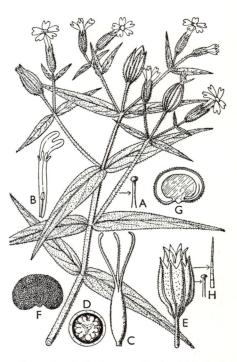

a free central placenta (D, $\times 4$); styles 3, hairy on the inside; fruit (E, $\times\frac{2}{3}$) a bell-shaped capsule opening at the top by 5 lobes; seeds (F, $\times 5$) kidney-shaped, closely warted, with a curved embryo (G, $\times 5$) (family *Caryophyllaceae*).

A common cornfield weed, flowering with the corn; native of central Europe. The flowers are fragrant when they open in the evening between 5 and 8 o'clock, and insect visitors are mainly moths. As the anthers mature long before the stigmas, self-pollination is virtually excluded.

Silene anglica L. ($\times\frac{1}{2}$)

Erect annual herb up to about 1 ft. high, clothed with glandular and non-glandular hairs; leaves opposite, connected by a rim at

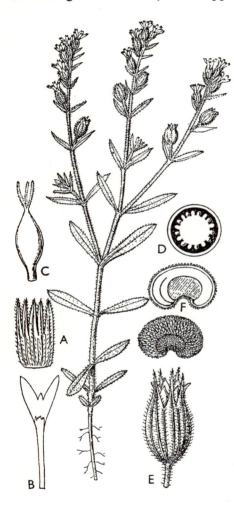

the base, narrowly oblanceolate, abruptly acute at the apex, the largest about 2 in. long, midrib very prominent below; flowers in the axils of leafy bracts and forming a more or less 1-sided raceme; stalks much shorter than the bracts; calyx (A, ×2) campanulate, 5-lobed, 10-ribbed, the ribs densely clothed with long hairs; lobes subulate; petals (B, ×2) 5, white, with long claws and a deeply lobed somewhat jagged limb; stamens 10; ovary (C, ×2) stalked, 1-locular, with numerous ovules on a free central placenta; styles 3, hairy; fruit (E, ×2) a 6-lobed capsule, enclosed by the persistent calyx; seeds (F, ×5) kidney-shaped, densely covered with bead-like warts (family *Carophyllaceae*).

Found in sandy and gravelly places and in waste ground; a native of Europe, introduced into other parts of the world.

Silene otites Smith (×½)

Perennial; stems 1–1½ ft. high, erect, slender, sticky; leaves (A, ×1) narrowly spoon-shaped, rather fleshy, minutely hairy on the margin and midrib below; stem-leaves few, opposite; flowers unisexual, on separate plants (dioecious), the males (B, ×½) (B, ×1) with conspicuous stamens, the females (E, ×½) with conspicuous styles, forming a loose narrow panicle; calyx (C, ×1½) tubular, shortly 5-lobed; petals (D, ×3) very narrow and green, with coiled tips; stamens in the male 10; anthers attached in the middle; rudimentary ovary with 3 styles in the male; female flowers without stamens and with an ellipsoid ovary (G, ×5) and 3 hairy styles; fruit an ovoid capsule rupturing the calyx (family *Caryophyllaceae*).

Found only in a few eastern counties and very local, flowering in July.

This species is pollinated mainly by the wind. It is almost completely dioecious, with more numerous male flowers than female, while bisexual flowers are few. Nectar is secreted in the base of the flowers, the sticky stem preventing small creeping insects from stealing it.

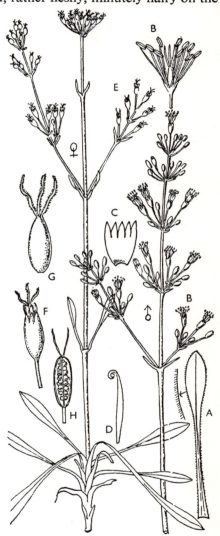

MOSS CAMPION
Silene acaulis L. ($\times \frac{1}{2}$)

Perennial mountain herb, much branched and forming dense moss-like clumps up to several inches in diameter; branches very short, covered by the remains of the old leaves and crowned by a rosette of about 8–10 spreading narrow linear leaves (A, $\times 2$) fringed with short teeth; no stipules; flowers numerous in each clump but single on each branch, shortly stalked; calyx tubular, 5-lobed, lobes ovate, obtuse; petals reddish-purple, obovate, provided with a short scale at the base of the limb; stamens (B, $\times 4$)

10; ovary (C, $\times 4$) 1-locular with free central placentation; styles 3; capsule (D, $\times 2\frac{1}{2}$) clasped by the persistent calyx, narrowly bell-shaped, opening at the top by 6 short teeth which become recurved; seeds (E, $\times 6$) kidney-shaped, brownish, finely transversely ridged (family *Caryophyllaceae*).

Found only in the mountains of northern Britain and Northern Ireland; widely distributed in mountains of Europe, Asia, and North America, sometimes at high elevations in southern and central Europe.

It forms lovely dense cushions on the face of the rocks and is a favourite plant for growing in rock gardens.

The flowers of this species are trioecious, the bisexual flowers being protrandrous and visited by many insects. In some places (according to Knuth) the flowers are quite dioecious. Clumps of *Silene acaulis* often show very strikingly the effect of exposure to the sun, for the southern half may present a dense mass of opened flowers whilst the northern half remains more or less in bud.

There are several varieties of this popular rock plant in cultivation, var. *alba* with white flowers, var. *aurea* with yellowish flowers.

Silene vulgaris (Moench) Garcke ($\times \frac{2}{5}$)

Perennial branched from the base; stems glabrous or rarely pubescent; leaves (A, ×1½) opposite, the lower withering before
flowering, sessile, lance-
olate, acute at the apex,
rounded at the base,
glabrous or very shortly
hairy, margins minutely
jagged; flowers few,
erect or drooping, in a
loose terminal cluster,
some male, some female
and some bisexual, each
sex possessing vestigial
organs of the other;
calyx about ½ in. long,
inflated and bladder-
like, much net-veined,
shortly 5-lobed (B,
×1¼); petals (C, ×1⅓)
white, deeply 2-lobed
with a pair of small
scales above the middle,
3-nerved from the base;
stamens usually 10, with
rather large anthers (D,
×1⅓) attached in the
middle; ovary (E, ×¾)
3-locular, with 3 slender

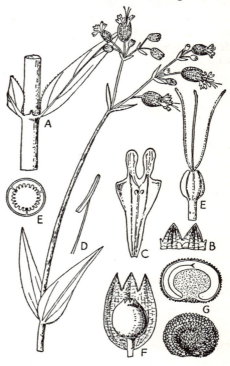

styles free to the base; capsule (F, ×1) shortly stalked within the
calyx, globose, opening by 6 small teeth at the top; seeds (G,
×6) kidney-shaped, closely covered with warts (family *Caryophyllaceae*).

Insect visitors are mainly moths and humble-bees, the nectar
being concealed at a depth of nearly half an inch. Humble-bees
often steal the nectar by perforating the calyx instead of by the
ordinary entrance between the deeply 2-lobed petals. Another
name for this species is *Silene inflata* Smith and *S. cucubalus* Wibel

Silene maritima (Hornem.) With. ($\times\frac{1}{2}$)

Perennial with numerous radiating and horizontally spreading glabrous stems, often tinged with dull purple up one side; leaves (A, ×1) opposite, sessile, lanceolate to ovate-lanceolate, rather acute and thick, bright glaucous-green, slightly joined at the base, not distinctly nerved; flowers few to each stem, terminal, on slender stalks; calyx (B, ×$\frac{3}{4}$) about $\frac{3}{4}$ in. long, inflated, green or tinged with crimson, distinctly veined, shortly 5-lobed; petals (C, ×1) 5,

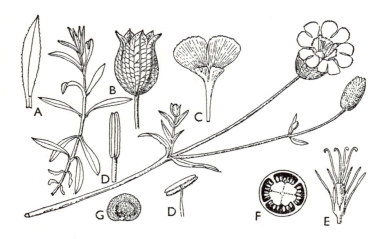

white, deeply 2-lobed, long-clawed, the claw with a bifid scale at the top; stamens 10; anthers (D, ×3) versatile (attached in the middle); ovary (E, ×1) 4-locular at the base, with numerous ovules on axile placentas (F, ×$2\frac{1}{2}$); styles 3–4, free to the base; fruit campanulate, nerved and reticulate; seeds (G, ×4) kidney-shaped, transversely striolate (family *Caryophyllaceae*).

In some *Floras* this is treated as a maritime variety of *Silene cucubalus* Wibel (fig. 345). It is very distinct in habit, however, the stems being prostrate and spreading. It grows in shingle by the sea or on the shores of maritime lochs.

Cucubalus baccifer L. ($\times \frac{1}{3}$)

A slender much-branched perennial; stems cylindric, slender, swollen at the nodes, covered with short reflexed hairs; leaves opposite, connected at the base by a rim, oblanceolate, narrowed into a short stalk, acute at the apex, up to about $1\frac{1}{2}$ in. long, entire, shortly hairy on both surfaces, with 2–3 pairs of lateral nerves; no stipules; flowers (A, $\times \frac{2}{3}$) solitary, terminal, shortly stalked, the one in the terminal fork soon maturing into fruit (ripe fruits and flowers present on the same plant); calyx bell-shaped, light green, $\frac{2}{3}$ in. long, 5-lobed, minutely hairy; petals (B, $\times 1$) 5, pale green, long-clawed, spreading, the limb split into 2 lobes, each lobe with

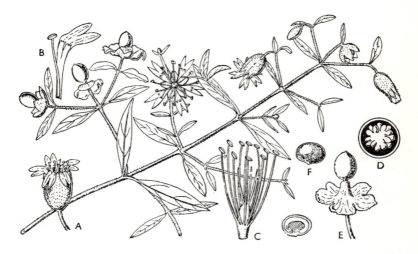

a whitish coronal appendage; stamens (C, $\times 3$) 10, united at the base to the stalk of the ovary (gynophore); anthers attached in the middle (versatile); ovary ellipsoid, 1-locular, with several ovules on a free central placenta (D, $\times 3$) styles 3, free; fruit (E, $\times \frac{2}{3}$) a shining black 'berry' nearly $\frac{1}{3}$ in. diam., exposed from the persistent calyx and containing several black brightly shining seeds (F, $\times 3$) (family *Caryophyllaceae*).

Druce says of this: 'possible native; borders of thickets and amid vegetation on sea-cliffs, very rare; formerly in Isle of Dogs'. It is a striking member of the family, being remarkable for its black berry-like fruits. Most of the flowers are bisexual, but some flowers may be female only, on the same or on separate plants.

SOAPWORT
Saponaria officinalis L. (×⅖)

Perennial with several rather stout leafy stems up to 2 ft. high; stems glabrous; leaves opposite, connected at the base across the

stem by a marked rim, ovate-lanceolate to lanceolate, gradually merging into bracts in the upper parts, strongly marked with 3–5 parallel nerves from the base, narrowed to the apex, very slightly roughened on the margins, but otherwise glabrous; no stipules; flowers large and handsome, arranged in a series of small cymes with leafy bracts, the ultimate stalks very short; a pair of narrow bracts just below each flower; calyx tubular, 5-lobed, the lobes in bud forming a narrow beak; petals (A, ×⅖) pale pink or nearly white, free, with a long claw and a broad blade notched at the top, the claw with a 2-toothed scale on the inside; stamens (C, ×⅘) 10, well exserted from the petals; ovary (B, ×3) glabrous, with only 2 styles, 1-locular, with numerous ovules arranged on the central axis; capsule (D, ×2) opening at the top by 4 teeth (family *Caryophyllaceae*).

To be found in flower in summer on banks, roadsides, and waste places, and it ranges far into western Asia; common around villages and probably only native in south-west England. It is easily recognized among British members of the family by the two styles. The fragrant odour of the flowers becomes much stronger in the evening, and hawk-moths are the chief pollinating agents, the nectar being secreted at the bottom of the calyx-tube. Double-flowered forms sometimes occur. As indicated by its common name, the plant was formerly used as soap, the leaves being boiled and macerated for the purpose.

Annual 1–2 ft. high with erect stems and few branches, shortly hairy all over; leaves opposite at the swollen nodes, linear, narrowed to the base, the larger 2–3 in. long and about $\frac{1}{4}$ in. broad, with prominent midrib below and fainter parallel side-nerves; flowers in clusters and forming a leafy cyme; calyx (A, $\times 1\frac{1}{3}$) subtended by nearly as long pointed bracts; tube $\frac{3}{4}$ in. long, very closely parallel-nerved; lobes 5, subulate-lanceolate; petals (B, $\times 1$) 5, with a long claw and spreading dentate limb; stamens (C, $\times 1$) 10; ovary (D, $\times 1$) 1-locular, with numerous ovules on a free central placenta (E, $\times 6$); styles 2; capsule (F, $\times 1\frac{1}{3}$) opening at the top by 4 valves; seeds (G, $\times 2\frac{1}{2}$) flattened, ovate, with a central hilum (family *Caryophyllaceae*).

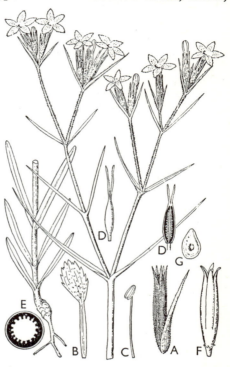

Flowers during summer in pastures, waste places, and under hedges, distributed eastward to the Caucasus and north to Sweden; introduced into North America.

The petals are bright red with clearer spots. Besides the normal bisexual flowers there are some in which one whorl of stamens is rudimentary, and others again that are purely female, the yellow anthers remaining enclosed in the corolla-tube and not opening. Nectar is secreted and concealed at the bottom of the tube formed by the long claws of the petals, and is accessible only to Lepidoptera which possess a very long proboscis.

A low-growing perennial herb with numerous ascending stems up to 1 ft. high or long, usually once forked above the middle; leaves

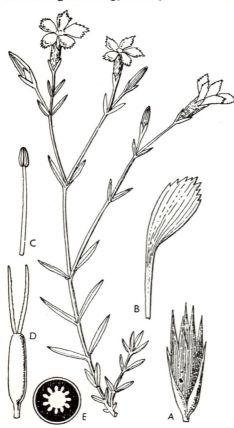

opposite, linear, obtuse at the apex, up to $\frac{3}{4}$ in. long, 3-nerved, the two lateral nerves very close to the margin very minutely hairy; flowers usually in pairs, all together forming a more or less flat-topped corymb, not scented; bracts 2–4, the innermost pair $\frac{1}{2}$–$\frac{3}{4}$ as long as the calyx, pointed; calyx (A, $\times 1\frac{3}{4}$) 5-lobed, with numerous closely parallel nerves, lobes very acute, of unequal length; petals (B, $\times 1\frac{1}{2}$) pink or white or spotted with white, with a jagged margin; stamens (C, $\times 1\frac{1}{2}$) 10; ovary (D, $\times 1\frac{1}{2}$) stalked, oblong, with numerous ovules on a free central placenta (E, $\times 4$); styles 2; capsule opening by 4 valves (family *Caryophyllaceae*).

Grows on banks and in open pastures, quite abundant in some localities, flowering during the whole summer.

The five outer stamens first elongate so that their anthers project from the corolla-tube when they have opened, and then the other five behave in the same way. After all the pollen is shed, the two styles, until now twisted together within the corolla-tube, elongate, and their stigma-bearing ends project from the flower, dominating its entrance and receiving the pollen from an insect which has previously visited other flowers.

Dianthus gratianopolitanus Vill. ($\times\frac{1}{2}$)

Perennial herb glaucous all over, in dense tufts from a woody rootstock; leaves in a dense cluster, with a few pairs up the flowering stem, linear, at most $1\frac{1}{2}$ in. long, 3-nerved, the lateral 2 nerves very near the margin; flowering stems with slightly swollen nodes, the leaves connate at their base; usually only one or two fragrant flowers out at a time; calyx (A, $\times1$) surrounded by an involucre of 4 broad bracts; calyx $\frac{3}{4}$ in. long, tubular, 5-lobed, very closely nerved lengthwise; petals (B, $\times1\frac{1}{2}$) pink, large and showy, veiny, with jagged margins; stamens (C, $\times1\frac{1}{2}$) 10, slightly exserted; ovary (D, $\times2$) elongated, with 2 free styles; capsule opening at the top by 4 short valves; seeds numerous (synonym *Dianthus caesius* Sm.) (family *Caryophyllaceae*).

Found on limestone rocks only in and near the Cheddar Gorge, Somerset; flowering in June and July; distributed in west, central, and southern Europe; a very interesting example of discontinuous distribution. According to International Rules the oldest specific name is used here, though it seems a pity that so lovely a species should be saddled with such a long one.

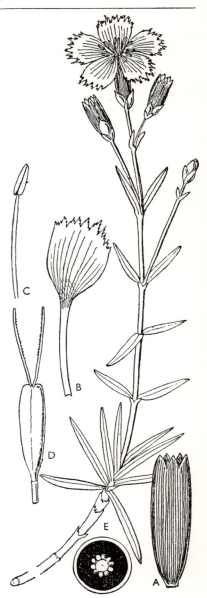

409

Dianthus prolifer L. ($\times \frac{1}{3}$)

A stiff erect wiry annual with slender forked roots, up to 1–1½ ft. high; leaves few, opposite, linear, up to 1½ in. long, margins more or less scabrid; flowers clustered at the top of the stems, surrounded by dry scarious broad brown bracts, opening in succession; calyx hidden by the bracts, very narrow, faintly ribbed; petals (A, ×2) touching each other, pink to purplish-red, oblanceolate, emarginate, the limb spreading; stamens usually 10, emerging and opening 5 at a time; disk elongated; ovary (B, ×3) narrowly oblong, 1-locular with numerous ovules on a central placenta (C, ×8); styles 2, free to the base, shortly hairy along the inner side; capsule (D, ×2) almost cylindric, 4-valved at the top, 1 cm. long; seeds (E, ×3) ellipsoid, black, minutely and closed pitted (family *Caryophyllaceae*). – Synonym *Tunica prolifera* (L.) Scop.

In gravelly pastures and grassy sand-dunes in the southern counties often near the sea; extends from Europe to Siberia, north Africa, and Canary Islands.

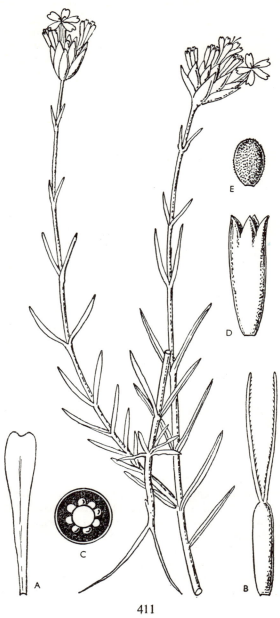

411

Annual or perennial herb up to 1 ft. high, rather succulent, quite glabrous; basal leaves on long stalks, broadly ovate-rhomboid, triangular at the apex or very slightly pointed, 3-nerved from the base, up to 2 in. long and broad; flowering stems with one pair of opposite ovate sessile leaves rather smaller than the blades of the basal leaves; racemes 2–3 at the top of each stem; bracts small and greenish; pedicels spreading, slender, up to 1 in. long in fruit; flowers (A, $\times 1\frac{1}{4}$) like those of *Stellaria*; sepals 2, rounded-ovate, enlarging a little and persistent around the fruit; petals (B, $\times 2$) 5, spreading, pale rose-pink or white tinged with pink, deeply bilobed; stamens 5, each opposite to a petal; anthers pink, facing outwards; ovary (C, $\times 3$) ovoid, greenish white; style deeply 3-lobed; capsule (D, $\times 2$) enclosed by the persistent sepals, ovoid; seeds (E, $\times 3$) 1–3 in each capsule, usually black and very shiny, minutely pitted (family *Portulacaceae*).

An introduced species, native of Siberia and north-western America; naturalized in many places from the midlands into Scotland, and here and there in more southern counties; found in abundance in some parts of the Lake District, in woods, by roadsides, and along the banks of streams; flowers from May until the autumn.

Annual in cultivated or waste ground; leaf-stalks and blades thick and fleshy, glabrous; basal leaves on long stalks, ovate or almost rhomboid, more or less wedge-shaped at the base, entire, up to about 1 in. long and broad, faintly 3-nerved from above the base; flowering stems with a pair of united opposite leaves at the top, in the middle of which a bunch or short raceme of flowers is borne; sepals (A, $\times2$) 2, green, broadly elliptic; petals (B, $\times4$) 5, white, shortly united at the base, shortly clawed and narrowly obovate, minutely notched at the apex; stamens (C, $\times6$) 5, opposite the petals (corolla-lobes); ovary (D, $\times5$) rounded, 1-locular, composed of 3 united carpels; style white, columnar, divided into three curved papillous stigmas; fruit (F, $\times1\frac{1}{2}$) splitting to the base into 3 valves; seeds (G, $\times3$) black and shining, in vertical section (H, $\times4$) showing the much curved embryo around the endosperm (E, flower bud, $\times1\frac{1}{2}$) (synonym *Claytonia perfoliata* Willd.) (family *Portulacaceae*).

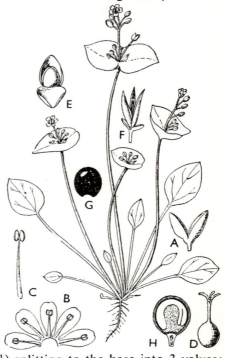

    In the latest classification of the genera of this family, this species is referred to the genus *Montia*, of which there is a second native species in Britain, *Montia fontana*, a tiny plant with spoon-shaped leaves, a zygomorphic corolla and only two stamens. The species of the genus *Claytonia*, in which *M. perfoliata* has usually been placed, are mostly perennials, whilst most species of *Montia* are annuals. *M. perfoliata* has also been placed in a third genus *Limnia*. It is a native of North America and naturalized in Britain.

Blackstonia perfoliata (L.) Huds. ($\times\frac{1}{2}$)

Erect annual up to $1\frac{1}{2}$ ft. high, glaucous (like the bloom on a grape) all over and without hairs (glabrous); leaves opposite, united at the base (perfoliate), each half broadly ovate and somewhat acute at the apex, the largest up to about $2\frac{1}{2}$ in. from tip to tip, each leaf 3-nerved; flowers in a dichotomous cyme (see drawing for this), the oldest flower in the first fork and subsequent forks; bracts becoming smaller upwards, like miniature leaves; calyx (A, $\times 1\frac{1}{2}$) divided to the base into 8 linear-subulate parts longer than the corolla-tube; corolla (B, $\times 1$) bright cream-yellow,

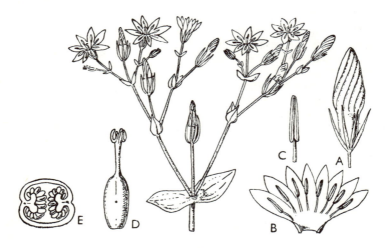

the 8 lobes twisted in bud to the right (A, $\times 1\frac{1}{2}$); stamens 8, inserted on the tube between the lobes; anthers (C, $\times 2$) linear; ovary (D, $\times 2\frac{1}{2}$) 1-locular, with numerous ovules on the 2 bilobed parietal (on the walls) placentas (E, $\times 5$); fruit a capsule with persistent style; seeds minute (synonym *Chlora perfoliata* L.) (family *Gentianaceae*).

In some seasons this is plentiful on the chalk downs and banks by the sea, and is a very pretty sight, often growing in the company of another member of the same family, *Centaurium minus* (fig. 361). It is only locally common, but is fairly widely distributed in England. It extends eastwards as far as the Caucasus.

This very attractive plant seems to be quite independent of insect visitors, for the flowers secrete no nectar. They close at night, and the two thick bilobed stigmas are self-pollinated.

Tiny glabrous annual, sometimes consisting of a single stem and 1 or 2 flowers; leaves very small, opposite, united at the base, shortly linear, glabrous; no stipules; flowers (A, $\times 1$) terminating the main stem and opposite branches, on slender (filiform) pedicels, the terminal pedicel up to 2 in. long in fruit; calyx campanulate, 5-lobed, lobes ovate, acute; corolla (B, $\times 1\frac{1}{2}$) golden yellow, shortly tubular, 4-lobed, lobes spirally folded in bud; stamens 4, inserted between the corollalobes; anthers shortly exserted from the tube; ovary (C, $\times 1$) ellipsoid, 1-locular, with numerous ovules on a free central placenta; style columnar, deciduous; fruit a capsule (family *Gentianaceae*). – Synonym *Microcala filiformis* Hoffm. & Link.

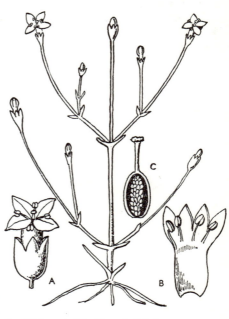

This is one of the smallest of British flowering plants which may be mistaken by the beginner for a member of the closely related family *Caryophyllaceae*; but its petals are united into a short tube and they are twisted (contorted) in bud. A very local species and often near the sea in some southern counties of England and Wales, south-west Eire, and the Channel Islands; extends to the Mediterranean and Morocco and the Near East.

There is only one species of this small genus in Britain, the second formerly included in it having been transferred to *Exaculum E. pusillum* (Lam.) Griseb. It differs from *Cicendia* by its pink corolla and bifid stigma. It is found only in the Channel Islands and as far south as North Africa.

Exaculum pusillum (Lam.) Caruel ($\times \frac{1}{2}$)

A very small annual with slender thread-like branches much re-sembling some members of the *Caryophyllaceae*, completely gla-brous all over; leaves opposite, linear, narrowed to the base, up to $\frac{1}{2}$ in. long, entire; no stipules; middle flower (A, $\times 3$) of the forked branches the oldest, on long slender pedicels; calyx 5-lobed, lobes spreading, oblong, apiculate; corolla (B, $\times 3$) pink, white, or pale yellow, tubular, the tube as long as the stamens

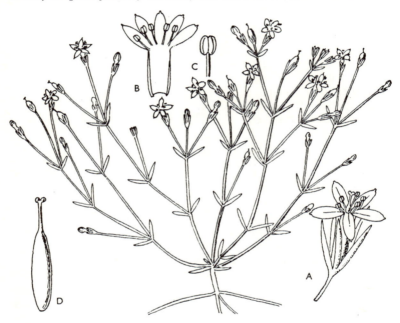

(C, $\times 6$) 5, inserted at the mouth of the tube and exserted, alter-nate with the lobes; filaments shorter than the corolla-lobes; an-thers (D, $\times 9$) ellipsoid, opening by slits lengthwise; ovary oblong, 1-locular, style deciduous, stigma 2-lobed, exserted; capsule opening by 2 valves (family *Gentianaceae*). – Synonyms *Microcala pusilla* L., *Cicendia pusilla* Griseb., *Cicendia candollei* Griseb.

In Britain found up to the present only in the Channel Islands and in the Hebrides; distributed through France and Spain to the western Mediterranean.

Gentiana pneumonanthe L. ($\times\frac{1}{2}$)

Perennial with thick spreading roots and stiff erect simple or little-branched stems up to 2 ft. high; leaves opposite, sessile, lanceolate to linear, glabrous and entire, the broader with three distinct parallel nerves; flowers (B, $\times\frac{3}{4}$) axillary, the lower branches 2–3, the upper axils with only one flower though several crowded at the top and the middle one the oldest and soon withering brown; calyx (A, $\times1\frac{1}{4}$) with 2 leafy bracts at the base, 5-lobed, lobes narrow and widely separate from each other, equal-sized; corolla $1\frac{1}{2}$ in. long, tinged with green outside but the lobes a beautiful deep blue, mottled with green spots inside and down the tube, but not hairy; lobes 5, ovate, with a sharp bent tip and with a short triangular lobe between each; stamens 5, the anthers (C, $\times2$) connivent in a cone around the style and facing outwards; ovary (D, $\times1$) stalked (stipitate), narrow, 1-locular, with numerous ovules on the two parietal placentas (E, $\times2$); cap-sule opening by 2 valves; seeds numerous (family *Gentianaceae*).

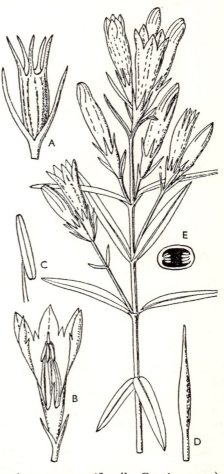

This is one of the few native species which has retained its popularity as a garden plant, and it is superior to many exotic kinds. Nevertheless, it should on no account be dug up. It is locally frequent in moist places on heaths, but not found in Scotland or Eire.

FIELD GENTIAN
Gentiana campestris L. ($\times \frac{2}{3}$)

Erect annual up to about 9 in. high with a slender taproot; leaves opposite, gradually increasing in size upwards, sessile, the largest

about 1 in. long and broadly lanceolate, prominently 3-nerved from the base, minutely papillous on the margin; flowers axillary and solitary or on short axillary branches; stalks up to $1\frac{1}{2}$ in. long; calyx (A, $\times 1\frac{1}{4}$) leaf-like, 4-lobed to about the middle, the two outer lobes ovate-lanceolate, much broader than the two inner linear sharp-pointed lobes, all minutely papillous on the margin; corolla (B, $\times 1\frac{3}{4}$) pale blue, twice as long as the calyx, 4-lobed, fringed with long blue hairs at the mouth; stamens 4, alternate with the corolla-lobes, and inserted well down the tube; anthers facing inwards; ovary (C, $\times 2$) nearly as long as the stamens, 1-locular, with the numerous ovules arranged on two placentas along the walls (D, $\times 6$); stigma deeply 2-lobed; fruit a capsule with numerous rounded seeds; flowers in late summer and autumn; in pastures and on commons mostly in limestone districts (family *Gentianaceae*).

Nectar is secreted at the bottom of the corolla and can only be reached by humble-bees and *Lepidoptera* because of the dense fringe of bristly hairs at the mouth of the corolla. This is the most common of the nine species of Gentian accredited to the British flora, and it is not likely to be mistaken for any except *Gentiana amarella* L. (fig. 360), which has 5 corolla-lobes, and 5 calyx-lobes all narrowly lanceolate, and of equal size.

Gentiana amarella L. (× ⅖)

Erect, simple or branched annual, with stiff erect branches, some-times only a few inches high or up to 15 in. and then very slender; stems often tinged with crimson or purple, glab-rous; leaves opposite, sessile, lanceolate to nar-rowly ovate, rounded and clasping the stem at the base, apex obtuse to somewhat acute, more or less 3-nerved from the base, entire; flowers few to numerous and crowded, sometimes so numerous as to form a leafy panicle; stalks variable, but up to ¾ in.; long in fruit; calyx (A, × 1¼) divided to the middle into 5 equal acute narrow lobes; co-rolla (B, × ⅘) pale purp-lish-blue, 2–2½ times as long as the calyx; lobes 5, with a dense fringe of erect stiff hairs within the mouth; stamens 5, alternate with the corol-la-lobes; ovary 1-locular, with 2 rows of ovules on

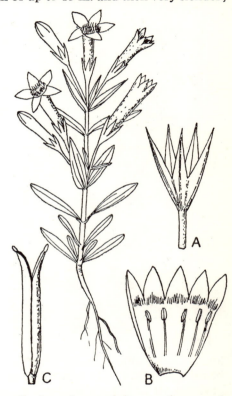

the walls; stigmas nearly sessile, broad, remaining on the capsule (C, × ⅘) like a little tongue, the capsule about ½ in. long and split-ting down the middle; seeds numerous, rounded, brown and very minutely pitted (family *Gentianaceae*).

This species is more common in some localities (dry hilly pas-tures, cliffs, and dunes), but not so widely distributed as *Gentiana campestris* L. (fig. 359). In *G. amarella* there are 5 calyx-lobes, all narrow and equal in size and shape. In *G. campestris*, however, there is a reduction to 4 calyx-lobes, and these are unequal in size and shape, two of them being broadly ovate and overlapping, the other two much narrower ones.

Centaurium erythraea Rafn. ($\frac{2}{5}$)

Erect annual, varying much in size according to situation from an inch up to a foot high, usually much-branched from the base;

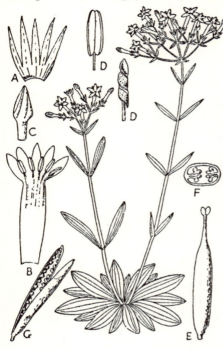

stems and branches narrowly ribbed, glabrous; leaves opposite, often forming also a basal rosette, these spoon - shaped - oblanceolate and prominently 3-nerved from the base; stem leaves sessile, lanceolate to almost linear, with 3-parallel nerves; flowers numerous in a rather dense repeatedly forked cyme, the middle flower of each branch nearly sessile; bracts paired below each lateral flower; calyx (A, ×2) deeply 5-lobed, the lobes very narrow and keeled; corolla pink, tube cylindric, narrow, contracted at the top and then spreading into a 5-lobed limb (B, ×5); lobes twisted in bud (C, ×1¾); stamens (D, ×5) 5, the anthers large and exserted from the tube, with a short slender 2-lobed style as high as the anthers, and with two placentas (F, ×5) projecting into the middle; ovules numerous on the two placentas; capsule (G, ×2) splitting along the placentas, with numerous seeds; grows in dry pastures, sandy banks, and by roadsides, flowering all the summer (family *Gentianaceae*).– Synonyms *C. umbellatum* Gilib. and *C. minus* Gars.

A striking feature is the spiral twisting of the anthers after opening. The stigma is mature when the flower opens, and the anthers discharge their pollen in succession, at which time the style is bent away to one side, whilst the stamens bend to the other side, when cross-pollination may take place. Later the stigma and anthers become erect and self-pollination is possible.

Herb growing in water, with a creeping rootstock and dense mat of roots; stem rather thick, creeping or floating, covered by the large sheathing bases of the leaves, the latter alternate, divided into 3 separate obovate leaflets rounded at the apex and with a few ascending looped lateral nerves; sheathing base up to about 2 in. long, membranous; flowers several in a raceme on a long stalk arising from below the tuft of leaves, each flower with a bract at the base shorter than its own stalk, the latter up to about 1 in. long; calyx deeply 5-lobed, lobes oblong, rounded at the apex; corolla (A, $\times 1\frac{1}{2}$) broadly tubular, 5-lobed, lobes not overlapping in bud (valvate),  densely clothed on the inside with numerous white hairs; stamens (B, $\times 2\frac{1}{4}$) 5, alternate with the corolla-lobes; ovary (C, $\times 2\frac{1}{4}$) with only 1 loculus and ovules arranged on the walls; fruit (D, E, $\times 1\frac{1}{2}$) a capsule bursting into 2 parts; seeds (F, $\times 2\frac{1}{2}$) few, rounded, slightly compressed, light brown and shining, $\frac{1}{8}$ in. diam. (family *Menyanthaceae*).

This plant is usually classified with the Gentians (*Gentianaceae*), but there are good reasons for treating it as a distinct family. In the Gentian family the leaves are always opposite and the corolla-lobes overlap and are twisted in bud, whilst in the Buckbean, and its related genus *Nymphoides* (*Limnanthemum*), the leaves are alternate and the corolla-lobes do not overlap or twist in bud. The flowers of the Buckbean are mostly of two kinds, a long-styled and a short-styled form, with a corresponding position for the anthers.

Aquatic plant with long stems creeping and rooting at the bottom of the water; leaf-blades floating on the surface, ovate-orbicular, deeply cordate at the base and slightly peltate, rather thick, undulate on the margin, pustulate when dry; leaf-stalks sheathing and stem-clasping at the base; flowers forming an umbel-like cluster with smaller leaves; pedicels up to 3 in. long; calyx deeply 5-lobed, lobes green, $\frac{1}{2}$ in. long; corolla (A, $\times \frac{1}{2}$) yellow, campanulate, with 5 spreading lobes with a narrow triangular middle portion and denticulate margins; stamens (B, $\times 3$) 5, alternate with the lobes and inserted towards the base of the tube; anthers (B, $\times 3$) exserted; ovary ovoid (C, $\times 2\frac{1}{2}$) with a style half as long;

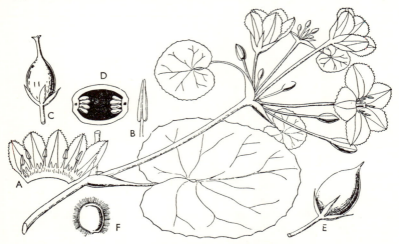

ovules (D, $\times 4$) on parietal placentas; fruit (E, $\times 1$) bursting irregularly when ripe, ovoid; seeds (F, $\times 4$) rounded, fringed with soft hairs (family *Menyanthaceae*).–Synonyms *Limnanthemum peltatum* Gmelin. *L. nymphaeoides* Link. *Villarsia nymphaeoides* Vent.

Widely distributed from Europe to China and Japan, in rivers and ponds, flowering in July and August. The flower buds are submerged, raising themselves above the surface when ready to open; later the pedicel bends again and the fruit develops and ripens under water. The flowers are of two forms, some with a longer style, others with a shorter style, and there is a corresponding difference in the length of the anthers, as in the Primrose; nectar is secreted at the base of the filaments.

Perennial with procumbent stems rooting at the lower nodes; leaves opposite, stalked, ovate, entire, up to 1½ in. long and nearly as much broad, 3-nerved from the base; no stipules; flowers solitary in the upper leaf-axils, on long slender stalks; sepals (A, ×2) 5, linear-lanceolate, acute; corolla (B, ×1½) yellow, with a short tube and 5 spreading lobes twisted (contorted) in bud; stamens (C, ×3) 5, inserted towards the base and opposite to the lobes;

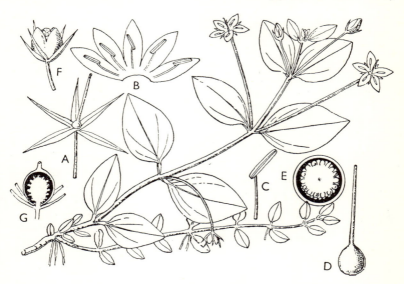

anthers linear, attached near the base, opening by slits lengthwise; ovary (D, G, ×3) above the calyx, rounded, 1-locular, with numerous ovules on a central basal placenta (E, ×4); fruit (F, × 1½) a capsule shorter than the sepals, and curling around on its stalk when ripe; seeds few on a fleshy placenta (family *Primulaceae*).

Grows in woods and shady places, sometimes forming a loose carpet amongst grasses, etc., flowering most of the summer, and in the south during late spring.

In the egg-yellow flowers of this species the diverging stamens are of equal length, and remote from the stigma, which is situated at a somewhat lower level, preventing self-pollination for some time.

Lysimachia vulgaris L. (×⅔)

Perennial with erect stems up to about 3 ft. high, growing on shady banks near water; leaves in whorls, the lower 4 or 3 in a whorl, the upper mostly in pairs, broadly to narrowly lanceolate, very shortly stalked at the base, gradually tapered to the apex, slightly pubescent below, with entire or undulate minutely jagged margins; flowers (B, ×⅔) in leafy terminal panicles; stalks slender, pubescent, with small narrow bracts at their base; sepals 5, broadly lanceolate, fringed with very short hairs; corolla yellow with a short broad tube, 5-lobed, the lobes (A, ×2) twisted (contorted) in bud, densely covered above by short glandular hairs; stamens (C, ×2½) 5, opposite the corolla-lobes, with rudiments of filaments between; anthers large; filaments covered with short gland-tipped hairs; ovary (D, ×2½) globose, 1-locular, with numerous ovules arranged on the central basal placenta (E, ×7); fruit a capsule (family *Primulaceae*). There are no nectaries in the flowers, but the abundant pollen in the very large anthers is collected by certain bees which carry it in balls on their hind legs.

The family *Primulaceae* is quite well represented in Britain with nine genera, *Lysimachia* having four species. The commonest is the one here described, another familiar one being the Creeping Jenny, *L. nummularia* L., which creeps on the ground, rooting at the nodes. The other two species, *L. thrysiflora* L., with axillary spike-like racemes, and *L. nemorum* L. resembling the Creeping Jenny, but with long slender flower-stalks, are much less common.

Perennial; stems prostrate, rooting at the lower nodes, with a broad groove alternately above and at the side between; leaves opposite, all spreading in the same plane, shortly stalked, very broadly ovate-rounded, not toothed (entire), with about 5 pairs of rather faint nerves, bright green, not hairy (glabrous); no stipules; flowers (A (bud), B, $\times\frac{3}{4}$) axillary, or rarely 2 in one of the leaf-axils; stalks erect, up to $1\frac{1}{2}$ in. long, smooth; sepals broadly ovate-triangular, eared (auriculate) at the base, pale green; corolla of

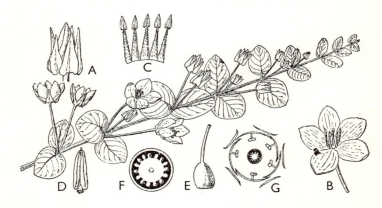

5 nearly separate petals, rich buttercup-yellow, about 1 in. diam. when fully expanded, the lobes twisted (contorted) in bud (A, $\times\frac{3}{4}$); stamens (C, $\times 2$) 5, opposite to the corolla-lobes; stalks (filaments) shortly united at the base, densely covered with short blunt hairs; anthers rounded to a short tip (mucronate) (D, $\times 3$); ovary (E, $\times 2$) free within the stamens, 1-locular (F, $\times 4$) with numerous ovules around the central axis, the latter reaching to the top of the chamber; fruit a capsule opening by 5 valves; seeds attached in the middle (G, floral diagram) (family *Primulaceae*).

Beginners may not see much in common between this plant and the common Primrose, though they both belong to the same family, *Primulaceae*. The best spotting feature of this family is that the stamens are inserted on and opposite to the more or less united petals.

This is a charming little plant and well worth a place in the rock garden or a hanging basket. It is scattered throughout Britain but becomes rarer in the north.

Lysimachia punctata L. ($\times \frac{1}{2}$)

Perennial, stems $1\frac{1}{2}$–2 ft., closely ribbed, softly pubescent; leaves mostly arranged in whorls of 4, shortly stalked, ovate-elliptic to ovate-lanceolate, more or less wedge-shaped at the base, tip hard and callus-like, the largest about 2 in. long and 1 in. broad, not toothed, very minutely hairy above, more obviously so below; main lateral nerves about 6 on each side of the midrib; no stipules; flowers 2 or 3 in each leaf axil (appearing to be whorled) from near the base of the stem to the top; stalks about $\frac{3}{4}$ in. long, softly hairy; calyx (A, $\times 2\frac{1}{2}$) of 5 narrow green sepals, with mostly gland-tipped hairs; corolla (B, $\times 1$) bright yellow with pale dull crimson centre, composed of 5 spreading petals united at the base and closely dotted with glands on the upper surface; stamens (C, $\times 3$) 5, united in a tube arising from the base of the corolla and falling away with it; anthers opposite to the corolla-lobes, arrow-shaped at the base; ovary (D, $\times 2\frac{1}{2}$) 1-locular, with numerous ovules arranged around a central column (E, $\times 6$); style undivided; (synonyms *L. quadrifolia* Mill.; *L. verticillata* Spreng.) (family *Primulaceae*).

Not a native, but naturalized and often found near dwellings, though occasionally growing, apparently quite naturally, in woods nearby. The species is distributed in a wild state from Austria to the Caucasus.

Besides the three native species of *Lysimachia* shown in figs. 364–366, there is one other native species *L. thrysiflora* L. (sometimes put in a separate genus *Naumburgia*) with flowers in axillary racemes and the lobes of the corolla narrow and short; and there are two other species which are naturalized besides the above *L. punctata*; these are *L. ciliata* L., sometimes found near buildings in northern England and Scotland, a native of North America; in this species the corolla-lobes are not ciliate on the margins, but they are densely glandular towards the base, and the filaments are free, alternating with small staminodes; the other introduced species is *L. terrestris* (L.) Britton, naturalized on the shores of Lake Windermere, a plant bearing numerous elongated bulbils in the axils of the narrowly lanceolate leaves and which rarely flowers.

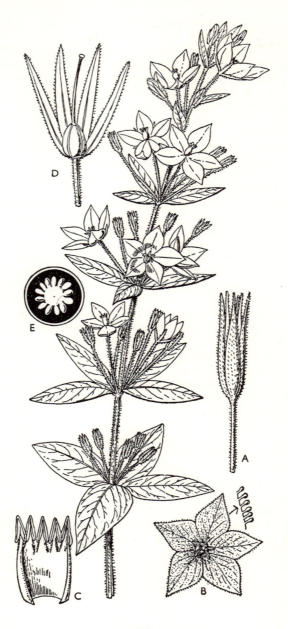

427

Hottonia palustris L. ($\times\frac{1}{2}$)

Aquatic perennial herb with a long trailing rhizome, the oldest part of this generally embedded in mud, with vertical aerial branches which may become detached by dying off of the older parts; leaves in a basal rosette, pinnate into many narrow lobes, above the leaves and at the base of the inflorescence a whorl of branches (A, $\times\frac{1}{2}$); after fruits are formed these separate from the parent plant, rest through the winter, and form the starting points for new plants the next spring when they may be found floating and often still without roots which develop later; flowers numerous in whorls on an upright axis and with linear bracts, the stalks decurved in fruit; calyx-lobes 5, narrow; corolla (B, $\times 1$) lilac with a yellow 'eye', 5-lobed; stamens 5, opposite the lobes and inserted in the tube; anthers (E, $\times 5$) at the mouth in the long-styled form (B, $\times 1$), well exserted in the short-styled form (C, $\times 1$); ovary superior, 1-locular, with a terminal undivided style (D, $\times 4$) varying in length according to the position of the anthers (E, $\times 5$); ovules numerous on a basal placenta (E, $\times 5$) with a barren tip; fruit (F, $\times 1$) a capsule opening by 5 vertical slits; seeds angular (family *Primulaceae*).

Flowers in early summer in ponds and marshes, but very rare in Scotland; distributed in central and northern Europe.

The whorl of branches at the base of the inflorescence is a very striking feature, and it is mostly well developed before the flowers open. Throughout the life of the latter, this whorl helps to maintain the vertical position of the inflorescence above the water. After fruits are formed these branches separate from the parent plant, rest through the winter, and then form the starting points for new plants in the spring, when they may be found floating about, often without roots, which develop later on. The seeds sink to the bottom within a week.

As may be seen from the drawings the flowers are of two kinds, some with a long style and the anthers almost hidden at the mouth of the corolla tube, others with a short style and well-exserted anthers. Thus pollen from the exserted anthers is transferred by insects to the stigma of the long-style, whilst pollen from the anthers hidden at the mouth of the tube pollinates the stigma of the short style, as in *Primula*. Nectar is secreted at the base of the ovary and stored up in the corolla-tube.

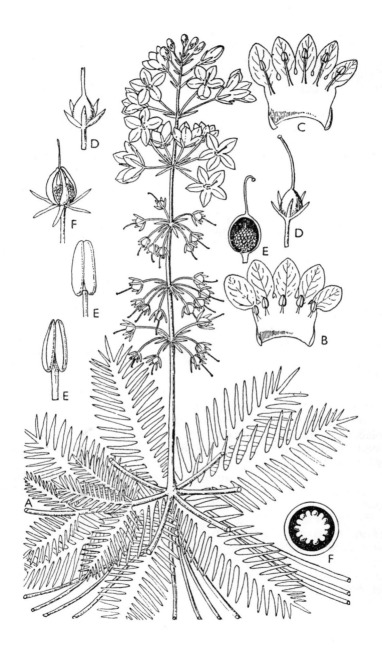

TRIENTALE
Trientalis europaea L. ($\times \frac{1}{2}$)

Perennial herb with slightly creeping rootstock; stem single, up to 6 in. high, bearing at the top a bunch of about half a dozen leaves, these broadly ob-lanceolate, averaging about 2 in. long, entire and with prominent looped nerves, often 2 or 3 smaller leaves on the stem below the larger leaves; flowers one or more (up to about 4) from the axils of the upper leaves, each with a slender stalk nearly as long as the leaves; no bracts; sepals (A, $\times 2$) 7–6, narrow; corolla 6–7 lobed, $\frac{3}{4}$ in. diam., white or pale

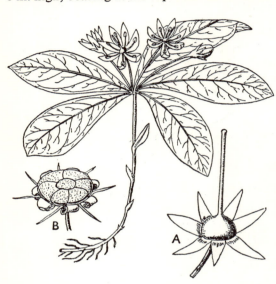

pink with a yellow ring; stamens as many as corolla-lobes and opposite to them; filaments slender; anthers short and recurved; ovary superior, 1-locular, with numerous ovules on a free central placenta; fruit a capsule (B, $\times 2$) opening by 5 recurved valves; seeds flattened, attached in the middle (peltate), with a greyish-white coat (family *Primulaceae*).

Grows in woods, often amongst pines and birches, from York-shire northwards, flowering in June and July; circumpolar in distribution.

Nectar is secreted by a thick fleshy ring around the ovary. The stigma is receptive as soon as the flower opens, the anthers being still closed. The stigma soon projects beyond the anthers, when cross-pollination is very probable. On withering the flower closes, pressing the stamens against the style so that self-pollination may be brought about.

Perennial herb with short tufted rootstock and rather long pale roots; leaves in a rosette, very variable in size according to situation, spathulate-oblanceolate, rounded at the top, up to 3 in. long and $\frac{3}{4}$ in. broad, finely dentate in the upper part, green above, densely covered below with a whitish or greenish-white meal; lateral nerves numerous but obscure, forked; common flower-stalk (peduncle) up to 1 ft. high, mealy towards the top, bearing an umbel of about a dozen or so lovely pale lilac flowers with a yellow 'eye'; bracts subulate-lanceolate, $\frac{1}{4}$ in. long; stalks (pedicels) slender, $\frac{1}{3}$ in. long; calyx (A, $\times 3$) 5-lobed nearly to the middle, mealy, lobes narrowly lanceolate; corolla with 5 deeply notched spreading lobes; anthers either inserted near the middle of the tube with the stigma at its mouth (B, $\times 3$), or just below its mouth with the stigma reaching only half way up the tube (C, $\times 3$); capsule a little longer than the calyx (family *Primulaceae*).

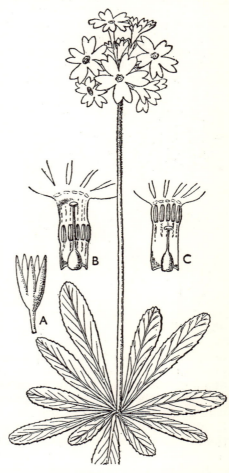

Mountains of northern England and Scotland; a species with a wide circumpolar distribution and in all the great mountain ranges of Europe and Asia.

Primula vulgaris Huds. (flower and leaf, $\times \frac{4}{5}$)

Perennial with a rosette of bright green leaves, these oblong-oblanceolate, with wavy and finely toothed margins, and wrinkled (bullate) reticulate upper surface, very coarsely reticulate below and with softly hairy nerves and veins (A, $\times 1\frac{1}{4}$); flowers sweet-scented, the stalks arising from the root, often as long as or longer than the leaves, softly hairy; calyx tubular, 5-ribbed and narrowly 5-lobed, softly hairy outside; corolla cream-yellow, tubular, the tube a little longer than the calyx, 5-lobed, the lobes (B, $\times \frac{4}{5}$)

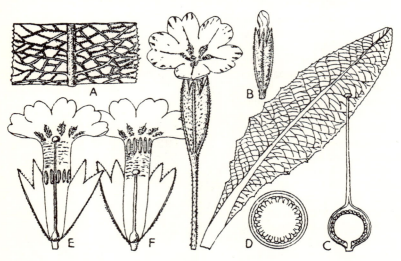

twisted (contorted) in bud, deeply notched and with wavy margins, suffused at the base with orange; stamens inserted either about the middle of the corolla-tube or within its throat, opposite the corolla-lobes; anthers facing inwards; ovary (C, $\times \frac{4}{5}$) rounded, with a slender style either reaching only to the middle of the corolla or to its mouth; ovules numerous, arranged around the central axis (D, $\times 2$) of the 1-locular ovary; fruit a capsule opening at the top by 5 teeth (family *Primulaceae*).

The flowers are of great biological interest and vertical sections of the two forms are shown. Figure E ($\times 1\frac{1}{4}$) shows the long-styled or pin-eyed form, with the stigma filling the throat of the corolla and the anthers attached in the middle of the tube. Figure F ($\times 1\frac{1}{4}$) shows the short-styled or thrum-eyed form, with the position of these organs reversed.

Perennial with a dense tuft of numerous slender roots; leaves all basal (radical) mostly ascending, oblong-oblanceolate to oblong-elliptic and often very abruptly narrowed into and decurrent on the stalks, finely toothed, very minutely pubescent; common flower stalks several from amongst the leaves and overtopping them considerably, very shortly and softly hairy, bearing at the top an umbel of several stalked, scented flowers, with a whorl of narrow bracts at the base of the stalks; calyx about ½ in. long, shortly 5-lobed, softly hairy; corolla cream-yellow usually with an orange patch at the base of each lobe, the tube expanded about the middle in the long-styled form (A,

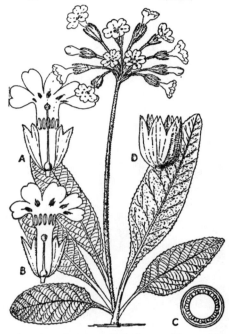

× 1¼) and towards the top in the short-styled form (B, × 1¼); lobes 5, notched; stamens 5, inserted either in the middle or towards the top of the tube; ovary superior, 1-locular (C, × 6), with a style reaching to the middle of the corolla-tube or nearly to the top (short- and long-styled forms respectively); fruit (D, × ⅔) a bell-shaped 5-lobed capsule about ⅔ in. long, enclosed by the persistent calyx (family *Primulaceae*).

The notes about the two forms of flowers in the Primrose (fig. 371) apply equally well to those of the Cowslip, and hybrids between them occur which have been and are easily mistaken for another species, the real Oxslip, *P. elatior* Schreb., which, however is much more rare and is found only in East Anglia. Nectar is secreted around the base of the ovary, and the corolla-tube is sometimes perforated by humble-bees.

SOWBREAD
Cyclamen hederifolium Ait. ($\times\frac{1}{2}$)

Rootstock a tuber up to 3 in. diam.; leaves appearing after the flowers, on long stalks, ovate-cordate, more or less angular and

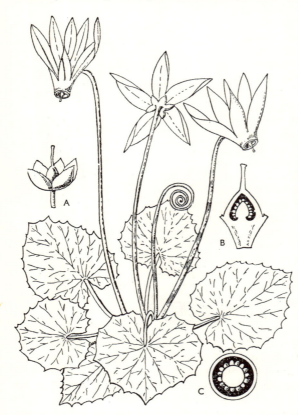

toothed, dark-green with a whitish mottled border above, often purplish or violet below; flowers white or pink, on long radical pedicels which become spirally coiled in the fruiting stage; calyx-lobes (A, $\times$2) ovate - lanceolate, acute; corolla-lobes 5, sharply reflexed on the short tube; stamens 5, inserted at the base of the corolla-tube; anthers included in the tube, pointed; ovary (B, C, $\times3\frac{1}{2}$) globose, 1-locular, with many ovules on a free basal placenta; style short, stigma undivided; capsule globular, 5-valved, many-seeded, valves reflexed; seeds angular, peltate; embryo with only one cotyledon (family *Primulaceae*). – Synonym *Cyclamen europeum* L.

Flowers in September, local and rare but doubtfully native from the midlands southwards; extends to the eastern Mediterranean.

Glaux maritima L. ($\times\frac{2}{3}$)

Small perennial with short decumbent branches often slightly fleshy, up to about 6 in. high; rootstock creeping, rooting at the nodes, which bear the remains of old leaves; lower leaves opposite, the upper alternate, ovate to oblong or even nearly linear, entire, glabrous; flowers (A, ×3) axillary, nearly sessile, forming a leafy spike-like raceme, the upper leaves only slightly reduced in size; sepals 5, pale pink and resembling petals (which are absent), narrowly obovate and shortly united at the base; stamens (B, ×3) 5, alternating with the sepals and about as long, with short broadly ovoid anthers; ovary (C, ×5) free from the calyx (superior), rounded and glabrous, 1-locular, with the several ovules arranged on a free basal placenta with no dividing walls (D, ×7); fruit a globose capsule opening by valves; seeds attached in the middle (peltate) (family *Primulaceae*).

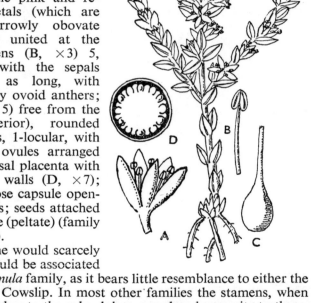

At first one would scarcely think this could be associated with the *Primula* family, as it bears little resemblance to either the Primrose or Cowslip. In most other families the stamens, when equal in number to the calyx-lobes, are placed opposite to them, and are therefore alternate with the petals. In other *Primulaceae*, however, they are opposite the petals, and in this genus without petals they stand in their place.

The pink flowers, with their coloured calyx, rather resemble those of some species of *Polygonum*, but then the absence of stipules at once distinguishes the plant from the latter, in which they are sheathing and very prominent (see figs. 385–391).

Anagallis arvensis L. ($\times \frac{2}{5}$)

A small often much-branched procumbent annual, with branches
from an inch or two up to a foot long, acutely angled or narrowly
winged; leaves opposite, sessile, ovate, rounded at the base, triangular at the apex, 3-nerved from the base, minutely roughened
on the margin; flowers (A, $\times 1\frac{3}{5}$), usually red, axillary, solitary,
with stalks longer than the leaves, the stalks recurving in fruit;
calyx (B, $\times 2\frac{2}{5}$) deeply 5-lobed nearly to the base, lobes lanceolate,

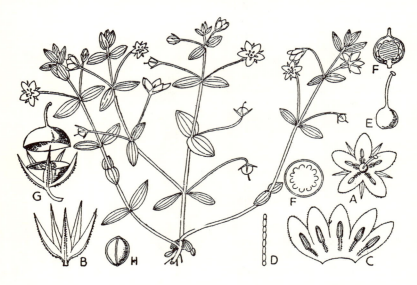

very acute, with a keel-like midrib and thin whitish margins;
corolla (C, $\times 2\frac{2}{5}$) with a very short tube, 5-lobed, lobes rounded
and very minutely fringed with glands; stamens 5, opposite the
corolla-lobes and inserted on the tube; stalks (filaments) fringed
with several-celled hairs (D, $\times 10$); ovary (E, $\times 2\frac{1}{2}$) globose, 1-
locular with several ovules arranged on a free central placenta
which does not reach the top of the loculus (F, $\times 3\frac{1}{2}$); fruit (G,
$\times 1\frac{3}{4}$) a dry capsule splitting transversely around the middle, the
upper part with the persistent style resembling a Chinaman's cap;
seeds (H, $\times 6$) several, triangular, and with narrowly winged margins (family *Primulaceae*).

BOG PIMPERNEL

Anagallis tenella (L.) Murr. ($\times \frac{1}{2}$)

A tiny creeping perennial growing in bogs and wet places chiefly beside brooks; stems rooting at the nodes; leaves opposite, shortly stalked, ovate-orbicular, entire, minutely speckled with brown (showing more when dried), glabrous; no stipules; flowers axillary, often together in the leaf-pairs, on slender stalks up to 1 in. long; sepals (A, $\times 2\frac{1}{2}$) 5, very narrowly lanceolate, acute; corolla 5-lobed, pale pink, tube short, the lobes twisted in bud; stamens (B, $\times 4$) 5, erect in the middle of the flower and held together by the very hairy filaments (C, $\times 12$); hairs on these jointed; ovary

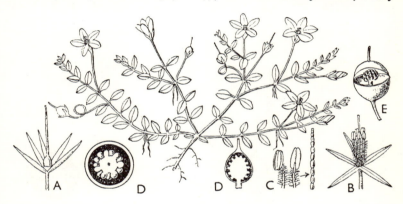

above the calyx, 1-locular, with several ovules on a free central placenta, which does not reach the top of the loculus (D, $\times 12$); style slender, undivided; fruit (E, $\times 2$) a capsule opening by a transverse slit (family *Primulaceae*).

Found mainly in the western counties of Britain and in Eire, flowering during summer. The hairs on the filaments of the stamens made a pretty microscopical object, with the cells forming a little chain. The interlacing of these peculiar hairs loosely holds together the stamens.

If these drawings of plants belonging to the Primula family, *Primulaceae*, be examined, it will be noticed that in the cross-section of the ovary (fig. E) no lines are shown dividing it up into separate compartments, or loculi, as botanists now call them. This is a good spotting feature for the family, the ovary being 1-locular, with the ovules arranged on what is called a *free basal placenta* (fig. D), which does not extend to the top of the ovary as in the related Pink family, *Caryophyllaceae* (compare figs. 317–352).

437

Centunculus minimus L. ($\times\frac{1}{2}$)

A tiny annual with several branches from the base; branches flattened and slightly winged, glabrous; leaves alternate, rounded-obovate, $\frac{1}{4}$–$\frac{1}{3}$ in. long, entire, glabrous, faintly nerved, very slightly stalked; flowers axillary, solitary, sessile; sepals 4, linear, acute; corolla (A, $\times 5$) pink, composed of united petals; tube short and globose, lobes 4, ovate-lanceolate, acute; stamens (B, $\times 5$) 4, opposite the corolla-lobes, inserted at the mouth of the tube; filaments short, anthers 2-locular, rounded; ovary (C, $\times 3$) superior, 1-locular, globose, with many ovules on a free basal placenta (D, $\times 9$); style undivided; fruit a capsule (E, F, $\times 4$)

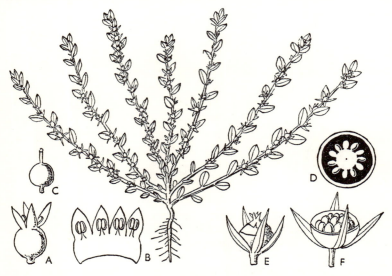

opening by a circular transverse slit, the lid falling off with the withered corolla encircling the style; seeds attached in the middle (peltate) (family *Primulaceae*).

In moist, sandy, or gravelly places, flowering in summer; distributed in various parts of the world.

A beginner in the study of classification might wonder why a tiny plant like this should be referred to the same family as the Primrose. This is because the petals are united into a tube with the stamens inserted *opposite* the lobes, and the ovules are attached to a *free central placenta*, characters shared by the Primrose and other members of the family.

Samolus valerandi L. (×½)

Perennial often flowering in the seedling stage; basal leaves (A, ×1) with longish and broad flat stalks, obovate-oblanceolate, slightly fleshy, glabrous, with about 3–4 pairs of ob-scure looped lateral nerves; stem-leaves be-coming less stalked and finally sessile, at the base of the inflorescence car-ried up on the stalk and becoming a leafy bracteole (see notes below); flowers (B, ×1½) in terminal racemes and terminating the upper branches; stalks bearing a leafy bracteole near the top; calyx 5-lobed, gland-dotted, shortly joined to the lower part of the ovary; corolla (C, ×2) white, of 5 partly united petals; sta-mens 5, in the corolla-tube and opposite the lobes, with small, white subulate staminodes be-tween the lobes; ovary (D, ×1½) half-inferior,

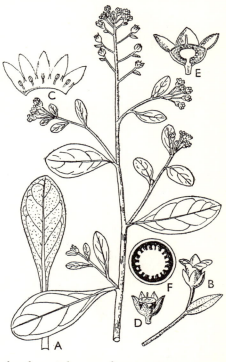

flat on top, with a short slender style; ovules numerous on a basal placenta, which is not carried to the top of the ovary (E, ×3); fruit girt by the persistent calyx-lobes, opening by 5 valves (F, cross-section of ovary, ×6) (family *Primulaceae*).

This is an exceptional genus in the *Primulaceae* because the ovary is partly united with the calyx, causing the former to be semi-inferior. In appearance the plant is rather like some species of *Myosotis* in *Boraginaceae*. As the leaves become bracts they are carried up some distance on the flower-bearing branchlets.

The corolla-tube is extremely short, and there is no nectar secretion. Insects visits are very rare. As the anthers are at the same level in the corolla-tube as the stigma, and mature at the same time, automatic self-pollination takes place, and is effective.

SEA LAVENDER
Limonium vulgare Mill. ($\times\frac{1}{3}$)

Perennial with short thick rootstock; old leaf-bases persistent and brown; leaves basal, oblanceolate to narrowly obovate, narrowed

at the base into a long stalk, almost nerveless except for the thick midrib below, glabrous but minutely pustulate on both surfaces, dull green; flowers (A, ×2) numerous and small, in repeatedly forked cymes on a stalk up to a foot or sometimes more high; bracts small and brown, half encircling the stem; calyx (A, ×2) tubular, shortly 5-lobed, blue and with crimson ribs, becoming the conspicuous part of the flower after withering of the 5 blue petals (B, ×2); stamens 5, opposite the petals; ovary (C, ×2) ellipsoid, 1-locular, with one pendulous ovule hanging from a basal stalk (D, ×2); styles 5, quite free from one another, glabrous (synonym *Statice limonium* L.) (family *Plumbaginaceae*).

Widely distributed in maritime sands and salt marshes, often in great quantity, in various temperate regions of the world.

A very interesting feature is that when the corolla withers the calyx takes on the function of attracting insects. Nectar is concealed and stored in the base of the corolla. The anthers mature first and after they have withered the styles elongate so that the now receptive stigmas project from the entrance to the flower. Cross-pollination then takes place, though self-pollination is possible.

Sea Lavender is one of the most decorative of our sea-side flowers, for it retains its form and colour for many months after gathering. The leaves are very bright green sometimes as much as a foot long, strongly nerved and with the sharp point bent backwards.

Armeria maritima Willd. ($\times \frac{2}{3}$)

A tufted perennial, rootstock branched, covered by the remains of the old leaf-bases; leaves numerous, grass-like, and forming a dense rosette, narrowly linear, entire, obtuse at the apex, minutely hairy; flowering stems single from each rosette, leafless, covered with short soft hairs, up to about 9 in. high, bearing at the top a globose head of usually pink or sometimes white flowers (A, $\times 1\frac{1}{4}$); outer bracts longer than the others and elongated at the base and forming a reflexed sheath around the top of the peduncle; inner bracts broader and becoming membranous, those below the flowers very thin and transparent; calyx (B, $\times 2$) tubular, of 5 lobes, lobes very narrow but united into a mem-

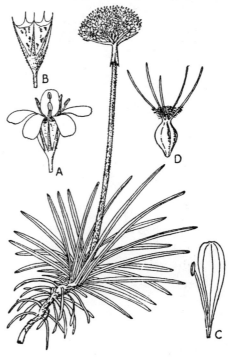

branous tube with the short sharp calyx teeth at the top, lower part green and pubescent; petals (C, $\times 2$) narrowly obovate, with narrow claws, free to the base; stamens 5, opposite to and inserted at the base of the petals; filaments slender, pale, anthers facing inwards, lemon yellow; ovary (D, $\times 6$) laterally 5-lobed, but with only one loculus and a single pendulous ovule; styles 5, free, with spreading rod-like hairs at the base (family *Plumbaginaceae*).

Very common around our coasts in muddy and sandy places and on maritime rocks; also high up in some of the Cumberland and Scottish mountains. The most striking feature is the basal prolongation of the outer bracts of the involucre to form a jagged tubular sheath around the top of the peduncle.

Plantago lanceolata L., *Plantago major* L., and *Plantago media* L.
(habit drawings much reduced, floral parts, ×2)

There are three common species of Plantain in Britain, and sketches of these are shown in the drawing, the other two being confined to maritime districts (*P. maritima* L. and *P. coronopus* L.). Of these three the most common is *P. lanceolata* (A), with erect or spreading lanceolate leaves minutely and distantly toothed on the margin with 3–6 longitudinal nerves and gradually narrowed into the petiole; the spikes are ovoid or oblong and not usually more than an inch long, and the fruit contains 2 seeds. In *P. major* (B) the leaves are ascending and very broadly ovate and stalked and lined with 5 or more nerves according to width; the

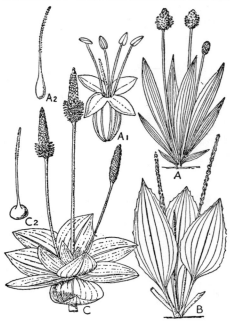

spike is narrow and slender and sometimes elongates up to about 15 in.; the fruit contains several seeds. In *P. media* (C) the leaves form a flat rosette on the ground, are very broad and sessile or with a wide very short stalk and usually 5 longitudinal nerves converging on the apex; the spike is intermediate between the other two species described here, at most about 2 in. long but narrower than in *P. lanceolata*. *P. media* is found mainly in limestone districts, but the other two are very abundant in almost any kind of soil. *P. lanceolata*, especially, is a very common pasture plant (family *Plantaginaceae*).

The flowers of Plantains are wind-pollinated, the stamens having long slender flexible filaments, and the styles feathery stigmas. Insects visit the flowers for the sake of their pollen.

Plantago maritima L. (×½)

Perennial with a woody rootstock and woolly hairs amongst the leaves at the base; leaves up to 1 ft. long, linear and flat, 3-nerved, or shorter and almost needle-like and resembling those of Sea Thrift (*Armeria*), glabrous and entire; flowers in dense slender spikes overtopping the leaves, the common stalk (p e d u n c l e) slightly hairy; sepals (A, ×4) 4, ovate; corolla (B, ×4) short, 4-lobed, dry and membranous, lobes spreading; stamens (C, ×3) 4, alternate with the lobes of the corolla and scarcely exserted; anthers (D, ×8) with a produced tip; ovary 2-locular, with 2 ovules; capsule (E, ×3) opening by a circular transverse slit, with 2 seeds (family *Plantaginaceae*).

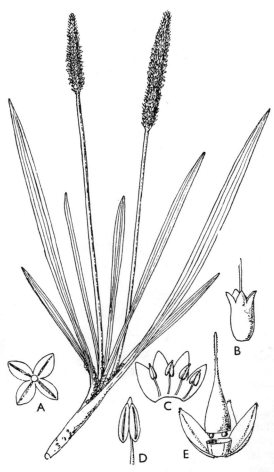

Found mainly near the sea on muddy shores and in salt marshes, but widely distributed in various parts of the world, sometimes on mountains inland.

Plantago coronopus L. ($\times \frac{2}{5}$)

Perennial with short thick upright rootstock; leaves spreading in a rosette, numerous, pilose, spoon-shaped or oblanceolate in

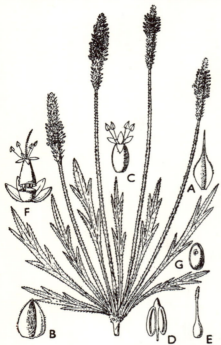

outline, deeply and pinnately divided into narrow acute lobes; common stalks of spikes densely villous when young, and the spike bristly with sharp-pointed bracts; spikes on slender stalks longer than the leaves; peduncles closely hairy; bracts (A, ×3) obovate, sharply and rather long-acuminate, shortly hairy on the margin; sepals (B, ×3) 4, with a broad darker midrib and thin hairy margins; corolla (C, ×3) bottle-shaped, 4-lobed, thin and membranous; stamens (D, ×4) 4, long-exserted from the corolla; ovary (E, ×4) bottle-shaped, with a long hairy style, 4-locular, each with 1 ovule; fruit (F, ×2½) splitting by a circular transverse slit; seeds (G, ×4) surrounded by a narrow white margin (family *Plantaginaceae*).

This is also a maritime species growing in dry, stony, or sandy places, flowering in summer and autumn.

The mode of opening of the fruits in order to set free the seeds is an interesting departure from the usual type found in flowering plants, and it is common also in the *Primula* family, to which the *Plantago* family is now considered to be related. This is by a transverse slit, a type described in botanical language as *circumscissile*.

Littorella uniflora (L.) Ascherson ($\times\frac{1}{2}$)

Perennial with a bunch of rather numerous stout roots; leaves all radical, narrowly linear, bright green, entire, up to $3\frac{1}{2}$ in. long; flowers of one sex, the males (A, ×3) on slender stalks up to 4 in. long, the females (C, ×3) at the base of the male flower-stalks, sessile and hidden amongst the bases of the leaves; male sepals 4, oblong-elliptic, with thin margins; corolla with 4 narrow lobes just above the sepals; stamens (B, ×1½) 4, with slender thread-like filaments up to $\frac{3}{4}$ in. long; anthers large and conspicuous; female flower with 3–4 unequal sepals, an urn-shaped corolla, and a small ovary

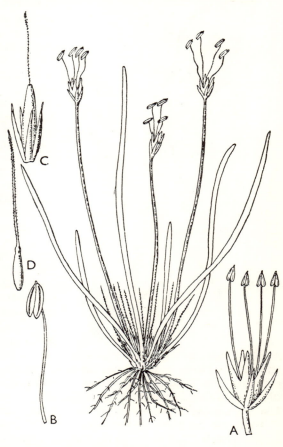

(D, ×3) with a thread-like style; fruit a hard nut with one erect seed (family *Plantaginaceae*) (synonym *Littorella lacustris* L.).

There are two kinds of flowers, those on slender stalks being male, the others hidden at the base being female and revealed by their long thread-like styles. It grows in mud and wet sand on the margins of pools, sometimes completely submerged, flowering during summer; widely distributed in Europe and in the Arctic.

Polygonum persicaria L. ($\times\frac{2}{3}$)

Annual, erect or spreading, with leggy branches from the base, reddish; leaves alternate, lanceolate, half acute, narrowed at the

base into a short petiole to which is adnate the thin tubular stipule about $\frac{1}{2}$ in. long; stipules fringed at the top with slender bristles; lateral nerves numerous; flowers (A, $\times 5$) red or greenish, in often paired spike-like racemes up to $1\frac{1}{2}$ in. long; flower-stalks very short, subtended by a small fringed bract like a miniature stipule; calyx (B, $\times 5$) 5-lobed to the middle; stamens 5 or 6; ovary (C, $\times 5$) broadly ovoid; styles 2, recurved; fruit (D, $\times 4$) slightly flattened, nearly black, shining (family *Polygonaceae*).

Common in ditches, by roadsides, and on waste ground and rubbish-heaps, flowering in summer and autumn.

The species of *Polygonum* included here (see also figs. 386–391) show in a striking way the peculiar nature of the stipule, which is a characteristic feature of the genus. It forms a sheath, sometimes of considerable size, within the leaf-stalk, and is called an *ochrea*. Usually this is fringed with long hairs or bristles.

There are no petals in the flowers of the family *Polygonaceae*, but the sepals often make up for this deficiency by being coloured. It is closely related to the Pink family, *Caryophyllaceae*.

Polygonum hydropiper L. ($\times\frac{1}{2}$)

A slender annual, common in wet places, stream, and pond-sides, and in damp gullies in woods; stems decumbent and rooting at the base, usually reddish or green and tinged with red, glabrous; leaves, alternate, very shortly stalked, the base of the stalk encircling the stem and prolonged upwards into a large sheathing stipule (ochrea), which is truncate at the top and fringed with slender bristles; blade lanceolate, fringed with very short hairs, otherwise glabrous; flowers in slender racemes in the axils of the leaves and at the top of each shoot, the short stalks jointed at the top; bract (A, ×2) like the stipule in shape, but much shorter, and not fringed with bristles; sepals (B, ×2½) 3, green and pink, pustulate; no petals; stamens (C, ×2½) usually 6, opposite the sepals; ovary (D, ×2½) flattened, with 2–3 short styles; fruit (E, ×2½) black, 3-angled, pitted when ripe (family *Polygonaceae*).

Polygonum hydropiper is called 'Smart-weed' in Canada, and is listed among the 'Pesky plants' of that country. The juice of the leaves and stems contains an irritant substance that produces burning and itching of the skin, especially between the fingers or on the back of the hand. When chewed, the leaves taste as hot as pepper.

The species has a wide range over the whole of Europe and most of Asiatic Russia, and Russian peasants use the fresh plant and other species of the genus as a poultice, gargle, etc.

Perennial with slender woody rootstock; stem erect or ascending, often in water; leaves stalked, with a large intrapetiolar sheath

(ochrea) at the base, lanceolate, gradually and rather broadly pointed, rounded at the base, up to about 4 or 5 in. long, minutely and closely toothed on the margin, lateral nerves numerous, repeatedly looped towards the margin; flowers numerous in rather thick spike-like racemes which are single or paired at the top of the stem; calyx (A, $\times2$) petaloid, pink to purple-red 5-lobed; stamens (B, $\times5$) 5, anthers broadly ellipsoid, attached near the middle; ovary (C, $\times2$) 1-locular, with 1 basal ovule; style deeply divided, with head-like stigmas; nut flattened (family *Polygonaceae*).

In ditches and ponds, flowering during summer; when growing away from the water, in dried up places, etc., stems creeping at the base, and the leaves often hairy.

Notes on the remarkable stipules accompanying fig. 385 apply also to this species. Two species of the genus grow in or near the water – that described above, and *P. hydropiper* L., shown in fig. 386.

The flowers smell like honey, nectar being secreted around the base of the ovary by 5 orange-yellow glands. The land form (var. *terrestre* Leers) possesses short hairs on the stalks secreting a viscid fluid which affords protection from creeping insects. The typical form is glabrous, the surrounding water giving access to none but flying insects.

A much-branched very wiry annual, usually prostrate, with stems or branches up to 2 ft. long when growing amongst crops or long grass; leaves very variable in size, from about $\frac{1}{3}$ in. to $1\frac{1}{2}$ in. but usually the smaller size, oblong-lanceolate to oblanceolate, narrowed to the short stalk to which are adnate the large membran-

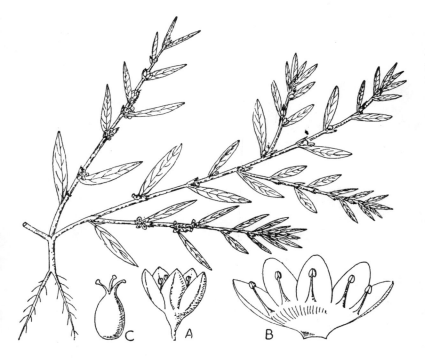

ous white stipules which soon become split and jagged on the margins; flowers (A, $\times$5) bisexual, axillary, shortly stalked, few together, pinkish; sepals (B, $\times$7) 5, connate at the base, overlapping in bud; stamens 8, five alternating with the sepals; ovary (C, $\times$6) with 3 styles; fruits surrounded by the persistent calyx-lobes which have whitish margins, triangular, beaked, very minutely pitted-reticulate (family *Polygonaceae*).

A troublesome weed which flowers and fruits nearly the whole season. It seems to thrive best where most trampled upon and ill-treated.

BLACK BINDWEED
Polygonum convolvulus L. ($\times \frac{1}{2}$)

An annual with a twining glabrous ribbed stem; leaves stipulate, alternate, stalked, rounded-ovate, very widely sagittate-heart-shaped (cordate) at the base, rather long-pointed, glabrous but minutely rugose, especially when dried in a plant-press; nerves looped and branched well within the entire margin; stipules encircling the stem, $\frac{1}{4}$ in. long, nerved longitudinally; flowers (A,

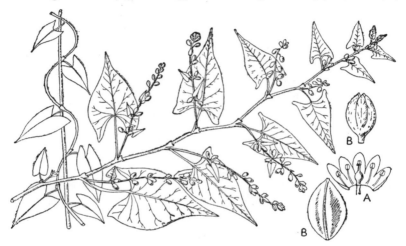

$\times 2\frac{1}{2}$) shortly stalked in axillary clusters, obovate in bud; sepals 5, glabrous, green with white margins, the outer 3 remaining around the fruit and narrowly keeled; no petals; stamens 5, opposite the sepals; ovary with 3 styles; fruit (B, $\times 3$) enclosed by the sepals, triangular, black and shining, the stalk jointed above the middle (family *Polygonaceae*).

This plant may prove injurious to stock fed on grain amongst which the fruits ('seeds') are very often mixed. Oats which contain too many of them may, by prolonged use, cause enteritis, with sometimes fatal results.

It grows in waste places and in arable land and gardens. It is generally distributed throughout the British Isles and has a wide range from Europe to temperate Asia, and is introduced into other countries. It is sometimes a frequent and very troublesome plant in cornfields, its long stems twining around the stalks of wheat and other crops and retarding growth.

Perennial; stems up to 3 ft., slender; basal leaves long-stalked, stalks winged, crimson towards the base; blade oblong-elliptic, right angled at the base, rounded to the apex, about 4–9 in. long and up to about 4 in. broad, glaucous and very minutely hairy-papillous below; lateral nerves spreading; stem-leaves few, the lanceolate-cordate blade more or less sessile on a long (2 in.) tubular sheath produced above the blade; spike-like racemes 2–2½ in. long, densely flowered; bracts (A, ×3) membranous; stalks as long as the 5 pink or rarely white sepals (B, ×4); stamens (C, ×5) with white exserted filaments; ovary (D, ×5) ellipsoid, styles 3; nut (E, ×3) 3-angled (family *Polygonaceae*).

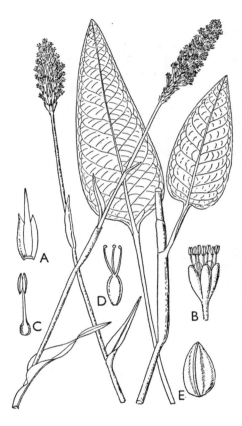

Grows in wet meadows and in woodlands, often in broad patches; widely distributed across the northern hemisphere.

The bright reddish-white flowers are collected into a dense spike-like inflorescence, which is very conspicuous and attracts numerous insects. It consists of small cymes made up of two, or rarely three, flowers, of which one is long-styled and bisexual, and the other male with a short style. In each cymule the bisexual flower opens first, starting from the bottom of the 'spike'. Later on all the males open and scatter their pollen on the still receptive stigmas of the bisexual flowers near them.

Perennial erect herb up to nearly 1 ft. high with a thick tuberous rootstock covered with the fibrous remains of the old leaf-sheaths;

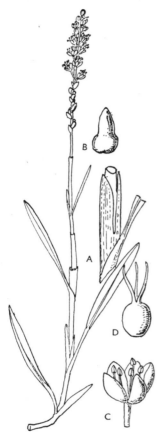

basal leaves on long slender stalks, lanceolate to oblong-lanceolate, subacute at each end, the blade up to $2\frac{1}{2}$ in. long, glabrous, with numerous much-branched side nerves; stem leaves few, narrowing to linear; flowers (C, $\times 3$) in a slender terminal solitary spike up to 3 in. long, pale flesh coloured, often the lower ones or all converted into little bulbils (B, $\times 3$) with crimson base and green tip; bracts large and persistent, ovate-lanceolate, sharply pointed; calyx-segments obovate; stamens usually 8; ovary (D, $\times 6$) with 3 styles; fruit a smooth nut (family *Polygonaceae*).

Only in the mountains of northern Britain and in Eire, widely spread in mountainous and Arctic regions of the northern hemisphere.

It grows on ledges of rocks and in wet places by streams. This species is remarkable for its tendency to propagate itself by bulbils by means of which it increases rapidly, while it rarely produces perfect seeds. These little bulbs are coloured green and crimson and are produced towards the base of the spike in place of the true flowers. They provide food for birds and small animals in the polar regions. The flowers appear in June and July.

Polygonum is one of the largest genera of British flowering plants, there being as many as 14 native species and 3 or 4 exotic species are sometimes naturalized, especially near dwellings in whose gardens they are grown.

Perennial; stems 2–3 ft. high, zigzag, ribbed; leaves alternate, stalked, lanceolate, rounded at the base, broadly pointed at the apex, entire or very faintly crenulate on the margin, with numerous looped and much-branched lateral nerves; stipules thin and sheathing within the leaf-stalk, soon withering, and leaving only a circular scar around the stem; flowers (A, $\times\frac{2}{3}$) bisexual, arranged in a leafy pyramidal panicle, clustered in little groups along the branches with here and there a leafy bract; stalks jointed between the middle and the base, the basal part persisting like little pegs; sepals 6, not tooth-

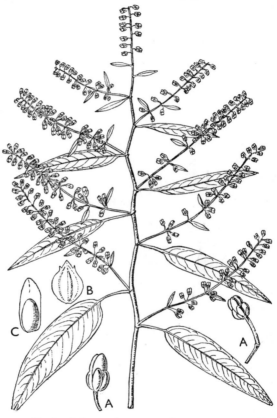

ed, the 3 outer very small, the 3 inner larger and erect around the fruit, in the latter state each with a large elliptic swelling (tubercle) in the lower half (C, $\times 3$); fruit (B, $\times 3$) a glossy triangular nut (family *Polygonaceae*).

This species may be recognized by the leaves never being arrow-shaped at the base, by the entire (not toothed) sepals, which are not cordate (heart-shaped) at the base, and by the swelling on the back of all three, and not only on one, as in *R. sanguineus* L.

Rumex obtusifolius L. ($\times\frac{1}{3}$)

Perennial; stems 2–3 ft. high, nearly straight, ribbed; lower leaves
(A, $\times\frac{1}{3}$) stalked, rather large, elliptic or elliptic-lanceolate, rounded to acute at the base, gradually and broadly pointed, distinctly
crenulate on the margin, with numerous looped and branched
lateral nerves; stipules membranous, sheathing within the petiole
(intrapetiolar); flowers very numerous in a stiff erect panicle, the
main axis and branches of which bear narrow lanceolate leaves

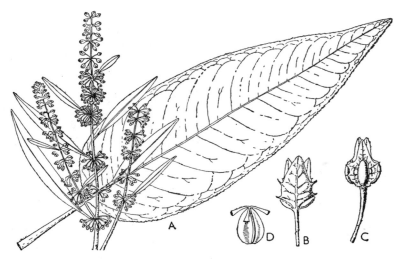

here and there; flower-stalks (B, $\times2\frac{1}{2}$) jointed just below the
middle, the lower part persisting like little pegs; inner sepals
broadly ovate, coarsely toothed, some of the teeth ending in a fine
point; in fruit these 3 inner sepals (C, $\times2$) closely appressed to the
3-sided shining nut (D, $\times2\frac{1}{2}$), and with an ellipsoid swelling
(tubercle) in the lower half, also coarsely reticulate (family
Polygonaceae).

On roadsides, in ditches, fields, and waste places, and widely
distributed in many parts of the world; flowers during summer.

Two species of Dock described in the present book belong to
different groups, one set of species, to which *R. obtusifolius* belongs, having the inner sepals toothed on the margin, whilst in the
other, to which *R. conglomeratus* (see fig. 392) belongs, the sepals
are not toothed, and all three of them have a swelling (tubercle) in
the lower part.

Erect, semi-aquatic, perennial herb up to about 5 ft. high; lower leaves long-stalked with an elliptic-lanceolate blade $1\frac{1}{2}$–2 ft. long

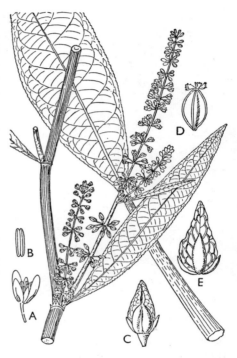

and 6 in. broad, slightly crenulate on the margin and with numerous looped lateral nerves spreading from the midrib almost at a right angle; stipules soon becoming torn and jagged but leaving a prominent transverse rim; upper leaves becoming bracts and scarcely stalked though narrowed to the base; flowers (A, ×2) in large terminal panicles with ascending branches each with a leaf-like bract at the base; sepals (C, ×2) 6, unequal, 3 larger and becoming winged and with a very prominent tubercle in the middle, wings reticulate (E, ×2½); stamens (B, ×2½) 6, anthers attached at the base; ovary (D, ×2) 3-sided; stigmas 3, becoming stag's-horn-like and persistent in fruit; nutlet sharply 3-angled, brown (family *Polygonaceae*).

Widely distributed in central and northern Europe, and in the Atlantic Islands, extending into Asiatic Russia; flowers during late summer and autumn, and pollination is by the wind.

This tall species is often common in ditches and on river banks and at one time had some reputation as an antiscorbutic. Its root is large and very astringent and a decoction was made from it and was used for washing the mouth. The fruits are very striking with their enlarged sepals bearing a large tubercle in the middle.

A very acid slender perennial plant; stems reddish or green and red; leaves alternate, stalked, narrowly lanceolate to oblanceolate, entire except for two spreading lobes (auricles) near the base, covered with minute wart-like protuberances; stalks usually shorter than the leaf-blade; stipules conspicuous, membranous, soon splitting up into segments; flowers very small, unisexual or sometimes bisexual, the males (A, $\times 3$) usually on one plant, the females on another (dioecious), arranged in slender lax terminal panicles, the pedicels in little clusters, those of the male very slender; bracts membranous; sepals small, obovate or elliptic, glabrous;

no petals; stamens (B, $\times 6$) (in the male) 6, with rather large anthers and very short filaments; female flowers with shorter stalks than the male; ovary (C, $\times 3$) globose with 3 deeply lobed fringe-like stigmas; nut (D, $\times 4$) enclosed by the inner sepals which do not become enlarged as in the closely related species *R. acetosa* L., and the outer sepals remain erect, not reflexed as in the latter (family *Polygonaceae*).

The flowers of this species are very small and are wind-pollinated, though sometimes visited by insects, the pollen being caught by the fringe-like stigmas. It is often a very troublesome weed and difficult to eradicate. As it contains oxalic acid it has been known to cause poisoning in stock.

Koenigia islandica L. (×½)

A very small glabrous annual herb with a few fibrous roots; stems very slender, sometimes in tufts, up to 4 in. long; upper leaves opposite, oblong to almost orbicular, up to ⅓ in. long, fleshy, obtuse at the apex, sessile or nearly so; stipules (ochrea) funnel - shaped, membranous; flowers (A, ×6) in a terminal cluster subtended by a whorl of leaves and sometimes a few axillary flowers in addition; calyx 2–4-partite, greenish white, segments valvate, equal;

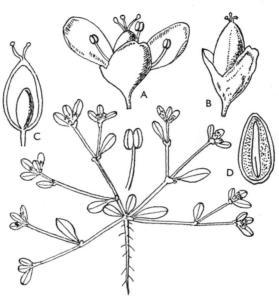

petals absent; stamens 4 or 2, alternate with the calyx-segments; anthers ovoid, on short filaments; ovary (C, ×8) 1-locular, with 1 erect ovule; style 2–3-partite; stigmas capitate; fruit (B, ×6) a small 3-sided nut; seed (D, ×8) with a straight embryo in the middle of the endosperm (family *Polygonaceae*).

A circumboreal species extending south to the Himalayas. This tiny plant was first collected in Britain in 1934, at 2,300 ft. in the Isle of Skye, but its identity was not discovered until several years later.* Skye is the most southerly station for the plant in Europe. It was not included in the latest British *Flora* (see p. xiv).

* See B. L. Burtt in Kew Bull. 1950 : 266.

BUCKWHEAT

Fagopyrum esculentum Moench. ($\times\frac{1}{3}$)

Annual herb up to about 2 ft. high; stem little branched, often crimson, glabrous; stipules encircling the stem obliquely cupu-

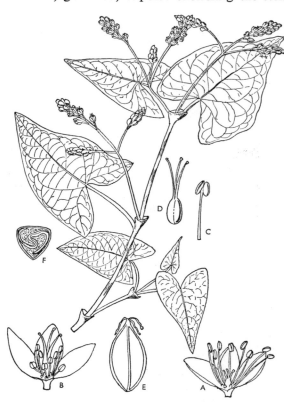

lar, thin and not fringed with bristles; leaves alternate, long-petiolate, rhomboid-ovate, sagittate at the base, triangular - acuminate at the apex, $2\frac{1}{2}$–3 in. long and nearly as broad, 5–7-nerved at the base, the nerves prominently looped and much branched within the margin, minutely mealy on the nerves; flowers (A, B, $\times$4) in axillary and terminal raceme-like cymes, often densely clustered in fruit; sepals 5, pinkish or cream-coloured, obovate; stamens (C, $\times$4) 8, alternating with 8 rounded glands; anther-loculi short and nearly separate; ovary (D, $\times$4) superior, 3-sided, with 3 free styles with globose terminal stigmas; fruit (E, $\times$4) a 3-sided 1-seeded nut, becoming black; seed (F, $\times$6) with much folded cotyledons and with endosperm (family *Polygonaceae*).

Cultivated as a farm crop mostly in the eastern counties and often found as a weed in other cornfields and waste places. Besides being a valuable poultry food, Buckwheat is an important honey plant, the flowers being rich in nectar.

KIDNEY SORREL

398

Oxyria digyna Hill (×⅓)

Perennial herb up to 1 ft. high; leaves mostly from the base of the plant, long-stalked, with large membranous stipules at the base; blade transversely oblong or kidney-shaped, up to 2½ in. broad, 1–1½ in. long, thin, glabrous, with about 7 nerves spreading from the base; flowers (A, ×4) in a terminal panicle subtended by a leaf, the branches raceme-like; bracts rather small and like stipules; pedicels short and slender; sepals 4, the outer 2 smaller, narrow, the inner 2 obovate, larger; stamens 6; ovary (B, ×4) with 2 much-divided stigmas; ovule 1, erect; fruit (C, ×4) flat, obovate and broadly winged; seed (D, E, ×8) with a straight embryo  in the middle of the endosperm (family *Polygonaceae*). – Synonym *Oxyria reniformis*.

In Britain only on the mountains of northern England and Wales and in Scotland; rare in Eire; flowers in summer; widely distributed in alpine and arctic regions of the northern hemisphere.

The flowers of this species are pollinated by the wind, hence the much-divided fan-like stigmas which readily catch the pollen.

STRAPWORT

Corrigiola littoralis L. ($\times\frac{1}{2}$)

A herb with often elongated weak branches, somewhat fleshy; stems rounded, glabrous; leaves (A, $\times$2) alternate, with a pair of membranous stipules at the base, sessile, lanceolate, acute, entire, dull green and glabrous; flowers (C, $\times$5) crowded towards the ends of the shoots and forming small corymbs rather like some *Cruciferae* but with small membranous bracts; stalks as long as the flower-buds, the latter (B, $\times$3) conspicuous by their white-margined but otherwise crimson 5 sepals; petals 5, white, not divided as in many of the closely related family *Caryophyllaceae*;

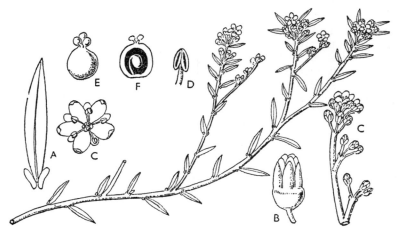

stamens (D, $\times$6) 5, alternate with the petals and inserted on a greenish disk; ovary (E, $\times$12) globose, 1-locular with 1 basal ovule suspended on a stalk (F, $\times$12); nuts enclosed when ripe in the persistent calyx (family *Illecebraceae*).

This is a very rare species, growing on shingly banks of pools near the coast in the south-west of England, flowering in summer and autumn. The small, white flowers are arranged in crowded corymbs and for the most part remain closed. The anthers are dark violet and they open at the side. As they project beyond the stigma self-pollination is easy and effective.

Herniaria glabra L. ($\times\frac{1}{3}$)

Herb with numerous prostrate radiating branches, rarely quite glabrous but at most very minutely pubescent on the branches and leaf-margins; lower leaves (A, $\times2\frac{1}{2}$) opposite, upper alternate, oblanceolate to elliptic, very small, at most $\frac{1}{3}$ in. long; stipules scarious, broad; flowers (B, $\times5$) very small, crowded on lateral often leaf-opposed branchlets, sessile or nearly so; calyx green, deeply 5-lobed, spreading in flower, closing up around the fruit; petals absent; stamens 5, alternating with as many bristle-like

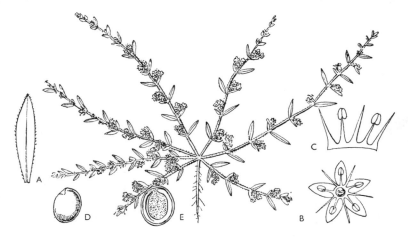

staminodes (C, $\times8$), joined with them into a ring at the base; anthers 2-locular; ovary globose, with 2 very small stigmas, 1-locular, with 1 erect ovule; fruit enclosed by the calyx, globose, 1-seeded; seed (D, E, $\times6$) black-brown, shining, with a horse-shoe-shaped embryo surrounding the endosperm (family *Illecebraceae*).

This species is not very appropriately named, for it is rarely quite glabrous. Owing to the reduction of one leaf in each pair of the upper leaves the flower-clusters appear to be leaf-opposed; grows in sandy places, flowering during summer.

Illecebrum verticillatum L. ($\times \frac{1}{2}$)

Small much-branched annual; branches almost thread-like, prostrate and spreading from the base, glabrous; leaves opposite, sessile, rounded-obovate, about $\frac{1}{5}$ in. diam., glabrous; flowers (A, $\times 8$) very small, whorled in the leaf-axils all along the branches, sessile; sepals 5, thick, oblong, white, bone-like structures with a very sharp tail-like tip and hooded, the whole much resembling a 5-valved capsule; petals (B, $\times 10$) 5, very minute; stamens (C, $\times 15$) 5, alternating with 5 filament-like staminodes; ovary (D,

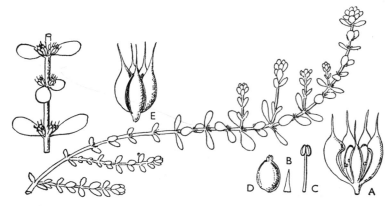

$\times 15$) with sessile stigmas; seed solitary in the capsule (E, $\times 6$) enclosed by the calyx and opening at the base by valves (family *Illecebraceae*).

Very local in sandy soil and sandy marshes, only in the southern counties of England; otherwise widely distributed in central and southern Europe, north Africa, Madeira, and the Canary Islands.

The silver-white cartilaginous sepals of this species contain air-conducting tracheids, and they greatly resemble free carpels such as occur in the family *Crassulaceae*. Automatic self-pollination takes place.

The family *Illecebraceae* is a small one merged by some botanists with *Caryophyllaceae*. They are more highly reduced types clearly derived from the same stock as the *Caryophyllaceae*, the ovary being reduced to one loculus with only one ovule and consequently a single seed.

Scleranthus annuus L. ($\times\frac{1}{2}$)

Very small much-branched annual herb; stems minutely pubescent, becoming pale and straw-coloured; leaves opposite, linear,
about 1 in. long, united at
the base into a short
membranous tube en-
circling the stem; flow-
ers (A, B, ×5) very small,
numerous and crowded
in small terminal cymes,
sessile in the repeated
forks; calyx-tube ovoid,
5-lobed, lobes acute, with
narrow thin margins;
petals absent; stamens 5,
alternating with 5 small
staminodes, inserted at
the base of the calyx-lobes
above the superior ovary,
the latter 1-locular, with
1 basal ovule pendulous
from a thread; styles 2,
free, stigmas capitate;
fruit (C, ×6) closed,
containing 1 seed (D,
×6) with much cur-
ved embryo surrounding
the endosperm (family *Illecebraceae*).

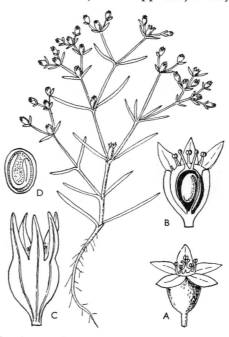

A weed in fields and waste places, flowering all the summer,
widely distributed in many other countries.

To those who know the South African flora, this plant would
probably recall species of *Thesium* in the family *Santalaceae*.

A second very rare species is found in Britain, *Scleranthus
perennis* L., a perennial plant with blunt calyx-lobes with broad
white margins, confined to eastern and southern England, flowering all the summer like *S. annuus*.

Atriplex patula L. (aggregate) ($\times \frac{1}{2}$)

Annual, very variable in size and leaf-shape, usually branched from the base, rather similar to *Chenopodium album* (fig. 404), but

the lower leaves mostly opposite; leaves stalked, the lower larger and more or less triangular with two spreading lobes (hastate) towards the base, the upper becoming much narrower and sometimes entire or coarsely toothed, glabrous or minutely mealy-papillous; flowers unisexual, the male (A, $\times 2$) and female (B, $\times 2$) on the same plant (monoecious), arranged in slender leafy spikes forming a terminal panicle, the females usually mixed with the males, mostly covered with mealy papillae; male flowers with 5 ovate-triangular entire sepals, and 5 stamens opposite to them; female flower consisting of two herbaceous toothed bracts which enlarge in fruit, the latter (C, $\times 3\frac{1}{2}$) slightly compressed, black and hard (family *Chenopodiaceae*).

Very similar in general appearance to the *Chenopodium* in fig. 404, but usually less mealy, and always to be distinguished in the fruiting stage. The fruits are little hard rounded structures and are enclosed in two closely appressed toothed bracts which make the clusters look rather prickly. Like the *Chenopodium* it is common in cultivated and waste ground.

An annual up to 2 ft. high, pale green or mealy white, especially the flowers and lower surfaces of the leaves; leaves alternate, stalked, the lowermost more or less triangular or almost rhomboid, and bluntly and coarsely toothed, gradually becoming narrower upwards to almost linear and entire, distinctly 3-nerved near the base; often completely covered below by rounded whitish papillae; flowers (A, $\times 3$) bisexual, arranged in short dense axillary spikes and forming a leafy spike-like panicle at the top of the shoot; calyx of 5 equal rounded lobes; no petals; stamens usually 5; ovary (B, $\times 4$) depressed; styles mostly 3; fruit depressed-globose, blackish, more or less covered by the persistent calyx-lobes; seeds spreading horizontally, black, rounded-kidney-shaped, with the embryo forming almost a ring around the endosperm (family *Chenopodiaceae*).

This is an abundant annual weed to be found on most rubbish-heaps. It multiplies rapidly by seed and spreads very quickly. Formerly this plant was used as a potherb and boiled and eaten like spinach, by which it has been replaced. The leaves are sometimes completely covered below by a rounded mealy substance, which makes the plant easy to recognize.

SEA BEET
Beta maritima L. ($\times\frac{1}{3}$)

Perennial with a tough narrow carrot-shaped rootstock; stem and branches erect or spreading, coarsely ribbed, glabrous; lowermost leaves long-petiolate, more or less triangular, about 5 in. long and $3\frac{1}{2}$ in. broad, the stem leaves gradually smaller and becoming sessile and cuneate at the base, wavy on the margin; flowers (A, $\times 3$) bisexual, small and green, sessile, single or clustered along the spike-like branches of a lax bracteate panicle; bract below the flower-clusters small and narrow, the lower ones larger and leaf-like; calyx green, deeply 5-lobed, spreading, lobes

with an incurved tip, persistent and becoming hard and angular or prickly in fruit; petals absent; stamens (B, $\times 8$) 5, opposite to the calyx-lobes, inserted around the nectar-secreting disk; ovary and fruit (C, $\times 5$) partly immersed in the base of the calyx; seed solitary, horizontal, with the embryo (D, $\times 4$) curled around the copious endosperm (family *Chenopodiaceae*).

Amongst rocks and in muddy sands by the seashore as far north as southern Scotland, flowering during summer and autumn. The cultivated Beetroot and Mangold Wurzel are derived from this wild species.

Obione portulacoides (L.) Moq. ($\times \frac{1}{2}$)

Low much-branched shrublet, branches often creeping and root-ing at the nodes, up to $1\frac{1}{2}$ ft. high, densely covered all over with a close mealy-scaly indumentum; leaves glaucous green, opposite, oblanceolate, narrowed at the base into a short petiole, entire, up to 2 in. long and $\frac{3}{4}$ in. broad, the nerves except the midrib scarcely evident; flowers (A, $\times 6$) minute, unisexual, numerous in a ter-minal panicle, sessile on the branches which bear leafy bracts; male flowers with a 5-lobed calyx; no petals; stamens 5; female

flowers (C, $\times 8$) with 2 flat triangular or orbicular segments which persist and become horny around the fruit; ovary (B, $\times 9$) covered with scales (family *Chenopodiaceae*). – Synonym *Atriplex portulacoides* L.

Found near the sea, north as far as the south of Scotland, often in salt marshes just below high water mark.

Obione is usually now separated from *Atriplex* because the two bracts of the female flower are united nearly to the top and remain small in fruit.

PRICKLY SALTWORT

Salsola kali L. (×⅓)

Annual with soft fleshy stems up to 1½ ft. high, much branched; stems solid but soft, marked with green parallel stripes, shortly

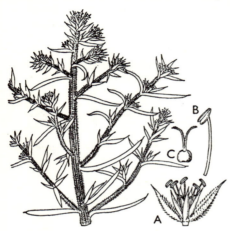

pubescent; leaves alternate to subopposite, narrow, flat above, triangular below, thick and fleshy, ending in a sharp hard point, minutely setulose on the margins and keel; flowers (A, ×6) small and axillary, each with a pair of sharp-pointed bracts; sepals 5, thin and membranous, acute; petals none; stamens (B, ×10) 5, anthers attached near the middle; ovary (C, ×10) glabrous, style deeply divided with 2 branches; ripe fruit enclosed by the calyx; embryo of the seed spirally coiled, with scarcely any endosperm (family *Chenopodiaceae*).

A common coastal species growing in sand and salt marshes, flowering in summer and autumn; widely distributed in the northern hemisphere. It was formerly burned for the use of soap-manufacturers, the ashes being known as 'barilla'.

Cross-pollination is effected by the wind, the stigma already projecting from the flower whilst still in bud, though it remains receptive after its own anthers have opened.

Salsola kali is the only native species, though *S. tragus* L., a more erect plant with almost thread-like leaves, occurs now and then as an introduction on waste ground. There is a form of *S. kali* with glabrous leaves and stems (var. *glabra*). *Salsola* is a genus of about forty species distributed from Europe through temperate Asia and in North and South Africa.

Suaeda vera J. F. Gmel. ($\times \frac{1}{2}$)

A shrubby perennial with numerous ascending herbaceous fleshy branchlets, glabrous; leaves alternate, narrowly oblong, thick and fleshy, slightly keeled below, almost flat above, bright glaucous-green, with a pair of small triangular membranous stipules at the base; flowers (A, $\times 6$) bisexual, axillary, solitary, sessile, globose; sepals 5, green, ovate-triangular; no petals; stamens (B, $\times 12$) 5, opposite the sepals; anthers short and very thick, opening at the sides; ovary (C, $\times 12$) sessile, 1-locular, with 1 ovule (D, $\times 12$) inserted on a distinct stalk and horizontal; styles 3, connate at the base and bifid at the apex (family *Chenopodiaceae*).

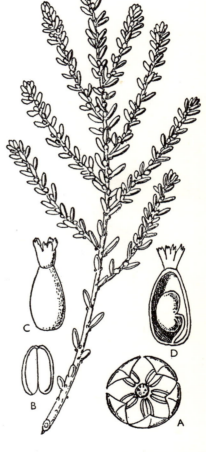

Grows in sand and in salt marshes at the seaside, confined to the eastern and southern coasts of England; widely distributed through the Mediterranean to central Asia and also in America. It is one of the plants burned in southern Europe for the manufacture of 'barilla', formerly used in glass-making. Synonym *S. fructicosa* Forssk. There is a second native species, *S. maritima* (L.) Dum., an annual herb with acute leaves narrowed to the base. It is more widely distributed than *S. fruticosa*. *Suaeda* is a genus of about forty species widely distributed in the world.

INDEX TO GENERA IN THE
TWO VOLUMES

(The numbers refer to volumes and illustrations)

INDEX TO NAMES OF GENERA

INDEX TO COMMON NAMES IN THE
TWO VOLUMES

(The numbers refer to volumes and illustrations)

NOTES

NOTES

NOTES

NOTES